READINGS IN MANAGEMENT INFORMATION SYSTEMS

READINGS IN MANAGEMENT INFORMATION SYSTEMS

1 2 3 4 5 6 7 8 9 0 WHWH 7 8 3 2 1 0 9 8 7 6

Library of Congress Cataloging in Publication Data
Main entry under title:

Readings in management information systems.

(McGraw-Hill series in management information systems)
Bibliography: p.
1. Management information systems — Addresses, essays, lectures.
I. Davis, Gordon Bitter.   II. Everest, Gordon C.
T58.6.R42   658.4'5   76-7954
ISBN 0-07-015835-5

The editor was Peter Nalle.
The Whitlock Press, Inc., was printer and binder.

CONTENTS

*no corresponding chapter in the Davis text.

PREFACE

This collection of readings is designed to support the MIS text by Gordon B. Davis entitled <u>Management Information Systems: Conceptual Foundations, Structure, and Development</u> (McGraw-Hill, 1974).

Each article was included because it satisfied one or more of six selection criteria. In the following list, the mention of authors under each criterion is illustrative, not exhaustive.

- classics widely read by people in MIS (Ackoff, Leavitt and Whisler, Miller, Pounds, Simon and Newell)

- provocative or polemic (Argyris, Dearden, Head)

- leading person in MIS (Emery, Glaser, Hanold, Head, Kriebel, Schwartz, Simon, Zani)

- significant research findings (Chervany and Dickson, Miller)

- notable case studies (Dickson and Simmons, Sprague)

- excellent summary (Andrus, Bello, Campbell, Everest, Ferrara and Nolan, Galbraith, Hirsch, Hunt and Newell, Katz and Kahn, Luke, Perrow)

Currency was only a secondary criterion. This set of criteria results in a collection of MIS readings substantially different from others which have been published in recent years. Even though the articles are selected and organized to support the Davis text, the book of readings can meaningfully be used by itself. By focusing on classics and polemics, etc., rather than articles only written in the last five years or so, the resulting collection should remain useful for a longer time period.

The selections have been reproduced from the original journal article. The page layouts have been altered in some cases to fit the page size of this collection. The entire article has been included except for Aron, Bello, Dzielinski, Hirsch, and Simon and Newell. In these cases, certain parts that were dated or otherwise of little interest were omitted. The resulting, shortened versions have a sharper focus relative to MIS.

This particular collection of readings has evolved over three years of teaching an introductory MIS course in the College of Business Administration at the University of Minnesota. We are particularly indebted to those students who used previous editions of these readings and reported their opinions as to the usefulness of each reading. Substantial weight was put on the student reading evaluations in making the final selections. If we thought an article was "important" but the students generally felt it was not very "useful," the reading was excluded from the final selection.

Each article is preceded by a preamble which explains why the article is included, gives a summary of the main points in the article, provides some suggestions for reading the article, and offers some questions for the reader. The reading suggestions and the questions tell the reader how to read the article and what to look for. After reading the article, the reader should refer back to the questions to test his/her own comprehension and understanding of the material.

Gordon B. Davis
Gordon C. Everest

BIBLIOGRAPHY OF ARTICLES BY AUTHOR

ACKOFF, Russell L., "Management Misinformation Systems," Management Science (14:4), 1967 December, pages B147-156; and rebuttal by Alfred RAPPAPORT, "Management Misinformation Systems -- Another Perspective," in Letters to the Editor, Management Science (15:4), 1968 December, pages B133-136.

ANDRUS, Roman R., "Approaches to Information Evaluation," MSU Business Topics (19:3), 1971 Summer, pages 40-46.

ARGYRIS, Chris, "Resistance to Rational Management Systems," Innovation 1970 Number 10, pages 28-35.

ARON, Joel D., "Information Systems in Perspective," Computing Surveys (1:4), 1969 December, pages 213-236 (extract of pages 213-221 and 233-235).

BELLO, Francis, "The Information Theory," Fortune (48:6), 1953 December, pages 136-141, 148ff (portions omitted).

CAMPBELL, John P., "Decision Making, Conflict Resolution, and the Steady State," Unpublished Working Paper, University of Minnesota, 1975 September.

CHERVANY, Norman L. and Gary W. DICKSON, "An Experimental Evaluation of Information Overload in a Production Environment," Management Science (20:10), 1974 June, pages 1335-1344.

DEARDEN, John, "MIS is a Mirage," Harvard Business Review (50:1), 1972 January-February, pages 90-99.

DEARDEN, John, "Myth of Real-Time Management Information," Harvard Business Review (44:3), 1966 May-June, pages 123-132.

DICKSON, Gary W. and John K. SIMMONS, "The Behavioral Side of MIS," Business Horizons (13:4), 1970 August, pages 59-71.

DZIELINSKI, Bernard P., "Abstracts of Financial Planning Programs," appendix to "A Guide to Financial Planning Tools and Techniques," IBM Systems Journal (12:2), 1973, pages 140-143.

EMERY, James C. and Christopher R. SPRAGUE, "MIS: Mirage or Misconception?" SMIS Newsletter (3:5), 1972 August, pages 2-6.

EVEREST, Gordon C., "Database Management Systems Tutorial," Fifth Annual Midwest AIDS Conference Proceedings, Vol. 1, Minneapolis, Minnesota, 1974 May 10-11, edited by Norman L. Chervany, Minneapolis: University of Minnesota, College of Business Administration, 1974, pages A1-A12.

FERRARA, Raymond and Richard L. NOLAN, "New Look at Computer Data Entry," Journal of Systems Management (24:2), 1973 February, pages 24-33.

sequently be related to achieve a better understanding of market response. For example, data on copy and format in company advertisements may be related to advertising performance measures in order to learn systematically how the market is responding to these characteristics of ads. Cox and Good [4] report that one large consumer goods company is doing precisely that, while Diamond [5] has developed an on-line model called ADFORS which utilizes the results of such analysis.

A key concept in the design of a data bank is to maintain data in its most elemental, disaggregated form. For salesmen's call reports, disaggregated data might be details such as person visited, time, place, sales aids used, etc. An aggregated form for such data might be simply the number of sales calls made by a salesman to accounts of a given type over some time period. Maintaining disaggregated data enhances the flexibility of its future use, to allow for organizing it differently for future, unknown purposes. Amstutz [3] discusses the benefits of future flexibility in his computerized portfolio selection system: "If initial data files had been structured to maintain information at the level of aggregation required when the system was begun, many operations of the present system would be precluded by data limitations."

Because of the high cost of physically storing disaggregated data, the data may not be maintained initially in computer disk storage, but on tapes, cards or even original work sheets. It is important, however, that it be preserved, to be accessed by model builders and managers when required.

The data bank should maintain information on who used which data and for what purposes. This should aid decisions on which data should be kept in high speed computer storage. Thus the data bank should gather information appropriate to adapting itself to better meet the needs of its users and developing specifications for the storage of disaggregated data.

Systems for Processing the Data

Two key issues in the development of the processing systems within the data bank are modularity and flexibility. Since the design of the data bank will be an evolving one rather than a one-shot, forever optimal system, the system must be readily adapted to change. Perfect foresight is not required if the system is flexible. Modularity in the processing systems (i.e., compartmentalization of the processing functions) will tend to minimize problems involved in adapting the processing systems to future requirements, since then existing moduals can be linked to meet the new demands.

Developing a variety of general commands to retrieve and manipulate data gives flexibility in data processing. These general commands may then operate on the data, whatever the data file may be. Although not specific to a particular data file, they greatly reduce the problems when a file is altered by additions, deletions, or reorganization. An example of an operational data handling

system using such general commands is the DATANAL system developed by Miller [13].

Security Systems

The data bank must have security systems at both the processing systems and data levels. At the systems level the system itself must be protected from the user, to prevent inadvertent altering of the system programs. Such accidents can be costly and frustrating. A more interesting aspect is the need for data security systems. The problem here is who may have access to what. It is clear that individuals below a certain level in the organization should not have access to certain types of information. But there may be data which should not be conveniently accessible to, say, the marketing vice president. A case in point is given by Amstutz [2] in which a sales vice president was able to access very detailed information on sales results in individual territories which distracted him from his real assignment, providing overall market planning and strategy.

In addition to vertical security, there is a need for horizontal security systems. As Ackoff [1] notes, organizational harmony and efficiency are not necessarily enhanced by letting, say, marketing and production have complete access to one another's data files. Horizontal security between firms becomes important with the emergence of the multi-firm marketing information system.

Communication of Data

A data bank must be accessible to the manager. An interactive man/system operation is an important system design aspect, to be discussed later. However, the capability a remote terminal provides a manager does allow the data bank to carry out one more function, "data browsing," where the manager can look at various aspects of operations data to find problems before they are severe enough to get management's attention through standard means such as exception reporting.

Although the ability to access data in a relevant form is important, it is not enough. Information systems must digest, analyze, and interpret data so the managers can improve decisions. If the data bank is more emphasized than analysis and models, the manager may suffer a data overload and receive little help in decision making. The model bank and the measurement-statistics bank are designed to help the manager analyze and make sense out of data.

THE MODEL BANK

The model bank provides the marketing information system with a capability to assist directly in decision making. It should contain many models appropriate for purposes such as understanding market behavior, diagnosis, control, prediction, and strategy formulation, all likely to be frequently used. Models for analysis of one-time market situations will remain, but they will often be "back-of-the-envelope" models like Hess' price timing model [7]. Unless they have potential for recurrent use they will not be made permanent in the computerized model bank, although they may temporarily reside there.

Some Model Bank Design Aspects

The model bank should contain models of varying levels of detail within each class of models and for each marketing problem area, to reflect alternate model cost/benefit tradeoffs. More model detail is generally useful, but as more variables are included in the model, more phenomena are considered, and more disaggregation takes place, the time and financial costs of model development, input generation, operation, maintenance, and testing rapidly increase. The best level of detail in a particular application will depend on time and resource constraints on model development and operation as compared to improvement in decision because of the higher level of detail.

The model bank concept presents a partial solution to this problem by making models of varying levels of detail for a particular problem available to the decision maker. For example, SPRINTER, a model for the analysis of frequently purchased consumer goods, exists in three levels. Mod I is a very simple description of the diffusion process. Mod II adds the controllable variables of advertising and price. Mod III uses a very detailed market response model based on the behavioral buying process and adds sampling, coupons, margins, and sales calls [18]. Mod I is simple but runs at 10% of the cost of Mod III, and 50% of the cost of Mod II. With these alternatives the manager can select the model which has the best cost/benefit tradeoff for his particular problem.

The model bank might even contain a number of models at a given level of detail for a given problem with each model particularly meaningful to specific managers and their decision styles. Thus, the model bank may ultimately have several levels of model detail and multiple models at each level to service the decision needs of various marketing managers. Development of the model bank must be an evolutionary, adaptive process which adjusts to the varied and changing needs of the managers.

The models should be compatible with models at other levels of detail. Simpler models could be used to evaluate a large number of alternatives and the more detailed ones to evaluate the specific outcomes of one or a few of the alternatives generated by the less detailed model. For example, an aggregate advertising budget model might be used to specify an annual budget. Then a media allocation model could be used to indicate the best media schedule and finally this schedule could be submitted to a micro-analytic simulation to obtain detailed attitude change and micro-purchase response results by market segment. The results might indicate the need for adjustment of the preceding analysis of budget level and media schedule and provide a benchmark for control purposes once a policy has been implemented. This compatible use of models allows low cost examination of many alternatives and a high level of model detail. It should strengthen the value of the model bank and improve its ability to serve decision makers.

Trends in Marketing Models

The model bank concept is supported by a number of new developments in modeling.[1] The first is the emergence of a problem-centered orientation. Much of the early work in marketing models could be characterized as techniques looking for problems, which often sacrificed marketing relevance to satisfy a given solution technique. The rush to formulate the media selection problem as a linear program is a case in point. There are now hopeful signs that marketing problems will begin to dominate techniques in the formulation of marketing models. This trend has been spurred by maturing experience in structuring marketing models, the realization that successful implementation and use depend on this approach, and steady progress in management science and operations research in approaching more realistic and complex problems. Although optimization techniques are improving, the trend in marketing is to non-algorithmic techniques such as heuristic programming and simulation. These are more capable of rich representation of the interdependent and dynamic nature of marketing problems.

Another development is the growing availability of data for estimating and testing models, which should bring more realistic, detailed, and valid model structures. The trend toward realistic market response representation is aided by inclusion of more behavioral phenomena, more variables, non-linear response functions, and stochastic elements in marketing models. Dynamic aspects of markets are also increasingly being incorporated. A significant model trend emerging from development of time shared computers is that toward interactive models. An interactive model operating on a time shared computer system enables a decision maker to quickly and efficiently explore implications of his judgments on given problems. The MEDIAC [9] and ADFORS [5] models provide marketing examples here.

A major development trend is towards inclusion of dynamic effects; Little [8] has proposed a model for adjusting an advertising budget in the face of a changing environment via a series of continuing market experiments, the results of which are used to update the budget decision.

Another model trend is emerging towards building models considering competitive effects. These will have a significant interaction with the data bank. The de-

---

[1] This section is designed to emphasize the directions of expansion of the state of the art, rather than the basic methodology of existing models. A detailed discussion of models is in [14].

velopment of competitive models must be supported by data bank capabilities in systematic monitoring and storing of competitive market data for developing, validating, and using these competitive models. It would seem important for firms to consider initiating a program of competitive data generation to match their future model intentions.

In addition to competitive and dynamic phenomena, there has been a trend towards including more behavioral content in mathematical models. For example, NOMAD has modeled the new product acceptance process basically as an updating of a brand preference vector on receipt of new advertising awareness, word-of-mouth communication, and product use experience [6]. This behavioral process approach has been utilized in SPRINTER: Mod III at a more aggregated level [18]. A general development of methods for use in behaviorally-based simulation models will play an important role in future models. While better solution methods will be evolved, principal developments will also occur in validity and sensitivity testing of complex behaviorally-based models.

The trend toward model banks with models which include competitive, dynamic, and behavioral phenomena will increase models' importance in the total information system.

THE MEASUREMENT-STATISTICS BANK

The measurement-statistics bank will provide a basis for measurement and estimation and methods for testing response functions and models. It should incorporate methods for both data-based and judgment-based estimation, such as procedures for estimating demand elasticities of marketing variables based on data in the data bank. It should also provide methods for judgmental assessments, such as the reference life cycle for a potential new product in an application of a new product model. In testing response functions and models it should provide techniques for assessing the adequacy of a postulated model or function in the light of available data.

Data-Based Measurement

The recent marketing literature makes the case for data-based measurement methods in marketing clear. The measurement-statistics bank should incorporate a wide variety of multivariate procedures, non-parametric methods, scaling techniques, and numerical estimation procedures [14].

Judgment-Based Methods

Marketing models, particularly normative models for planning marketing strategy, often require a certain amount of judgmental input. While much remains to be learned about effectively obtaining judgmental information, these methods should be incorporated into the system as they evolve.

One obvious example of a judgment-based method applicable in marketing is statistical decision theory. A barrier to its use, however, is the computational burden involved in problems large enough to be meaningful. A program which will perform the numerical analysis, preferably in real time from a remote console, should increase the use of this procedure. If a convenient mode is made available to marketing managers, there should be an increasingly widespread use of decision theory in marketing. Some simple steps have been made in this direction [17].

The importance and utility of judgmental inputs and systems for their evaluation can be illustrated by examples. The first of these, which must remain anonymous for competitive reasons, relates to an application in a company whose problem was to determine which items to feature at what prices in weekly ads to increase store traffic, sales, and profits, as well as how much ad space to allocate to each featured item. Store managers and a consultant developed a simple model describing how the market would respond to this form of promotion. It was made operative on a time shared computer and made available to managers for planning their weekly promotional strategy. It required judgmental inputs from managers, and has produced excellent results in use. The consultant attributes this success to the managers' ability to provide meaningful judgmental inputs to this simple marketing model. This case reinforces the notion that useful judgmental inputs to formal analysis can be obtained from marketing managers.

Another example of the use of judgmental inputs is represented by an application of the SPRINTER: Mod O model to a new chemical product. In this case managers gave good subjective estimates of market response components, but without a model they could not combine them effectively to make the GO, ON, or NO decision and specify a best pricing strategy. Their overall subjective decision was GO for the product, but by combining their component inputs in the model and using their criteria and structure, a NO decision was indicated. Their overall subjective decision was not consistent with the logical combination of their market response judgments. A model can help produce more consistent decision procedures. In this particular case the subjective market response input and the model were also used to identify a pricing strategy predicted to generate 50% more profit.

In view of subjective inputs' importance, the system should include procedures for monitoring their performance from individuals in the firm to help identify individuals who are particularly knowledgeable and help adjust for bias in individual estimates.[2] For example, one company in a rapidly growing area combined judgmental inputs and market data in selecting sites for new outlets. In

---

[2] This is similar in concept to the monitoring and adjustment of judgment in applications of PERT.

this case, monitoring of the performance of individuals supplying judgmental inputs indicated that the operations vice president tended to supply better judgmental inputs than any of the personnel on the real estate staff. When he subsequently resigned, the company not only lost a competent executive but also a valuable source of judgmental marketing information. The system should also correct any systematic bias in the estimates given by each individual. Claycamp has developed such a procedure for a manufacturer of electronic components, who asks salesmen to report an a product-by-product and customer-by-customer basis their subjective probability of realizing a sale in 30, 60, and 90 days. Each salesman's subjective probabilities are then adjusted on the basis of his past prediction performance. When aggregated across salesmen, subjective probability estimates are the basis of a short run sales forecast used by the production department.

Judgmental inputs are being used in systematic analysis of marketing problems. Interesting work has been done by Winkler on the use of experts and group judgments [19, 20]. He has also proposed some incentives for managers to supply their best judgments, but more research is needed to develop procedures generating good subjective estimates.

Some Design Aspects of the Measurement-Statistics Bank

Computerized statistical analysis has greatly lowered the computational burden in perfoming such analyses. The proliferation of readily available programs for statisical analysis makes it important that a proposed measurement-statistics bank be designed to minimize danger of misuse [10].

As an example, consider regression analysis. The measurement-statistics bank should incorporate complete econometric capability in all the available tests of assumptions which underlie the model. The measurement-statistics bank itself should warn the user of potential pitfalls and recommend appropriate tests and courses of action. Such system warnings and recommendations should help prevent naive use of this method. Sometimes the system can automatically get the user out of trouble. For example, the on-line statistical package DATANAL automatically performs a Fisher exact test when the user has specified a chi-square contingency analysis with insufficient data [13].

The design of the measurement-statistical bank is especially important since model outputs are only as good as their input. A good measurement capability is necessary for effective operation of a decision-information operation.

THE USER-SYSTEM INTERFACE

The last major component is the subsystem which provides the user-system interface, or system input/output capability. As the only direct contact between the user and the system, it is crucial that this interface be designed to provide for convenient, efficient user-system interaction if the marketing information system is to have impact on management.

While the more traditional batch processing operations will continue to play a useful and important role in marketing information systems of the future, our attention will focus on the newer capacity for a closely coupled relationship between manager or user and the system, made feasible by the advent of time shared computers. Time shared systems allow many users to access and use a computer simultaneously. At present the most common form of interactive communication is the remote typewriter. While this form of input/output has been enormously useful and will continue to be so, computer graphics will come to play a much larger role in the future, because graphical display is often a more convenient medium in which to communicate with management.

Morton has described the use of such a graphical "management terminal system" in coordinating marketing and production planning in the consumer appliance division of Westinghouse [15]. This process originally absorbed three weeks of calendar time and six days of executive time. The new graphical system used the same data, models, and analytic approaches, adding nothing more than the capacity for interactive graphical display of such items as forecasted and observed sales, production, and inventory over several time periods by product. The graphical system changed the decision making style drastically: the three top managers coordinating marketing and production would now do so by having a session at the interactive video console. Calendar time required was reduced from three weeks to one half day, executive time from six man-days to one. Thus valuable executive time was released and the organization became more responsive to planning errors since the correction time was dramatically reduced. In addition to these objective results, it was also felt that decision making had improved as a result of the use of this system.

Consider also the problem of sales territory definition for a large sales force. A map of the area to be partitioned could be projected on a graphical display device connected to a computer containing relevant information about the area and the salesman (e.g., distribution of present and potential customers in the area). With a light pen, the sales manager could partition the graphic display area into sales territories. Once at a territory definition which he would like to consider, the computer could take the graphic input and evelute sales and marketing implications of the proposed territorial definitions with a sales model or models using area information stored in the data bank. If the manager approved of his current territorial definition, he might decide to adopt it. Probably he would like to explore several alternatives to achieve a satisfactory (even if not globally optimal) definition. This method of user-machine interaction

The authors of information theory

Norbert Wiener of M.I.T., ex-child prodigy and one of the world's foremost mathematicians, was the first to grasp clearly that communication of information is a problem in statistics.

Claude Shannon of Bell Laboratories, a thirty-seven-year-old engineer and mathematician, published his brilliant work, *A Mathematical Theory of Communication*, in 1948.

to be prepared to vary the intensity of every dot on every one of the 525 scanning lines thirty times a second. To do this required a bandwidth of some four million cycles, or nearly 1,000 times that required for ordinary radio. Shannon recalls that one of the questions motivating his early work was: could television be compressed into a smaller bandwidth, or couldn't it?

While information theory now shows that it can, no one has progressed much beyond paper plans, for the job is extremely tricky and takes a lot of hardware, as the diagram and caption on Fig. 8 suggest.

It is precisely here that the value and power of a good theory become difficult to describe. A theory builds no machinery. But inevitably, when good theories are enunciated, they make machinery easier to build. "Before we had the theory a lot of us were deeply troubled," says Jerome Wiesner, director of M.I.T.'s Research Laboratory of Electronics. "We had been dealing with a commodity that we could never see or really define. We were in the situation petroleum engineers would be in if they didn't have a measuring unit like the gallon. We had intuitive feelings about these matters, but we didn't have a clear understanding."

One "bit" of information

To provide a measure for information, which makes it possible to measure the "something" in different sorts of messages, information theory builds from the simplest of all bases. It considers two symbols, say A and B, and the way they may be combined into messages. We have already seen that an endless string of A's presents nothing that needs transmitting. Information begins with uncertainty—with the first B. As more B's are mixed in with the A's the engineer has to send out more signals. In the extreme case when there are as many B's as A's and they appear at random, i.e., unpredictably, the flow of signals—hence the flow of information—reaches a maximum. The simplest possible code for A and B is 0 and 1. If the engineer sends the 1 over a channel as one electric impulse, and the 0 as "no impulse," he has achieved all the economy possible.

Thus the engineer is working hardest, in the simplest case, when transmitting two symbols of equal probability. This suggested to Wiener and Shannon that *the unit of information be defined as that which makes a decision between two equally probable events*. This unit was baptized the "bit" because the symbols 0 and 1 are technically known as "binary digits," which someone had previously abbreviated to "bits." Thus to transmit a random string of A's and B's the engineer has to transmit one full bit of information, either 0 or 1, every time the message source utters one letter or the other.

By stringing together code groups composed of bits—just as Morse used dots and dashes—it is possible to code the entire alphabet of twenty-six letters, or "alphabets" of any desired length. A code group two bits long provides four combinations, 00, 01, 10, 11, hence can be used to encode a four-letter "alphabet," say, A, B, C, D. A three-bit code can be arranged in eight possible combinations: 000, 001, 010, 011, 100, 101, 110, 111, hence will specify an eight-letter alphabet. Note that as the code lengthens by *one* bit, the number of combinations *doubles*. Thus an eight-bit code provides 256 combinations starting with 00000000 and ending with 11111111.

Information theory tells the engineer that his codes are efficient only when each 0 and 1, i.e., each bit, is working just as hard as it can. When this is achieved, says the theory, the engineer can count up the number of bits he has used, and this will tell him the *net* amount of information in the original message.

Since the engineer, obviously, cannot be expected to sit down and test every possible way of encoding a message into 0's and 1's, the theory provides him with an equation that gives, in bits, the amount of information per symbol in any message—be it speech, music, or pictures.* All the engineer has to put into the equation is the relative frequency with which each symbol appears in the message. This is not hard to do for a single message, but the answer obtained in this way is not very useful. What should go into the equation are frequencies with which *groups of symbols* are used in a large sample of messages.

This concept is easiest to follow if we consider written English. Morse dealt only with frequencies for each letter. However, he might have counted the frequencies of letter *pairs*, of which there are 676 possibilities from AA to ZZ. These he could have ranked in decreasing order of frequency, assigning a longer code to each as he went down the list. (Had he done this, of course, telegraphers would have given up in despair.) If letter pairs were coded into binary digits, with no regard to frequencies, the average code length would be about 9.4 bits. Such a code could be devised by drawing up a "code mobile" similar to that shown for the twenty-six-letter alphabet on Fig. 4. If the mobile were extended to support 676 symbols (i.e., 676 letter pairs), the number of bits needed to specify each would usually be nine, though some symbols would require ten.

If, however, the 676 symbols were hung, according to frequency, on what Fig. 3 describes as an asymmetrical "mobile," some commonplace letter pairs (for example, TH and IE) would be assigned codes only two or three bits long, while the least frequent pairs would carry codes sixteen or seventeen bits long. If ordinary English were translated into such a code, a count would show that, on the average, only

---

In written messages the symbols are the letters of the alphabet; in spoken messages the symbols are the various phonetic sounds, of which there are about forty; in pictures the symbols are the number of distinguishable tones from white to black of which each "dot" of the picture is composed. In played music, the number of possible symbols may be obtained by "quantizing" the complex sound wave of the music into a succession of numerical values. How this may be done is illustrated in Fig. 6.

7.1 instead of 9.4 bits had been used to encode each pair of letters. This works out to 3.56 bits per letter as against the 4.7 bits required when the code is assigned without *any* reference to frequencies.

The question that fascinated Shannon was how *little* information does ordinary English really contain. If he could determine this he would know how tightly English might theoretically be encoded. With existing frequency tables he could go only one step beyond two-letter frequencies, to three-letter frequencies (calculated as an aid to cryptographers). These, in Shannon's equation, reduced the code requirement to 3.3 bits per letter.

It is easy to see why no one ever carried the frequency tables beyond three-letter groups: there are 17,576 possible ways to arrange twenty-six letters into groups of three, and nearly half a million combinations of four-letter groups, from AAAA to ZZZZ. Shannon, however, was determined to press further, so he reasoned that any average speaker of English ought to have a tremendous "built-in" knowledge of English statistics. To tap this knowledge, Shannon resorted to ingenious guessing games.

The guessing game

In one game he would pick a passage at random, from a book, and ask someone to guess the letters, one by one. He would tell the subject only if he were wrong, and the subject would continue until he finally guessed the right letter (or space). Shannon quickly discovered that the average person requires substantially fewer than 3.3 guesses to identify the correct letter in ordinary text. The relation between guesses and bits of information should become clearer in what follows.*

One of Shannon's favorite passages for this type of game was *"There is no reverse on a motorcycle a friend of mine found this out rather dramatically the other day."* In this

Information theorists view the game Twenty Questions as an exercise in their theory. If the game were played perfectly, they say, each yes or no should provide the contestant with one bit of information. In this view, twenty bits would suffice to identify 2^{20}, or one out of a million-plus, possible objects. This indicates why the twenty-first question would frequently be so helpful; with twenty-one questions it should be possible to identify one of 2^{21}, or over two million objects.

passage there are 102 letters and spaces, including a final space after "day." Going through the passage letter by letter, one of Shannon's subjects guessed right on his first guess 79 times, and correctly identified all 102 letters and spaces with only 198 guesses, or less than two guesses per letter or space.

In Joyce, a compression?

After mathematical analysis of many such experiments Shannon concluded that in ordinary literary English the long-range statistical effects reduce the information content to about *one bit per letter*. That is to say, if one sees the first 50 or 100 letters of a message, he can be reasonably certain, on the average, that the next following letter (which he hasn't seen) will be one of only two equally probable letters. To remove this much uncertainty requires, by definition, only one bit of information.

Naturally, the amount of uncertainty, hence amount of information, varies among different samples of English. In his basic paper on communication theory, Shannon writes: "Two [opposite] extremes of redundancy in English prose are represented by Basic English and by James Joyce's book, *Finnegans Wake.* The Basic English vocabulary is limited to 850 words and the redundancy is very high. This is reflected in the expansion that occurs when a passage is translated into Basic English. Joyce on the other hand enlarges the vocabulary and is alleged to achieve a compression of semantic content."

Shannon's calculation that the average letter of English (in a long passage) contains only one bit of information has this surprising implication. It says that with proper encoding it should be possible to translate any page of ordinary English into a succession of binary digits, 0 and 1, so that there are no more digits than there were letters in the original text. In other words, twenty-four of the twenty-six letters of the alphabet are superfluous. So far as printed English is concerned, this is the goal that information theory establishes for the communication engineer.*

To help engineers visualize how English might be tightly encoded, Shannon asks them to imagine a

However, the theory recognizes that redundancy often has value. It is English's high redundancy, for example, that makes typographical errors fairly easy to catch. By using a few extra binary digits, it is possible to design error-checking and error-correcting codes.

communication system in which the transmitting device "guesses" upcoming letters in the way his subject guesses the letters in *"There is no reverse on a motorcycle."* The numbers under each of the following letters (and spaces) indicate the number of guesses the human subject required for the first words:

T H E R E   I S   N O
1 1 1 5 1 1 2   1 1 2   1 1

R E V E R S E
15 1 17 1 1 1 2

In theory, one could build a transmitter or encoding device that would approach this performance by providing it with a suitable set of operating instructions or program. It might, for example, be programed to guess T to start every message. After T it might always guess H, then E. After E, however, its programed sequence of guesses, in order, might be space, S, I, Y, and R. Presumably the human subject ran through some such sequence before guessing R. Like the human, the machine finds that its program of first and second choices works fine until it reaches the R and V in REVERSE.

With such a transmitter, the symbols that go over the channel are not the letters in the message but the numbers (in binary code) corresponding to the transmitter's guesses. (Naturally, strings of 1's would be coded into more economical form.) The receiver at the other end is an "identical twin" of the transmitter, hence it "knows," for example, that its own fifth guess after T-H-E would be R, and so on.

To reach the goal of two bits per letter—let alone the theoretical one bit—such a transmitter should not even start to guess until it had inspected at least the first ten letters of the message. Once it starts guessing it should make every guess on the basis of probabilities established by the preceding ten letters. This means that to program such a transmitter someone would have to establish these probabilities by tabulating all combinations of eleven letters in a fair sample of all the English ever written. Since there are nearly four million billion ways to arrange twenty-six letters in groups of eleven, the task is all but unthinkable. Even so it might be done electronically if anyone thought the project worth while.

The speaking machines

Meanwhile, communication engineers will concentrate their efforts on fatter targets. Two of the fattest

are present-day telephone and television systems, which, as one Bell Labs engineer phrases it, "ignore the past and pretend each [message] sample is a complete surprise."

Long before information theory, Bell Labs perceived that speech involved great redundancies of its own, independent of the redundancies existing in language itself. The Vocoder, described and diagramed in Fig. 7, represents an early and continuing effort to code speech into more economical form for transmission.

So far, however, there are no plans to use the Vocoder in the telephone system—in part because one technical problem is still unsolved, that of establishing pitch with 100 per cent accuracy. Meanwhile, Bell Labs has worked out another speech-compression system called Vobanc, which makes a bandwidth saving of only 50 per cent, but does it with equipment which is simpler than the Vocoder's, and without remaking speech from hisses and buzzes.

An ear for speech

For the distant future, Bell researchers are experimenting with systems that promise to compress speech even more tightly than the Vocoder. One, now in early development, involves a machine that will recognize spoken sounds. This machine, called AUDREY.

Originally just an "automatic digit recognizer," AUDREY has now been equipped to recognize sixteen of the most important phonetic sounds. When AUDREY recognizes a phonetic sound she signals a hiss-buzz generator (like the Vocoder's) to reproduce it. The result, while not yet equal to the Vocoder product, is surprisingly good. When AUDREY was expected only to recognize digits she frequently had trouble with digits spoken by anyone but her two inventors. Now, however, she can surmount this difficulty. Whereas she may still be unable to recognize a poorly spoken digit, she can signal the hiss-buzz generator to reproduce it accurately enough so it can be recognized as a poorly spoken digit.

If hooked into a phone system, the only signal AUDREY would send over the line would be a four-bit code identifying, in sequence, the particular phonetic sounds uttered by the speaker. Since an average speaker produces about ten of these per second, the channel need have a capacity of only about forty bits per second. This happens to be very close to the capacity needed to send the same message at the same rate by ordinary telegraphy.

Television is predictable

In television the room for improvement is about as great, and the incentive to do something about it is possibly greater. It is much easier to visualize the redundancy in pictures on a TV screen than in a telephone conversation. As in a sequence of movie frames, there is usually very little difference in the successive pictures beamed onto a TV screen. Bell scientists estimate that frequently the redundancy in TV runs as high as 99 per cent. When this happens, the signal, in theory, could be transmitted on a 40,000-cycle, instead of four-million-cycle, channel.

Since the Bell System has almost sole responsibility for piping network television around the country, it is more eager than anyone else to slice away at the redundancy. With a compression of perhaps 100-to-1 it might be possible to send television signals across the ocean in one hop as is now done with short-wave radio. Bell Labs is designing experimental equipment that may achieve the first practical compression of a TV signal. As a first step, Bell has already demonstrated that there are several ways to code a TV signal to reduce power consumption. One of these methods is illustrated in Fig. 8.

The battle against noise

The communication art changes rapidly, however, and it is conceivable that ten or twenty years from now channel capacity will be much cheaper than it is today, and the Bell System may no longer feel any urgency about compressing television signals. Reason: Bell has in the laboratory new types of signal-carrying systems that will accommodate—in a single "pipe" called a wave guide—hundreds of standard TV channels. Nothing, however, is gained without cost. In the new "pipes" high capacity is achieved by speeding up the signaling process. This makes the signal more vulnerable to imperfections in transmission, which cause what the communication engineer calls noise. The term "noise" covers a host of electric disturbances that degrade a signal. The ultimate unavoidable source of noise is the "thermal" motion of electrons (the hum) in the electronic equipment itself.

Noise, basically a random phenomenon, is another fundamental problem to which information theory

has applied the powerful tools of statistics. The theory tells the engineer how to establish the accuracy with which a message may be transmitted through a noisy channel. As Wiener points out, if there were no noise, the engineer could, in theory, transmit a perfectly measured voltage and thereby transmit an infinity of information. Thus a voltage measured precisely out to the billionth decimal place could represent a coded message a billion digits long.

If the engineer finds he must pass a TV signal through a wide but noisy channel he will probably turn to a relatively new coding system called "pulse code modulation," or PCM, which minimizes the effects of noise. PCM (as explained on Fig. 6) can be used to encode music, pictures, or any other type of message into the pulse-and-no-pulse of a binary code. PCM is effective in combating noise because it is extremely difficult for noise to give rise to a spurious pulse, or to blur out an existing pulse. The checkered wheel in Fig. 1 is designed to code information into PCM's nearly blur-proof form. (Photo transistors lined up along the radius of the wheel transmit pulses when they are behind white (clear) segments of the wheel, "no pulses" if black segments come between them and a light source.)

While the first U.S. patent on PCM was issued in 1942, there is reason to believe that PCM's virtues would have gone largely unappreciated if it had not been for information theory. Shannon showed for the first time precisely how the capacity of a channel in bits is related to the bandwidth, the signal power, and the noise. His equation showed that noise could be combated either by raising the signal power, by increasing the bandwidth, or by changing the signaling method. The theory also suggests that signaling methods even better than PCM remain to be discovered.

How perfect?

It is the mark of a great theory that, beginning with certain intuitive concepts, it erects a series of relationships, which, rigorously extended, lead to propositions that are not at all self-evident. Thus the intuitive basis of relativity theory would have seemed reasonable to Aristotle, but its conclusion that energy and mass are exchangeable would not.

While information theory does not contain anything so dramatic as $E=mc^2$, it does contain one

conclusion of great subtlety that continues to astonish its most diligent students. It is a conclusion that, by extension, has great significance for designers of computers and automatic factories, on the one hand, and neurophysiologists on the other. And there are those who believe it may one day have significance in the everyday (i.e., non-electronic) affairs of men.

The striking conclusion is this: After setting up the relationship between channel capacity, bandwidth, power, and noise, Shannon goes on to prove that if an information source produces information at a rate that does not exceed the channel capacity, there exists a method for putting the information through the channel and recovering it at the other side with negligibly small error. Simply stated, this means that a channel, *no matter how noisy*, can give, as a limit, ideal performance—in short, perfection from imperfection. "This to me," says M.I.T.'s Robert Fano, who teaches information theory, "is still a very astonishing thing. It has been definitely proved, but, except for trivial cases, we don't know how to do it."

Evidence is accumulating that living organisms long ago acquired the secret for obtaining near-perfect performance from relatively imperfect apparatus. For example, generations of physiologists have puzzled over the ability of the ear, which seems quite grossly designed, to distinguish two tones almost identical in pitch. Recently, W. H. Huggins obtained his doctorate at M.I.T. with a brilliant theory of hearing that seems to explain the mystery. What the ear employs, evidently, is an extremely clever encoding system. While Huggins made no direct use of information theory, his work is generally included in information theory's fast growing body of literature, for it speaks of an information-handling mechanism.

Man as communicator

Some of the most interesting applications of information theory, outside of electrical engineering, are being made in experimental psychology. To the psychologist, man may be considered as a message source or as a channel, but not very readily as a transmitter or a receiver. If you try to measure his abilities purely as a transmitter or receiver, you find you are really using him as a channel. Thus there seems to be no good way to ascertain the rate at which the eye or ear may receive information except by

measuring the amount that is remembered or otherwise played back.

In tests run at M.I.T., subjects were asked to point to numbered squares as fast as they could read numbers flashed in random sequence. The test was run with two numbers and two squares, four numbers and four squares, and so on up to 4,096 numbers and 4,096 squares. As might be expected, the subject can hit quite a few squares per second when he has only a few to choose from, but when he has 1,024 (each worth ten bits) he does well to average 1.5 per second. In terms of information theory, it turns out that the average person can handle about fifteen bits per second.

The highest human channel capacity that M.I.T. psychologists have measured is forty-five bits per second, determined by a variant of the experiment just described. The world's fastest typist, in typing 149 words per minute, is handling just about twenty-five bits per second, if each letter be given a value of two bits. (This seems fair since she probably cannot grasp the long-range clues that, according to Shannon, reduce the information to one bit per letter.) The world's shorthand record is 282 words per minute, which, on the same basis, works out to about forty-seven bits per second.

These figures provide an upper limit for the amount of information a person may handle in a lifetime. The upper limit: roughly 50 billion bits.* One can now appreciate the immense channel capacity used to transmit television. The information handled in the most diligently spent lifetime could, if suitably encoded, be transmitted over a television channel in about sixteen minutes. The information handled in an *average* lifetime could hardly keep a TV channel occupied more than ten seconds.

There are dangers, of course, in overworking any concept, no matter how helpful. Some psychologists who originally encouraged their colleagues to study information theory and to apply it in their experiments now feel that the theory is frequently misapplied by psychologists—and almost inevitably misapplied by sociologists.

Inside the nerve

As Norbert Wiener perceived with his characteristic great enthusiasm, the concepts of information theory apply directly to neurophysiology. Largely as a result of his

Fifty bi. per second, twelve hours a day for sixty years.

inspiration, M.I.T. has become one of the leading centers for the study of the central nervous system. The work, which comes under the Research Laboratory of Electronics, not only has high significance in its own right, but since biological reflexes are the most economical known, it may suggest ways to improve man-made systems.

To learn more of fundamental nerve circuitry, the M.I.T. investigators insert dozens of ultra-tiny electrodes into the spinal cords of anesthetized animals to chart the detailed flow of nerve messages. In the old technique for recording nerve impulses, a relatively large electrode was clamped outside a bundle of nerve fibers. This method, explains one M.I.T. scientist, was about as helpful as trying to analyze the communication network of the entire U.S. using only the signals picked up by ships stationed off the coast. The new electrode-insertion method requires complex electronic recording gear that is available only at a relatively few places like M.I.T., and the work goes slowly.

Information and life

So far no mention has been made of a word that appears in information theory with great frequency. The word is "entropy," and Shannon uses it as synonymous with "amount of information." When Shannon had derived his equation for calculating "amount of information," he found it was precisely the same equation that physicists use to calculate the quantity known as "entropy" in thermodynamics. What the physicist means by "entropy" has stumped freshman physics students for well over seventy-five years, but it is really not too difficult a concept. In thermodynamics, entropy measures the degree of randomness, or disorder, in atomic and molecular systems. The more disorder, the higher the entropy. The famous second law of thermodynamics states that in an isolated system, entropy may stay constant or increase, but never decrease. For an analogy, consider a shoebox into which one puts a handful of white beads at one end and a handful of black beads at the other. If the box is never touched, the beads will stay in their respective ends, i.e., entropy (disorder) will stay constant. However, the moment the box is disturbed the beads will begin to mix, and disorder, i.e., entropy, will increase.

In Shannon's view, entropy (or amount of information) reaches a maximum when all the symbols in a message appear independently with equal probability, i.e., in random order.* Shannon does not suggest that there is any real identity between his entropy and thermodynamic entropy. Other scientists, however, have speculated that some deep, underlying identity *may* exist.

The identity seems tantalizingly real when one considers the nature of life. Life appears to refute the second law of thermodynamics, until one considers that life cannot continue in a closed system. In his book, *What Is Life?*, Erwin Schrödinger, the Austrian-born physicist, stated a view that has gained popularity when he observed that life feeds on high-grade energy or negative entropy, that is, on substances with highly ordered structures. But the question remains: How does a simple leaf utilize solar energy to erect the primary ordered structures (e.g., sugar, starch, proteins)? It does this, Wiener and others suspect, because photosynthesis employs catalysts that somehow have the power to suspend the second law of thermodynamics, locally and temporarily. Such sorting agents, first proposed by Clerk Maxwell, have been called "Maxwell Demons." For the demon (catalyst) to operate it has to obtain information about the particles it is sorting. If life is thus viewed as a manipulation of energy and information, Wiener and others consider it fitting that both carry "entropy" as a common measure.

Information and meaning

While some extremely gifted minds have tried to use information theory as the foundation for a new theory of meaning, they have not been too successful, or at least they have not convinced their colleagues of their success. Yet even many of the unconvinced continue to hope that a foundation exists. One of the most hopeful is Warren Weaver, president-elect of the American Association for the Advancement of Science. Soon after Shannon's work appeared, Weaver wrote: "The theory . . . has so penetratingly cleared the air that one is now perhaps for the first time ready for a real theory of meaning. . . . One

Some information theorists, including Wiener, prefer to view information as equivalent to negative entropy —seemingly because information, to them, represents order not disorder. It is doubtful, however, if this reflects anything more than a bookkeeping difference.

has the vague feeling . . . that information and meaning may be subject to some joint restriction that compels the sacrifice of one if you insist on having much of the other."

Until Warren Weaver's hope is fulfilled, perhaps the hardest thing for the average person to keep steadily in mind is that information theory says nothing whatever about meaning. It is content to tell the engineer that a surprisingly large part of any English sentence (or of any other ordinary message) is predictable. But with all its quaint redundancies the English sentence is still, in Churchill's phase, "a noble thing." The mind cannot conceive its all but infinite variety. In a billion years even television's capacious channel could not transmit more than a subsubmicroscopic fraction of the ways Churchill

might have written a single speech.

The power of the theory lies in its ability to cope with messages of any nature. It will, for example, help the neurologist analyze communication networks that transmit apparently meaningless strings of coded symbols. Indeed, neurologists have already discovered that the signals that transmit information from the eye to the brain appear to be wholly random. However, to the brain, which knows the code, the signals are not meaningless; their apparent randomness simply reflects a high degree—conceivably the optimum degree—of compression. It is this same compression that information theory invites the communication engineer to achieve.

It is hard to see how information theory can fail to rank with the enduring great. For it goes to the heart of what appears to be life's most essential feature—the ability to communicate information. END

"THE VALUE OF INFORMATION"

The Journal of Accountancy (125:6), 1968 June, pages 41-45 (extract of pages 41-44).

The Hirsch article is included because of its practical, well written, and to-the-point exposition of the value of information in an organizational environment. The article points out why all decisions are made with imperfect information and then describes how the value of information may be calculated. This cost/value justification is divided into justification with calculable benefits and justification without calculable benefits. In the latter case, since benefits are not calculable, the approach by Hirsch is a set of six value guidelines:

1. Information must influence decisions
2. More accuracy means higher costs
3. Timeliness influences costs
4. Shorter delay means higher costs
5. The system's capacity affects the value of information
6. What is the actionability of information?

The article explains and illustrates each of these guidelines. The last section of the article on the cost of information processing equipment is somewhat dated and, therefore, omitted.

READING SUGGESTIONS

There are three main points in the article: (1) the reason for operating with imperfect information, (2) the cost justification of information with calculable benefits, and (3) the cost justification of information without calculable benefits. The major problem is in the latter situation, and the major emphasis is on the six value guidelines. His explanations are especially pertinent regarding accuracy, timeliness (processing interval), and delay (response time).

QUESTIONS

1. What are the reasons for operating with imperfect information?
2. What is the justification yardstick if cost and benefit can be calculated?
3. List the six value guidelines for nondollar measurable information.
4. Name the advantages of short and long information intervals.
5. What is meant by actionability of information?

BY RUDOLPH E. HIRSCH

THE VALUE
OF INFORMATION

A discussion of when information value
can and cannot be calculated, what
determines information costs, and some
techniques for controlling them.

RUDOLPH HIRSCH *is Manager, Management Advisory Services, at the New York office of Price Waterhouse & Co. He graduated from Swarthmore in 1950 with a bachelor of arts degree and from George Washington University in 1955 with a master of arts degree. Mr. Hirsch is also an Instructor at the New School for Social Research. This article is based on talks given at the National Association of Accountants Seminars on Value Analysis in Chicago and Cleveland.*

INFORMATION has become one of the main ingredients of business activity. The great increase of white-collar workers is legendary, and most of them concentrate on producing information and/or consuming it. The growth of government lends further importance to information as such, since government on all levels is a voracious consumer of tax data, operating reports and other business data while turning out imposing amounts of statistical information. Information in the form of specialized knowledge has also become, according to many economists, the decisive factor in the survival of many large, complex enterprises.

In this article, an attempt will be made to study the use of information in business and to present a number of guidelines for determining whether and what kind of information is needed, the value it has for its organization, and those costs of producing it which it justifies.

Ideally information is the sum total of data needed for decision-making. In practice, virtually all decisions are made with too little of some kinds of information and/or too much of others. Any item of information is needed if without it a decision would be different; leading to the conclusion that an item of information has no value if it cannot at least potentially influence a decision.

The fact that all decisions are made with imperfect information is almost a truism when it is considered that perfect information would involve an ability to foretell or control the future. Not being able to do this is not the only reason for operating with imperfect information. The others are:

1. The needed information is unavailable. It would be impossible, for example, to obtain precise statistics on last year's typewriter sales in Matsubililand.

2. The effort to get the information may be unrealistically great or costly. An example would be data on last year's typewriter sales in Chicago.

3. There is no knowledge of the availability of the information. It appears that the existence of a large part of the U. S. government's statistics is not known to its potential users.

4. The information is not available in the form needed. For example, sales analysis information may be available by customer rather than by type of item sold.

For all of these reasons, decisions must be made with imperfect information. Therefore more or different information always has value, which must be analyzed to determine whether the costs of providing it are justified.

VALUE JUSTIFICATION WITH CALCULABLE BENEFITS

The justification yardstick for information is that, if its cost is less than its contribution to profit or reduction of other costs, the information is justified. This yardstick is useful in cases where the information has a *concrete measurable objective,* and although these cases are probably in the minority, many of them do exist. An historical example is that of Nathan Rothschild, who in 1815 foresaw the influence which the outcome of the battle of Waterloo, then about to start, would have on the price of British government bonds. In order to get the earliest possible information about the outcome of the battle, he provided his private and extremely costly courier service from the battlefield to London. He was thus the first to have information about the French defeat and gained a large fortune through his dealings in British government bonds during the brief time in which only he had the correct information.

Another example of measurable information value comes from the installation of computers by the Internal Revenue Service for processing income tax returns Yields were approximately $3 billion above forecast in 1965, the first year of full computer use. If the link between computers, higher tax yields and taxpayer honesty may be assumed, then the cost of providing the new computerized information was amortized several times over during the first year, and the computers' information and their costs were fully and spectacularly justified.

A more conventional instance of measurable information value would be changes in accounting systems permitting earlier billings and hence earlier payments. Calculation of how much faster payments are then received and of the resulting interest implications is an easy matter. If the expense increase brought about by faster billing is less than the amount of additional interest collected (or interest payments foregone), the expense of the faster billing system is justified.

Value justification of information is a relatively simple matter in cases such as these, where objectives are clear-cut and the extent to which they are achieved can be exactly determined. Unfortunately this holds true in only a minority of cases.

VALUE JUSTIFICATION WITHOUT CALCULABLE BENEFITS

Most cases of information value determination are less clear-cut than the preceding examples. Typically improvements in information systems are designed to bring benefits such as faster order processing. Changes of this kind are intended to be beneficial and usually are, but it is difficult and in most cases impossible to make a firm calculation of their dollar impact. An example of this situation would be the major airlines, most of which have or are about to install computer-based reservation systems. Though invariably costly, no attempt is made to profit-justify them. Their justification is instead that they will enable the airline to continue operating at all with rapidly and constantly increasing passenger volumes, and to prevent competing airlines using such systems from gaining a competitive advantage.

Cases such as these, in which the estimation of benefits obtained cannot be a concrete matter, contain an element of risk: it takes a long time to determine whether or not the expected benefits are being obtained; i.e., an information system may be operated for quite a long time before it can be decided to discontinue it. Most computer professionals can cite examples of abandonment of computerization projects after futile installation efforts measured in man-years and rolled heads.

Following are some value guidelines for non-dollar-measurable information:

1. **Information must influence decisions.** No information is worth producing if it does not influence management decisions or functional operations of the organization.

2. **More accuracy means higher costs.** Therefore the amount of accuracy provided by the information should be kept down to the point below which decisions or operations would be different.

The costliness of additional accuracy is demonstrated by the following incident from my work in a bank shortly after graduation. At the time I joined the bank, state law required banks to balance exactly at the end of each business day. After a few months, though hopefully not as a direct result of my having entered banking, the law was changed to permit balancing to within $10 followed by an adjusting entry. As a result of $10 less of accuracy, closings occurred 1-2 hours earlier at a saving of that much overtime per clerk per day.

A high level of accuracy is costly in large part because most accuracy-increasing techniques are based on duplication: verifying punched cards, double-entry bookkeeping, proofing, etc.

One of the most difficult tasks in analyzing the value of information is to determine the point of decreasing returns of accuracy. It is, of course, a brave value analyst who will go on record as recommending less accuracy.

3. **Timeliness influences costs.** Virtually all information is produced repeatedly. In general, the

shorter the interval between two appearances of the information, the more costly that information becomes, since any production process—including production of information—has its set-up costs. The oftener the information is produced in a year, the oftener these set-up costs are incurred and the higher the annual information bill becomes. No general rule can, of course, be given for calculating the most appropriate information interval. Arguments exist for both shorter and longer ones and can be summarized as follows:

Advantages of Short Information Intervals

a. Short intervals decrease the amount of information which must be stored until the next production cycle, thus lowering the cost of information storage devices needed, such as computer discs, filing cabinets, etc.

b. Information appearing at frequent intervals makes possible early identification and correction of emergency conditions.

c. If information is not produced often enough, "bootleg" records will be kept by the recipients. It will be uncontrolled and inaccurate. Conversely, "bootlegging" is invariably a danger signal that the information system it duplicates is in some way inadequate.

d. Shorter information intervals mean fresher news which will more effectively draw the attention of those receiving it.

Advantages of Long Information Intervals

a. As already mentioned, longer intervals mean fewer information production cycles in the course of the year and thus lower total production set-up costs and lower overall information expense.

b. Reports covering longer periods reduce the importance of unusual one-time or few-time events to their proper magnitude, while in short-interval reports such events can appear unduly serious. In short, reports produced less often permit easier recognition of trends.

c. Reports produced at longer intervals tend to be reviewed thoroughly. If a report appears too often, its recipient tends to collect and summarize it rather than read it, or to ignore it altogether.

Since many enterprises are influenced by seasonal or other predictable variations, varying of intervals should be considered but for whatever reason seldom is. Whoever makes, let alone adopts, this suggestion is unlikely to become popular with his chief accountant or computer operations super-

visor, but this approach often has its merits. An example is a well-known newspaper for ice hockey enthusiasts which appears weekly in the winter and monthly in the summer.

4. Shorter delays mean higher costs. A certain amount of time always elapses between the end of an event and the appearance of the information about it. Examples of this are the times needed for closing books, sending data to keypunching, keypunching itself, verifying, proving the cards, waiting to gain computer access for these cards, running the computer and decollating, bursting, binding and distributing the computer-produced information. The cost of an information system is greatly influenced by the length of its delay; the shorter the delay, the higher the costs.

Representatives of the computer manufacturer involved once told me that if the maximum response time of an airline reservation system they were about to deliver had been 5 seconds instead of 3, the multimillion dollar programing expense could have been reduced by half. If anything, I believe that they were conservative in their estimate.

The cost/delay relationship can be demonstrated more conventionally: the use of more bookkeepers for earlier closings, the use of local computing facilities to avoid the delay in sending data to and from central facilities, the use of faster and hence more costly computers to reduce turnaround time. Not surprisingly, the ultimate reduction in delay, "real-time" computer-based information systems which reduce delays to a few seconds, is probably the most costly of all.

When it appears that the value of information can be increased by minimizing its delay, it should be considered that the time spent by recipients in reviewing information contributes to the delay. It does not end until a decision has been made. Exception reporting, in which only those items falling outside specified limits are the ones reported, receives far more lip service than actual application. Nevertheless it is a delay-cutting device since it permits recipients to review information more rapidly. Another way of cutting delay is to keep a manager behind his desk rather than on the road so that his reports reach him earlier.

5. The system's capacity affects the value of the information. The capacity of an information system has a direct bearing on its cost and hence on the value its information must have before the system can be justified. The fixed costs of an information system are almost directly proportional to its ability to handle peak volumes. The considerations are almost the same as those of peak-volume considerations of other systems: ability to handle any peak means unused assets in off-peak times. Therefore organizations with high and predictable peaks in information requirements will often do well to consider using temporary office personnel at peak times and/or then using service bureaus to handle peak computer loads. It is then possible to settle for a smaller and less costly in-house information system which can be more fully and evenly utilized throughout the year.

Data recipients will often insist that the additional delays of using a service bureau are unacceptable; the question of the dollar value of reducing delays is thus in effect raised once more. When information peaks are widely spaced and large, the expense of full in-house information processing becomes large and the demands for it should be evaluated critically. In situations such as these, it is often useful to consider how the situation was handled before the availability of computers and other high-speed information processing systems.

6. What is the actionability of information? The implication in the use of this British term is that information is of value only if it influences policy or operations, and thus has no value if prepared for individuals without the appropriate influence. Many reports exist, some founded on fact, of office boys who made better marketing decisions than their sales managers, but any sales information produced only for these exceptional office boys is totally wasted until they receive their deserved promotions. In this connection it may be appropriate to include a rhetoric warning against the sin, often committed, of producing information not because of the recipient's ability to influence the events reported but because he would otherwise feel bypassed. Politically produced information has no dollar value.

THE COST OF INFORMATION-PROCESSING EQUIPMENT

The higher the cost of the information-producing system is, the greater the value of its information to justify that system must be. Let us therefore for the moment assume the value of information as fixed and consider methods of reducing the cost of the system producing it.

Since most major information-producing systems by now involve computers in one way or another, it becomes relevant to discuss various ways in which their cost can be kept under control. Though the cost of computing systems has decreased and will decrease further, data processing expense can easily assume Wagnerian proportions. While cost/throughput ratios have become favorable and most computers are now produced in program-compatible "families" of machines, acquiring (and programming) the first machine is expensive and capacity can only be increased in large and costly increments.

Further, the costs of systems design, programing and startup usually exceed those of the equipment itself. Additional fixed costs of computer usage such as space, management salaries and the like can also be substantial, can only vary in large increments and, in any event, do not change as does data volume.

. . . .

It is, of course, true that many computers are used primarily as printing presses instead of information-producing machines. Invoices, checks, mailing labels, premium notices and the like account for a substantial part of all computer output. Value justification in such cases is usually superfluous since the output must be produced in any case. The question of whether or not to use computers reduces itself to a simple comparison of the cost of producing the output conventionally against the cost of using a computer. No computer should be used entirely for this kind of noninformation production since every organization has uses for information which even a "printing-press" computer can well produce.

It is also possible to mechanize some parts of the executive decision-making process itself. Obvious yes-or-no decisions in fields such as granting credit or processing insurance applications can well be made by computer, leaving only the "gray areas" to managerial discretion. In granting personal credit, for instance, a computer could well produce rejection notices to applicants requesting loans clearly too large for their incomes and approval notices for those wanting loans in obviously reasonable proportion to income. The details of all other loan applications would be printed for managerial decisions on them.

"Printing-press" applications apart, however, value justification should be required for all business information. The need for this has been increased, if possible, by the advent of computers: they have reduced the cost per unit of output but have also dramatically increased information production capacity to the point where an organization can be choked to death in its own reports.

"HUMAN PROBLEM SOLVING: THE STATE OF THE THEORY IN 1970"

American Psychologist (26:2), 1971 February, pages 145-159
(extract of pages 148-159).

This survey article is by two of the best-known and most productive researchers in human problem solving -- Simon and Newell. Simon's other contributions to the field of MIS include: the notion of administrative man as a better model of a decision-making manager, the satisficing behavior of managers in contrast to optimizing behavior, the notion of bounded rationality, and a theory of complexity.

The first part of this article, describing the state of the theory in 1958 and the development of their research strategy (referred to as the "Elements" paper), is largely omitted because the purpose of including the article is to survey the theory in 1970.

The theory of human problem solving makes reference to three fundamental elements: a human information processing system, a task environment, and a problem space. The state of the theory as of 1970 is surveyed with respect to these three elements. The article concludes with some ideas about research needed. Three main research questions are outlined: how do problem solvers generate problem spaces (discussed in some detail), the neurological basis for human information processing, and the application of human problem solving processes to the practice of education.

The major points to be obtained from the article are the state of theory with respect to the characteristics of the human information processing system, the structure of task environments, and problem spaces. The problem space discussion also considers objections that have been made to the problem space approach to a theory of problem solving.

READING SUGGESTIONS

The article is organized well for study. There is first a discussion of the three elements of the problem solving theory (the human information system, task environment, and problem space) then a discussion of the direction in which the theory and research might be expected to go.

To enhance understanding of one of the major experimental tasks used for research in problem solving, try to solve the following arithmetic problem before reading the article.

    DONALD
  + GERALD
    ROBERT

Assign the numerals 0 - 9 uniquely to the letters such that the sum is arithmetically correct. Start with D = 5. Carefully reflect on the process used to solve this problem.

The problem space discussion has several fundamental ideas that should be carefully studied. Problem spaces are too large for a sequential search of possibilities. Rather, there appears to be a heuristic for locating feasible regions and examining them. Note the discussion of the types of information and search strategies. The future theory section continues the emphasis on problem space by considering the incomplete evidence on the generation of problem spaces.

QUESTIONS

1. What are the characteristics of the human information-processing system?
2. What is the difference between task environment and problem space?
3. Define problem space.
4. What is meant by hill climbing?
5. What types of information are available in a problem space?
6. What is the difference between scan-and-search and progressive deepening?
7. What are the sources of information for constructing problem spaces?

HUMAN PROBLEM SOLVING:
THE STATE OF THE THEORY IN 1970 [1]

HERBERT A. SIMON AND ALLEN NEWELL [2]

Carnegie-Mellon University

What questions should a theory of problem solving answer? First, it should predict the performance of a problem solver handling specified tasks. It should explain how human problem solving takes place: what processes are used, and what mechanisms perform these processes. It should predict the incidental phenomena that accompany problem solving, and the relation of these to the problem-solving process. . . . It should show how changes in the attendant conditions—both changes "inside" the problem solver and changes in the task confronting him—alter problem-solving behavior. It should explain how specific and general problem-solving skills are learned, and what it is that the problem solver "has" when he has learned them [p. 151].

THEORY OF PROBLEM SOLVING—1958

Now I have been quoting—

—from a paper published in the *Psychological Review* in 1958 (Newell, Shaw, & Simon, 1958). In that paper, titled "Elements of a Theory of Human Problem Solving," our research group reported on the results of its first two years of activity in programming a digital computer to perform problem-solving tasks that are difficult for humans. Problem solving was regarded by many, at that time, as a mystical, almost magical, human activity—as though the preservation of human dignity depended on man's remaining inscrutable to himself.

. . . Psychology is now taking the road taken earlier by other sciences: it is introducing essential formalisms to describe and explain its phenomena. Natural language formulations of the phenomena of human thinking did not yield explanations of what was going on; formulations in

information-processing languages appear to be yielding such explanations. And the pain and cost of acquiring the new tools must be far less than the pain and cost of trying to master difficult problems with inadequate tools.

Our account today will be framed in ordinary language. But we must warn you that it is a translation from information-processing languages which, like most translations, has probably lost a good deal of the subtlety of the original. In particular, we warn you against attaching magical meanings to terms that refer to entirely concrete and operational phenomena taking place in fully defined and operative information-processing systems. The account will also be Pittsburgh-centric. It will refer mainly to work of the Carnegie-RAND group, although information-processing psychology enlists an ever-growing band of research psychologists, many of whom are important contributors of evidence to the theory presented here.

THEORY OF PROBLEM SOLVING—1970

The dozen years since the publication of the "Elements" paper has seen a steady growth of activity in information-processing psychology—both in the area of problem solving and in such areas as learning, concept formation, short-term memory phenomena, perception, and language behavior. Firm contact has been made with more traditional approaches, and information-processing psychology has joined (or been joined by) the mainstream of scientific inquiry in experimental psychology today.[3] Instead of tracing history here, we should like to give a brief account of the product of the history, of the theory of human problem solving that has emerged from the research.

The theory makes reference to an *information-processing system*, the problem solver, confronted by a task. The task is defined objectively (or from the viewpoint of an experimenter, if you prefer) in terms of a *task environment*. It is defined by the problem solver, for purposes of attacking it, in terms of a *problem space*. The shape of the theory can be captured by four propositions (Newell & Simon, in press, Ch. 14):

1. A few, and only a few, gross characteristics of the human information-processing system are invariant over task and problem solver.

2. These characteristics are sufficient to determine that a task environment is represented (in the information-processing system) as a problem space,

[1] The research reported here was supported in part by United States Public Health Service Research Grant MH-07722, from the National Institute of Mental Health.

[2] Since the Distinguished Scientific Contribution Award citation last year recognized that the work for which it was awarded was done by a team, rather than an individual, Dr. Simon thinks it appropriate that Allen Newell, with whom he has been in full partnership from the very beginning of the effort, should be enlisted into coauthorship of this report on it. Both authors would like to acknowledge their debts to the many others who have been members of the team during the past decade and a half, but especially to J. C. Shaw and Lee W. Gregg. This article is based on the final chapter of the authors' forthcoming book, *Human Problem Solving* (Englewood Cliffs, N. J.: Prentice-Hall, in press).

[3] The authors have undertaken a brief history of these developments in an Addendum to their book, *Human Problem Solving* (Newell & Simon, in press).

and that problem solving takes place in a problem space.

3. The structure of the task environment determines the possible structures of the problem space.

4. The structure of the problem space determines the possible programs that can be used for problem solving.

These are the bones of the theory. In the next pages, we will undertake to clothe them in some flesh.

Characteristics of the Information-Processing System

When human beings are observed working on well-structured problems that are difficult but not unsolvable for them, their behaviors reveal certain broad characteristics of the underlying neurophysiological system that supports the problem-solving processes; but at the same time, the behaviors conceal almost all of the detail of that system.

The basic characteristics of the human information-processing system that shape its problem-solving efforts are easily stated: The system operates essentially serially, one-process-at-a-time, not in parallel fashion. Its elementary processes take tens or hundreds of milliseconds. The inputs and outputs of these processes are held in a small short-term memory with a capacity of only a few symbols. The system has access to an essentially infinite long-term memory, but the time required to store a symbol in that memory is of the order of seconds or tens of seconds.

These properties—serial processing, small short-term memory, infinite long-term memory with fast retrieval but slow storage—impose strong constraints on the ways in which the system can seek solutions to problems in larger problem spaces. A system not sharing these properties—a parallel system, say, or one capable of storing symbols in long-term memory in milliseconds instead of seconds—might seek problem solutions in quite different ways from the system we are considering.

The evidence that the human system has the properties we have listed comes partly from problem-solving behavior itself. No problem-solving behavior has been observed in the laboratory that seems interpretable in terms of simultaneous rapid search of disjoint parts of the solver's problem space. On the contrary, the solver always appears to search sequentially, adding small successive ac-

cretions to his store of information about the problem and its solution.[4]

Additional evidence for the basic properties of the system as well as data for estimating the system parameters come from simpler laboratory tasks. The evidence for the 5 or 10 seconds required to store a symbol in long-term memory comes mainly from rote memory experiments; for the seven-symbol capacity of short-term memory, from immediate recall experiments; for the 200 milliseconds needed to transfer symbols into and out of short-term memory, from experiments requiring searches down lists or simple arithmetic computations.[5]

These things we *do* learn about the information-processing system that supports human thinking—but it is significant that we learn little more, that the system might be almost anything as long as it meets these few structural and parametral specifications. The detail is elusive because the system is adaptive. For a system to be adaptive means that it is capable of grappling with whatever task environment confronts it. Hence, to the extent a system is adaptive, its behavior is determined by the demands of that task environment rather than by its own internal characteristics. Only when the environment stresses its capacities along some dimension—presses its performance to the limit—do we discover what those capabilities and limits are, and are we able to measure some of their parameters (Simon, 1969, Ch. 1 and 2).

Structure of Task Environments

If the study of human behavior in problem situations reveals only a little about the structure of the information-processing system, it reveals a great deal about the structure of task environments.

---

[4] Claims that human distractability and perceptual capability imply extensive parallel processing have been refuted by describing or designing serial information-processing systems that are distractable and possess such perceptual capabilities. (We are not speaking of the initial "sensory" stages of visual or auditory encoding, which certainly involve parallel processing, but of the subsequent stages, usually called perceptual.) For further discussion of this issue, see Simon (1967) and Simon and Barenfeld (1969). Without elaborating here, we also assert that incremental growth of knowledge in the problem space is not incompatible with experiences of sudden "insight." For further discussion of this point, see Newell, Shaw, and Simon (1962) and Simon (1966).

[5] Some of this evidence is reviewed in Newell and Simon (in press, Ch. 14).

Consider the cryptarithmetic problem

DONALD
+GERALD

ROBERT

which has been studied on both shores of the Atlantic, in England by Bartlett (1958), and in the United States in our own laboratory (Newell, 1967; Newell & Simon, in press, Part II). The problem is to substitute numbers for the letters in the three names in such a way as to produce a correct arithmetic sum. As the problem is usually posed, the hint is given that $D = 5$. If we look at the protocols of subjects who solve the problem, we find that they all substitute numbers for the letters in approximately the same sequence. First, they set $T = 0$, then $E = 9$ and $R = 7$, then $A = 4$ and $L = 8$, then $G = 1$, then $N = 6$ and $B = 3$, and, finally, $O = 2$.

To explain this regularity in the sequence of assignments, we must look first at the structure of the task itself. A cryptarithmetic problem may be tackled by trying out various tentative assignments of numbers to letters, rejecting them and trying others if they lead to contradictions. In the DONALD + GERALD problem, hundreds of thousands of combinations would have to be tried to find a solution in this way. (There are $9! = 362,880$ ways of assigning nine digits to nine letters.) A serial processor able to make and test five assignments per minute would require a month to solve the problem; many humans do it in 10 minutes or less.

But the task structure admits a heuristic that involves processing first those columns that are most constrained. If two digits in a single column are already known, the third can be found by applying the ordinary rule of arithmetic. Hence, from $D = 5$, we obtain the right-most column: $5 + 5 = T$, hence $T = 0$, with a carry of 1 to the next column. Each time a new assignment is made in this way, the information can be carried into other columns where the same letter appears, and then the most-constrained column of those remaining can be selected for processing. For the DONALD + GERALD problem (but not, of course, for all cryptarithmetic problems), it turns out that the correct assignments for T, E, R, A, L, and G can all be found in this way without any trial-and-error search whatsoever, leaving only N, B, and O for the possible permutations of 6, 3, and 2.

Not only does this heuristic of processing the most-constrained columns first almost eliminate the need for search, but it also reduces the demands on the short-term memory of the problem solver. All the information he has acquired up to any given point can be represented on a single external display, simply by replacing each letter by the digit assigned to it as soon as the assignment is made. Since the assignments are definite, not tentative, no provision need be made by an error-free processing system for correcting wrong assignments, nor for keeping track of assignments that were tried previously and failed. The human information-processing system is subject to error, however, hence requires back-up capabilities not predictable from the demands of the task environment.

Hence, from our knowledge of properties of this task environment, we can predict that an error-free serial information-processing system using the heuristic we have described *could* solve the DONALD + GERALD problem rather rapidly, and without using much short-term memory along the way. But if it solved the problem by this method, it would have to make the assignments in the particular order we have indicated.

The empirical fact that human solvers do make the assignments in roughly this same order provides us with one important piece of evidence (we can obtain many others by analyzing their thinking-aloud protocols and eye movements) that they are operating as serial systems with limited short-term memories. But the empirical data show that there are few task-independent invariants of the human processor beyond the basic structural features we have mentioned. Since the problem solver's behavior is adaptive, we learn from his protocol the shape of the task environment of DONALD + GERALD—the logical interdependencies that hold among the several parts of that problem. We also learn from the protocol the structure of the problem space that the subject uses to represent the task environment, and the program he uses to search the problem space. Though the problem space and program are not task-invariant, they constitute the adaptive interface between the invariant features of the processor and the shape of the environment, and can be understood by considering the functional requirements that such an interface must satisfy.

Problem Spaces

Subjects faced with problem-solving tasks represent the problem environment in internal memory as a space of possible situations to be searched in order to find that situation which corresponds to the solution. We must distinguish, therefore, between the task environment—the omniscient observer's way of describing the actual problem "out there"—and the problem space—the way a particular subject represents the task in order to work on it.

Each node in a problem space may be thought of as a possible state of knowledge to which the problem solver may attain. A state of knowledge is simply what the problem solver knows about the problem at a particular moment of time—knows in the sense that the information is available to him and can be retrieved in a fraction of a second. After the first step of the DONALD + GERALD problem, for example, the subject knows not only that $D = 5$, but also that $T = 0$ and that the carry into the second column from the right is 1. The problem solver's search for a solution is an odyssey through the problem space, from one knowledge state to another, until his current knowledge state includes the problem solution—that is, until he knows the answer.

Problem spaces, even those associated with relatively "simple" task environments, are enormous. Since there are $9! = 362,880$ possible assignments of nine digits to nine letters, we may consider the basic DONALD + GERALD space to be $9!$ in size, which is also the size of the space of tic-tac-toe. The sizes of problem spaces for games like chess or checkers are measured by very large powers of ten—10^{120}, perhaps, in the case of chess. The spaces associated with the problem called "life" are, of course, immensely larger.

For a serial information-processing system, however, the exact size of a problem space is not important, provided the space is very large. A serial processor can visit only a modest number of knowledge states (approximately 10 per minute, the thinking-aloud data indicate) in its search for a problem solution. If the problem space has even a few thousand states, it might as well be infinite—only highly selective search will solve problems in it.

Many of you have tried to solve the Tower of Hanoi problem. (This is very different from the problem of Hanoi in your morning newspaper, but fortunately much less complex.) There are

three spindles, on one of which is a pyramid of wooden discs. The discs are to be moved, one by one, from this spindle, and all placed, in the end, on one of the other spindles, with the constraint that a disc may never be placed on another that is smaller than it is. If there are four discs, the problem space comprised of possible arrangements of discs on spindles contains only $3^4 = 81$ nodes, yet the problem is nontrivial for human adults. The five-disc problem, though it admits only 243 arrangements, is very difficult for most people; and the problems with more than five discs almost unsolvable—until the right heuristic is discovered!

Problems like this one—where the basic problem space is *not* immense—tell us how little trial-and-error search the human problem solver is capable of, or is willing to endure. Problems with immense spaces inform us that the amount of search required to find solutions, making use of available structure, bears little or no relation to the size of the entire space. To a major extent, the power of heuristics resides in their capability for examining small, promising regions of the entire space and simply ignoring the rest. We need not be concerned with how large the haystack is, if we can identify a small part of it in which we are quite sure to find a needle.

Thus, to understand the behavior of a serial problem solver, we must turn to the structure of problem spaces and see just how information is imbedded in such spaces that can be extracted by heuristic processes and used to guide search to a problem solution.

Sources of Information in Problem Spaces

Problem spaces differ not only in size—a difference we have seen to be usually irrelevant to problem difficulty—but also in the kinds of structure they possess. Structure is simply the antithesis of randomness, providing redundancy that can be used to predict the properties of parts of the space not yet visited from the properties of those already searched. This predictability becomes the basis for searching selectively rather than randomly.

The security of combination safes rests on the proposition that there is no way, short of exhaustive search, to find any particular point in a fully random space. (Of course, skilled safecrackers know that complete randomness is not always achieved in the construction of real-world safes, but that is another matter.)

Nonrandomness is information, and information can be exploited to search a problem space in promising directions and to avoid the less promising. A little information goes a long way to keep within bounds the amount of search required, on average, to find solutions.

Hill climbing. The simplest example of information that can be used to solve problems without exhaustive search is the progress test—the test that shows that one is "getting warmer." In climbing a (not too precipitous) hill, a good heuristic rule is always to go upward. If a particular spot is higher, reaching it probably represents progress toward the top. The time it takes to reach the top will depend on the height of the hill and its steepness, but not on its circumference or area—not on the size of the total problem space.

Types of information. There is no great mystery in the nature of the information that is available in many typical problem spaces; and we now know pretty well how humans extract that information and use it to search selectively. For example, in the DONALD + GERALD problem, we saw how information was obtained by arithmetic and algebraic operations. Now, abstracting from particular examples, can we characterize the structure of problem spaces in more general terms?

Each knowledge state is a node in the problem space. Having reached a particular node, the problem solver can choose an *operator* from among a set of operators available to him, and can apply it to reach a new node. Alternatively, the problem solver can abandon the node he has just reached, select another node from among those previously visited, and proceed from that node. Thus, he must make two kinds of choices: choice of a node from which to proceed, and choice of an operator to apply at that node.

We can think of information as consisting of one or more evaluations (not necessarily numerical, of course) that can be assigned to a node or an operator. One kind of evaluation may rank nodes with respect to their promise as starting points for further search. Another kind of evaluation may rank the operators at a particular node with respect to *their* promise as means for continuing from that node. The problem-solving studies have disclosed examples of both kinds of evaluations: for node and operator selection, respectively.

When we examine how evaluations are made—what information they draw on—we again discover several varieties. An evaluation may depend only on properties of a single node. Thus, in theorem-proving tasks, subjects frequently decline to proceed from their current node because "the expression is too complicated to work with." This is a judgment that the node is not a promising one. Similarly, we find frequent statements in the protocols to the effect that "it looks like Rule 7 would apply here."

In most problem spaces, the choice of an efficient next step cannot be made by absolute evaluation of the sorts just illustrated, but instead is a function of the problem that is being solved. In theorem proving, for example, what to do next depends on what theorem is to be proved. Hence, an important technique for extracting information to be used in evaluators (of either kind) is to compare the current node with characteristics of the desired state of affairs and to extract *differences* from the comparison. These differences serve as evaluators of the node (progress tests) and as criteria for selecting an operator (operator relevant to the differences). Reaching a node that differs less from the goal state than nodes visited previously is progress; and selecting an operator that is relevant to a particular difference between current node and goal is a technique for (possibly) reducing that difference.

The particular heuristic search system that finds differences between current and desired situations, finds an operator relevant to each difference, and applies the operator to reduce the difference is usually called means-ends analysis. Its common occurrence in human problem-solving behavior has been observed and discussed frequently since Duncker (1945). Our own data analyses reveal means-ends analysis to be a prominent form of heuristic organization in some tasks—proving theorems, for example. The procedure is captured in the General Problem Solver (GPS) program which has now been described several times in the psychological literature.[6] The GPS find-and-reduce-difference heuristic played the central role in our theory of problem solving for a decade beginning with its

---

[6] Brief descriptions of GPS can be found in Hilgard and Bower (1966) and Hilgard and Atkinson (1967). For an extensive analysis of GPS, see Ernst and Newell (1969). The relation of GPS to human behavior is discussed in Newell and Simon (in press, Ch. 9).

discovery in 1957, but more extensive data from a wider range of tasks have now shown it to be a special case of the more general information-extracting processes we are describing here.

Search strategies. Information obtained by finding differences between already-attained nodes and the goal can be used for both kinds of choices the problem solver must make—the choice of node to proceed from, and the choice of operator to apply. Examining how this information can be used to organize search has led to an explanation of an important phenomenon observed by de Groot (1965) in his studies of choice in chess. De Groot found that the tree of move sequences explored by players did not originate as a bushy growth, but was generated, instead, as a bundle of spindly explorations, each of them very little branched. After each branch had been explored to a position that could be evaluated, the player returned to the base position to pick up a new branch for exploration. De Groot dubbed this particular kind of exploration, which was universal among the chessplayers he studied, "progressive deepening."

The progressive deepening strategy is not imposed on the player by the structure of the chess task environment. Indeed, one can show that a different organization would permit more efficient search. This alternative method is called the scan-and-search strategy, and works somewhat as follows: Search proceeds by alternation of two phases: (*a*) in the first phase, the node that is most promising (by some evaluation) is selected for continuation; (*b*) in the second phase, a few continuations are pursued from that node a short distance forward, and the new nodes thus generated are evaluated and placed on a list for Phase 1. The scan-search organization avoids stereotypy. If search has been pursued in a particular direction because it has gone well, the direction is reviewed repeatedly against other possibilities, in case its promise begins to wane.

A powerful computer program for finding checkmating combinations, called MATER, constructed with the help of the scan-search strategy, appears a good deal more efficient than the progressive deepening strategy (Baylor & Simon, 1966). Nevertheless, in chess and the other task environments we have studied, humans do not use the scan-search procedure to organize their efforts. In those problems where information about the current node is preserved in an external memory, they tend to proceed almost always from the current knowledge state, and back up to an earlier node only when they find themselves in serious trouble (Newell & Simon, in press, Ch. 12 and 13). In task environments where the information about the current node is not preserved externally (e.g., the chessboard under rules of touch-move), and especially if actions are not reversible, humans tend to preserve information (externally or internally) about a base node to which they return when evaluation rejects the current node. This is essentially the progressive deepening strategy.

We can see now that the progressive deepening strategy is a response to limits of short-term memory, hence provides additional evidence for the validity of our description of the human information-processing system. When we write a problem-solving program without concern for human limitations, we can allow it as much memory of nodes on the search tree as necessary—hence we can use a scan-search strategy. To the human problem solver, with his limited short-term memory, this strategy is simply not available. To use it, he would have to consume large amounts of time storing in his long-term memory information about the nodes he had visited.

That, in sum, is what human heuristic search in a problem space amounts to. A serial information processor with limited short-term memory uses the information extractable from the structure of the space to evaluate the nodes it reaches and the operators that might be applied at those nodes. Most often, the evaluation involves finding differences between characteristics of the current node and those of the desired node (the goal). The evaluations are used to select a node and an operator for the next step of the search. Operators are usually applied to the current node, but if progress is not being made, the solver may return to a prior node that has been retained in memory—the limits of the choice of prior node being set mostly by short-term memory limits. These properties have been shown to account for most of the human problem-solving behaviors that have been observed in the three task environments that have been studied intensively: chess playing, discovering proofs in logic, and cryptarithmetic; and programs have been written to implement problem-solving systems with these same properties.

Alternative Problem Spaces

Critics of the problem-solving theory we have sketched above complain that it explains too little. It has been tested in detail against behavior in only three task environments—and these all involving highly structured symbolic tasks.[7] More serious, it explains behavior only after the problem space has been postulated—it does not show how the problem solver constructs his problem space in a given task environment. How, when he is faced with a cryptarithmetic problem, does he enter a problem space in which the nodes are defined as different possible assignments of letters to numbers? How does he become aware of the relevance of arithmetic operations for solving the problem? What suggests the "most-constrained-column-first" heuristic to him?

Although we have been careful to distinguish between the task environment and the problem space, we have not emphasized how radical can be the differences among alternative problem spaces for representing the same problem. Consider the following example: An elimination tournament, with 109 entries, has been organized by the local tennis club. Players are paired, the losers eliminated, and the survivors re-paired until a single player emerges victorious. How should the pairings be arranged to minimize the total number of individual matches that will have to be played? An obvious representation is the space of all possible "trees" of matchings of 109 players—an entirely infeasible space to search. Consider an alternative space in which each node is a possible sequence of matches constituting the tournament. This is, again, an enormous space, but there is a very simple way to solve the problem without searching it. Take an arbitrary sequence in the space, and note the number of surviving players after each match. Since the tournament begins with 109 players, and since each match eliminates one player, there must be exactly 108 matches to eliminate all but one player—no matter which sequence we have chosen. Hence, the minimum number of matches is 108, and any tree we select will contain exactly this number.

There are many "trick" problems of this kind where selection of the correct problem space permits the problem to be solved without any search

[7] The empirical findings, only some of which have been published to date, are collected in Parts II, III, and IV, of Newell and Simon (in press).

whatsoever. In the more usual case, matters are not so extreme, but judicious selection of the problem space makes available information that reduces search by orders of magnitude in comparison with what is required if a less sophisticated space is used.

We cannot claim to have more than fragmentary and conjectural answers to the questions of representation. The initial question we asked in our research was: "What processes do people use to solve problems?" The answer we have proposed is: "They carry out selective search in a problem space that incorporates some of the structural information of the task environment." Our answer now leads to the new question: "How do people generate a problem space when confronted with a new task?" Thus, our research, like all scientific efforts, has answered some questions at the cost of generating some new ones.

By way of parenthesis, however, we should like to refute one argument that seems to us exaggerated. It is sometimes alleged that search in a well-defined problem space is not problem solving at all—that the *real* problem solving is over as soon as the problem space has been selected. This proposition is easily tested and shown false. Pick a task environment and a particular task from it. To do the task, a person will first have to construct a problem space, then search for a solution in that space. Now give him a second task from the same environment. Since he can work in the problem space he already has available, all he needs to do this time is to search for a solution. Hence, the second task—if we are to accept the argument—is no problem at all. Observation of subjects' behavior over a sequence of chess problems, cryptarithmetic puzzles, or theorem-finding problems shows the argument to be empirically false. For the subjects do not find that all the problems become trivial as soon as they have solved the first one. On the contrary, the set of human behaviors we call "problem solving" encompasses both the activities required to construct a problem space in the face of a new task environment, and the activities required to solve a particular problem in some problem space, new or old.

WHERE IS THE THEORY GOING?

Only the narrow seam of the present divides past from future. The theory of problem solving in 1970

—and especially the part of it that is empirically validated—is primarily a theory that describes the problem spaces and problem-solving programs, and shows how these adapt the information-processing system to its task environment. At the same time that it has answered some basic questions about problem-solving processes, the research has raised new ones: how do problem solvers generate problem spaces; what is the neurological substrate for the serial, limited-memory information processor; how can our knowledge of problem-solving processes be used to improve human problem solving and learning? In the remaining pages of this article, we should like to leave past and present and look briefly—using Milton's words—into "the never-ending flight of future days."

Constructing Problem Spaces

We can use our considerable knowledge about the problem spaces subjects employ to solve problems in particular task environments as our taking-off place for exploring how the problem spaces come into being, how the subjects construct them.

Information for construction. There are at least six sources of information that can be used to help construct a problem space in the face of a task environment:

1. The task instructions themselves, which describe the elements of the environment more or less completely, and which may also provide some external memory—say, in the form of a chessboard.
2. Previous experience with the same task or a nearly identical one. (A problem space available from past experience may simply be evoked by mention of the task.)
3. Previous experience with analogous tasks, or with components of the whole task.
4. Programs stored in long-term memory that generalize over a range of tasks.
5. Programs stored in long-term memory for combining task instructions with other information in memory to construct new problem spaces and problem-solving programs.
6. Information accumulated while solving a problem, which may suggest changing the problem space. (In particular, it may suggest moving to a more abstract and simplified planning space.)

The experience in the laboratory with subjects confronting a new task, and forced, thereby, to generate within a few minutes a problem space for tackling the task, suggests that the first source—task instructions and illustrative examples accompanying them—plays a central role in generation of the problem space. The array presented with the cryptarithmetic problem, for example, suggests immediately the form of the knowledge state (or at least the main part of it); namely, that it consists of the same array modified by the substitution in it of one or more digits for letters.

The second source—previous experience with the same task—is not evident, of course, in the behavior of naive subjects, but the third source—analogous and component tasks—plays an important role in cryptarithmetic. Again, the form of the external array in this task is sufficient to evoke in most subjects the possible relevance of arithmetic processes and arithmetic properties (odd, even, and so on).

The fourth source—general purpose programs in long-term memory—is a bit more elusive. But, as we have already noted, subjects quite frequently use means-ends programs in their problem-solving endeavors, and certainly bring these programs to the task from previous experience. We have already mentioned the General Problem Solver, which demonstrates how this generality can be achieved by factoring the specific descriptions of individual tasks from the task-independent means-ends analysis processes.

The fifth and sixth sources on the list above are mentioned because common sense tells us that they must sometimes play a role in the generation of problem spaces. We have no direct evidence for their use.

What evidence we have for the various kinds of information that are drawn on in constructing problem spaces is derived largely from comparing the problem spaces that subjects are observably working in with the information they are known to have access to. No one has, as yet, really observed the process of generation of the space—a research task that deserves high priority on the agenda.

Some simulation programs. Some progress has been made, however, in specifying for computers several programs that might be regarded as candidate theories as to how it is done by humans. Two of these programs were constructed, by Tom Williams (1965) and Donald Williams (1969), respectively, in the course of their doctoral research.

A General Game Playing Program (GGPP), designed by Tom Williams, when given the instructions for a card or board game (somewhat as these are written in Hoyle, but with the language simplified and smoothed), is able, by interpreting these instructions, to play the game—at least legally if not well. GGPP relies primarily on the first, fourth, and fifth sources of information from the list above. It has stored in memory general information about such objects as "cards," "hands," "boards," "moves," and is capable of combining this general information with information derived from the specific instructions of the game.

The Aptitude Test Taker, designed by Donald Williams, derives its information from worked-out examples of items on various kinds of aptitude tests (letter series, letter analogies, number series and analogies, and so on) in order to construct its own programs capable of taking the corresponding tests.

These programs put us into somewhat the same position with respect to the generation of problem spaces that LT did with respect to problem solving in a defined problem space: that is to say, they demonstrate that certain sets of information-processing mechanisms are sufficient to do the job over some range of interesting tasks. They do not prove that humans do the same job in the same way, using essentially the same processes, or that these processes would suffice for all tasks. It should be noted that the programs written by the two Williamses employ the same kind of basic information-processing system that was used for earlier cognitive simulations. They do not call for any new magic to be put in the hat.

Planning and abstracting processes. The processes for generating problem spaces are not unrelated to some other processes about which we *do* have empirical data—planning processes. In several of the tasks that have been studied, and especially in the logic task, subjects are often observed to be working in terms more abstract than those that characterize the problem space they began with. They neglect certain details of the expressions they are manipulating (e.g., the operations or connectives), and focus on features they regard as essential.

One way of describing what they are doing is to say that they are abstracting from the concrete detail of the initial problem space in order to construct a *plan* for a problem solution in a simpler abstract planning space. Programs have been written, in the context of GPS, that are also capable of such abstracting and planning, hence are capable of constructing a problem space different from the one in which the problem solving begins.

The evidence from the thinking-aloud protocols in the logic task suggests, however, that the human planning activities did not maintain as sharp a boundary between task space and abstract planning space as the simulation program did. The human subjects appeared able to move back and forth between concrete and abstract objects without treating the latter as belonging to a separate problem space. In spite of this difference, the data on planning behavior give us additional clues as to how problem spaces can be generated and modified.

Production Systems

A hypothesis about the structure of a complex system—like a human problem-solving program—becomes more plausible if we can conceive how a step-by-step development could have brought about the finished structure. Minerva sprang full-grown from the brow of Zeus, but we expect terrestrial systems to evolve in a more gradual and lawful fashion—our distrust of the magician again.

Anyone who has written and debugged a large computer program has probably acquired, in the process, a healthy skepticism that such an entangled, interconnected structure could have evolved by small, self-adapting steps. In an evolving system, a limited, partial capability should grow almost continuously into a more powerful capability. But most computer programs have an all-or-none character: disable one subroutine and a program will probably do nothing useful at all.

A development of the past few years in computer language construction has created an interesting possible solution to this difficulty. We refer to the languages known as *production systems*. In a production system, each routine has a bipartite form, consisting of a *condition* and an *action*. The condition defines some test or set of tests to be performed on the knowledge state. (E.g., "Test if it is Black's move.") If the test is satisfied, the action is executed; if the test is not satisfied, no action is taken, and control is transferred to some other production. In a pure production system, the individual productions are simply listed in some order, and considered for execution in turn.

47

The attraction of a production system for our present concerns—of how a complex program could develop step by step—is that the individual productions are independent of each other's structures, and hence productions can be added to the system one by one. In a new task environment, a subject learns to notice conditions and make discriminations of which he was previously unaware (a chessplayer learns to recognize an open file, a passed pawn, and so on). Each of these new discriminations can become the condition part of a production, whose action is relevant to that condition.

We cannot pursue this idea here beyond noting its affinity to some classical stimulus-response notions. We do not wish to push the analogy too far, for productions have some complexities and subtleties of structure that go beyond stimulus-response ideas, but we do observe that linking a condition and action together in a new production has many similarities to linking a stimulus together with its response. One important difference is that, in the production, it is the condition—that is, the tests—and not the stimulus itself that is linked to the response. In this way, the production system illuminates the problem of defining the effective stimulus, an old bugaboo of stimulus-response theory.

Perception and Language

We have seen that research on problem solving has begun to shift from asking how searches are conducted in problem spaces, a subject on which we have gained a considerable understanding, to asking how problem spaces—internal representations of problems—are built up in human minds. But the subject of internal representation links problem-solving research with two other important areas of psychology: perception and psycholinguistics. The further extension of this linkage (see Step 8 in the strategy outlined in our introductory section) appears to be one of the principal tasks for the next decade.

Elsewhere, one of us has described briefly the main connections between problem-solving theory and the theories of perception and psycholinguistics (Simon, 1969, pp. 42–52). We will simply indicate these connections even more briefly here.

Information comes to the human problem solver principally in the form of statements in natural language and visual displays. For information to be exchanged between these external sources and the mind, it must be encoded and decoded. The information as represented externally must be transformed to match the representations in which it is held inside. It is very difficult to imagine what these transformations might be as long as we have access only to the external representations, and not to the internal. It is a little like building a program to translate from English to Language X, where no one will tell us anything about Language X.

The research on problem solving has given us some strong hypotheses about the nature of the internal representations that humans use when they are solving problems. These hypotheses define for us, therefore, the endpoint of the translation process—they tell us something about Language X. The hypotheses should provide strong clues to the researcher in perception and to the psycholinguist in guiding their search for the translation process. Indeed, we believe that these cues have already been used to good advantage in both areas, and we anticipate a great burgeoning of research along these lines over the coming decade.

Links to Neurophysiology

The ninth step in the strategy set forth in our introduction was to seek the neurophysiological counterparts of the information processes and data structures that the theory postulates. In this respect, we are in the position of nineteenth-century chemistry which postulated atoms on the basis of observations of chemical reactions among molecules, and without any direct evidence for their existence; or in the position of classical genetics, which postulated the gene before it could be identified with any observed microscopic structures in the cell.

Explanation in psychology will not rest indefinitely at the information-processing level. But the explanations that we can provide at that level will narrow the search of the neurophysiologist, for they will tell him a great deal about the properties of the structures and processes he is seeking. They will put him on the lookout for memory fixation processes with times of the order of five seconds, for the "bottlenecks" of attention that account for the serial nature of the processing, for memory structures of small capacity capable of storing a few symbols in a matter of a couple of hundred milliseconds.

All of this is a prospect for the future. We cannot claim to see in today's literature any firm bridges between the components of the central nervous system as it is described by neurophysiologists and the components of the information-processing system we have been discussing here. But bridges there must be, and we need not pause in expanding and improving our knowledge at the information-processing level while we wait for them to be built.

The Practice of Education

The professions always live in an uneasy relation with the basic sciences that should nourish and be nourished by them. It is really only within the present century that medicine can be said to rest solidly on the foundation of deep knowledge in the biological sciences, or the practice of engineering on modern physics and chemistry. Perhaps we should plead the recency of the dependence in those fields in mitigation of the scandal of psychology's meager contribution to education.

It is, of course, incorrect to say that there has been no contribution. Psychology has provided to the practice of education a constant reminder of the importance of reinforcement and knowledge of results for effective learning. And particularly under the influence of the Skinnerians, these principles have seen increasingly systematic and conscious application in a variety of educational settings.

Until recently, however, psychology has shown both a reluctance and an inability to address itself to the question of "what is learned." At a common sense level, we know perfectly well that rote learning does not provide the same basis for lasting and transferable skills that is provided by "meaningful" learning. We have even a substantial body of laboratory evidence—for example, the research by Katona (1940), now 30 years old—that shows clearly the existence and significance of such differences in kinds of learning. But we have largely been unable to go beyond common sense in characterizing what is rote and what is meaningful. We have been unable because we have not described what is learned in these two different modes of learning—what representation of information or process has been stored in memory. And we have

not described how that stored information and those stored programs are evoked to perform new tasks.

The theory of problem solving described here gives us a new basis for attacking the psychology of education and the learning process. It allows us to describe in detail the information and programs that the skilled performer possesses, and to show how they permit him to perform successfully. But the greatest opportunities for bringing the theory to bear upon the practice of education will come as we move from a theory that explains the structure of human problem-solving programs to a theory that explains how these programs develop in the face of task requirements—the kind of theory we have been discussing in the previous sections of this article.

It does not seem premature at the present stage of our knowledge of human problem solving to undertake large-scale development work that will seek to bring that theory to bear upon education. Some of the tasks that have been studied in the basic research programs—proving theorems in logic and geometry, playing chess, doing cryptarithmetic problems, solving word problems in algebra, solving letter-series completion problems from intelligence tests—are of a level of complexity comparable to the tasks that face students in our schools and colleges.[8]

The experience of other fields of knowledge teaches us that serious attempts at practical application of basic science invariably contribute to the advance of the basic science as well as the area of application. Unsuspected phenomena are discovered that can then be carried back to the laboratory; new questions are raised that become topics for basic research. Both psychology and education stand to benefit in major ways if we make an earnest effort over the next decade to draw out the practical lessons from our understanding of human information processes.

IN CONCLUSION

We have tried to describe some of the main things that are known about how the magician produces the rabbit from the hat. We hope we have dispelled the illusion, but we hope also that you are not disappointed by the relative simplicity of the

[8] For the first three of these tasks, see Newell and Simon (in press); for algebra, Paige and Simon (1966); for letter series, Simon and Kotovsky (1963) and Klahr and Wallace (1970).

phenomena once explained. Those who have the instincts and esthetic tastes of scientists presumably will not be disappointed. There is much beauty in the superficial complexity of nature. But there is a deeper beauty in the simplicity of underlying process that accounts for the external complexity. There is beauty in the intricacy of human thinking when an intelligent person is confronted with a difficult problem. But there is a deeper beauty in the basic information processes and their organization into simple schemes of heuristic search that make that intricate human thinking possible. It is a sense of this latter beauty—the beauty of simplicity—that we have tried to convey to you.

REFERENCES

BARTLETT, F. C. *Thinking.* New York: Basic Books, 1958.

BAYLOR, G. W., JR., & SIMON, H. A. A chess mating combinations program. *AFIPS Conference Proceedings,* 1966 Spring Joint Computer Conference, Boston, April 26–28, **28**, 431–447. Washington, D. C.: Spartan Books, 1966.

DE GROOT, A. *Thought and choice in chess.* The Hague: Mouton, 1965.

DUNCKER, K. On problem solving. *Psychological Monographs,* 1945, **58**(5, Whole No. 270).

ERNST, G. W., & NEWELL, A. *GPS: A case study in generality and problem solving.* New York: Academic Press, 1969.

HILGARD, E. R., & BOWER, G. W. *Theories of learning.* (3rd ed.) New York: Appleton-Century-Crofts, 1966.

HILGARD, E. R., & ATKINSON, R. C. *Introduction to psychology.* (4th ed.) New York: Harcourt, Brace & World, 1967.

KATONA, G. *Organizing and memorizing.* New York: Columbia University Press, 1940.

KLAHR, D., & WALLACE, J. G. Development of serial completion strategy: Information processing analysis. *British Journal of Psychology,* 1970, **61**, 243–257.

NEWELL, A. Studies in problem solving: Subject 3 on the cryptarithmetic task: DONALD + GERALD = ROBERT. Pittsburgh: Carnegie-Mellon University, 1967.

NEWELL, A., & SHAW, J. C. Programming the Logic Theory Machine. *Proceedings of the 1957 Western Joint Computer Conference,* February 26–28, 1957, 230–240.

NEWELL, A., SHAW, J. C., & SIMON, H. A. Empirical explorations of the Logic Theory Machine: A case study in heuristics. *Proceedings of the 1957 Western Joint Computer Conference,* February 26–28, 1957, 218–230.

NEWELL, A., SHAW, J. C., & SIMON, H. A. Elements of a theory of human problem solving. *Psychological Review,* 1958, **65**, 151–166.

NEWELL, A., SHAW, J. C., & SIMON, H. A. The processes of creative thinking. In H. E. Gruber & M. Wertheimer (Eds.), *Contemporary approaches to creative thinking.* New York: Atherton Press, 1962.

NEWELL, A., & SIMON, H. A. The Logic Theory Machine: A complex information processing system. *IRE Transactions on Information Theory,* 1956, IT-2, **3**, 61–79.

NEWELL, A., & SIMON, H. A. *Human problem solving.* Englewood Cliffs, N. J.: Prentice-Hall, 1971, in press.

PAIGE, J. M., & SIMON, H. A. Cognitive processes in solving algebra word problems. In B. Kleinmuntz (Ed.), *Problem solving.* New York: Wiley, 1966.

SIMON, H. A. Scientific discovery and the psychology of problem solving. In R. C. Colodny (Ed.), *Mind and cosmos: Essays in contemporary science and philosophy.* Pittsburgh: University of Pittsburgh Press, 1966.

SIMON, H. A. An information-processing explanation of some perceptual phenomena. *British Journal of Psychology,* 1967, **58**, 1–12.

SIMON, H. A. *The sciences of the artificial.* Cambridge: M.I.T. Press, 1969.

SIMON, H. A., & BARENFELD, M. Information-processing analysis of perceptual processes in problem solving. *Psychological Review,* 1969, **76**, 473–483.

SIMON, H. A., & KOTOVSKY, K. Human acquisition of concepts for sequential patterns. *Psychological Review,* 1963, **70**, 534–546.

WILLIAMS, D. S. Computer program organization induced by problem examples. Unpublished doctoral dissertation, Carnegie-Mellon University, 1969.

WILLIAMS, T. G. Some studies in game playing with a digital computer. Unpublished doctoral dissertation, Carnegie Institute of Technology, 1965.

George A. Miller   Davis Chapter 3

"THE MAGICAL NUMBER SEVEN, PLUS OR MINUS TWO:
SOME LIMITS ON OUR CAPACITY FOR PROCESSING INFORMATION"

The Psychological Review (63:2), 1956 March, pages 81-97.

Miller's cogent summary of research relating to the limits on human information processing has become a classic. It has been widely reprinted and the phrase, "seven, plus or minus two," is now part of the terminology in several fields including MIS.

This article discusses several different experiments relating to the human capacity to process information. The experiments are grouped into single variable experiments and multiple variable experiments. All the experiments discussed tend to support the notion of "seven, plus or minus two" as a limit on human information processing capacity. The summary of research emphasizes the span of immediate memory and the use of recoding in order to reduce information processing requirements.

Even though the span of absolute judgment is very limited, there are a variety of techniques for increasing the accuracy of human judgments. In multi-dimensional experiments, the human information processor does some additional processing to handle the multiple variables; for example, coding, recoding, and subitizing. With fewer than seven observations, the human tends to count but with more than seven, one tends to "chunk". In human information processing the amount of information is not 7 bits, 7 digits, or 7 characters; rather it is 7 chunks. A chunk may be a digit, a character, a word, or any other unit. Human information processing capacity is increased by the human processor recoding data into larger chunks. The process of memorization can be related to the summation of chunks.

READING SUGGESTIONS

Rather than concentrate on the precise details of the various experiments, the reader should observe the degree of uniformity in the results of seemingly diverse experiments. In other words, skim over the details of the experiment and focus in on the results. Note how consistently the single variable experiments approximate at seven. Note also the use of logarithms to the base two for measuring the information processing capacity. The log of seven to the base two equals about 2.5.

QUESTIONS

1. Define a bit in the measurement of information processing capacity. Why is information processing capacity calculated by using the log to the base 2?
2. What is the effect of multiple stimuli on the human ability to process information?
3. How does human learning influence the limit of "seven, plus or minus two"?
4. Name the three most important techniques for overcoming the span of absolute judgment and increasing the accuracy of our judgments.
5. Explain the difference between bits of information and chunks of information.
6. Explain the use of recoding to increase the number of bits of information that can be held in memory.

VOL. 63, No. 2   MARCH, 1956

THE PSYCHOLOGICAL REVIEW

THE MAGICAL NUMBER SEVEN, PLUS OR MINUS TWO: SOME LIMITS ON OUR CAPACITY FOR PROCESSING INFORMATION [1]

Harvard University

My problem is that I have been persecuted by an integer. For seven years this number has followed me around, has intruded in my most private data, and has assaulted me from the pages of our most public journals. This number assumes a variety of disguises, being sometimes a little larger and sometimes a little smaller than usual, but never changing so much as to be unrecognizable. The persistence with which this number plagues me is far more than a random accident. There is, to quote a famous senator, a design behind it, some pattern governing its appearances. Either there really is something unusual about the number or else I am suffering from delusions of persecution.

I shall begin my case history by telling you about some experiments that tested how accurately people can assign numbers to the magnitudes of various aspects of a stimulus. In the traditional language of psychology these would be called experiments in absolute judgment. Historical accident, however, has decreed that they should have another name. We now call them experiments on the capacity of people to transmit information. Since these experiments would not have been done without the appearance of information theory on the psychological scene, and since the results are analyzed in terms of the concepts of information theory, I shall have to preface my discussion with a few remarks about this theory.

INFORMATION MEASUREMENT

The "amount of information" is exactly the same concept that we have talked about for years under the name of "variance." The equations are different, but if we hold tight to the idea that anything that increases the variance also increases the amount of information we cannot go far astray.

The advantages of this new way of talking about variance are simple enough. Variance is always stated in terms of the unit of measurement—inches, pounds, volts, etc.—whereas the amount of information is a dimensionless quantity. Since the information in a discrete statistical distribution does not depend upon the unit of measurement, we can extend the concept to situations where we have no metric and we would not ordinarily think of using the variance. And it also enables us to compare results obtained in quite different experimental situations where it would be meaningless to compare variances based on different metrics. So there are some good reasons for adopting the newer concept.

The similarity of variance and amount of information might be explained this way: When we have a large variance, we are very ignorant about what is going to happen. If we are very ignorant, then when we make the observation it gives us a lot of information. On the other hand, if the variance is very small, we know in advance how our observation must come out, so we get little information from making the observation.

If you will now imagine a communication system, you will realize that there is a great deal of variability about what goes into the system and also a great deal of variability about what comes out. The input and the output can therefore be described in terms of their variance (or their information). If it is a good communication system, however, there must be some systematic relation between what goes in and what comes out. That is to say, the output will depend upon the input, or will be correlated with the input. If we measure this correlation, then we can say how much of the output variance is attributable to the input and how much is due to random fluctuations or "noise" introduced by the system during transmission. So we see that the measure of transmitted information is simply a measure of the input-output correlation.

There are two simple rules to follow. Whenever I refer to "amount of information," you will understand "variance." And whenever I refer to "amount of transmitted information," you will understand "covariance" or "correlation."

The situation can be described graphically by two partially overlapping cir-

[1] This paper was first read as an Invited Address before the Eastern Psychological Association in Philadelphia on April 15, 1955. Preparation of the paper was supported by the Harvard Psycho-Acoustic Laboratory under Contract N5ori-76 between Harvard University and the Office of Naval Research, U. S. Navy (Project NR142–201, Report PNR–174). Reproduction for any purpose of the U. S. Government is permitted.

cles. Then the left circle can be taken to represent the variance of the input, the right circle the variance of the output, and the overlap the covariance of input and output. I shall speak of the left circle as the amount of input information, the right circle as the amount of output information, and the overlap as the amount of transmitted information.

In the experiments on absolute judgment, the observer is considered to be a communication channel. Then the left circle would represent the amount of information in the stimuli, the right circle the amount of information in his responses, and the overlap the stimulus-response correlation as measured by the amount of transmitted information. The experimental problem is to increase the amount of input information and to measure the amount of transmitted information. If the observer's absolute judgments are quite accurate, then nearly all of the input information will be transmitted and will be recoverable from his responses. If he makes errors, then the transmitted information may be considerably less than the input. We expect that, as we increase the amount of input information, the observer will begin to make more and more errors; we can test the limits of accuracy of his absolute judgments. If the human observer is a reasonable kind of communication system, then when we increase the amount of input information the transmitted information will increase at first and will eventually level off at some asymptotic value. This asymptotic value we take to be the *channel capacity* of the observer: it represents the greatest amount of information that he can give us about the stimulus on the basis of an absolute judgment. The channel capacity is the upper limit on the extent to which the observer can match his responses to the stimuli we give him.

Now just a brief word about the *bit* and we can begin to look at some data. One bit of information is the amount of information that we need to make a decision between two equally likely alternatives. If we must decide whether a man is less than six feet tall or more than six feet tall and if we know that the chances are 50–50, then we need one bit of information. Notice that this unit of information does not refer in any way to the unit of length that we use—feet, inches, centimeters, etc.

However you measure the man's height, we still need just one bit of information.

Two bits of information enable us to decide among four equally likely alternatives. Three bits of information enable us to decide among eight equally likely alternatives. Four bits of information decide among 16 alternatives, five among 32, and so on. That is to say, if there are 32 equally likely alternatives, we must make five successive binary decisions, worth one bit each, before we know which alternative is correct. So the general rule is simple: every time the number of alternatives is increased by a factor of two, one bit of information is added.

There are two ways we might increase the amount of input information. We could increase the rate at which we give information to the observer, so that the amount of information per unit time would increase. Or we could ignore the time variable completely and increase the amount of input information by increasing the number of alternative stimuli. In the absolute judgment experiment we are interested in the second alternative. We give the observer as much time as he wants to make his response; we simply increase the number of alternative stimuli among which he must discriminate and look to see where confusions begin to occur. Confusions will appear near the point that we are calling his "channel capacity."

Absolute Judgments of Unidimensional Stimuli

Now let us consider what happens when we make absolute judgments of tones. Pollack (17) asked listeners to identify tones by assigning numerals to them. The tones were different with respect to frequency, and covered the range from 100 to 8000 cps in equal logarithmic steps. A tone was sounded and the listener responded by giving a numeral. After the listener had made his response he was told the correct identification of the tone.

When only two or three tones were used the listeners never confused them. With four different tones confusions were quite rare, but with five or more tones confusions were frequent. With fourteen different tones the listeners made many mistakes.

These data are plotted in Fig. 1. Along the bottom is the amount of in-

put information in bits per stimulus. As the number of alternative tones was increased from 2 to 14, the input information increased from 1 to 3.8 bits. On the ordinate is plotted the amount of

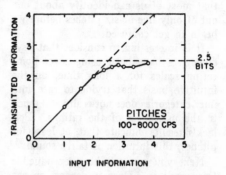

FIG. 1. Data from Pollack (17, 18) on the amount of information that is transmitted by listeners who make absolute judgments of auditory pitch. As the amount of input information is increased by increasing from 2 to 14 the number of different pitches to be judged, the amount of transmitted information approaches as its upper limit a channel capacity of about 2.5 bits per judgment.

transmitted information. The amount of transmitted information behaves in much the way we would expect a communication channel to behave; the transmitted information increases linearly up to about 2 bits and then bends off toward an asymptote at about 2.5 bits. This value, 2.5 bits, therefore, is what we are calling the channel capacity of the listener for absolute judgments of pitch.

So now we have the number 2.5 bits. What does it mean? First, note that 2.5 bits corresponds to about six equally likely alternatives. The result means that we cannot pick more than six different pitches that the listener will never confuse. Or, stated slightly differently, no matter how many alternative tones we ask him to judge, the best we can expect him to do is to assign them to about six different classes without error. Or, again, if we know that there were N alternative stimuli, then his judgment enables us to narrow down the particular stimulus to one out of $N/6$.

Most people are surprised that the number is as small as six. Of course, there is evidence that a musically sophisticated person with absolute pitch can identify accurately any one of 50 or 60 different pitches. Fortunately, I do not have time to discuss these remarkable exceptions. I say it is fortunate because I do not know how to explain their superior performance. So I shall stick to the more pedestrian fact that most of us can identify about one out of only five or six pitches before we begin to get confused.

It is interesting to consider that psychologists have been using seven-point rating scales for a long time, on the intuitive basis that trying to rate into finer categories does not really add much to the usefulness of the ratings. Pollack's results indicate that, at least for pitches, this intuition is fairly sound.

Next you can ask how reproducible this result is. Does it depend on the spacing of the tones or the various conditions of judgment? Pollack varied these conditions in a number of ways. The range of frequencies can be changed by a factor of about 20 without changing the amount of information transmitted more than a small percentage. Different groupings of the pitches decreased the transmission, but the loss was small. For example, if you can discriminate five high-pitched tones in one series and five low-pitched tones in another series, it is reasonable to expect that you could combine all ten into a single series and still tell them all apart without error. When you try it, however, it does not work. The channel capacity for pitch seems to be about six and that is the best you can do.

While we are on tones, let us look next at Garner's (7) work on loudness. Garner's data for loudness are summarized in Fig. 2. Garner went to some trouble to get the best possible spacing of his tones over the intensity range from 15 to 110 db. He used 4, 5, 6, 7, 10, and 20 different stimulus intensities.

The results shown in Fig. 2 take into account the differences among subjects and the sequential influence of the immediately preceding judgment. Again we find that there seems to be a limit. The channel capacity for absolute judgments of loudness is 2.3 bits, or about five perfectly discriminable alternatives.

Since these two studies were done in different laboratories with slightly different techniques and methods of analysis, we are not in a good position to argue whether five loudnesses is significantly different from six pitches. Probably the difference is in the right direction, and absolute judgments of pitch are slightly more accurate than absolute judgments of loudness. The important point, however, is that the two answers are of the same order of magnitude.

The experiment has also been done for taste intensities. In Fig. 3 are the results obtained by Beebe-Center, Rogers, and O'Connell (1) for absolute judgments of the concentration of salt solutions. The concentrations ranged from 0.3 to 34.7 gm. NaCl per 100 cc. tap water in equal subjective steps. They used 3, 5, 9, and 17 different concentrations. The channel capacity is 1.9 bits, which is about four distinct concentrations. Thus taste intensities seem a little less distinctive than auditory stimuli, but again the order of magnitude is not far off.

On the other hand, the channel capacity for judgments of visual position seems to be significantly larger. Hake and Garner (8) asked observers to interpolate visually between two scale markers. Their results are shown in Fig. 4. They did the experiment in two ways. In one version they let the observer use any number between zero and 100 to describe the position, al-

though they presented stimuli at only 5, 10, 20, or 50 different positions. The results with this unlimited response technique are shown by the filled circles on the graph. In the other version the observers were limited in their responses to reporting just those stimulus values that were possible. That is to say, in the second version the number of different responses that the observer could make was exactly the same as the number of different stimuli that the experimenter might present. The results with this limited response technique are shown by the open circles on the graph. The two functions are so similar that it seems fair to conclude that the number of responses available to the observer had nothing to do with the channel capacity of 3.25 bits.

The Hake-Garner experiment has been repeated by Coonan and Klemmer. Although they have not yet published their results, they have given me permission to say that they obtained channel capacities ranging from 3.2 bits for very short exposures of the pointer position to 3.9 bits for longer exposures. These values are slightly higher than Hake and Garner's, so we must conclude that there are between 10 and 15 distinct positions along a linear interval. This is the largest channel capacity that has been measured for any unidimensional variable.

At the present time these four experiments on absolute judgments of simple, unidimensional stimuli are all that have appeared in the psychological journals. However, a great deal of work on other stimulus variables has not yet appeared in the journals. For example, Eriksen and Hake (6) have found that the channel capacity for judging the sizes of squares is 2.2 bits, or about five

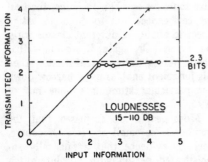

FIG. 2. Data from Garner (7) on the channel capacity for absolute judgments of auditory loudness.

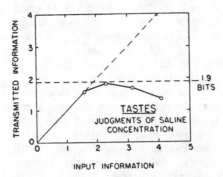

FIG. 3. Data from Beebe-Center, Rogers, and O'Connell (1) on the channel capacity for absolute judgments of saltiness.

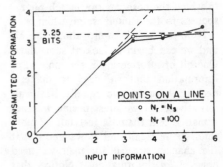

FIG. 4. Data from Hake and Garner (8) on the channel capacity for absolute judgments of the position of a pointer in a linear interval.

categories, under a wide range of experimental conditions. In a separate experiment Eriksen (5) found 2.8 bits for size, 3.1 bits for hue, and 2.3 bits for brightness. Geldard has measured the channel capacity for the skin by placing vibrators on the chest region. A good observer can identify about four intensities, about five durations, and about seven locations.

One of the most active groups in this area has been the Air Force Operational Applications Laboratory. Pollack has been kind enough to furnish me with the results of their measurements for several aspects of visual displays. They made measurements for area and for the curvature, length, and direction of lines. In one set of experiments they used a very short exposure of the stimulus—1/40 second—and then they repeated the measurements with a 5-second exposure. For area they got 2.6 bits with the short exposure and 2.7 bits with the long exposure. For the length of a line they got about 2.6 bits with the short exposure and about 3.0 bits with the long exposure. Direction, or angle of inclination, gave 2.8 bits for the short exposure and 3.3 bits for the long exposure. Curvature was apparently harder to judge. When the length of the arc was constant, the result at the short exposure duration was 2.2 bits, but when the length of the chord was constant, the result was only 1.6 bits. This last value is the lowest that anyone has measured to date. I should add, however, that these values are apt to be slightly too low because the data from all subjects were pooled before the transmitted information was computed.

Now let us see where we are. First, the channel capacity does seem to be a valid notion for describing human observers. Second, the channel capacities measured for these unidimensional variables range from 1.6 bits for curvature to 3.9 bits for positions in an interval. Although there is no question that the differences among the variables are real and meaningful, the more impressive fact to me is their considerable similarity. If I take the best estimates I can get of the channel capacities for all the stimulus variables I have mentioned, the mean is 2.6 bits and the standard deviation is only 0.6 bit. In terms of distinguishable alternatives, this mean

corresponds to about 6.5 categories, one standard deviation includes from 4 to 10 categories, and the total range is from 3 to 15 categories. Considering the wide variety of different variables that have been studied, I find this to be a remarkably narrow range.

There seems to be some limitation built into us either by learning or by the design of our nervous systems, a limit that keeps our channel capacities in this general range. On the basis of the present evidence it seems safe to say that we possess a finite and rather small capacity for making such unidimensional judgments and that this capacity does not vary a great deal from one simple sensory attribute to another.

ABSOLUTE JUDGMENTS OF MULTI-DIMENSIONAL STIMULI

You may have noticed that I have been careful to say that this magical number seven applies to one-dimensional judgments. Everyday experience teaches us that we can identify accurately any one of several hundred faces, any one of several thousand words, any one of several thousand objects, etc. The story certainly would not be complete if we stopped at this point. We must have some understanding of why the one-dimensional variables we judge in the laboratory give results so far out of line with what we do constantly in our behavior outside the laboratory. A possible explanation lies in the number of independently variable attributes of the stimuli that are being judged. Objects, faces, words, and the like differ from one another in many ways, whereas the simple stimuli we have considered thus far differ from one another in only one respect.

Fortunately, there are a few data on what happens when we make absolute judgments of stimuli that differ from one another in several ways. Let us look first at the results Klemmer and Frick (13) have reported for the absolute judgment of the position of a dot in a square. In Fig. 5 we see their results. Now the channel capacity seems to have increased to 4.6 bits, which means that people can identify accurately any one of 24 positions in the square.

The position of a dot in a square is clearly a two-dimensional proposition. Both its horizontal and its vertical po-

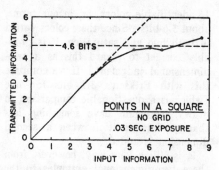

FIG. 5. Data from Klemmer and Frick (13) on the channel capacity for absolute judgments of the position of a dot in a square.

sition must be identified. Thus it seems natural to compare the 4.6-bit capacity for a square with the 3.25-bit capacity for the position of a point in an interval. The point in the square requires two judgments of the interval type. If we have a capacity of 3.25 bits for estimating intervals and we do this twice, we should get 6.5 bits as our capacity for locating points in a square. Adding the second independent dimension gives us an increase from 3.25 to 4.6, but it falls short of the perfect addition that would give 6.5 bits.

Another example is provided by Beebe-Center, Rogers, and O'Connell. When they asked people to identify both the saltiness and the sweetness of solutions containing various concentrations of salt and sucrose, they found that the channel capacity was 2.3 bits. Since the capacity for salt alone was 1.9, we might expect about 3.8 bits if the two aspects of the compound stimuli were judged independently. As with spatial locations, the second dimension adds a little to the capacity but not as much as it conceivably might.

A third example is provided by Pollack (18), who asked listeners to judge both the loudness and the pitch of pure tones. Since pitch gives 2.5 bits and loudness gives 2.3 bits, we might hope to get as much as 4.8 bits for pitch and loudness together. Pollack obtained 3.1 bits, which again indicates that the second dimension augments the channel capacity but not so much as it might.

A fourth example can be drawn from the work of Halsey and Chapanis (9) on confusions among colors of equal luminance. Although they did not analyze their results in informational terms, they estimate that there are about 11 to

15 identifiable colors, or, in our terms, about 3.6 bits. Since these colors varied in both hue and saturation, it is probably correct to regard this as a two-dimensional judgment. If we compare this with Eriksen's 3.1 bits for hue (which is a questionable comparison to draw), we again have something less than perfect addition when a second dimension is added.

It is still a long way, however, from these two-dimensional examples to the multidimensional stimuli provided by faces, words, etc. To fill this gap we have only one experiment, an auditory study done by Pollack and Ficks (19). They managed to get six different acoustic variables that they could change: frequency, intensity, rate of interruption, on-time fraction, total duration, and spatial location. Each one of these six variables could assume any one of five different values, so altogether there were 5^6, or 15,625 different tones that they could present. The listeners made a separate rating for each one of these six dimensions. Under these conditions the transmitted information was 7.2 bits, which corresponds to about 150 different categories that could be absolutely identified without error. Now we are beginning to get up into the range that ordinary experience would lead us to expect.

Suppose that we plot these data, fragmentary as they are, and make a guess about how the channel capacity changes with the dimensionality of the stimuli. The result is given in Fig. 6. In a moment of considerable daring I sketched the dotted line to indicate roughly the trend that the data seemed to be taking.

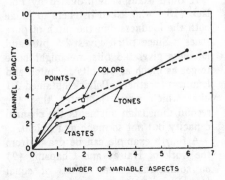

FIG. 6. The general form of the relation between channel capacity and the number of independently variable attributes of the stimuli.

Clearly, the addition of independently variable attributes to the stimulus increases the channel capacity, but at a decreasing rate. It is interesting to note that the channel capacity is increased even when the several variables are not independent. Eriksen (5) reports that, when size, brightness, and hue all vary together in perfect correlation, the transmitted information is 4.1 bits as compared with an average of about 2.7 bits when these attributes are varied one at a time. By confounding three attributes, Eriksen increased the dimensionality of the input without increasing the amount of input information; the result was an increase in channel capacity of about the amount that the dotted function in Fig. 6 would lead us to expect.

The point seems to be that, as we add more variables to the display, we increase the total capacity, but we decrease the accuracy for any particular variable. In other words, we can make relatively crude judgments of several things simultaneously.

We might argue that in the course of evolution those organisms were most successful that were responsive to the widest range of stimulus energies in their environment. In order to survive in a constantly fluctuating world, it was better to have a little information about a lot of things than to have a lot of information about a small segment of the environment. If a compromise was necessary, the one we seem to have made is clearly the more adaptive.

Pollack and Ficks's results are very strongly suggestive of an argument that linguists and phoneticians have been making for some time (11). According to the linguistic analysis of the sounds of human speech, there are about eight or ten dimensions—the linguists call them *distinctive features*—that distinguish one phoneme from another. These distinctive features are usually binary, or at most ternary, in nature. For example, a binary distinction is made between vowels and consonants, a binary decision is made between oral and nasal consonants, a ternary decision is made among front, middle, and back phonemes, etc. This approach gives us quite a different picture of speech perception than we might otherwise obtain from our studies of the speech spectrum and of the ear's ability to discriminate

relative differences among pure tones. I am personally much interested in this new approach (15), and I regret that there is not time to discuss it here.

It was probably with this linguistic theory in mind that Pollack and Ficks conducted a test on a set of tonal stimuli that varied in eight dimensions, but required only a binary decision on each dimension. With these tones they measured the transmitted information at 6.9 bits, or about 120 recognizable kinds of sounds. It is an intriguing question, as yet unexplored, whether one can go on adding dimensions indefinitely in this way.

In human speech there is clearly a limit to the number of dimensions that we use. In this instance, however, it is not known whether the limit is imposed by the nature of the perceptual machinery that must recognize the sounds or by the nature of the speech machinery that must produce them. Somebody will have to do the experiment to find out. There is a limit, however, at about eight or nine distinctive features in every language that has been studied, and so when we talk we must resort to still another trick for increasing our channel capacity. Language uses sequences of phonemes, so we make several judgments successively when we listen to words and sentences. That is to say, we use both simultaneous and successive discriminations in order to expand the rather rigid limits imposed by the inaccuracy of our absolute judgments of simple magnitudes.

These multidimensional judgments are strongly reminiscent of the abstraction experiment of Külpe (14). As you may remember, Külpe showed that observers report more accurately on an attribute for which they are set than on attributes for which they are not set. For example, Chapman (4) used three different attributes and compared the results obtained when the observers were instructed before the tachistoscopic presentation with the results obtained when they were not told until after the presentation which one of the three attributes was to be reported. When the instruction was given in advance, the judgments were more accurate. When the instruction was given afterwards, the subjects presumably had to judge all three attributes in order to report on any one of them and the accuracy was correspondingly lower. This is in complete accord with the results we have just been considering, where the accuracy of judgment on each attribute decreased as more dimensions were added. The point is probably obvious, but I shall make it anyhow, that the abstraction experiments did *not* demonstrate that people can judge only one attribute at a time. They merely showed what seems quite reasonable, that people are less accurate if they must judge more than one attribute simultaneously.

SUBITIZING

I cannot leave this general area without mentioning, however briefly, the experiments conducted at Mount Holyoke College on the discrimination of number (12). In experiments by Kaufman, Lord, Reese, and Volkmann random patterns of dots were flashed on a screen for 1/5 of a second. Anywhere from 1 to more than 200 dots could appear in the pattern. The subject's task was to report how many dots there were.

The first point to note is that on patterns containing up to five or six dots the subjects simply did not make errors. The performance on these small numbers of dots was so different from the performance with more dots that it was given a special name. Below seven the subjects were said to *subitize;* above seven they were said to *estimate.* This is, as you will recognize, what we once optimistically called "the span of attention."

This discontinuity at seven is, of course, suggestive. Is this the same basic process that limits our unidimensional judgments to about seven categories? The generalization is tempting, but not sound in my opinion. The data on number estimates have not been analyzed in informational terms; but on the basis of the published data I would guess that the subjects transmitted something more than four bits of information about the number of dots. Using the same arguments as before, we would conclude that there are about 20 or 30 distinguishable categories of numerousness. This is considerably more information than we would expect to get from a unidimensional display. It is, as a matter of fact, very much like a two-dimensional display. Although the dimensionality of the random dot patterns is not entirely clear, these results are in the same range as Klemmer and

Frick's for their two-dimensional display of dots in a square. Perhaps the two dimensions of numerousness are area and density. When the subject can subitize, area and density may not be the significant variables, but when the subject must estimate perhaps they are significant. In any event, the comparison is not so simple as it might seem at first thought.

This is one of the ways in which the magical number seven has persecuted me. Here we have two closely related kinds of experiments, both of which point to the significance of the number seven as a limit on our capacities. And yet when we examine the matter more closely, there seems to be a reasonable suspicion that it is nothing more than a coincidence.

THE SPAN OF IMMEDIATE MEMORY

Let me summarize the situation in this way. There is a clear and definite limit to the accuracy with which we can identify absolutely the magnitude of a unidimensional stimulus variable. I would propose to call this limit the *span of absolute judgment,* and I maintain that for unidimensional judgments this span is usually somewhere in the neighborhood of seven. We are not completely at the mercy of this limited span, however, because we have a variety of techniques for getting around it and increasing the accuracy of our judgments. The three most important of these devices are (a) to make relative rather than absolute judgments; or, if that is not possible, (b) to increase the number of dimensions along which the stimuli can differ; or (c) to arrange the task in such a way that we make a sequence of several absolute judgments in a row.

The study of relative judgments is one of the oldest topics in experimental psychology, and I will not pause to review it now. The second device, increasing the dimensionality, we have just considered. It seems that by adding more dimensions and requiring crude, binary, yes-no judgments on each attribute we can extend the span of absolute judgment from seven to at least 150. Judging from our everyday behavior, the limit is probably in the thousands, if indeed there is a limit. In my opinion, we cannot go on compounding dimensions indefinitely. I suspect that there is also a *span of perceptual*

dimensionality and that this span is somewhere in the neighborhood of ten, but I must add at once that there is no objective evidence to support this suspicion. This is a question sadly needing experimental exploration.

Concerning the third device, the use of successive judgments, I have quite a bit to say because this device introduces memory as the handmaiden of discrimination. And, since mnemonic processes are at least as complex as are perceptual processes, we can anticipate that their interactions will not be easily disentangled.

Suppose that we start by simply extending slightly the experimental procedure that we have been using. Up to this point we have presented a single stimulus and asked the observer to name it immediately thereafter. We can extend this procedure by requiring the observer to withhold his response until we have given him several stimuli in succession. At the end of the sequence of stimuli he then makes his response. We still have the same sort of input-output situation that is required for the measurement of transmitted information. But now we have passed from an experiment on absolute judgment to what is traditionally called an experiment on immediate memory.

Before we look at any data on this topic I feel I must give you a word of warning to help you avoid some obvious associations that can be confusing. Everybody knows that there is a finite span of immediate memory and that for a lot of different kinds of test materials this span is about seven items in length. I have just shown you that there is a span of absolute judgment that can distinguish about seven categories and that there is a span of attention that will encompass about six objects at a glance. What is more natural than to think that all three of these spans are different aspects of a single underlying process? And that is a fundamental mistake, as I shall be at some pains to demonstrate. This mistake is one of the malicious persecutions that the magical number seven has subjected me to.

My mistake went something like this. We have seen that the invariant feature in the span of absolute judgment is the amount of information that the observer can transmit. There is a real operational similarity between the absolute judgment experiment and the immediate memory experiment. If immediate memory is like absolute judgment, then it should follow that the invariant feature in the span of immediate memory is also the amount of information that an observer can retain. If the amount of information in the span of immediate memory is a constant, then the span should be short when the individual items contain a lot of information and the span should be long when the items contain little information. For example, decimal digits are worth 3.3 bits apiece. We can recall about seven of them, for a total of 23 bits of information. Isolated English words are worth about 10 bits apiece. If the total amount of information is to remain constant at 23 bits, then we should be able to remember only two or three words chosen at random. In this way I generated a theory about how the span of immediate memory should vary as a function of the amount of information per item in the test materials.

The measurements of memory span in the literature are suggestive on this question, but not definitive. And so it was necessary to do the experiment to see. Hayes (10) tried it out with five different kinds of test materials: binary digits, decimal digits, letters of the alphabet, letters plus decimal digits, and with 1,000 monosyllabic words. The lists were read aloud at the rate of one item per second and the subjects had as much time as they needed to give their responses. A procedure described by Woodworth (20) was used to score the responses.

The results are shown by the filled circles in Fig. 7. Here the dotted line indicates what the span should have been if the amount of information in the span were constant. The solid curves represent the data. Hayes repeated the experiment using test vocabularies of different sizes but all containing only English monosyllables (open circles in Fig. 7). This more homogeneous test material did not change the picture significantly. With binary items the span is about nine and, although it drops to about five with monosyllabic English words, the difference is far less than the hypothesis of constant information would require.

There is nothing wrong with Hayes's experiment, because Pollack (16) repeated it much more elaborately and

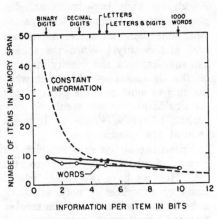

FIG. 7. Data from Hayes (10) on the span of immediate memory plotted as a function of the amount of information per item in the test materials.

got essentially the same result. Pollack took pains to measure the amount of information transmitted and did not rely on the traditional procedure for scoring the responses. His results are plotted in Fig. 8. Here it is clear that the amount of information transmitted is not a constant, but increases almost linearly as the amount of information per item in the input is increased.

And so the outcome is perfectly clear. In spite of the coincidence that the magical number seven appears in both places, the span of absolute judgment and the span of immediate memory are quite different kinds of limitations that are imposed on our ability to process information. Absolute judgment is limited by the amount of information. Immediate memory is limited by the number of items. In order to capture this distinction in somewhat picturesque terms, I have fallen into the custom of distinguishing between *bits* of information and *chunks* of information. Then I can say that the number of bits of information is constant for absolute judgment and the number of chunks of information is constant for immediate memory. The span of immediate memory seems to be almost independent of the number of bits per chunk, at least over the range that has been examined to date.

The contrast of the terms *bit* and *chunk* also serves to highlight the fact that we are not very definite about what constitutes a chunk of information. For example, the memory span of five words that Hayes obtained when each word was drawn at random from a set of 1000 English monosyllables might just as ap-

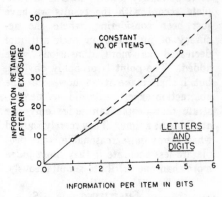

FIG. 8. Data from Pollack (16) on the amount of information retained after one presentation plotted as a function of the amount of information per item in the test materials.

propriately have been called a memory span of 15 phonemes, since each word had about three phonemes in it. Intuitively, it is clear that the subjects were recalling five words, not 15 phonemes, but the logical distinction is not immediately apparent. We are dealing here with a process of organizing or grouping the input into familiar units or chunks, and a great deal of learning has gone into the formation of these familiar units.

RECODING

In order to speak more precisely, therefore, we must recognize the importance of grouping or organizing the input sequence into units or chunks. Since the memory span is a fixed number of chunks, we can increase the number of bits of information that it contains simply by building larger and larger chunks, each chunk containing more information than before.

A man just beginning to learn radio-telegraphic code hears each *dit* and *dah* as a separate chunk. Soon he is able to organize these sounds into letters and then he can deal with the letters as chunks. Then the letters organize themselves as words, which are still larger chunks, and he begins to hear whole phrases. I do not mean that each step is a discrete process, or that plateaus must appear in his learning curve, for surely the levels of organization are achieved at different rates and overlap each other during the learning process. I am simply pointing to the obvious fact that the dits and dahs are organized by learning into patterns and that as these larger chunks emerge the amount of message that the operator can remember increases correspondingly. In the terms I am proposing to use, the operator learns to increase the bits per chunk.

In the jargon of communication theory, this process would be called *recoding*. The input is given in a code that contains many chunks with few bits per chunk. The operator recodes the input into another code that contains fewer chunks with more bits per chunk. There are many ways to do this recoding, but probably the simplest is to group the input events, apply a new name to the group, and then remember the new name rather than the original input events.

Since I am convinced that this process is a very general and important one for psychology, I want to tell you about a demonstration experiment that should make perfectly explicit what I am talking about. This experiment was conducted by Sidney Smith and was reported by him before the Eastern Psychological Association in 1954.

Begin with the observed fact that people can repeat back eight decimal digits, but only nine binary digits. Since there is a large discrepancy in the amount of information recalled in these two cases, we suspect at once that a recoding procedure could be used to increase the span of immediate memory for binary digits. In Table 1 a method for grouping and renaming is illustrated. Along the top is a sequence of 18 binary digits, far more than any subject was able to recall after a single presentation. In the next line these same binary digits are grouped by pairs. Four possible pairs can occur: 00 is renamed 0, 01 is renamed 1, 10 is renamed 2, and 11 is renamed 3. That is to say, we recode from a base-two arithmetic to a base-four arithmetic. In the recoded sequence there are now just nine digits to remember, and this is almost within the span of immediate memory. In the next line the same sequence of binary digits is regrouped into chunks of three. There are eight possible sequences of three, so we give each sequence a new name between 0 and 7. Now we have recoded from a sequence of 18 binary digits into a sequence of 6 octal digits, and this is well within the span of immediate memory. In the last two lines the binary digits are grouped by fours and by fives and are given decimal-digit names from 0 to 15 and from 0 to 31.

TABLE 1
WAYS OF RECODING SEQUENCES OF BINARY DIGITS

Binary Digits (Bits)		1 0 1 0 0 0 1 0 0 1 1 1 0 0 1 1 1 0							
2:1	Chunks	10	10	00	10	01	11	00	11	10
	Recoding	2	2	0	2	1	3	0	3	2
3:1	Chunks	101		000	100		111	001		110
	Recoding	5		0	4		7	1		6
4:1	Chunks	1010			0010		0111		0011	10
	Recoding	10			2		7		3	
5:1	Chunks	10100				01001		11001		110
	Recoding	20				9		25		

It is reasonably obvious that this kind of recoding increases the bits per chunk, and packages the binary sequence into a form that can be retained within the span of immediate memory. So Smith assembled 20 subjects and measured their spans for binary and octal digits. The spans were 9 for binaries and 7 for octals. Then he gave each recoding scheme to five of the subjects. They studied the recoding until they said they understood it—for about 5 or 10 minutes. Then he tested their span for binary digits again while they tried to use the recoding schemes they had studied.

The recoding schemes increased their span for binary digits in every case. But the increase was not as large as we had expected on the basis of their span for octal digits. Since the discrepancy increased as the recoding ratio increased, we reasoned that the few minutes the subjects had spent learning the recoding schemes had not been sufficient. Apparently the translation from one code to the other must be almost automatic or the subject will lose part of the next group while he is trying to remember the translation of the last group.

Since the 4:1 and 5:1 ratios require considerable study, Smith decided to imitate Ebbinghaus and do the experiment on himself. With Germanic patience he drilled himself on each recoding successively, and obtained the results shown in Fig. 9. Here the data follow along rather nicely with the results you would predict on the basis of his span for octal digits. He could remember 12 octal digits. With the 2:1 recoding, these 12 chunks were worth 24 binary digits. With the 3:1 recoding they were worth 36 binary digits. With the 4:1 and 5:1 recodings, they were worth about 40 binary digits.

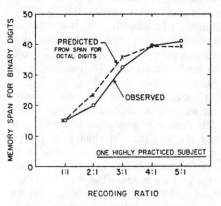

FIG. 9. The span of immediate memory for binary digits is plotted as a function of the recoding procedure used. The predicted function is obtained by multiplying the span for octals by 2, 3 and 3.3 for recoding into base 4, base 8, and base 10, respectively.

It is a little dramatic to watch a person get 40 binary digits in a row and then repeat them back without error. However, if you think of this merely as a mnemonic trick for extending the memory span, you will miss the more important point that is implicit in nearly all such mnemonic devices. The point is that recoding is an extremely powerful weapon for increasing the amount of information that we can deal with. In one form or another we use recoding constantly in our daily behavior.

In my opinion the most customary kind of recoding that we do all the time is to translate into a verbal code. When there is a story or an argument or an idea that we want to remember, we usually try to rephrase it "in our own words." When we witness some event we want to remember, we make a verbal description of the event and then remember our verbalization. Upon recall we recreate by secondary elaboration the details that seem consistent with the particular verbal recoding we happen to have made. The well-known experiment by Carmichael, Hogan, and Walter (3) on the influence that names have on the recall of visual figures is one demonstration of the process.

The inaccuracy of the testimony of eyewitnesses is well known in legal psychology, but the distortions of testimony are not random—they follow naturally from the particular recoding that the witness used, and the particular recoding he used depends upon his whole life history. Our language is tremendously useful for repackaging material into a few chunks rich in information. I suspect that imagery is a form of recoding, too, but images seem much harder to get at operationally and to study experimentally than the more symbolic kinds of recoding.

It seems probable that even memorization can be studied in these terms. The process of memorizing may be simply the formation of chunks, or groups of items that go together, until there are few enough chunks so that we can recall all the items. The work by Bousfield and Cohen (2) on the occurrence of clustering in the recall of words is especially interesting in this respect.

Summary

I have come to the end of the data that I wanted to present, so I would like now to make some summarizing remarks.

First, the span of absolute judgment and the span of immediate memory impose severe limitations on the amount of information that we are able to receive, process, and remember. By organizing the stimulus input simultaneously into several dimensions and successively into a sequence of chunks, we manage to break (or at least stretch) this informational bottleneck.

Second, the process of recoding is a very important one in human psychology and deserves much more explicit attention than it has received. In particular, the kind of linguistic recoding that people do seems to me to be the very lifeblood of the thought processes. Recoding procedures are a constant concern to clinicians, social psychologists, linguists, and anthropologists and yet, probably because recoding is less accessible to experimental manipulation than nonsense syllables or T mazes, the traditional experimental psychologist has contributed little or nothing to their analysis. Nevertheless, experimental techniques can be used, methods of recoding can be specified, behavioral indicants can be found. And I anticipate that we will find a very orderly set of relations describing what now seems an uncharted wilderness of individual differences.

Third, the concepts and measures provided by the theory of information provide a quantitative way of getting at some of these questions. The theory provides us with a yardstick for calibrating our stimulus materials and for measuring the performance of our subjects. In the interests of communication I have suppressed the technical details of information measurement and have tried to express the ideas in more familiar terms; I hope this paraphrase will not lead you to think they are not useful in research. Informational concepts have already proved valuable in the study of discrimination and of language; they promise a great deal in the study of learning and memory; and it has even been proposed that they can be useful in the study of concept formation. A lot of questions that seemed fruitless twenty or thirty years ago may now be worth another look. In fact, I feel that my story here must stop just as it begins to get really interesting.

And finally, what about the magical number seven? What about the seven wonders of the world, the seven seas, the seven deadly sins, the seven daughters of Atlas in the Pleiades, the seven ages of man, the seven levels of hell, the seven primary colors, the seven notes of the musical scale, and the seven days of the week? What about the seven-point rating scale, the seven categories for absolute judgment, the seven objects in the span of attention, and the seven digits in the span of immediate memory? For the present I propose to withhold judgment. Perhaps there is something deep and profound behind all these sevens, something just calling out for us to discover it. But I suspect that it is only a pernicious, Pythagorean coincidence.

REFERENCES

1. Beebe-Center, J. G., Rogers, M. S., & O'Connell, D. N. Transmission of information about sucrose and saline solutions through the sense of taste. *J. Psychol.*, 1955, **39**, 157–160.

2. Bousfield, W. A., & Cohen, B. H. The occurrence of clustering in the recall of randomly arranged words of different frequencies-of-usage. *J. gen. Psychol.*, 1955, **52**, 83–95.

3. Carmichael, L., Hogan, H. P., & Walter, A. A. An experimental study of the effect of language on the reproduction of visually perceived form. *J. exp. Psychol.*, 1932, **15**, 73–86.

4. Chapman, D. W. Relative effects of determinate and indeterminate *Aufgaben*. *Amer. J. Psychol.*, 1932, **44**, 163–174.

5. Eriksen, C. W. Multidimensional stimulus differences and accuracy of discrimination. *USAF, WADC Tech. Rep.*, 1954, No. 54–165.

6. Eriksen, C. W., & Hake, H. W. Absolute judgments as a function of the stimulus range and the number of stimulus and response categories. *J. exp. Psychol.*, 1955, **49**, 323–332.

7. Garner, W. R. An informational analysis of absolute judgments of loudness. *J. exp. Psychol.*, 1953, **46**, 373–380.

8. Hake, H. W., & Garner, W. R. The effect of presenting various numbers of discrete steps on scale reading accuracy. *J. exp. Psychol.*, 1951, **42**, 358–366.

9. Halsey, R. M., & Chapanis, A. Chromaticity-confusion contours in a complex viewing situation. *J. Opt. Soc. Amer.*, 1954, **44**, 442–454.

10. Hayes, J. R. M. Memory span for several vocabularies as a function of vocabulary size. In *Quarterly Progress Report*, Cambridge, Mass.: Acoustics Laboratory, Massachusetts Institute of Technology, Jan.–June, 1952.

11. Jakobson, R., Fant, C. G. M., & Halle, M. *Preliminaries to speech analysis.* Cambridge, Mass.: Acoustics Laboratory, Massachusetts Institute of Technology, 1952. (Tech. Rep. No. 13.)

12. Kaufman, E. L., Lord, M. W., Reese. T. W., & Volkmann, J. The discrimination of visual number. *Amer. J. Psychol.*, 1949, **62**, 498–525.

13. Klemmer, E. T., & Frick, F. C. Assimilation of information from dot and matrix patterns. *J. exp. Psychol.*, 1953, **45**, 15–19.

14. Külpe, O. Versuche über Abstraktion. *Ber. ü. d. I Kongr. f. exper. Psychol.*, 1904, 56–68.

15. Miller, G. A., & Nicely, P. E. An analysis of perceptual confusions among some English consonants. *J. Acoust. Soc. Amer.*, 1955, **27**, 338–352.

16. Pollack, I. The assimilation of sequentially encoded information. *Amer. J. Psychol.*, 1953, **66**, 421–435.

17. Pollack, I. The information of elementary auditory displays. *J. Acoust. Soc. Amer.*, 1952, **24**, 745–749.

18. Pollack, I. The information of elementary auditory displays. II. *J. Acoust. Soc. Amer.*, 1953, **25**, 765–769.

19. Pollack, I., & Ficks, L. Information of elementary multi-dimensional auditory displays. *J. Acoust. Soc. Amer.*, 1954, **26**, 155–158.

20. Woodworth, R. S. *Experimental psychology.* New York: Holt, 1938.

Norman L. Chervany and Gary W. Dickson   Davis Chapter 3

"AN EXPERIMENTAL EVALUATION OF INFORMATION OVERLOAD IN A PRODUCTION ENVIRONMENT"

<u>Management Sciences</u> (20:10), 1974 June, pages 1335-1344.

This article reports some significant research findings on the effects of information overload on human decision makers. Many writers in the field have noted the problem. For example, Ackoff contends that information systems too often present an over-abundance of data rather than filtering and condensing data for use in decision making. Although often mentioned, there has not been much research on the problem of information overload. The article is important both because it reports research on information overload and also because of the findings.

Two randomly selected and evenly matched groups of decision makers made periodic decisions relating to manufacturing production schedules, labor force changes, and raw material orders in a production environment. A computerized production simulator processed these decisions by "running" the plant for a week and reporting results back to the decision makers at the end of each week. The reported information consisted of production costs, production volume, finished goods inventory, raw material inventory, and labor status and utilization. Each test group received the information in a different form. The raw data group received detailed daily data while the statistically summarized data group received only mean, variance, and range data for each of several variables.

The criteria for measuring the performance of the two groups included production costs, time to make a decision, and the decision maker's level of confidence in each decision made. The experimental results showed that the decisions of the group receiving the statistically summarized data produced better and more consistent performance, that is, lower and stabler production costs. At the same time, they took longer to make their decisions and had less confidence in those decisions than the group receiving the raw data.

READING SUGGESTIONS

Do not concentrate on the details of the experiment; it is the results that are important and their implications for information systems design. Read enough to understand how the experiment was performed and to be able to make your own judgment on the validity of the research results.

QUESTIONS

1. Describe the two different forms in which information was presented to the two groups in this experiment.
2. What information was gathered to measure the performance and behavior of the decision makers? Are these the most significant measures?
3. What resulted in the group making decisions with a reduced amount of information? Which of these results are unexpected?
4. What were some of the differences between the two groups when comparing their behavior early in the decision making process and then later in the process?
5. Based upon the results of this experiment, would you recommend that an information system analyst always give decision makers the information they say they want?
6. What other options are open to the information systems designer for reducing information overload?

MANAGEMENT SCIENCE
Vol. 20, No. 10, June, 1974
Printed in U.S.A.

AN EXPERIMENTAL EVALUATION OF INFORMATION OVERLOAD IN A PRODUCTION ENVIRONMENT*

NORMAN L. CHERVANY AND GARY W. DICKSON

University of Minnesota

This paper reports the results of an experimental study of the relationship between the effectiveness of aggregate production planning decisions and the form of the information system used to support the decision making. The experiment, involving twenty-two graduate business administration students devoting an entire weekend to the decision making activity in a simulated, computer based environment, generated results showing significantly different performance according to the form in which information was presented. Decision makers given data summarized through the use of simple descriptive statistics (1) made higher quality decisions than those receiving the same data in standard formats, (2) had less confidence in the quality of their decisions, and (3) took longer to make their decisions.

At the Founding Conference of the Society for Management Information Systems held at the University of Minnesota, management information systems (MIS) professionals were asked to rank twenty-six potential research projects. The two projects receiving the highest rankings were: (1) development of methods for determining what the content of an information system should be, and (2) investigation into the characteristics of decision makers which affect MIS design [3].

Motivated by these opinions, this paper describes the first in a series of experimental research projects concerning the interface between decision effectiveness and the decision maker, his decision problem, and the information system provided to him. The experiment to be described specifically addressed the relationship between the form in which information is presented and several specific characteristics of the decisions that were made.

Research Background

In recent years, organizations have spent a great deal of effort developing computer based information systems to aid the management process. Unfortunately, many individuals express dissatisfaction with the benefits resulting from these systems ([1], [6], [16]). One of the basic reasons for this dissatisfaction is that MIS's are being designed under a condition in which little is known about the relationship between the effectiveness of managerial decisions and the information systems used to support the decisions.

Very few researchers have focused directly on the relationship between decision making and information systems (Dickson, Chervany and Kozar [5], Mason and Mitroff [11]). Among those few studies undertaken in this area, many have shortcomings which limit their usefulness. Some studies employ decision situations that are different from those encountered within complex organizations (Newman & Rogers [13]). In other cases, the research is frequently a case study of the implementation of one type of information system rather than a controlled evaluation of alternative

* Processed by Professor Richard L. Van Horn, Departmental Editor for Information Systems; received October 18, 1972, revised August 15, 1973. The work described in this article was supported by ONR Contract N000 14-67-A-0113-0017 and by the Management Information Systems Research Center, University of Minnesota. Special appreciation goes to Kenneth Kozar and James Johnson for their assistance in facilitating the computer processing in this project.

information systems (Gerrity [9], Morton [12], and Ferguson and Jones [7]). One specific study that employed a design capable of producing transferable results is reported by Prokop and Brooks [14]. Their study provided decision makers with a simulation model to aid in inventory control decisions. Beyond the provision of the decision aid, this study compared the impact of using alternative media (a CRT display versus batch paper output for the decision aid). Because of the controlled, experimental nature of their study, some generalizable insights into causal relationships in MIS design are available.

The Nature of the Experiment

A common problem identified in information system usage is that of information overload. Information systems too often present an over-abundance of data rather than filtering and condensing data for use in decision making [1]. In view of this contention, the independent variable chosen for investigation was the form in which information is presented. In particular, we investigated the differences in performance associated with using raw data (RD) versus statistically summarized data (SSD) as the controllable features of the information system.

The decision setting chosen for the investigation was an operations management situation. Decisions concerning production, inventory, and workforce levels had to be made. The setting was selected for two reasons. First, a relatively unambiguous, decision criterion (cost minimization) could be measured. Second, these decisions involve a heavy reliance upon quantitative data and thus permit an analysis of the use of summary statistics for reducing information overload.

The research method employed to conduct these investigations was experimental gaming. Twenty-two graduate students[1] in business administration interacted with a computerized operations management simulator in a controlled experimental setting. Based upon scores obtained in the Admission Test for Graduate Study in Business, two matched groups were selected and members of each group were randomly assigned to one of two information form treatments (RD versus SSD). The experiment required each subject to devote an entire weekend to making decisions in the simulated environment. They were induced to participate in the experiment by partial course credit, a $20 payment per subject for taking part, and prizes ($20 and $10) for the two best performances (minimum production costs) in a treatment.[2]

Saturday was devoted to a familiarization session. The subjects were given an opportunity to ask questions on the case material that described the decision setting. They were then presented with the information system reports they would be using. Each report was explained in detail. Finally, the decisions to be made, the form used to record their decisions, and the logistics of the experiment were discussed. After this, each subject made three weekly decisions.

On Sunday, each participant was given a set of initial conditions and firm parametric characteristics that were different from those employed in the familiarization session. Each subject than made ten weekly decisions. Subjects were not informed as to the number of decisions that they would be required to make. This was done to avoid any attempt on the subjects' part to "end play" the simulation. The simulator was con-

---

[1] Pretests of the experiment indicated that 10–12 hours of subject time would be required to complete the total experiment. Because of computer requirements, the experiment had to be conducted over a weekend. These costs in subject time (given the exploratory nature of the research) were felt to be too excessive to consider using managers as subjects.

[2] The only costs included in the simulator were production costs.

structed to allow individual subjects to be working in different decision periods. Thus, subjects were able to make decisions at their own speed. No noticeable, indirect peer pressure tending to force the slower subjects to speed up their decision making process was observed. Analysis of a post-experiment questionnaire confirmed the absence of any pressure to make faster decisions.

When a subject completed a decision, the time to make the decision was recorded. In addition, each subject marked on a continuum the level of confidence (low to high) he felt in the decision. After the subject's decisions were processed and his information system reports returned, a new cycle was begun.

Experimental Task

The vehicle serving as the basis for the experiment is a FORTRAN IV computer program which processes decisions in a simulated manufacturing plant environment [4]. The hypothetical manufacturing facility produces three products (resinoid, resinforced, and vitrified). Orders for these products arrive daily and finished good units to fill these orders are shipped at the end of each day. Each of the three products takes an associated type of raw material. Orders for raw materials, in any quantity, can be placed once per day. The time between placement of an order for raw material and its arrival varies randomly.

The plant has one type of machine for each product, but the machine operators can operate all types. Another class of worker, the material handler, has the job of delivering raw material to the machines, removing finished products from the machines, and taking them to the finished goods inventory area.

The objective of the production manager (the subject) is to make the decisions necessary to operate the plant at a minimum cost. To attain this objective, he must consider: (1) labor costs (salaries and hire/fire costs), (2) raw material costs, and (3) inventory costs (raw material order costs, raw material and finished goods carrying costs, and finished goods stockout costs). At the beginning of the week the production manager makes a set of operating decisions which consist of:

1. *Production Schedules*: Production is scheduled by specifying how many products of each type are to be produced each day of the week.

2. *Labor Force Changes*: The size of the work force is determined by specifying the number of workers in each of the two classes to be hired or terminated for each day of the week.

3. *Raw Material Orders*: Raw material is ordered by specifying the size of the order (by raw material type) for each day of the week

Experimental Treatments

The information necessary to make the decisions outlined above consisted of paper copy, batch processed reports detailing both weekly process results and end-of-the-week status In particular, the subjects received five classes of reports: (1) production costs, (2) finished goods production, (3) finished goods inventory, (4) raw material inventory, and (5) labor status/utilization. The information was provided in terms of the total operation and on a product-by-product basis for the four most recent weeks.

The experimental treatment investigated in this study consisted of different forms of the same information while content, presentation mode, and time availability remained the same. In neither treatment were decision aids given to the subjects. Abbreviated samples from the two treatments are presented in Exhibit 1. As can be seen, the same categories of information are contained in both reports. The RD

EXHIBIT 1
Information System Treatments

A. *Raw Data Treatment*   FINISHED GOODS INVENTORY HISTORY

INVENTORY LEVELS	WEEK 1 OF MONTH 3			WEEK 2 OF MONTH 3			WEEK 3
	RESINOID	R-FORCED	VITRIFID	RESINOID	R-FORCED	VITRIFID	RESINOID
MONDAY	0	371	0	0	120	481	0
TUESDAY	30	102	82	0	153	191	0
WEDNESDAY	0	0	198	0	202	0	29
THURSDAY	34	36	299	38	267	0	52
FRIDAY	71	84	393	79	188	38	79
STOCKOUTS							
	RESINOID	R-FORCED	VITRIFID	RESINOID	R-FORCED	VITRIFID	
MONDAY	285	0	58	354	0	0	
TUESDAY	0	0	0	423	0	0	
WEDNESDAY	379	221	0	144	0	201	
THURSDAY	0	0	0	0	0	121	
FRIDAY	0	0	0	0	0	0	
DEMAND							
	RESINOID	R-FORCED	VITRIFID	RESINOID	R-FORCED		
MONDAY	420	414	381	425	420		

B. *Statistically Summarized Treatment*

FINISHED GOODS INVENTORY HISTORY
SUMMARY STATISTICS CALCULATED
FROM OPERATIONS FOR PERIOD
WEEK 1 OF MONTH 3 THROUGH WEEK 4 OF MONTH 3

	DAILY INVENTORY LEVELS (END OF DAY)				STOCKOUTS		
	RESINOID	R-FORCED	VITRIFID		RESINOID	R-FORCED	VITRIFID
MEAN	23.25	140.80	92.85	MEAN	171.30	38.20	123.70
COEF VAR	6.28	4.18	7.97	COEF VAR	5.63	14.77	7.09
MAXIMUM	79.00	371.00	481.00	MAXIMUM	427.00	392.00	484.00
RANGE	79.00	371.00	481.00	RANGE	427.00	392.00	484.00

	DAILY DEMAND		
	RESINOID	R-FORCED	VITRIFID
MEAN	430.20	399.50	415.60
COEF VAR	.09	.23	.50
MAXIMUM	442.00	424.00	484.00
RANGE	24.00	49.00	140.00

report contains the information in what might be described as a "typical" managerial report form. The SSD report presents the information summarized by the arithmetic mean, coefficient of variation, maximum value and range; no detailed daily or weekly data are available. The total set of RD reports required ten pages of computer output; the SSD reports, seven pages. For the RD reports there were 1040 data items reported; for the SSD reports; 449 data items. These two treatments represent *one* of the options for reducing information overload open to the information systems analyst.

Hypotheses and Experimental Measures

The hypotheses tested in the study concerns three performance areas: cost, decision making time, and decision confidence. The belief was held that the performance of the RD subjects would differ from the SD subjects in: (1) average total cost, (2) average time to make a decision, and (3) average confidence in decisions made. Further-more, it was believed that the inter-subject variation in all three measures would be different between the treatment groups.

To test these beliefs, three basic types of performance data were collected:

1. *Production Costs*: Data on each of the seven cost categories were collected for each subject for each weekly decision period and summarized in terms of total cost.

2. *Decision Time*: The decision making time was calculated by elapsed time be-tween when a subject received his output reports and submitted his next decision.

3. *Decision Confidence*: Each time a subject submitted a set of weekly decisions he recorded his confidence in his current decisions on a seven point scale.

In addition to above data collected during the experiment, post-experimental ques-tionnaire data were also obtained. These data consisted of a subject (1) evaluating the contents of each report available to him with respect to its importance and/or usefulness in his decision process, (2) describing other information he would like to have had, and (3) evaluating the experimental setting and experimental task.

Results of the Experiment

The results presented here focus upon the RD versus SSD treatment effect. For each experimental measure—total cost, decision time, and decision confidence—differences in average treatment performance and variability in average treatment performance were examined.

Statistical Results

As described in the preceding section, the basic data were collected for thirteen time periods—three familiarization decisions and ten experimental decisions. To test the hypotheses, the data for periods three through ten of the experimental session were used. The data for the first two periods of the experimental session were omitted because they were substantially influenced by the initial conditions (which were beyond the subjects' control) of the simulator and subject learning. The nature of the simulator is such that by the beginning of the second week all of the initial con-ditions were overcome. In particular, the longest decision lead times involved are a one week delay in hiring machine operators and a maximum one week raw material order/receipt lead time. The data for the second experimental period were omitted because subjects were still becoming "familiar" with the new decision environments and we did not want to confound the results with this learning effect. The temporal patterns supporting these omissions are shown on the total cost portion of Exhibit 3.

For these eight time periods the average performance on each measure for each subject was calculated. The two treatments were compared on each measure by employing (a) *t*-tests on the paired differences for the treatment averages, and (b) *F*-tests on the ratio of treatment variances.[3] The results of the statistical tests are presented in Exhibit 2. These data show that:

1. The subjects using the SSD reports had weekly total costs that averaged $1483 less than the subjects that used the RD reports ($32,215–$30,732). This difference, relative to the $32,215 total cost for the RD treatment, represents approximately a 4.6% reduction in average total costs.

2. Although their cost performance was superior, the subjects using the SSD took

---

[3] Analysis of the individual subject data did not indicate any substantial departures from nor-mality that would invalidate the use of these tests. The matched pairs design was felt to be a sufficient control on the caliber of the subjects. An extensive analysis using a general linear model to incorporate a variety of subject attributes is currently in progress.

EXHIBIT 2

Treatment Effects

	Total Cost	Decision Time	Decision Confidence
Average Performance:			
Sample Difference*	$1,483	−47 min.	0.636
Level of Significance	0.18	0.05	0.12
Variance in Average Performance:			
Sample Ratio	1.984**	1.057***	5.307***
Level of Significance	0.15	NS	0.02

* All differences RD-SSD.

** Ratio computed as RD/SSD.

*** Ratio computed as SSD/RD.

an average of 4.7 minutes longer per decision (18.3 minutes — 23.0 minutes) and rated their confidence 0.6 scale points lower (4.9 — 4.3). The average time spent by the SSD subjects was approximately 25 % longer than that of the RD subjects.

3. The variance in the average total cost per subject using the RD reports was approximately 2.0 times (20,488/10,304) that of the subjects using the SSD reports.

4. With respect to the variability in the subjects' average confidence, the subjects using the SSD demonstrated much more variability (1.97/.37) than the RD subjects.

Interpretation of the Statistical Results

Before discussing "why" these effects occurred, one point needs to be emphasized: The only data available are the costs incurred, times spent, decisions recorded, and post-experimental questionnaire responses. There are no data available on what the subjects were thinking *during* the experiment. Similarly, no data are available on why the subjects made specific decisions or what decision strategy was employed.[4]

Analysis of the simulated decision problem with respect to the administrative parameters for demand, cost, and production suggests that concentrating upon minimizing stockouts (by attempting accurate demand forecasting and using more conservative raw material ordering policies) is the "key" to the problem as configured for this study. For all subjects, the average weekly stockout costs ($9987) represent 31 % of the average weekly total costs ($31,473). Examination of the seven cost categories reveals an important fact. *For all categories but stockout costs,* average costs for the SSD subjects were higher than for the RD subjects. But the average finished good stockout costs were significantly lower (0.08 level of significance) for the SSD subject ($11,444 — $8,531). Furthermore the minimum *average* finished goods stockout cost over all SSD subjects was $512.00; for the RD subjects, $3,129. We hypothesize that the RD subjects either had a more difficult time identifying the stockout problem or solving it once identified. This "ability" to focus on the "key" problem may also explain the reduction in the variability in average subject cost performance and average decision time.

The post-experiment questionnaire data provided evidence to support this idea of the increased ability of the SSD subjects to identify and resolve the major problem

[4] These are valuable types of information. They were not, however, the prime objective of this study. Since this experiment, some work into modeling a decision strategy for the operations management simulator has been undertaken (see Johnson [10]).

in the decision setting. In response to the question:

"How do you feel about the form in which the information was provided by the reports?"

a. Very poor, substantial changes should be made.

b. Adequate, but could be improved by a few changes.

c. Good, should be left as it is.

Both treatment groups split about equally between responses b and c (5–6 for the RD subjects and 6-5 for the SSD subjects). Of those that desired "a few changes," however, there was a substantive difference among the requests by treatment. Four of the six of the SSD subjects requesting changes wanted additional information concerning demand forecasts and scheduled arrival dates of raw material orders. None of the five RD subjects desiring changes requested anything remotely connected to solving the stockout problem.

Another source of evidence supporting the contention that the SSD subjects were better able to "solve" the decision problem is found in the subjects ranking of the reports available to them in terms of their importance and usefulness in making their decisions. Average ranks of the reports by experimental treatment were developed.

EXHIBIT 3. Temporal Patterns in Cost Performance (Cumulative Averages).

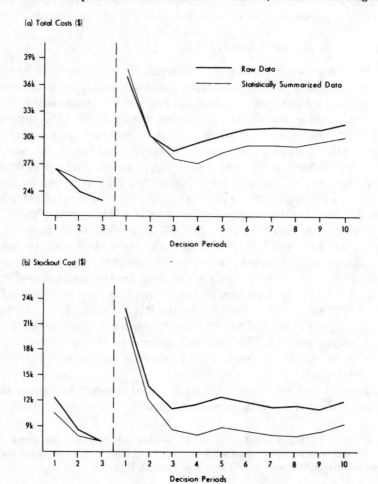

Rank correlation analysis of these rankings indicated that the two sets of rankings were independent. Only for the SSD subjects do the reports ranked highest provide a means of analyzing and solving the demand forecasting/inventory control problem.

The essence of the above discussion is that the RD subjects did not (or perhaps could not) transform their data into the form given in the SSD reports. These findings (or hypotheses) are in agreement with a large number of research findings discussed in the experimental psychology literature that deals with man's limited information processing capabilities [15].

The results with respect to the decision time and confidence are troublesome. Even though the SSD subjects did better, the increased average time and reduced average confidence lead to the tentative conclusion that they did not realize they had a "handle" on the problem. Perhaps, these phenomena would "correct" themselves over a larger number of decisions. This cannot be deduced, however, from this experiment.

Additional insight into the above differences in the average performance by treatment can be seen by examining Exhibits 3 and 4. They reveal that, on a cumulative average basis, the SSD subjects did better (costwise) starting with the third decision

EXHIBIT 4. Temporal Patterns in Decision Time and Confidence (Cumulative Averages).

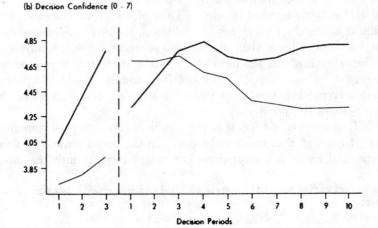

(a) Decision Time (min.)

Raw Data
Statistically Summarized Data

Decision Periods

(b) Decision Confidence (0 - 7)

Decision Periods

in the experimental session.[5] The time and decision confidence performance data reveal an interesting pattern. The RD subjects initially took longer and had lower confidence than the SSD subjects. As of the third experimental decision, however, this pattern reversed itself. This reversal in time and confidence took place in spite of the fact that they were not doing as well (costwise). When asked to rate the difficulty of their middle decision and final decision as a percentage of the difficulty of their first decision, e.g., twice as difficult or half as difficult, the average responses of the RD subjects were 0.62 and 0.61 respectively. The average responses of the SSD subjects to these same questions were 0.83 and 0.52 respectively. Perceived learning (but not necessarily confidence) had increased more in the SSD subjects than in the RD subjects.

Conclusions

For the MIS practitioner, the experimental data support the general contention that the reduction in information overload via the use of descriptive statistics can both improve performance and make performance more predictable, i.e., reduced performance variability. The results further suggest two potentially undesirable consequences of the use of statistical summarization. First, the projected savings in user time may not occur; second, uncomfortable (if not dissatisfied) users may be encountered. The first problem may be overcome by the long run use of the statistically summarized information. In evaluating the economic costs and benefits of a planned system, however, user time savings benefits may have to be discounted. The latter problem implies the need for a thorough user education program.

Some potential problems with the implementation of the above analysis and design guidelines can be identified in the experimental results. In particular, consider the problems foreshadowed by the paradoxical results that the RD subjects performed worse (higher average total costs) but took less time making decisions and had higher confidence in their decisions. These findings lead one to doubt that a user would request the SSD reports over the RD reports.

Additional support for the idea that users would not be likely to request a statistically summarized information system is found in the post-experiment questionnaire data. In response to the question:

"How sufficient was the content of the information in order to allow you to make the necessary decisions?"

a. There was insufficient information to make the decisions.

b. The information was just about right to make the decisions.

c. There was much more information that was needed to make the decisions.

Ten of the RD subjects selected b; one, a. The SSD subjects, however, were split 3, 4 and 4 among a, b and c respectively. In addition, the SSD subjects rated the decision setting as more artificial than did the RD subjects. Since the only difference in the experimental setting was the form of the information, this is equivalent to their rating the reports as less realistic These two facts coupled together support the conclusion that user participation *alone* in systems design may not select the "best" information systems [16, pp. 37–38].

For the MIS researcher, we feel that the results of this study point unambiguously to *one* type of research that needs to be done. In the broad sense, this study shows that experimental research can produce instructive insights into the interrelations

---

[5] The rising cost curves reflect the increasing total demand experienced during the course of the simulation.

among factors that impinge upon the success or failure of an MIS. From the specific results of the study several direct "follow-on" projects are suggested. For example, one extension would involve the replication of the experiment using managers as subjects. We recognize the potential problems of using student subjects as surrogates for managers ([2], [8]). The results of this current study are seen as providing the motivation for managers to make the necessary time commitment.

References

1. ACKOFF, R. L., "Management Misinformation Systems," *Management Science*, Vol. 14 (December, 1967), pp. B147–B156.
2. ALPERT, B., "Nonbusinessmen as Surrogates for Businessmen in Behavioral Research," *Journal of Business*, Vol. 15 (April, 1967), pp. 203–207.
3. DICKSON, G. W., "Management Information Systems: Definitions, Problems, and Research," *SMIS Newsletter*, Vol. 1 (July, 197), pp. 6–12.
4. ——, CHERVANY, N. L., AND DAVITT, P., "An Interactive Decision Environment Simulator For Use in Experimentally Evaluating Factors in Information Systems Design," *Management Information Systems Research Center Working Paper Series*, MISRC-WP-71-13, University of Minnesota, Minneapolis, Minnesota, 1972.
5. ——, ——, AND KOZAR, K. A., "An Experimental Gaming Framework For Investigating the Influence of Management Information Systems on Decision Effectiveness," *Management Information Systems Research Center Working Paper Series*, MISRC-WP-71-12, University of Minnesota, Minneapolis, Minnesota, 1972.
6. DIEBOLD, J., "Bad Decisions on Computer Use," *Harvard Business Review*, Vol. 47 (January-February, 1969), pp. 14–28.
7. FERGUSON, R. L., AND JONES, C. H., "A Computer Aided Decision System," *Management Science*, Vol. 15 (June, 1969), pp. B550–B561.
8. FLEMMING, J. E., "Managers as Subjects in Business Decisions Research," *Academy of Management Journal*, Vol. 12 (March, 1969), pp. 59–66.
9. GERRITY, T. P., "Design of Man-Machine Decision Systems: An Application to Portfolio Management," *Sloan Management Review*, Vol. 12 (Winter, 1971), pp. 59–75.
10. JOHNSON, J. C., "Production Decision: A Heuristic Approach," *Management Information Systems Research Center Working Paper Series*, MISRC-WP-72-1, University of Minnesota, Minneapolis, Minnesota, 1972.
11. MASON, R. O., AND MITROFF, I. I., "A Program for Research on Management Information & Information Systems," *Management Science*, Vol. 19 No. 5 (January, 1973) pp. 475–487.
12. MORTON, M. S. S., "Interactive Visual Display Systems and Management Problem Solving," *Industrial Management Review*, Vol. 9 (Fall, 1967), pp. 69–81.
13. NEWMAN, J. R. AND ROGERS, M. S., "Experiments in Computer-Aided Inductive Reasoning," *TM-3227/000/00*, System Development Corporation, Santa Monica, California, 1966.
14. PROKOP, J. S. AND BROOKS, F. P., JR., "Decision Making With Computer Graphics," *Proceedings of the Fall Joint Computer Conference*, Vol. 37 (1970), pp. 599–607.
15. SLOVIC, P., "From Shakespear to Simon: Speculations—And Some Evidence—About Man's Ability to Process Information." A paper presented to the XIX International Meeting of the Institute of Management Sciences, Houston, Texas, April 5, 1972.
16. "Unlocking the Computer's Profit Potential," A Research Report to Management, McKinsey and Company, New York, 1968.

Daniel Katz and Robert L. Kahn   Davis Chapter 4

"ORGANIZATIONS AND THE SYSTEM CONCEPT"

The Social Psychology of Organizations, Chapter 2,
New York: John Wiley and Sons, 1966, pages 14-29.

The relatively recent theory of open systems seeks to
explain why some types of systems survive and thrive in a
rapidly changing environment and in the face of a through-
put of material, energy, and information. Katz and Kahn
have summarized the nine major characteristics of open systems and discussed them in terms of human organizations.
An open systems view focuses attention on the problems of
relationships, of structure, and of interdependence.
Living organisms, humans, and collections of individuals in
society exhibit these characteristics. Such systems also
exhibit very complex relationships internally and with
their environment. The systems are acutely dependent upon
their external environment and so must be conceived as open
systems.

In contrast to the traditional goal-oriented view of
an organization, an open system approach to an organization
begins by identifying and mapping the repeated cycles of
input, transformation, output, and renewed input. These
comprise the pattern of organizational behavior.

Several consequences stem from viewing the organization as an open system. An organization is continually dependent upon inputs from the environment; but the inflow of
materials and human energy is not constant. Flexibility
may therefore be more important to the continued existence
of an organization than a high degree of internal integration and coordination. The theory suggests that there is
more than one best way to accomplish organizational tasks,
and that it is vital for an organization to develop feedback mechanisms to gather information about changes in environmental forces.

READING SUGGESTIONS

Read to obtain an understanding of the nature and characteristics of open systems. Open systems should be understood in relationship to closed systems. Relate the open
system view of organization to traditional views of organizations. It is not necessary to obtain a detailed understanding of the characteristics of open systems, but do understand what each characteristic means when related to
social organizations. In particular, note the importance
of energy importation, information (coding and feedback),
dynamic homeostasis, and equifinality as these concepts

apply to organizations. All this should produce an appreciation for the complexity of social organizations and the
resulting challenge in the development of information systems in organizations.

QUESTIONS

1. Explain the weaknesses in the traditional approaches
    to understanding organizations relating to boundaries
    and purposes.

2. Describe the underlying model of an open system.

3. What is the limitation of saying that "businesses
    exist to make money, that is, to make a profit"?

4. Contrast the open systems view inherent in biological
    and social systems with the closed systems view of the
    physical sciences.

5. List the nine major characteristics of open systems
    and match some feature or attribute of social organi-
    zations with each one.

6. What are the possible consequences on an organization
    of developing bureaucratic structures and standard
    procedures?

7. What are some implications for MIS design stemming
    from open systems theory as applied to organizations?
    What is the effect of having an inflexible MIS?

ORGANIZATIONS AND THE SYSTEM CONCEPT

Daniel KATZ and Robert L. KAHN

D. Katz and R. L. Kahn, *The Social Psychology of Organizations*, chapter 2, Wiley, 1966, pp. 14–29.

The aims of social science with respect to human organizations are like those of any other science with respect to the events and phenomena of its domain. The social scientist wishes to understand human organizations, to describe what is essential in their form, aspects, and functions. He wishes to explain their cycles of growth and decline, to predict their effects and effectiveness. Perhaps he wishes as well to test and apply such knowledge by introducing purposeful changes into organizations – by making them, for example, more benign, more responsive to human needs.

Such efforts are not solely the prerogative of social science, however; common-sense approaches to understanding and altering organizations are ancient and perpetual. They tend, on the whole, to rely heavily on two assumptions: that the location and nature of an organization are given by its name; and that an organization is possessed of built-in goals – because such goals were implanted by its founders, decreed by its present leaders, or because they emerged mysteriously as the purposes of the organizational system itself. These assumptions scarcely provide an adequate basis for the study of organizations and at times can be misleading and even fallacious. We propose, however, to make use of the information to which they point.

The first problem in understanding an organization or a social system is its location and identification. How do we know that we are dealing with an organization? What are its boundaries? What behavior belongs to the organization and what behavior lies outside it? Who are the individuals whose actions are to be studied and what segments of their behavior are to be included?

The fact that popular names exist to label social organizations is both a help and a hindrance. These popular labels represent the socially accepted stereotypes about organizations and do not specify their role structure, their psychological nature, or their boundaries. On the other hand, these names help in locating the area of behavior in which we are interested. Moreover, the fact that people both within and without an organization accept stereotypes about its nature and functioning is one determinant of its character.

The second key characteristic of the common-sense approach to understanding an organization is to regard it simply as the epitome of the purposes of its designer, its leaders, or its key members. The teleology of this approach is again both a help and a hindrance. Since human purpose is deliberately built into organizations and is specifically recorded in the social compact, the by-laws, or other formal protocol of the undertaking, it would be inefficient not to utilize these sources of information. In the early development of a group, many processes are generated which have little to do with its rational purpose, but over time there is a cumulative recognition of the devices for ordering group life and a deliberate use of these devices.

Apart from formal protocol, the primary mission of an organization as perceived by its leaders furnishes a highly informative set of clues for the researcher seeking to study organizational functioning. Nevertheless, the stated purposes of an organization as given by its by-laws or in the reports of its leaders can be misleading. Such statements of objectives may idealize, rationalize, distort, omit, or even conceal some essential aspects of the functioning of the organization. Nor is there always agreement about the mission of the organization among its leaders and members. The university president may describe the purpose of his institution as one of turning out national leaders; the academic dean sees it as imparting the cultural heritage of the past, the academic vice-president as enabling students to move toward self-actualization and development, the graduate dean as creating new knowledge, the dean of men as training youngsters in technical and professional skills which will enable them to earn their living, and the editor of the student newspaper as inculcating the conservative values which will preserve the status quo of an outmoded capitalistic society.

The fallacy here is one of equating the purposes of goals of organizations with the purposes and goals of individual members. The organization as a system has an output, a product, or an outcome, but this is not necessarily identical with the individual purposes of group members. Though the founders of the organization and its key members do think in teleological terms about organizational objectives, we should not accept such practical thinking, useful as it may be, in place of a theoretical set of constructs for purposes of scientific analysis. Social science, too frequently in the past, has been misled by such short-cuts and has equated popular phenomenology with scientific explanation.

In fact, the classic body of theory and thinking about organizations has assumed a teleology of this sort as the easiest way of identifying organizational structures and their functions. From this point of view an organization is a social device for efficiently accomplishing through group means some stated purpose; it is the equivalent of the blueprint for the design of the machine which is to be created for some practical objective. The essential difficulty with this purposive or design approach is that an organization characteristically includes more and less than is indicated by the design of its founder or the purpose of its leader. Some of the factors assumed in the design may be lacking or so distorted in operational practice as to be meaningless, while unforeseen embellishments dominate the organizational structure. Moreover, it is not always possible to ferret out the designer of the organization or to discover the intricacies of the design which he carried in his head. The attempt by Merton (1957) to deal with the latent function of the organization in contrast with its manifest function is one way of dealing with this problem. The study of unanticipated consequences as well as anticipated consequences of organizational functioning is a similar way of handling the matter. Again, however, we are back to the purposes of the creator or leader, dealing with unanticipated consequences on the assumption that we can discover the consequences anticipated by him and can lump all other outcomes together as a kind of error variance.

It would be much better theoretically, however, to start with concepts which do not call for identifying the purposes of the designers and then correcting for them when they do not seem to be fulfilled. The theoretical concepts should begin with the input, output, and functioning of the organization as a system and not with the rational purposes of its leaders. We may want to utilize such purposive notions to lead us to sources of data or as subjects of special study, but not as our basic theoretical constructs for understanding organizations.

Our theoretical model for the understanding of organizations is that of an energic input–output system in which the energic return from the output reactivates the system. Social organizations are flagrantly open systems in that the input of energies and the conversion of output into further energic input consist of transactions between the organization and its environment.

All social systems, including organizations, consist of the patterned activities of a number of individuals. Moreover, these patterned activities are complementary or interdependent with respect to some common output or outcome; they are repeated, relatively enduring, and bounded in space and time. If the activity pattern occurs only once or at unpredictable intervals, we could not speak of an organization. The stability or recurrence of activities can be examined in relation to the *energic input* into the system, the *transformation of energies within the system*, and the *resulting product or energic output*. In a factory the raw materials and the human labor are the energic input, the patterned activities of production the transformation of energy, and the finished product the output. To maintain this patterned activity requires a continued renewal of the inflow of energy. This is guaranteed in social systems by the energic return from the product or outcome. Thus the outcome of the cycle of activities furnishes new energy for the initiation of a renewed cycle. The company which produces automobiles sells them and by doing so obtains the means of securing new raw materials, compensating its labor force, and continuing the activity pattern.

In many organizations outcomes are converted into money and new energy is furnished through this mechanism. Money is a convenient way of handling energy units both on the output and input sides, and buying and selling represent one set of social rules for regulating the exchange of money. Indeed, these rules are so effective and so widespread that there is some danger of mistaking the business of buying and selling for the defining cycles of organization. It is a commonplace executive observation that businesses exist to make money, and the observation is usually allowed to go unchallenged. It is, however, a very limited statement about the purposes of business.

Some human organizations do not depend on the cycle of selling and buying to maintain themselves. Universities and public agencies depend rather on bequests and legislative appropriations, and in so-called voluntary organizations the output re-energizes the activity of organization members in a more direct fashion. Member activities and accomplishments are rewarding in themselves and tend therefore to be continued, without the mediation of the outside environment. A society of bird watchers can wander into the hills and engage in the rewarding activities of identifying birds for their mutual edification and enjoyment. Organizations thus differ on this important dimension of the source of energy renewal, with the great majority utilizing both intrinsic and extrinsic sources in varying degree. Most large-scale organizations are not as self-contained as small voluntary groups and are very dependent upon the social effects of their output for energy renewal.

Our two basic criteria for identifying social systems and determining their functions are (1) tracing the pattern of energy exchange or activity of people as it results in some output and (2) ascertaining how the output is translated into energy which reactivates the pattern. We shall refer to organizational functions or objectives not as the conscious purposes of group leaders or group members but as the outcomes which are the energic source for a maintenance of the same type of output.

This model of an energic input–output system is taken from the open system theory as promulgated by von Bertalanffy (1956). Theorists have pointed out the applicability of the system concepts of the natural sciences to the problems of social science. It is important, therefore, to examine in more detail the constructs of system theory and the characteristics of open systems.

System theory is basically concerned with problems of relationships, of structure, and of interdependence rather than with the constant attributes of objects. In general approach it resembles field theory except that its dynamics deal with temporal as well as spatial patterns. Older formulations of system constructs dealt with the closed systems of the physical sciences, in which relatively self-contained structures could be treated successfully as if they were independent of external forces. But living systems, whether biological organisms or social organizations, are acutely dependent upon their external environment and so must be conceived of as open systems.

Before the advent of open-system thinking, social scientists tended to take one of two approaches in dealing with social structures; they tended either (1) to regard them as closed systems to which the laws of physics applied or (2) to endow them with some vitalistic concept like entelechy. In the former case they ignored the environmental forces affecting the organization and in the latter case they fell back upon some magical purposiveness to account for organizational functioning. Biological theorists, however, have rescued us from this trap by pointing out that the concept of the open system means that we neither have to follow the laws of traditional physics, nor in deserting them do we have to abandon science. The laws of Newtonian physics are correct generalizations but they are limited to closed systems. They do not apply in the same fashion to open systems which maintain themselves through constant commerce with their environment, i.e. a continuous inflow and outflow of energy through permeable boundaries.

One example of the operation of closed versus open systems can be seen in the concept of entropy and the second law of thermodynamics. According to the second law of thermodynamics, a system moves toward equilibrium; it tends to run down, that is, its differentiated structures tend to move toward dissolution as the elements composing them become arranged in random disorder. For example, suppose that a bar of iron has been heated by the application of a blowtorch on one side. The arrangement of all the fast (heated) molecules on one side and all the slow molecules on the other is an unstable state, and over time the distribution of molecules becomes in effect random, with the resultant cooling of one side and heating of the other, so that all surfaces of the iron approach the same temperature. A similar process of heat exchange will also be going on between the iron bar and its environment, so that the bar will gradually approach the temperature of the room in which it is located, and in doing will elevate somewhat the previous temperature of the room. More technically, entropy increases toward a maximum and equilibrium occurs as the physical system attains the state of the most probable distribution of its elements. In social systems, however, structures tend to become more elaborated rather than less differentiated. The rich may grow richer and the poor may grow poorer. The open system does not run down, because it can import energy from the world around it. Thus the operation of entropy is counteracted by the importation of energy and the living system is characterized by negative rather than positive entropy.

Common Characteristics of Open Systems

Though the various types of open systems have common characteristics by virtue of being open systems, they differ in other characteristics. If this were not the case, we would be able to obtain all our basic knowledge about social organizations through studying the biological organisms or even through the study of a single cell.

The following nine characteristics seem to define all open systems:

1. Importation of energy

Open systems import some form of energy from the external environment. The cell receives oxygen from the blood stream; the body similarly takes in oxygen from the air and food from the external world. The personality is dependent upon the external world for stimulation. Studies of sensory deprivation show that when a person is placed in a darkened soundproof room, where he has a minimal amount of visual and auditory stimulation, he develops hallucinations and other signs of mental stress (Solomon et al., 1961). Deprivation of social stimulation also can lead to mental disorganization (Spitz, 1945). Köhler's (1944, 1947) studies of the figural after-effects of continued stimulation show the dependence of perception upon its energic support from the external world. Animals deprived of visual experience from birth for a prolonged period never fully recover their visual capacities (Melzack and Thompson, 1956). In other words, the functioning personality is heavily dependent upon the continuous inflow of stimulation from the external environment. Similarly, social organizations must also draw renewed supplies of energy from other institutions, or people, or the material environment. No social structure is self-sufficient or self-contained.

2. The through-put

Open systems transform the energy available to them. The body converts starch and sugar into heat and action. The personality converts chemical and electrical forms of stimulation into sensory qualities, and information into thought patterns. The organization creates a new product, or processes materials, or trains people, or provides a service. These activities entail some reorganization of input. Some work gets done in the system.

3. The output

Open systems export some product into the environment, whether it be the invention of an inquiring mind or a bridge constructed by an engineering firm. Even the biological organism exports physiological products such as carbon dioxide from the lungs which helps to maintain plants in the immediate environment.

4. Systems as cycles of events

The pattern of activities of the energy exchange has a cyclic character. The product exported into the environment furnishes the sources of energy for the repetition of the cycle of activities. The energy reinforcing the cycle of activities can derive from some exchange of the product in the external world or from the activity itself. In the former instance, the industrial concern utilizes raw materials and human labor to turn out a product which is marketed, and the monetary return is used to obtain more raw materials and labor to perpetuate the cycle of activities. In the latter instance, the voluntary organization can provide expressive satisfactions to its members so that the energy renewal comes directly from the organizational activity itself.

The problem of structure, or the relatedness of parts, can be observed directly in some physical arrangement of things where the larger unit is physically bounded and its subparts are also bounded within the larger structure. But how do we deal with social structures, where physical boundaries in this sense do not exist? It was the genius of F. H. Allport (1962) which contributed the answer, namely that the structure is to be found in an interrelated set of events which return upon themselves to complete and renew a cycle of activities. It is events rather than things which are structured, so that social structure is a dynamic rather than a static concept. Activities are structured so that they comprise a unity in their completion or closure. A simple linear stimulus–response exchange between two people would not constitute social structure. To create structure, the responses of A would have to elicit B's reactions in such a manner that the responses of the latter would stimulate A to further responses. Of course the chain of events may involve many people, but their behavior can be characterized as showing structure only when there is some closure to the chain by a return to its point of origin with the probability that the chain of events will then be repeated. The repetition of the cycle does not have to involve the same set of phenotypical happenings. It may expand to include more subevents of exactly the same kind or it may involve similar activities directed toward the same outcomes. In the individual organism the eye may move in such a way as to have the point of light fall upon the center of the retina. As the point of light moves, the movements of the eye may also change but to complete the same cycle of activity, i.e. to focus upon the point of light.

A single cycle of events of a self-closing character gives us a simple form of structure. But such single cycles can also combine to give a larger structure of events or an event system. An event system may consist of a circle of smaller cycles or hoops, each one of which makes contact with several others. Cycles may also be tangential to one another from other types of subsystems. The basic method for the identification of social structures is to follow the energic chain of events from the input of energy through its transformation to the point of closure of the cycle.

5. Negative entropy

To survive, open systems must move to arrest the entropic process; they must acquire negative entropy. The entropic process is a universal law of nature in which all forms of organization move toward disorganization or death. Complex physical systems move toward simple random distribution of their elements and biological organisms also run down and perish. The open system, however, by importing more energy from its environment than it expends, can store energy and can acquire negative entropy. There is then a general trend in an open system to maximize its ratio of imported to expended energy, to survive and even during periods of crisis to live on borrowed time. Prisoners in concentration camps on a starvation diet will carefully conserve any form of energy expenditure to make the limited food intake go as far as possible (Cohen, 1954). Social organizations will seek to improve their survival position and to acquire in their reserves a comfortable margin of operation.

The entropic process asserts itself in all biological systems as well as in closed physical systems. The energy replenishment of the biological organism is not of a qualitative character which can maintain indefinitely the complex organizational structure of living tissue. Social systems, however, are not anchored in the same physical constancies as biological organisms and so are capable of almost indefinite arresting of the entropic process. Nevertheless the number of organizations which go out of existence every year is large.

6. Information input, negative feedback, and the coding process

The inputs into living systems consist not only of energic materials which become transformed or altered in the work that gets done. Inputs are also informative in character and furnish signals to the structure about the environment and about its own functioning in relation to the environment. Just as we recognize the distinction between cues and drives in individual psychology, so must we take account of information and energic inputs for all living systems.

The simplest type of information input found in all systems is negative feedback. Information feedback of a negative kind enables the system to correct its deviations from course. The working parts of the machine feed back information about the effects of their operation to some central mechanism or subsystem which acts on such information to keep the system on target. The thermostat which controls the temperature of the room is a simple example of a regulatory device which operates on the basis of negative feedback. The automated power plant would furnish more complex examples. Miller (1955) emphasizes the critical nature of negative feedback in his proposition: '*When a system's negative feedback discontinues, its steady state vanishes, and at the same time its boundary disappears and the system terminates*' (p. 529). If there is no corrective device to get the system back on its course, it will expend too much energy or it will ingest too much energic input and no longer continue as a system.

The reception of inputs into a system is selective. Not all energic inputs are capable of being absorbed into every system. The digestive system of living creatures assimilates only those inputs to which it is adapted. Similarly, systems can react only to those information signals to which they are attuned. The general term for the selective mechanisms of a system by which incoming materials are rejected or accepted and translated for the structure is coding. Through the coding process the 'blooming, buzzing confusion' of the world is simplified into a few meaningful and simplified categories for a given system. The nature of the functions performed by the system determines its coding mechanisms, which in turn perpetuate this type of functioning.

7. The steady state and dynamic homeostasis

The importation of energy to arrest entropy operates to maintain some constancy in energy exchange, so that open systems which survive are characterized by a steady state. A steady state is not motionless or a true equilibrium. There is a continuous inflow of energy from the external environment and a continuous export of the products of the system, but the character of the system, the ratio of the energy exchanges and the relations between parts, remains the same. The catabolic and anabolic processes of tissue breakdown and restoration within the body preserve a steady state so that the organism from time to time is not the identical organism it was but a highly similar organism. The steady state is seen in clear form in the homeostatic processes for the regulation of body temperature; external conditions of humidity and temperature may vary, but the temperature of the body remains the same. The endocrine glands are a regulatory mechanism for preserving an evenness of physiological functioning. The general principle here is that of Le Chatelier (see Bradley and Calvin, 1956) who maintains that any internal or external factor making for disruption of the system is countered by forces which restore the system as closely as possible to its previous state. Krech and Crutchfield (1948) similarly hold, with respect to psychological organization, that cognitive structures will react to influences in such a way as to absorb them with minimal change to existing cognitive integration.

The homeostatic principle does not apply literally to the functioning of all complex living systems, in that in counteracting entropy they move toward growth and expansion. This apparent contradiction can be resolved, however, if we recognize the complexity of the subsystems and their interaction in anticipating changes necessary for the maintenance of an overall steady state. Stagner (1951) has pointed out that the initial disturbance of a given tissue constancy within the biological organism will result in mobilization of energy to restore the balance, but that recurrent upsets will lead to actions to anticipate the disturbance:

> We eat before we experience intense hunger pangs . . . energy mobilization for forestalling tactics must be explained in terms of a *cortical tension* which reflects the visceral-proprioceptic pattern of the original biological disequilibrium . . . *Dynamic homeostasis* involves the maintenance of tissue constancies by establishing a constant physical environment – by reducing the variability and disturbing effects of external stimulation. Thus the organism does not simply restore the prior equilibrium. A new, more complex and more comprehensive equilibrium is established (p. 5).

Though the tendency toward a steady state in its simplest form is homeostatic, as in the preservation of a constant body temperature, the basic principle is *the preservation of the character of the system*. The equilibrium which complex systems approach is often that of a quasi-stationary equilibrium, to use Lewin's concept (1947). An adjustment in one direction is countered by a movement in the opposite direction and both movements are approximate rather than precise in their compensatory nature. Thus a temporal chart of activity will show a series of ups and downs rather than a smooth curve.

In preserving the character of the system, moreover, the structure will tend to import more energy than is required for its output, as we have already noted in discussing negative entropy. To insure survival, systems will operate to acquire some margin of safety beyond the immediate level of existence. The body will store fat, the social organization will build up reserves, the society will increase its technological and cultural base. Miller (1955) has formulated the proposition that the rate of growth of a system – within certain ranges – is exponential if it exists in a medium which makes available unrestricted amounts of energy for input.

In adapting to their environment, systems will attempt to cope with external forces by ingesting them or acquiring control over them. The physical boundedness of the single organism means that such attempts at control over the environment affect the behavioral system rather than the biological system of the individual. Social systems will move, however, toward incorporating within their boundaries the external resources essential to survival. Again the result is an expansion of the original system.

Thus, the steady state which at the simple level is one of homeostasis over time, at more complex levels becomes one of preserving the character of the system through growth and expansion. The basic type of system does not change directly as a consequence of expansion. The most common type of growth is a multiplication of the same type of cycles or subsystems – a change in quantity rather than in quality. Animals and plant species grow by multiplication. A social system adds more units of the same essential type as it already has. Haire (1959) has studied the ratio between the sizes of different subsystems in growing business organizations. He found that though the number of people increased in both the production subsystem and the subsystem concerned with the external world, the ratio of the two groups remained constant. Qualitative change does occur, however, in two ways. In the first place, quantitative growth calls for supportive subsystems of a specialized character not necessary when the system was smaller. In the second place, there is a point where quantitative changes produce a qualitative difference in the functioning of a system. A small college which triples its size is no longer the same institution in terms of the relation between its administration and faculty, relations among the various academic departments, or the nature of its instruction.

In fine, living systems exhibit a growth or expansion dynamic in which they maximize their basic character. They react to change or they anticipate change through growth which assimilates the new energic inputs to the nature of their structure. In terms of Lewin's quasi-stationary equilibrium the ups and downs of the adjustive process do not always result in a return to the old level. Under certain circumstances a solidification or freezing occurs during one of the adjustive cycles. A new base line level is thus established and successive movements fluctuate around this plateau which may be either above or below the previous plateau of operation.

8. Differentiation

Open systems move in the direction of differentiation and elaboration. Diffuse global patterns are replaced by more specialized functions. The sense organs and the nervous system evolved as highly differentiated structures from the primitive nervous tissues. The growth of the personality proceeds from primitive, crude organizations of mental functions to hierarchically structured and well-differentiated systems of beliefs and feelings. Social organizations move toward the multiplication and elaboration of roles with greater specialization of function. In the United States today medical specialists now outnumber the general practitioners.

One type of differentiated growth in systems is what von Bertalanffy (1956) terms progressive mechanization. It finds expression in the way in which a system achieves a steady state. The early method is a process which involves an interaction of various dynamic forces, whereas the later development entails the use of a regulatory feedback mechanism. He writes:

It can be shown that the *primary* regulations in organic systems, that is, those which are most fundamental and primitive in embryonic development as well as in evolution, are of such nature of dynamic interaction . . . Superimposed are those regulations which we may call *secondary*, and which are controlled by fixed arrangements, especially of the feedback type. This state of affairs is a consequence of a general principle of organization which may be called progressive mechanization. At first, systems – biological, neurological, psychological or social – are governed by dynamic interaction of their components; later on, fixed arrangements and conditions of constraint are established which render the system and its parts more efficient, but also gradually diminish and eventually abolish its equipotentiality (p. 6).

9. Equifinality

Open systems are further characterized by the principle of equifinality, a principle suggested by von Bertalanffy in 1940. According to this principle, a system can reach the same final state from differing initial conditions and by a variety of paths. The well-known biological experiments on the sea urchin show that a normal creature of that species can develop from a complete ovum, from each half of a divided ovum, or from the fusion product of two whole ova. As open systems move toward regulatory mechanisms to control their operations, the amount of equifinality may be reduced.

Some Consequences of Viewing Organizations as Open Systems

In the following chapter we shall inquire into the specific implications of considering organizations as open systems and into the ways in which social organizations differ from other types of living systems. At this point, however, we should call attention to some of the misconceptions which arise both in theory and practice when social organizations are regarded as closed rather than open systems.

The major misconception is the failure to recognize fully that the organization is continually dependent upon inputs from the environment and that the inflow of materials and human energy is not a constant. The fact that organizations have built-in protective devices to maintain stability and that they are notoriously difficult to change in the direction of some reformer's desires should not obscure the realities of the dynamic interrelationships of any social structure with its social and natural environment. The very efforts of the organization to maintain a constant external environment produce changes in organizational structure. The reaction to changed inputs to mute their possible revolutionary implications also results in changes.

The typical models in organizational theorizing concentrate upon principles of internal functioning as if these problems were independent of changes in the environment and as if they did not affect the maintenance inputs of motivation and morale. Moves toward tighter integration and coordination are made to insure stability, when flexibility may be the more important requirement. Moreover, coordination and control become ends in themselves rather than means to an end. They are not seen in full perspective as adjusting the system to its environment but as desirable goals within a closed system. In fact, however, every attempt at coordination which is not functionally required may produce a host of new organizational problems.

One error which stems from this kind of misconception is the failure to recognize the equifinality of the open system, namely that there are more ways than one of producing a given outcome. In a closed physical system the same initial conditions must lead to the same final result. In open systems this is not true even at the biological level. It is much less true at the social level. Yet in practice we insist that there is one best way of assembling a gun for all recruits, one best way for the baseball player to hurl the ball in from the outfield, and that we standardize and teach these best methods. Now it is true under certain conditions that there is one best way, but these conditions must first be established. The general principle, which characterizes all open systems, is that there does not have to be a single method for achieving an objective.

A second error lies in the notion that irregularities in the functioning of a system due to environmental influences are error variances and should be treated accordingly. According to this conception, they should be controlled out of studies of organizations. From the organization's own operations they should be excluded as irrelevant and should be guarded against. The decisions of officers to omit a consideration of external factors or to guard against such influences in a defensive fashion, as if they would go away if ignored, is an instance of this type of thinking. So is the now outmoded 'public be damned' attitude of businessmen toward the clientele upon whose support they depend. Open system theory, on the other hand, would maintain that environmental influences are not sources of error variance but are integrally related to the functioning of a social system, and that we cannot understand a system without a constant study of the forces that impinge upon it.

Thinking of the organization as a closed system, moreover, results in a failure to develop the intelligence or feedback function of obtaining adequate information about the changes in environmental forces. It is remarkable how weak many industrial companies are in their market research departments when they are so dependent upon the market. The prediction can be hazarded that organizations in our society will increasingly move toward the improvement of the facilities for research in assessing environmental forces. The reason is that we are in the process of correcting our misconception of the organization as a closed system.

Emery and Trist (1960) have pointed out how current theorizing on organizations still reflects the older closed system conceptions. They write:

In the realm of social theory, however, there has been something of a tendency to continue thinking in terms of a 'closed' system, that is, to regard the enterprise as sufficiently independent to allow most of its problems to be analysed with reference to its internal structure and without reference to its external environment . . . In practice the system theorists in social science . . . did 'tend to focus on the statics of social structure and to neglect the study of structural change'. In an attempt to overcome this bias, Merton suggested that 'the concept of dysfunction, which implied the concept of strain, stress and tension on the structural level, provides an analytical approach to the study of dynamics and change'. This concept has been widely accepted by system theorists but while it draws attention to sources of imbalance within an organization it does not conceptually reflect the mutual permeation of an organization and its environment that is the cause of such imbalance. It still retains the limiting perspectives of 'closed system' theorizing. In the administrative field the same limitations may be seen in the otherwise invaluable contributions of Barnard and related writers (p. 84).

Summary

The open-system approach to organizations is contrasted with common-sense approaches, which tend to accept popular names and stereotypes as basic organizational properties and to identify the purpose of an organization in terms of the goals of its founders and leaders.

The open-system approach, on the other hand, begins by identifying and mapping the repeated cycles of input, transformation, output, and renewed input which comprise the organizational pattern. This approach to organizations represents the adaptation of work in biology and in the physical sciences by von Bertalanffy and others.

Organizations as a special class of open systems have properties of their own, but they share other properties in common with all open systems. These include the importation of energy from the environment, the through-put or transformation of the imported energy into some product form which is characteristic of the system, the exporting of that product into the environment, and the re-energizing of the system from sources in the environment.

Open systems also share the characteristics of negative entropy, feedback, homeostasis, differentiation, and equifinality. The law of negative entropy states that systems survive and maintain their characteristic internal order only so long as they import from the environment more energy than they expend in the process of transformation and exportation. The feedback principle has to do with information input, which is a special kind of energic importation, a kind of signal to the system about environmental conditions and about the functioning of the system in relation to

its environment. The feedback of such information enables the system to correct for its own malfunctioning or for changes in the environment, and thus to maintain a steady state or homeostasis. This is a dynamic rather than a static balance, however. Open systems are not at rest but tend toward differentiation and elaboration, both because of subsystem dynamics and because of the relationship between growth and survival. Finally, open systems are characterized by the principle of equifinality, which asserts that systems can reach the same final state from different initial conditions and by different paths of development.

Traditional organizational theories have tended to view the human organization as a closed system. This tendency has led to a disregard of differing organizational environments and the nature of organizational dependency on environment. It has led also to an overconcentration on principles of internal organizational functioning, with consequent failure to develop and understand the processes of feedback which are essential to survival.

References

ALLPORT, F. H. (1962), 'A structuronomic conception of behavior: individual and collective. I. Structural theory and the master problem of social psychology', *Journal of Abnormal and Social Psychology*, vol. 64, pp. 3–30.

BRADLEY, D. F., and CALVIN, M. (1956), 'Behavior: imbalance in a network of chemical transformations', *General Systems*, Yearbook of the Society for the Advancement of General System Theory, vol. 1, pp. 56–65.

COHEN, E. (1954), *Human Behavior in the Concentration Camp*, Jonathan Cape.

EMERY, F. E., and TRIST, E. L. (1960), 'Socio-technical systems', in *Management Sciences Models and Techniques*, vol. 2, Pergamon Press.

HAIRE, M. (1959), 'Biological models and empirical histories of the growth of organizations', in M. Haire (ed.), *Modern Organization Theory*, Wiley, pp. 272–306.

KOEHLER, W., and EMERY, D. (1947), 'Figural after-effects in the third dimension of visual space', *American Journal of Psychology*, vol. 60, pp. 159–201.

KOEHLER, W., and WALLACH, H. (1944), 'Figural after-effects: an investigation of visual processes', *Proceedings of the American Philosophical Society*, vol. 88, pp. 269–357.

KRECH, D., and CRUTCHFIELD, R. (1948), *Theory and Problems of Social Psychology*, McGraw-Hill.

LEWIN, K. (1947), 'Frontiers in group dynamics', *Human Relations*, vol. 1, pp. 5–41.

MELZACK, R., and THOMPSON, W. (1956), 'Effects of early experience on social behaviour', *Canadian Journal of Psychology*, vol. 10. pp. 82–90.

MERTON, R. K. (1957), *Social Theory and Social Structure*, Free Press, rev. edn.

MILLER, J. G. (1955), 'Toward a general theory for the behavioral sciences', *American Psychologist*, vol. 10. pp. 513–31.

SOLOMON, P. *et al.* (1961), *Sensory Deprivation*, Harvard University Press.

SPITZ, R. A. (1945), 'Hospitalism: an inquiry into the genesis of psychiatric conditions in early childhood', *Psychoanalytic Study of the Child*, vol. 1. pp. 53–74.

STAGNER, R. (1951), 'Homeostasis as a unifying concept in personality theory', *Psychological Review*, vol. 58. pp. 5–17.

VON BERTALANFFY, L. (1940), 'Der organismus als physikalisches system betrachtet', *Naturwissenschaften*, vol. 28. pp. 521ff.

VON BERTALANFFY, L. (1956), 'General system theory', *General Systems*, Yearbook of the Society for the Advancement of General System Theory, vol. 1. pp. 1–10.

Charles Perrow   Davis Chapter 5

"THE SHORT AND GLORIOUS HISTORY OF ORGANIZATIONAL THEORY"

Organizational Dynamics (2:1), 1973 Summer, pages 2-15.

An understanding of organizational theory is important
in designing organizational information systems. Yet, the
theory has been evolving so rapidly that it is easy to become confused. This article does an excellent job of sur-
veying the different streams of organizational theory.

The history covers the major schools of thought in organization theory:
    Scientific management
    The human relations school
    Bureaucracy
    Institutional school
    Contingency view (based on technology)
    Integrative mechanisms
    Systems view
The conclusions at the end of the article summarize present
thought. Note the statement (in the next to last paragraph)
that controls on information received is one of the methods
for changing organizational behavior.

READING SUGGESTIONS

Perrow's analogy of the forces of light and darkness
is irrelevant, but adds a light touch some may appreciate.
In reading the article, there are two main points: 1) the
flow of ideas and argument from the early part of this century until now, and 2) the ideas advocated by each of the
major schools or major researchers in organizational theory.
Note the trend to a recognition that organizations vary considerably in goals, technology, internal power groups, etc.
and that these factors affect the kind of organization that
appears to work best.

QUESTIONS

1. What are the major tenents regarding organizational
    theory of:
    a. The scientific management school
    b. The human relations school
    c. The bureaucratic school
    d. The systems view
    e. The neo-Weberian bureaucratic model
2. How does level of technology affect organizational
    design?
3. What is the role of integrating mechanisms?

4. What has research discovered about the value of human
    relations mechanisms for promoting efficiency?
5. What has research discovered about the best leader?

The Short and Glorious History of Organizational Theory

Charles Perrow

From the beginning, the forces of light and the forces of darkness have polarized the field of organizational analysis, and the struggle has been protracted and inconclusive. The forces of darkness have been represented by the mechanical school of organizational theory—those who treat the organization as a machine. This school characterizes organizations in terms of such things as:

- centralized authority
- clear lines of authority
- specialization and expertise
- marked division of labor
- rules and regulations
- clear separation of staff and line

The forces of light, which by mid-twentieth century came to be characterized as the human relations school, emphasizes people rather than machines, accommodations rather than machine-like precision, and draws its inspiration from biological systems rather than engineering systems. It has emphasized such things as:

- delegation of authority
- employee autonomy
- trust and openness
- concerns with the "whole person"
- interpersonal dynamics

THE RISE AND FALL OF SCIENTIFIC MANAGEMENT

The forces of darkness formulated their position first, starting in the early part of this century. They have been characterized as the scientific management or classical management school. This school started by parading simple-minded injunctions to plan ahead, keep records, write down policies, specialize, be decisive, and keep your span of control to about six people. These injunctions were needed as firms grew in size and complexity, since there were few models around beyond the railroads, the military, and the Catholic Church to guide organizations. And their injunctions worked. Executives began to delegate, reduce their span of control, keep records, and specialize. Planning ahead still is difficult, it seems, and the modern equivalent is Management by Objectives.

But many things intruded to make these simple-minded injunctions less relevant:

1. Labor became a more critical factor in the firm. As the technology increased in sophistication it took longer to train people, and more varied and specialized skills were needed. Thus, labor turnover cost more and recruitment became more selective. As a consequence, labor's power increased. Unions and strikes appeared. Management adjusted by beginning to speak of a cooperative system of capital, management, and labor. The machine model began to lose its relevancy.

2. The increasing complexity of markets, variability of products, increasing number of branch plants, and changes in technology all required more adaptive organization.

The scientific management school was ill-equipped to deal with rapid change. It had presumed that once the proper structure was achieved the firm could run forever without much tampering. By the late 1930s, people began writing about adaptation and change in industry from an organizational point of view and had to abandon some of the principles of scientific management.

3. Political, social, and cultural changes meant new expectations regarding the proper way to treat people. The dark, satanic mills needed at the least a white-washing. Child labor and the brutality of supervision in many enterprises became no longer permissible. Even managers could not be expected to accept the authoritarian patterns of leadership that prevailed in the small firm run by the founding father.

4. As mergers and growth proceeded apace and the firm could no longer be viewed as the shadow of one man (the founding entrepreneur), a search for methods of selecting good leadership became a preoccupation. A good, clear, mechanical structure would no longer suffice. Instead, firms had to search for the qualities of leadership that could fill the large footsteps of the entrepreneur. They tacitly had to admit that something other than either "sound principles" or "dynamic leadership" was needed. The search for leadership traits implied that leaders were made, not just born, that the matter was complex, and that several skills were involved.

ENTER HUMAN RELATIONS

From the beginning, individual voices were raised against the implications of the scientific management school. "Bureaucracy" had always been a dirty word, and the job design efforts of Frederick Taylor were even the subject of a congressional investigation. But no effective counterforce developed until 1938, when a business executive with academic talents named Chester Barnard proposed the first new theory of organizations: Organizations are cooperative systems, not the products of mechanical engineering. He stressed natural groups within the organization, upward communication, authority from below rather than from above, and leaders who functioned as a cohesive force. With the spectre of labor unrest and the Great Depression upon him, Barnard's emphasis on the cooperative nature of organizations was well-timed. The year following the publication of his *Functions of the Executive* (1938) saw the publication of F. J. Roethlisberger and William Dickson's *Management and the Worker*, reporting on the first large-scale empirical investigation of productivity and social relations. The research, most of it conducted in the Hawthorne plant of the Western Electric Company during a period in which the workforce was reduced, highlighted the role of informal groups, work restriction norms, the value of decent, humane leadership, and the role of psychological manipulation of employees through the counseling system. World War II intervened, but after the war the human relations movement, building on the insights of Barnard and the Hawthorne studies, came into its own.

The first step was a search for the traits of good leadership. It went on furiously at university centers but at first failed to produce more than a list of Boy Scout maxims: A good leader was kind, courteous, loyal, courageous, etc. We suspected as much. However, the studies did turn up a distinction between "consideration," or employee-centered aspects of leadership, and job-centered, technical aspects labeled "initiating structure." Both were important, but the former received most of the attention and the latter went undeveloped. The former led directly to an examination of group processes, an investigation that has culminated in T-group programs and is moving forward still with encounter groups. Meanwhile, in England, the Tavistock Institute sensed the importance of the influence of the kind of task a group had to perform on the social relations within the group. The first important study, conducted among coal miners, showed that job simplification and specialization did not work under conditions of uncertainty and nonroutine tasks.

As this work flourished and spread, more adventurous theorists began to extend it beyond work groups to organizations as a whole. We now knew that there were a number of things that were bad for the morale and loyalty of groups—routine tasks, submission to authority, specialization of task, segregation of task sequence, ignorance of the goals of the firm, centralized decision making, and so on. If these were bad for groups, they were likely to be bad for groups of groups—i.e., for organizations. So people like Warren Bennis began talking about innovative, rapidly changing organizations that were made up of temporary groups, temporary authority systems, temporary leadership and role assignments, and democratic access to the goals of the firm. If rapidly changing technologies and unstable, turbulent environments were to characterize industry, then the structure of firms should be temporary and decentralized. The forces of light, of freedom, autonomy, change, humanity, creativity, and democracy were winning. Scientific management survived only in outdated text books. If the evangelizing of some of the human relations school theorists was excessive, and if Likert's System 4 or MacGregor's Theory Y or Blake's 9 x 9 evaded us, at least there was a rationale for confusion, disorganization, scrambling, and stress: Systems should be temporary.

BUREAUCRACY'S COMEBACK

Meanwhile, in another part of the management forest, the mechanistic school was gathering its forces and preparing to outflank the forces of light. First came the numbers men—the linear programmers, the budget experts, and the financial analysts—with their PERT systems and cost-benefit analyses. From another world, unburdened by most of the scientific management ideology and untouched by the human relations school, they began to parcel things out and give some meaning to those truisms, "plan ahead" and "keep records." Armed with emerging systems concepts, they carried the "mechanistic" analogy to its fullest—and it was very productive. Their work still goes on, largely untroubled by organizational theory; the theory, it seems clear, will have to adjust to them, rather than the other way around.

Then the works of Max Weber, first translated from the German in the 1940s—he wrote around 1910, incredibly—began to find their way into social science thought. At first, with his celebration of the efficiency of bureaucracy, he was received with only reluctant respect, and even with hostility. All writers were against bureaucracy. But it turned out, surprisingly, that managers were not. When asked, they acknowledged that they preferred clear lines of communication, clear specifications of authority and responsibility, and clear knowledge of whom they were responsible to. They were as wont to say "there ought to be a rule about this," as to say "there are too many rules around here," as wont to say "next week we've got to get organized," as to say "there is too much red tape." Gradually, studies began to show that bureaucratic organizations could change faster than nonbureaucratic ones, and that morale could be higher where there was clear evidence of bureaucracy.

What was this thing, then? Weber had showed us, for example, that bureaucracy was the most effective way of ridding organizations of favoritism, arbitrary authority, discrimination, payola and kick-backs, and yes, even incompetence. His model stressed expertise, and the favorite or the boss' nephew or the guy who burned up resources to make his performance look good was *not* the one with expertise. Rules could be changed; they could be dropped in exceptional circumstances; job security promoted more innovation. The sins of bureaucracy began to look like the sins of failing to follow its principles.

ENTER POWER, CONFLICT, AND DECISIONS

But another discipline began to intrude upon the confident work and increasingly elaborate models of the human relations theorists (largely social psychologists) and the uneasy toying with bureaucracy of the "structionalists" (largely sociologists). Both tended to study economic organizations. A few, like Philip Selznick, were noting conflict and differences in goals (perhaps because he was studying a public agency, the Tennessee Valley Authority), but most ignored conflict or treated it as a pathological manifestation of breakdowns in communication or the ego trips of unreconstructed managers.

But in the world of political parties, pressure groups, and legislative bodies, conflict was not only rampant, but to be expected —it was even functional. This was the domain of the political scientists. They kept talking about power, making it a legitimate concern for analysis. There was an open acknowledgement of "manipulation." These were political scientists who were "behaviorally" inclined—studying and recording behavior rather than constitutions and formal systems of government—and they came to a much more complex view of organized activity. It spilled over into the area of economic organizations, with the help of some economists like R. A. Gordon and some sociologists who were studying conflicting goals of treatment and custody in prisons and mental hospitals.

The presence of legitimately conflicting goals and techniques of preserving and using power did not, of course, sit well with a cooperative systems view of organizations. But it also puzzled the bureaucratic school (and what was left of the old scientific management school), for the impressive Weberian principles were designed to settle questions of power through organizational design and to keep conflict out through reliance on rational-legal authority and systems of careers, expertise, and hierarchy. But power was being overtly contested and exercised in covert ways, and conflict was bursting out all over, and even being creative.

Gradually, in the second half of the 1950s and in the next decade, the political science view infiltrated both schools. Conflict could be healthy, even in a cooperative sys-

tem, said the human relationists; it was the mode of resolution that counted, rather than prevention. Power became reconceptualized as "influence," and the distribution was less important, said Arnold Tannenbaum, than the total amount. For the bureaucratic school —never a clearly defined group of people, and largely without any clear ideology—it was easier to just absorb the new data and theories as something else to be thrown into the pot. That is to say, they floundered, writing books that went from topic to topic, without a clear view of organizations, or better yet, producing "readers" and leaving students to sort it all out.

Buried in the political science viewpoint was a sleeper that only gradually began to undermine the dominant views. This was the idea, largely found in the work of Herbert Simon and James March, that because man was so limited—in intelligence, reasoning powers, information at his disposal, time available, and means of ordering his preferences clearly—he generally seized on the first acceptable alternative when deciding, rather than looking for the best; that he rarely changed things unless they really got bad, and even then he continued to try what had worked before; that he limited his search for solutions to well-worn paths and traditional sources of information and established ideas; that he was wont to remain preoccupied with routine, thus preventing innovation. They called these characteristics "cognitive limits on rationality" and spoke of "satisficing" rather than maximizing or optimizing. It is now called the "decision making" school, and is concerned with the basic question of how people make decisions.

This view had some rather unusual implications. It suggested that if managers were so limited, then they could be easily controlled. What was necessary was not to give direct orders (on the assumption that subordinates were idiots without expertise) or to leave them to their own devices (on the assumption that they were supermen who would somehow know what was best for the organization, how to coordinate with all the other supermen, how to anticipate market changes, etc.). It was necessary to control only the *premises* of their decisions. Left to themselves, with those premises set, they could be predicted to rely on precedent, keep things stable and smooth, and respond to signals that reinforce the behavior desired of them.

To control the premises of decision making, March and Simon outline a variety of devices, all of which are familiar to you, but some of which you may not have seen before in quite this light. For example, organ-

izations develop vocabularies, and this means that certain kinds of information are highlighted, and others are screened out—just as Eskimos (and skiers) distinguish many varieties of snow, while Londoners see only one. This is a form of attention directing. Another is the reward system. Change the bonus for salesmen and you can shift them from volume selling to steady-account selling, or to selling quality products or new products. If you want to channel good people into a different function (because, for example, sales should no longer be the critical function as the market changes, but engineering applications should), you may have to promote mediocre people in the unrewarded function in order to signal to the good people in the rewarded one that the game has changed. You cannot expect most people to make such decision on their own because of the cognitive limits on their rationality, nor will you succeed by giving direct orders, because you yourself probably do not know whom to order where. You presume that once the signals are clear and the new sets of alternatives are manifest, they have enough ability to make the decision but you have had to change the premises for their decisions about their career lines.

It would take too long to go through the dozen or so devices, covering a range of decision areas (March and Simon are not that clear or systematic about them, themselves, so I have summarized them in my own book), but I think the message is clear.

It was becoming clear to the human relations school, and to the bureaucratic school. The human relationists had begun to speak of changing stimuli rather than changing personality. They had begun to see that the rewards that can change behavior can well be prestige, money, comfort, etc., rather than trust, openness, self-insight, and so on. The alternative to supportive relations need not be punishment, since behavior can best be changed by rewarding approved behavior rather than by punishing disapproved behavior. They were finding that although leadership may be centralized, it can function best through indirect and unobtrusive means such as changing the premises on which decisions are made, thus giving the impression that the subordinate is actually making a decision when he has only been switched to a different set of alternatives. The implications of this work were also beginning to filter into the human relations school through an emphasis on behavioral psychology (the modern version of the much maligned stimulus-response school) that was supplanting personality theory (Freudian in its roots, and drawing heavily, in the human relations school, on Maslow).

For the bureaucratic school, this new line of thought reduced the heavy weight placed upon the bony structure of bureaucracy by highlighting the muscle and flesh that make these bones move. A single chain of command, precise division of labor, and clear lines of communication are simply not enough in themselves. Control can be achieved by using alternative communication channels, depending on the situation; by increasing or decreasing the static or "noise" in the system; by creating organizational myths and organizational vocabularies that allow only selective bits of information to enter the system; and through monitoring performance through indirect means rather than direct surveillance. Weber was all right for a starter, but organizations had changed vastly, and the leaders needed many more means of control and more subtle means of manipulation than they did at the turn of the century.

THE TECHNOLOGICAL QUALIFICATION

By now the forces of darkness and forces of light had moved respectively from midnight and noon to about 4 A.M. and 8 A.M. But any convergence or resolution would have to be on yet new terms, for soon after the political science tradition had begun to infiltrate the established schools, another blow struck both of the major positions. Working quite independently of the Tavistock Group, with its emphasis on sociotechnical systems, and before the work of Burns and Stalker on mechanistic and organic firms, Joan Woodward was trying to see whether the classical scientific principles of organization made any sense in her survey of 100 firms in South Essex. She tripped and stumbled over a piece of gold in the process. She picked up the gold, labeled it "technology," and made sense out of her otherwise hopeless data. Job-shop firms, mass-production firms, and continuous-process firms all had quite different structures because the type of tasks, or the "technology," was different. Somewhat later, researchers in America were coming to very similar conclusions based on studies of hospitals, juvenile correctional institutions, and industrial firms. Bureaucracy appeared to be the best form of organization for routine operations; temporary work groups, decentralization, and emphasis on interpersonal processes appeared to work best for nonroutine operations. A raft of studies appeared and are still appearing, all trying to show how the nature of the task affects the structure of the organization.

This severely complicated things for the human relations school, since it suggested that openness and trust, while good things in themselves, did not have much impact, or perhaps were not even possible in some kinds of work situations. The prescriptions that were being handed out would have to be drastically qualified. What might work for nonroutine, high-status, interesting, and challenging jobs performed by highly educated people might not be relevant or even beneficial for the vast majority of jobs and people.

It also forced the upholders of the revised bureaucratic theory to qualify their recommendations, since research and development units should obviously be run differently from mass-production units, and the difference between both of these and highly programmed and highly sophisticated continuous-process firms was obscure in terms of bureaucratic theory. But the bureaucratic school perhaps came out on top, because the forces of evil—authority, structure, division of labor, etc.—no longer looked evil, even if they were not applicable to a minority of industrial units.

The emphasis on technology raised other questions, however. A can company might be quite routine, and a plastics division nonroutine, but there were both routine and nonroutine units within each. How should they be integrated if the prescription were followed that, say, production should be bureaucratized and R&D not? James Thompson began spelling out different forms of interdependence among units in organizations, and Paul Lawrence and Jay Lorsch looked closely at the nature of integrating mechanisms. Lawrence and Lorsch found that firms performed best when the differences between units were *maximized* (in contrast to both the human relations and the bureaucratic school), as long as the integrating mechanisms stood half-way between the two—being neither strongly bureaucratic nor nonroutine. They also noted that attempts at participative management in routine situations were counterproductive, that the environments of some kinds of organizations were far from turbulent and customers did not want innovations and changes, that cost reduction, price, and efficiency were trivial considerations in some firms, and so on. The technological insight was demolishing our comfortable truths right and left. They were also being questioned from another quarter.

ENTER GOALS, ENVIRONMENTS, AND SYSTEMS

The final seam was being mined by the sociologists while all this went on. This was the concern with organizational goals and the environment. Borrowing from the political scientists to some extent, but pushing ahead on their own, this "institutional school" came to see that goals were not fixed; conflicting goals could be pursued simultaneously, if there were enough slack resources, or sequentially (growth for the next four years, then cost-cutting and profit-taking for the next four); that goals were up for grabs in organizations, and units fought over them. Goals were, of course, not what they seemed to be, the important ones were quite unofficial; history played a big role; and assuming profit as the pre-eminent goal explained almost nothing about a firm's behavior.

They also did case studies that linked the organization to the web of influence of the environment; that showed how unique organizations were in many respects (so that, once again, there was no one best way to do things for all organizations); how organizations were embedded in their own history, making change difficult. Most striking of all, perhaps, the case studies revealed that the stated goals usually were not the real ones; the official leaders usually were not the powerful ones; claims of effectiveness and efficiency were deceptive or even untrue; the public interest was not being served; political influences were pervasive; favoritism, discrimination, and sheer corruption were commonplace. The accumulation of these studies presented quite a pill for either the forces of light or darkness to swallow, since it was hard to see how training sessions or interpersonal skills were relevant to these problems, and it was also clear that the vaunted efficiency of bureaucracy was hardly in evidence. What could they make of this wad of case studies?

We are still sorting it out. In one sense, the Weberian model is upheld because organizations are not, *by nature,* cooperative systems; top managers must exercise a great deal of effort to control them. But if organizations are tools in the hands of leaders, they may be very recalcitrant ones. Like the broom in the story of the sorcerer's apprentice, they occasionally get out of hand. If conflicting goals, bargaining, and unofficial leadership exists, where is the structure of Weberian bones and Simonian muscle? To what extent are organizations tools, and to what extent are they products of the varied interests and group strivings of their members? Does it vary by organization, in terms of some typological alchemy we have not discovered? We don't know. But at any rate, the bureaucratic model suffers again; it simply has not reckoned on the role of the environment. There are enormous sources of variations that the neat, though by now quite complex, neo-Weberian model could not account for.

The human relations model has also been badly shaken by the findings of the institutional school, for it was wont to assume that goals were given and unproblematical, and that anything that promoted harmony and efficiency for an organization also was good for society. Human relationists assumed that the problems created by organizations were largely limited to the psychological consequences of poor interpersonal relations within them, rather than their impact on the environment. Could the organization really promote the psychological health of its members when by necessity it had to define psychological health in terms of the goals of the organization itself? The neo-Weberian model at least called manipulation "manipulation" and was skeptical of claims about autonomy and self-realization.

But on one thing all the varied schools of organizational analysis now seemed to be agreed: organizations are systems—indeed, they are open systems. As the growth of the field has forced ever more variables into our consciousness, flat claims of predictive power are beginning to decrease and research has become bewilderingly complex. Even consulting groups need more than one or two tools in their kit-bag as the software multiplies.

The systems view is intuitively simple. Everything is related to everything else, though in uneven degrees of tension and reciprocity. Every unit, organization, department, or work group takes in resources, transforms them, and sends them out, and thus interacts with the larger system. The psychological, sociological, and cultural aspects of units interact. The systems view was explicit in the institutional work, since they tried to study whole organizations; it became explicit in the human relations school, because they were so concerned with the interactions of people. The political science and technology viewpoints also had to come to this realization, since they dealt with parts affecting each other (sales affecting production; technology affecting structure).

But as intuitively simple as it is, the systems view has been difficult to put into practical use. We still find ourselves ignoring the tenets of the open systems view, possibly because of the cognitive limits on our rationality. General systems theory itself has not lived up to its heady predictions; it remains rather nebulous. But at least there is a model for calling us to account and for stretching our minds, our research tools, and our troubled nostrums.

Some Conclusions

Where does all this leave us? We might summarize the prescriptions and proscriptions for management very roughly as follows:

1. A great deal of the "variance" in a firm's behavior depends on the environment. We have become more realistic about the limited range of change that can be induced through internal efforts. The goals of organizations, including those of profit and efficiency, vary greatly among industries and vary systematically by industries. This suggests that the impact of better management by itself will be limited, since so much will depend on market forces, competition, legislation, nature of the work force, available technologies and innovations, and so on. Another source of variation is, obviously, the history of the firm and its industry and its traditions.

2. A fair amount of variation in both firms and industries is due to the type of work done in the organization—the technology. We are now fairly confident in recommending that if work is predictable and routine, the necessary arrangement for getting the work done can be highly structured, and one can use a good deal of bureaucratic theory in accomplishing this. If it is not predictable, if it is nonroutine and there is a good deal of uncertainty as to how to do a job, then one had better utilize the theories that emphasize autonomy, temporary groups, multiple lines of authority and communications, and so on. We also know that this distinction is important when organizing different parts of an organization.

We are also getting a grasp on the question of what is the most critical function in different types of organizations. For some organizations it is production; for others, marketing; for still others, development. Furthermore, firms go through phases whereby the initial development of a market or a product or manufacturing process or accounting scheme may require a non-bureaucratic structure, but once it comes on stream, the structure should change to reflect the changed character of the work.

3. In keeping with this, management should be advised that the attempt to produce change in an organization through managerial grids, sensitivity training, and even job enrichment and job enlargement is likely to be fairly ineffective for all but a few organizations. The critical reviews of research in all these fields show that there is no scientific evidence to support the claims of the proponents of these various methods; that research has told us a great deal about social psychol-ogy, but little about how to apply the highly complex findings to actual situations. The key word is *selectivity*: We have no broad-spectrum antibiotics for interpersonal relations. Of course, managers should be sensitive, decent, kind, courteous, and courageous, but we have known that for some time now, and beyond a minimal threshold level, the payoff is hard to measure. The various attempts to make work and interpersonal relations more humane and stimulating should be applauded, but we should not confuse this with solving problems of structure, or as the equivalent of decentralization or participatory democracy.

4. The burning cry in all organizations is for "good leadership," but we have learned that beyond a threshold level of adequacy it is extremely difficult to know what good leadership is. The hundreds of scientific studies of this phenomenon come to one general conclusion: Leadership is highly variable or "contingent" upon a large variety of important variables such as nature of task, size of the group, length of time the group has existed, type of personnel within the group and their relationships with each other, and amount of pressure the group is under. It does not seem likely that we'll be able to devise a way to select the best leader for a particular situation. Even if we could, that situation would probably change in a short time and thus would require a somewhat different type of leader.

Furthermore, we are beginning to realize that leadership involves more than smoothing the paths of human interaction. What has rarely been studied in this area is the wisdom or even the technical adequacy of a leader's decision. A leader does more than lead people; he also makes decisions about the allocation of resources, type of technology to be used, the nature of the market, and so on. This aspect of leadership remains very obscure, but it is obviously crucial.

5. If we cannot solve our problems through good human relations or through good leadership, what are we then left with? The literature suggests that changing the structures of organizations might be the most effective and certainly the quickest and cheapest method. However, we are now sophisticated enough to know that changing the formal structure by itself is not likely to produce the desired changes. In addition, one must be aware of a large range of subtle, unobtrusive, and even covert processes and change devices that exist. If inspection procedures are not working, we are now unlikely to rush in with sensitivity training, nor would we send down authoritative communications telling people to do a better job. We are more likely

to find out where the authority really lies, whether the degree of specialization is adequate, what the rules and regulations are, and so on, but even this very likely will not be enough.

According to the neo-Weberian bureaucratic model, as it has been influenced by work on decision making and behavioral psychology, we should find out how to manipulate the reward structure, change the premises of the decision-makers through finer controls on the information received and the expectations generated, search for interdepartmental conflicts that prevent better inspection procedures from being followed, and after manipulating these variables, sit back and wait for two or three months for them to take hold. This is complicated and hardly as dramatic as many of the solutions currently being peddled, but I think the weight of organizational theory is in its favor.

We have probably learned more, over several decades of research and theory, about the things that do *not* work (even though some of them obviously *should* have worked), than we have about things that do work. On balance, this is an important gain and should not discourage us. As you know, organizations are extremely complicated. To have as much knowledge as we do have in a fledgling discipline that has had to borrow from the diverse tools and concepts of psychology, sociology, economics, engineering, biology, history, and even anthropology is not really so bad.

SELECTED BIBLIOGRAPHY

This paper is an adaptation of the discussion to be found in Charles Perrow, *Complex Organizations: A Critical Essay*, Scott, Foresman & Co., Glenville, Illinois, 1972. All the points made in this paper are discussed thoroughly in that volume.

The best overview and discussion of classical management theory, and its changes over time is by Joseph Massie—"Management Theory" in the *Handbook of Organizations* edited by James March, Rand McNally & Co., Chicago, 1965, pp. 387–422.

The best discussion of the changing justifications for managerial rule and worker obedience as they are related to changes in technology, etc., can be found in Reinhard Bendix's *Work and Authority in Industry*, John Wiley & Sons, Inc., New York, 1956. See especially the chapter on the American experience.

Some of the leading lights of the classical view—F. W. Taylor, Col. Urwick, and Henry Fayol—are briefly discussed in *Writers on Organizations* by D. S. Pugh, D. J. Hickson and C. R. Hinings, Penguin, 1971. This brief, readable,

and useful book also contains selections from many other schools that I discuss, including Weber, Woodward, Cyert and March, Simon, the Hawthorne Investigations, and the Human Relations Movement as represented by Argyris, Herzberg, Likert, McGregor, and Blake and Mouton.

As good a place as any to start examining the human relations tradition is Rensis Likert, *The Human Organization*, McGraw-Hill, New York, 1967. See also his *New Patterns of Management*, McGraw-Hill Book Company, New York, 1961.

The Buck Rogers school of organizational theory is best represented by Warren Bennis. See his *Changing Organizations*, McGraw-Hill Book Company, New York, 1966, and his book with Philip Slater, *The Temporary Society*, Harper & Row, Inc., New York, 1968. Much of this work is linked into more general studies, e.g., Alvin Toffler's very popular paperback *Future Shock*, Random House, 1970, and Bantam Paperbacks, or Zibigniew Brzezinsky's *Between Two Ages: America's Role in the Technitronic Era*, the Viking Press, New York, 1970. One of the first intimations of the new type of environment and firm and still perhaps the most perceptive is to be found in the volume by Tom Burns and G. Stalker, *The Management of Innovation*, Tavistock, London, 1961, where they distinguished between "organic" and "mechanistic" systems. The introduction, which is not very long, is an excellent and very tight summary of the book.

The political science tradition came in through three important works. First, Herbert Simon's *Administrative Behavior*, The MacMillan Co., New York, 1948, followed by the second half of James March and Herbert Simon's *Organizations*, John Wiley & Sons, Inc., New York, 1958, then Richard M. Cyert and James March's *A Behavioral Theory of the Firm*, Prentice-Hall, Inc. Englewood Cliffs, N.J., 1963. All three of these books are fairly rough going, though chapters 1, 2, 3, and 6 of the last volume are fairly short and accessible. A quite interesting book in this tradition, though somewhat heavygoing, is Michael Crozier's *The Bureaucratic Phenomenon*, University of Chicago, and Tavistock Publications, 1964. This is a striking description of power in organizations, though there is a somewhat dubious attempt to link organization processes in France to the cultural traits of the French people.

The book by Joan Woodward *Industrial Organisation: Theory and Practice*, Oxford University Press, London, 1965, is still very much worth reading. A fairly popular attempt to discuss the implications for this for management can be found in my own book, *Organizational Analysis: A Sociological View*, Tavistock, 1970, Chapters 2 and 3. The impact of technology on structure is still fairly controversial. A number of technical studies have found both support and nonsupport, largely because the concept is defined so differently, but there is general agree-

ment that different structures and leadership techniques are needed for different situations. For studies that support and document this viewpoint see James Thompson, *Organizations in Action*, McGraw-Hill Book Company, New York, 1967, and Paul Lawrence and Jay Lorsch, *Organizations and Environment*, Harvard University Press, Cambridge, Mass., 1967.

The best single work on the relation between the organization and the environment and one of the most readable books in the field is Philip Selznick's short volume *Leadership in Administration*, Row, Peterson, Evanston, Illinois, 1957. But the large number of these studies are scattered about. I have summarized several in my *Complex Organizations: A Critical Essay*.

Lastly, the most elaborate and persuasive argument for a systems view of organizations is found in the first 100 pages of the book by Daniel Katz and Robert Kahn, *The Social Psychology of Organizations*, John Wiley and Co., 1966. It is not easy reading, however.

While Charles Perrow's *primary affiliation has been with sociology departments in a variety of universities (Michigan, Pittsburgh, Wisconsin, and now, the State University of New York at Stony Brook), he has tempered his theorizing by also teaching in professional schools at these universities. "Business students want to know what difference theory makes, and it is a salutory discipline for the sociologists," he notes. This resulted in a book for business managers,* Organizational Analysis: A Sociological View, *in 1970. He has published three other books dealing with organizations, as well as more than 20 scholarly articles. The present article has grown out of his recent volume,* Complex Organizations: A Critical Essay *(1972).*

He has consulted with business, government and voluntary agencies (but very modestly), spent a year at the Industrial Relations Institute in Berkeley and the Business School there, in the year of the People's Park and the Cleaver demonstrations. Currently he is spending this year at the London Business School and is running two-day training sessions on the structural analysis of organizations for managers. He is also working with some groups on the social responsibilities of business. Professor Perrow is on the editorial board of Administrative Science Quarterly *and the* American Sociological Review. *His other books are* The Radical Attack on Business, *1972, and* Organization for Treatment, *1966, with D. Street and R. Vinter.*

Jay R. Galbraith   Davis Chapter 5

"ORGANIZATION DESIGN: AN INFORMATION PROCESSING VIEW"

TIMS Interfaces (4:3), 1974 May, pages 28-36.

With the emergence of information systems technology
and the increasingly vital role information plays in complex organizations, it is useful to view an organization
in terms of the flow and processing of information. Galbraith is one of the major proponents of the information
processing view of organizations. His ideas are even more
important because they lead to a consideration of alternative strategies for designing organizations.

The cognitive limits on human information processing
are a basic limiting factor in determining organizational
structures. More uncertainty in organizational tasks requires more information for decision making and more exchange of information among decision makers during task
execution to achieve a given level of performance. Inability to process more information or to reduce the need
for information results in reduced performance.

In large, complex organizations the basic problem is
to subdivide the tasks among several specialist groups and
then integrate the subtasks to accomplish the global organizational task. With a traditional mechanistic model of an
organization three strategies are possible to coordinate
and integrate subtasks -- develop standard operating procedures and decision rules, establish a hierarchy within
which exceptions to the rules can be referred to the next
higher level, or set the goal or target of each subtask
and delegate the method of accomplishing the goal to the
personnel in the subtask.

Eventually, when the organization faces greater uncertainty, the result is more exceptions, an overloaded hierarchy, and a need for more information processing. At this
point the organization can reduce the need for information
processing through the creation of slack resources or the
creation of self-contained tasks. Alternatively, it can
increase the capacity to process information by developing
vertical information systems or creating lateral organizational relations. Galbraith provides a detailed discussion
of these four organization design strategies.

READING SUGGESTIONS

This article is a concise summarization of Galbraith's
book entitled Designing Complex Organizations (Addison-
Wesley, 1973). Therefore, it must be read carefully to retain the rapid development of logical thought. Figure 1
provides a helpful summary of the organization of the paper.
Focus on the description of the four design strategies for
reducing the need for information processing or increasing
the capacity for information processing to handle increased
uncertainty. Look at each strategy to discover its differences and its benefits and costs. Must an organization always pick one of these strategies? As you read, consider
how a computer-based information system could support each
of the organization design strategies.

QUESTIONS

1. Looking at the three coordination strategies and the
   four organization design strategies, how does each
   strategy affect the information flows in an organization?
2. How does each of the three coordination strategies
   break down under increased uncertainty?
3. What are the benefits and costs of each of the four
   design strategies?
4. If an organization does nothing to redesign in the
   face of increased uncertainty, which strategy will
   happen by default?
5. The use of computers and the development of MIS are
   chiefly part of which strategy of organizational design?
6. List and contrast the evolutionary stages in the development of lateral organizational relations.
7. What types of organizations and organizational tasks
   are most suitable for a matrix organization?
8. How can an MIS support each of the organizational design strategies for handling uncertainty?

INTERFACES
Vol. 4, No. 3
May 1974

ORGANIZATION DESIGN:
AN INFORMATION PROCESSING VIEW

JAY R. GALBRAITH
European Institute for Advanced Studies

JAY R. GALBRAITH is currently serving as Professor of Organizational Behavior at the European Institute for Advanced Studies in Management. Formerly, he was affiliated with the Sloan School of Management, M.I.T. Professor Galbraith is interested in the design of organization structures and his most recent work is *Designing Complex Organizations* (Addison-Wesley, 1973).

The Information Processing Model

A basic proposition is that the greater the uncertainty of the task, the greater the amount of information that has to be processed between decision makers during the execution of the task. If the task is well understood prior to performing it, much of the activity can be preplanned. If it is not understood, then during the actual task execution more knowledge is acquired which leads to changes in resource allocations, schedules, and priorities. All these changes require information processing *during* task performance. Therefore the greater the task uncertainty, the greater the amount of information that must be processed among decision makers during task execution in order to achieve a given level of performance. The basic effect of uncertainty is to limit the ability of the organization to preplan or to make decisions about activities in advance of their execution. Therefore it is hypothesized that the observed variations in organizational forms are variations in the strategies of organizations to 1) increase their ability to preplan, 2) increase their flexibility to adapt to their inability to preplan, or, 3) to decrease the level of performance required for continued viability. Which strategy is chosen depends on the relative costs of the strategies. The function of the framework is to identify these strategies and their costs.

The Mechanistic Model

This framework is best developed by keeping in mind a hypothetical organization. Assume it is large and employs a number of specialist groups and resources in providing the output. After the task has been divided into specialist substasks, the problem is to integrate the subtasks around the completion of the global task. This is the problem of organization design. The behaviors that occur in one subtask cannot be judged as good or bad *per se*. The behaviors are more effective or ineffective depending upon the behaviors of the other subtask performers. There is a design problem because the executors of the behaviors cannot communicate with all the roles with whom they are interdependent. Therefore the design problem is to create mechanisms that permit coordinated action across large numbers of interdependent roles. Each of these mechanisms, however, has a limited range over which it is effective at handling the information requirements necessary to coordinate the interdependent roles. As the amount of uncertainty increases, and therefore information processing increases, the organization must adopt integrating mechanisms which increase its information processing capabilities.

1. Coordination by Rules or Programs

For routine predictable tasks March and Simon have identified the use of rules or programs to coordinate behavior between interdependent subtasks [March and Simon, 1958, Chap. 6]. To the extent that job related situations can be predicted in advance, and behaviors specified for these situations, programs allow an interdependent set of activities to be performed without the need for inter-unit communication. Each role occupant simply executes the behavior which is appropriate for the task related situation with which he is faced.

2. Hierarchy

As the organization faces greater uncertainty its participants face situations for which they have no rules. At this point the hierarchy is employed on an exception basis. The recurring job situations are programmed with rules while infrequent situations are referred to that level in the hierarchy where a global perspective exists for all affected subunits. However, the hierarchy also has a limited range. As uncertainty increases the number of exceptions increases until the hierarchy becomes overloaded.

3. Coordination by Targets or Goals

As the uncertainty of the organization's task increases, coordination increasingly takes place by specifying outputs, goals or targets [March and Simon, 1958, p. 145]. Instead of specifying specific behaviors to be enacted, the organization undertakes processes to set goals to be achieved and the employees select the behaviors which lead to goal accomplishment. Planning reduces the amount of information processing in the hierarchy by increasing the amount of discretion exercised at lower levels. Like the use of rules, planning achieves integrated action and also eliminates the need for continuous communication among interdependent subunits as long as task performance stays within the planned task specifications, budget limits and within targeted completion dates. If it does not, the hierarchy is again employed on an exception basis.

The ability of an organization to coordinate interdependent tasks depends on its ability to compute meaningful subgoals to guide subunit action. When uncertainty increases because of introducing new products, entering new markets, or employing new technologies these subgoals are incorrect. The result is more exceptions, more information processing, and an overloaded hierarchy.

Design Strategies

The ability of an organization to successfully utilize coordination by goal setting, hierarchy, and rules depends on the combination of the frequency of exceptions and the capacity of the hierarchy to handle them. As the task uncertainty increases the organization must again take organization design action. It can proceed in either of two general ways. First, it can act in two ways to reduce the amount of information that is processed. And second, the organization can act in two ways to increase its capacity to handle more information. The two methods for reducing the need for information and the two methods for increasing processing capacity are shown schematically in Figure 1. The effect of all these actions is to reduce the number of exceptional cases referred upward into the organization through hierarchical channels. The assumption is that the critical limiting factor of an organizational form is its ability to handle the non-routine, consequential events that cannot be anticipated and planned for in advanced. The non-programmed events place the greatest communication load on the organization.

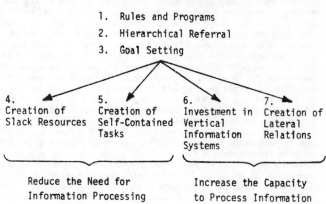

FIGURE 1. Organization Design Strategies

1. Creation of Slack Resources

As the number of exceptions begin to overload the hierarchy, one response is to increase the planning targets so that fewer exceptions occur. For example, completion dates can be extended until the number of exceptions that occur are within the existing information processing capacity of the organization. This has been the practice in solving job shop scheduling problems [Pounds, 1963]. Job shops quote delivery times that are long enough to keep the scheduling problem within the computational and information processing limits of the organization. Since every job shop has the same problem standard lead times evolve in the industry. Similarly budget targets could be raised, buffer inventories employed, etc. The greater the uncertainty, the greater the magnitude of the inventory, lead time or budget needed to reduce an overload.

All of these examples have a similar effect. They represent the use of slack resources to reduce the amount of interdependence between subunits [March and Simon, 1958, Cyert and March, 1963]. This keeps the required amount of information within the capacity of the organization to process it. Information processing is reduced because an exception is less likely to occur and reduced interdependence means that fewer factors need to be considered simultaneously when an exception does occur.

The strategy of using slack resources has its costs. Relaxing budget targets has the obvious cost of requiring more budget. Increasing the time to completion date has the effect of delaying the customer. Inventories require the investment of capital funds which could be used elsewhere. Reduction of design optimization reduces the performance of the article being designed. Whether slack resources are used to reduce information or not depends on the relative cost of the other alternatives.

The design choices are: 1) among which factors to change (lead time, overtime, machine utilization, etc.) to create the slack, and 2) by what amount should the factor be changed. Many operations research models are useful in choosing factors and amounts. The time-cost trade off problem in project networks is a good example.

2. Creation of Self-Contained Tasks

The second method of reducing the amount of information processed is to change the subtask groupings from resource (input) based to output based categories and give each group the resources it needs to supply the output. For example, the functional organization could be changed to product groups. Each group would have its own product engineers, process engineers, fabricating and assembly operations, and marketing activities. In other situations, groups can be created around product lines, geographical areas, projects, client groups, markets, etc., each of which would contain the input resources necessary for creation of the output.

The strategy of self-containment shifts the basis of the authority structure from one based on input, resource, skill, or occupational categories to one based on output or geographical categories. The shift reduces the amount of information processing through several mechanisms. First, it reduces the amount of output diversity faced by a single collection of resources. For example, a professional organization with multiple skill specialties providing service to three different client groups must schedule the use of these specialties across three demands for their services and determine priorities when conflicts occur. But, if the organization changed to three groups, one for each client category, each with its own full compliment of specialties, the schedule conflicts across client groups disappears and there is no need to process information to determine priorities.

The second source of information reduction occurs through a reduced division of labor. The functional or resource specialized structure pools the demand for skills across all output categories. In the example above each client generates approximately one-third of the demand for each skill. Since the division of labor is limited by the extent of the market, the division of labor must decrease as the demand decreases. In the professional organization, each client group may have generated a need for one-third of a computer programmer. The functional organization would have hired one programmer and shared him across the groups. In the self-contained structure there is insufficient demand in each group for a programmer so the professionals must do their own programming. Specialization is reduced but there is no problem of scheduling the programmer's time across the three possible uses for it.

The cost of the self-containment strategy is the loss of resource specialization. In the example, the organization foregoes the benefit of a specialist in computer programming. If there is physical equipment, there is a loss of economies of scale. The professional organization would require three machines in the self-contained form but only a large time-shared machine in the functional form. But those resources which have large economies of scale or for which specialization is necessary may remain centralized. Thus, it is the degree of self-containment that is the variable. The greater the degree of uncertainty, other things equal, the greater the degree of self-containment.

The design choices are the basis for the self-contained structure and the number of resources to be contained in the groups. No groups are completely self-contained or they would not be part of the same organization. But one product divisionalized firm may have eight of fifteen functions in the division while another may have twelve of fifteen in the divisions. Usually accounting, finance, and legal services are centralized and shared. Those functions which have economies of scale, require specialization or are necessary for control remain centralized and not part of the self-contained group.

The first two strategies reduced the amount of information by lower performance standards and creating small autonomous groups to provide the output. Information is reduced because an exception is less likely to occur and fewer factors need to be considered when an exception does occur. The next two strategies accept the performance standards and division of labor as given and adapt the organization so as to process the new information which is created during task performance.

3. Investment in Vertical Information Systems

The organization can invest in mechanisms which allow it to process information acquired during task performance without overloading the hierarchical communication channels. The investment occurs according to the following logic. After the organization has created its plan or set of targets for inventories, labor utilization, budgets, and schedules, unanticipated events occur which generate exceptions requiring adjustments to the original plan. At some point when the number of exceptions becomes substantial, it is preferable to generate a new plan rather than make incremental changes with each exception. The issue is then how frequently should plans be revised — yearly, quarterly, or monthly? The greater the frequency of replanning the greater the resources, such as clerks, computer time, input-output devices, etc., required to process information about relevant factors.

The cost of information processing resources can be minimized if the language is formalized. Formalization of a decision-making language simply means that more information is transmitted with the same number of symbols. It is assumed that information processing resources are consumed in proportion to the number of symbols transmitted. The accounting system is an example of a formalized language.

Providing more information, more often, may simply overload the decision maker. Investment may be required to increase the capacity of the decision maker by employing computers, various man-machine combinations, assistants-to, etc. The cost of this strategy is the cost of the information processing resources consumed in transmitting and processing the data.

The design variables of this strategy are the decision frequency, the degree of formalization of language, and the type of decision mechanism which will make the choice. This strategy is usually operationalized by creating redundant information channels which transmit data from the point of origination upward in the hierarchy where the point of decision rests. If data is formalized and quantifiable, this strategy is effective. If the relevant data are qualitative and ambiguous, then it may prove easier to bring the decisions down to where the information exists.

4. Creation of Lateral Relationships

The last strategy is to employ selectively joint decision processes which cut across lines of authority. This strategy moves the level of decision making down in the organization to where the information exists but does so without reorganizing around self-contained groups. There are several types of lateral decision processes. Some processes are usually referred to as the informal organization. However, these informal processes do not always arise spontaneously out of the needs of the task. This is particularly true in multi-national organizations in which participants are separated by physical barriers, language differences, and cultural differences. Under these circumstances lateral processes need to be designed. The lateral processes evolve as follows with increases in uncertainty.

4.1. *Direct Contact* between managers who share a problem. If a problem arises on the shop floor, the foreman can simply call the design engineer, and they can jointly agree upon a solution. From an information processing view, the joint decision prevents an upward referral and unloads the hierarchy.

4.2. *Liaison Roles* — when the volume of contacts between any two departments grows, it becomes economical to set up a specialized role to handle this communication. Liaison men are typical examples of specialized roles designed to facilitate communication between two interdependent departments and to bypass the long lines of communication involved in upward referral. Liaison roles arise at lower and middle levels of management.

4.3. *Task Forces.* Direct contact and liaison roles, like the integration mechanisms before them, have a limited range of usefulness. They work when two managers or functions are involved. When problems arise involving seven or eight departments, the decision making capacity of direct contacts is exceeded. Then these problems must be referred upward. For uncertain, interdependent tasks such situations arise frequently. Task forces are a form of horizontal contact which is designed for problems of multiple departments.

The task force is made up of representatives from each of the affected departments. Some are full-time members, others may be part-time. The task force is a temporary group. It exists only as long as the problem remains. When a solution is reached, each participant returns to his normal tasks.

To the extent that they are successful, task forces remove problems from higher levels of the hierarchy. The decisions are made at lower levels in the organization. In order to guarantee integration, a group problem solving approach is taken. Each affected subunit contributes a member and therefore provides the information necessary to judge the impact on all units.

4.4. *Teams.* The next extension is to incorporate the group decision process into the permanent decision processes. That is, as certain decisions consistently arise, the task forces become permanent. These groups are labeled teams. There are many design issues concerned in team decision making such as at what level do they operate, who participates, etc. [Galbraith, 1973, Chapters 6 and 7]. One design decision is particularly critical. This is the choice of leadership. Sometimes a problem exists largely in one department so that the department manager is the leader. Sometimes the leadership passes from one manager to another. As a new product moves to the market place, the leader of the new product team is first the technical manager followed by the production and then the marketing manager. The result is that if the team cannot reach a consensus decision and the leader decides, the goals of the leader are consistent with the goals of the organization for the decision in question. But quite often obvious leaders cannot be found. Another mechanism must be introduced.

4.5. *Integrating Roles.* The leadership issue is solved by creating a new role — an integrating role [Lawrence and Lorsch, 1967, Chapter 3]. These roles carry the labels of product managers, program managers, project managers, unit managers (hospitals), materials managers, etc. After the role is created, the design problem is to create enough power in the role to influence the decision process. These roles have power even when no one reports directly to them. They have some power because they report to the general manager. But if they are selected so as to be unbiased with respect to the groups they integrate and to have technical competence, they have expert power. They collect information and equalize power differences due to preferential access to knowledge and information. The power equalization increases trust and the quality of the joint decision process. But power equalization occurs only if the integrating role is staffed with someone who can exercise expert power in the form of persuasion and informal influences rather than exert the power of rank or authority.

4.6. *Managerial Linking Roles.* As tasks become more uncertain, it is more difficult to exercise expert power. The role must get more power of the formal authority type in order to be effective at coordinating the joint decisions which occur at lower levels of the organization. This position power changes the nature of the role which for lack of a better name is labeled a managerial linking role. It is not like the integrating role because it possesses formal position power but is different from line managerial roles in that participants do not report to the linking manager. The power is added by the following successive changes:

a) The integrator receives approval power of budgets formulated in the departments to be integrated.

b) The planning and budgeting process starts with the integrator making his initiation in budgeting legitimate.

c) Linking manager receives the budget for the area of responsibility and buys resources from the specialist groups.

FIGURE 2. A Pure Matrix Organization

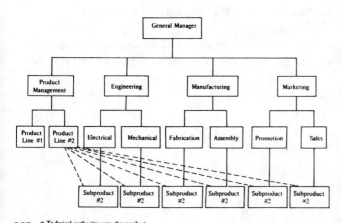

- - - = Technical authority over the product
——— = Formal authority over the product (in product organization, these relationships may be reversed)

These mechanisms permit the manager to exercise influence even though no one works directly for him. The role is concerned with integration but exercises power through the formal power of the position. If this power is insufficient to integrate the subtasks and creation of self-contained groups is not feasible, there is one last step.

4.7. *Matrix Organization.* The last step is to create the dual authority relationship and the matrix organization [Galbraith, 1971]. At some point in the organization some roles have two superiors. The design issue is to select the locus of these roles. The result is a balance of power between the managerial linking roles and the normal line organization roles. Figure 2 depicts the pure matrix design.

The work of Lawrence and Lorsch is highly consistent with the assertions concerning lateral relations [Lawrence and Lorsch, 1967, Lorsch and Lawrence, 1968]. They compared the types of lateral relations undertaken by the most successful firm in three different industries. Their data are summarized in Table 1. The plastics firm has the greatest rate of new product introduction (uncertainty) and the greatest utilization of lateral processes. The container firm was also very successful but utilized only standard practices because its information processing task is much less formidable. Thus, the greater the uncertainty the lower the level of decision making and the integration is maintained by lateral relations.

TABLE 1

	Plastics	Food	Container
% new products in last ten years	35%	20%	0%
Integrating Devices	Rules	Rules	Rules
	Hierarchy	Hierarchy	Hierarchy
	Planning	Planning	Planning
	Direct Contact	Direct Contact	Direct Contact
	Teams at 3 levels	Task forces	
	Integrating Dept.	Integrators	
% Integrators/Managers	22%	17%	0%

[Adopted from Lawrence and Lorsch, 1967, pp. 86–138 and Lorsch and Lawrence, 1968].

Table 1 points out the cost of using lateral relations. The plastics firm has 22% of its managers in integration roles. Thus, the greater the use of lateral relations the greater the managerial intensity. This cost must be balanced against the cost of slack resources, self-contained groups and information systems.

Choice of Strategy

Each of the four strategies has been briefly presented. The organization can follow one or some combination of several if it chooses. It will choose that strategy which has the least cost in its environmental context. [For an example, see Galbraith, 1970]. However, what may be lost in all of the explanations is that the four strategies are hypothesized to be an exhaustive set of alternatives. That is, if the organization is faced with greater uncertainty due to technological change, higher performance standards due to increased competition, or diversifies its product line to reduce dependence, the amount of information processing is increased. *The organization must adopt at least one of the four strategies when faced with greater uncertainty.* If it does not consciously choose one of the four, then the first, reduced performance standards, will happen automatically. The task information requirements and the capacity of the organization to process information are always matched. If the organization does not consciously match them, reduced performance through budget overruns, schedule overruns will occur in order to bring about equality. Thus the organization should be planned and designed simultaneously with the planning of the strategy and resource allocations. But if the strategy involves introducing new products, entering new markets, etc., then some provision for increased information must be made. Not to decide is to decide, and it is to decide upon slack resources as the strategy to remove hierarchical overload.

There is probably a fifth strategy which is not articulated here. Instead of changing the organization in response to task uncertainty, the organization can operate on its environment to reduce uncertainty. The organization through strategic decisions, long term contracts, coalitions, etc., can control its environment. But these maneuvers have costs also. They should be compared with costs of the four design strategies presented above.

Summary

The purpose of this paper has been to explain why task uncertainty is related to organizational form. In so doing the cognitive limits theory of Herbert Simon was the guiding influence. As the consequences of cognitive limits were traced through the framework various organization design strategies were articulated. The framework provides a basis for integrating organizational interventions, such as information systems and group problem solving, which have been treated separately before.

BIBLIOGRAPHY

Cyert, Richard, and March, James, *The Behavioral Theory of the Firm*, Prentice-Hall, Englewood Cliffs, N. J., 1963.
Galbraith, Jay, "Environmental and Technological Determinants of Organization Design: A Case Study" in Lawrence and Lorsch (ed.) *Studies in Organization Design*, Richard D. Irwin Inc., Homewood, Ill., 1970.
Galbraith, Jay, "Designing Matrix Organizations", *Business Horizons*, (Feb. 1971), pp. 29-40.
Galbraith, Jay, *Organization Design*, Addison-Wesley Pub. Co., Reading, Mass., 1973.
Lawrence, Paul, and Lorsch, Jay, *Organization and Environment*, Division of Research, Harvard Business School, Boston, Mass., 1967.
Lorsch, Jay, and Lawrence, Paul, "Environmental Factors and Organization Integration", Paper read at the Annual Meeting of the American Sociological Association, August 27, 1968, Boston, Mass.
March, James, and Simon, Herbert, *Organizations*, John Wiley & Sons, New York, N. Y., 1958.
Pounds, William, "The Scheduling Environment" in Muth and Thompson (eds.) *Industrial Scheduling*, Prentice-Hall Inc., Englewood Cliffs, N. J., 1963.
Simon, Herbert, *Models of Man*, John Wiley & Sons, New York, N. Y., 1957.

John P. Campbell   Davis Chapter 6

"DECISION MAKING, CONFLICT RESOLUTION, AND THE STEADY STATE"

Unpublished Working Paper, University of Minnesota, 1975 September.

The paper by Campbell has two parts: the first is a
survey of decision making concepts which help to explain
decision making behavior, and the second explores means
for changing decision making behavior. Although somewhat
long, the paper provides a perceptive survey of decision
making models, their problems, and what might be done
to improve the situation.

For the purposes of the survey, Campbell classifies
ideas about decision making behavior into four themes:
1. Classic economic model
2. Administrative model
3. Skinnerian model
4. Controlled anarchist model

The classic economic model of decision making is a
useful explanation for large populations; it is not a good
description of individual behavior. The administrative
model stresses expectations, cost of search for alternatives, uncertainty of outcomes, and the willingness of
decision makers to satisfice. The Skinnerian model con-
centrates on rewards or reinforcement to explain choice
behavior. The incremental or controlled anarchy model of
decision behavior says that decision behavior is not based
on a rational or satisficing approach, but is based on a
complex set of factors such as current state and status
or power of those involved. Due to these complex and
interrelated factors, decisions may appear somewhat random.

Campbell differentiates between simple decision
makers in a decision situation and multiple decision
makers in conflict resolution. In changing individual
decision behavior one approach focuses on providing the
decision maker with more information about the decision
process, a second approach provides more information about
outcomes, a third changes reinforcement characteristics.
Conflict in group decision making can be constructive or
destructive. Conflict can be resolved in several ways;
two effective methods are changing of reinforcers and controlled confrontation between the conflicting parties.

READING SUGGESTIONS

The framework and viewpoint of the article needs to
be kept in mind. The author emphasizes a behavioral approach in the discussion of decision making. The first
part of the paper is not how decisions are made; it is a
survey of explanations for observed decision making behavior. The second part of the paper focuses on how decision behavior is changed. The decision behavior modification is divided into individual and group decisions,
the latter being identified as conflict resolution.

QUESTIONS

1. How does the administrative model of decision be-
    havior differ from the classic economic model?
2. What is the decision behavior of the Skinnerian model?
3. Name four ways individual decision behavior may be
    changed.
4. How does a stereotype assist in decision making?
5. How can group conflict (decision making) be resolved?

DECISION MAKING, CONFLICT RESOLUTION, AND THE STEADY STATE*

John P. Campbell

University of Minnesota

Not too many years ago asking whether it is possible for the planet earth to achieve a "steady state" condition would have been regarded as an overly cosmic and sophomoric question. Many would have laughed derisively. Some still do. Others feel that we have only a very few years left before the point of no return is passed and it will no longer be possible to stabilize our civilization at any relatively comfortable level of existence.

Whether we can ever reach the steady state will be a function of many factors. For example, there is the not so small question of whether the available technology will permit it, *given a particular population size, nutritional level, standard of living, etc.* Notice that just this brief example illustrates another fundamental set of problems. Whether we can achieve a steady state in the systems or ecological sense is dependent upon how we define an acceptable "quality of life" and upon the decisions we make about population size, standard of living, etc. Thus a second set of factors consists of the processes by which we make these various decisions and the processes by which we resolve the conflicts that surround them. Will such processes permit a satisfactory allocation of resources such that a steady state will be achieved? All of which brings me to the objectives of this paper.

What I would like to do first is briefly outline some descriptive models that have been used to describe the decision making process and consider where each might point the finger relative to defects in ecological choice behavior. Second, it would be appropriate to consider a list of possible ways to change our decision making behavior and to say something about the feasibility of doing it. Finally, I want to make a distinction between decision making and conflict resolution and also consider how we might attack the latter. At the outset, I should state that I have come to an almost fatalistic position regarding the probability of changing our decision making habits, almost but not quite. These are not the remarks of an optimist.

Trying to define decision making or distinguishing it from other kinds of behavior is a difficult task

and probably not all that useful. Let me say simply that what I want to talk about is the *act* of choosing among alternatives when the choice cannot be made via some objective rule or algorithm; that is, when completely programmed standard operating procedures can't make the decision for us. Under these conditions, all good capitalists, socialists, etc., tend to avoid decision making for as long as possible, just as they try to avoid competition by whatever means are at hand. On the surface this avoidance behavior may seem irrational since nothing may get done and bad situations are prolonged. Viewed another way, such behavior is eminently rational since the longer one waits the more information becomes available. However, a preliminary point I wish to argue is that we not think in terms of whether humans act rationally or irrationally. Rather we should adopt an evolutionary model as a superordinate view of the whole thing and constantly ask ourselves why specific choices are *adaptive* for people and organizations. As a good determinist, I think we should assume that *all* behavior is rational and that it is the responsibility of the researcher, politician, and voter to figure out the adaptive mechanisms involved. I think this removes the necessity of an "evil person" theory of polluters or an "ecology freak" model of environmentalists. Reasonable people are quite capable of getting us into environmental trouble.

DECISION MAKING MODELS

There are many descriptive models of the decision making process but most of these are variations of four major themes concerning what individuals do. I've labeled them as follows:

1. Classical economic model
2. Administrative model
3. Skinnerian model
4. Controlled anarchist model

For the moment, let's put aside a number of obvious parametric questions such as whether certain subsets of decision makers are better described by some models than others and whether there are different kinds of decision situations for which some models are more accurate descriptions than others. Most of these models make use of some form of the following picture.

*An earlier version of this paper was prepared originally for a lecture series entitled "Spaceship Earth and the Steady State," sponsored by the Division of Social Sciences, University of Minnesota, 1971.

Figure 1

Possible courses of action	Probability that some outcome will occur, given the selection of a particular course action	Value of outcomes (consequences, rewards, payoffs) resulting from each course of action
Alternative 1	$P(O_1/A_1) \longrightarrow$	$V(O_1/A_1)$
	$P(O_2/A_1) \longrightarrow$	$V(O_2/A_1)$
	$P(O_3/A_1) \longrightarrow$	$V(O_3/A_1)$
Alternative 2	$P(O_1/A_2) \longrightarrow$	$V(O_1/A_2)$
	$P(O_2/A_2) \longrightarrow$	$V(O_2/A_2)$
$\vdots$		
Alternative N	$P(O_1/A_N) \longrightarrow$	$V(O_1/A_N)$
	$P(O_2/A_N) \longrightarrow$	$V(O_2/A_N)$
	$P(O_3/A_N) \longrightarrow$	$V(O_3/A_N)$
	$P(O_4/A_N) \longrightarrow$	$V(O_4/A_N)$

It says that a decision maker is faced with a number of alternative actions. Each action, if pursued, will lead to a certain set of outcomes (here labeled O_i). For example, alternative means of mass transit are associated with different outcomes such as whether or not people will actually use it, the cost, what kinds of people it would benefit most, and relative efficiency. In like manner, an undergraduate trying to choose a graduate school is faced with certain outcomes flowing from each choice (large classes, high caliber student body, large stipend, etc.).

Each outcome has a value to the decision maker. An economist calls this value utility, a social psychologist might use the term valence. The important thing is that we realize that these assignments of utility are value judgements. Even though a prospective graduate student knows the stipend will be exactly $9,450 (tax free), the student must still decide what that's worth to him or her personally. Values can be positive or negative.

Besides taking on a particular value, each outcome is also characterized by the probability that it will indeed occur if a specific alternative is chosen. For example, what's the probability that choosing the University of Minnesota will stick you with larger classes? These probabilities (even if we don't know them very precisely) are matters of *fact* rather than personal preference. Mushy though it is, we should keep this particular distinction between fact and value in mind.

The total worth, or total utility, of a particular

alternative is then some function of the individual utilities of the outcomes associated with it and the probability that each of these outcomes will occur. Different models propose different methods for combining these individual variables into total utility and the method of combination constitutes one of the major distinctions among theories. Other distinctions revolve around how value and probability estimates are made and how alternatives are compared, once their utility has been determined.

Classical Economic Model

The traditional view of the decision maker comes from the economists in the form of variations on the theme of classic economic man. Early classic decision theory had the following ingredients (Taylor, 1965):

1. The probabilities of all outcomes, given an alternative selection, were assumed to be 1.0 (i.e., decision making under certainty).

2. Information about available alternatives and the outcomes associated with them is complete. That is, the theory assumed we had all the information we needed.

3. Outcomes can be at least ordered on a utility continuum. A cardinal (ratio) scale is not really necessary, but the utility continuum is assumed to be continuous such that two different outcomes can always be distinguished. That is, the individual is infinitely sensitive.

4. Alternatives are selected which maximize utility for the decision maker.

In this form, the classic model was used to derive some rather basic dicta of how a profit seeking organization should behave.

Later developments in the classic theory took up the case of so called *risky decisions* where the probability of an outcome given an alternative is not 1.0 but is known. For example, what's the probability of any one graduate student receiving a teaching assistantship if 500 students are accepted and there are 125 teaching assistant positions? Obviously, it is .25. Under these conditions, the model predicts that individuals will attempt to maximize expected value (their expected utility). The expected value of any particular alternative is equal to the products of individual outcome values and the probability of their occurence summed across outcomes. This says that the decision to pollute is taken because the organization has determined that the positive outcome values outweigh the negative outcome values and/or the probabilities that the negative outcomes will occur are less. Notice that something more

than an ordinal scale for value or utility was re-
introduced. That is, if people are going to be making
this multiplication and summation in their heads, they
have to be able to judge outcome utilities on something
more than an ordinal scale.

In sum, the classic theory portrays the decision
maker as being completely knowledgeable, infinitely
sensitive to differences in utility, and a maximizer
of something (profits, stockholders equity, or some
other variable directly tied to the firm's carefully
circumscribed self-interest). In a very macro sense,
the theory has worked and some predictions can be made
about what various sectors of the economy will do, faced
with certain factors such as investment credits, tax
incentives, and the like. However, for a single organization or individual it's another matter. The assumptions are questionable and the model as a descriptor
of individual behavior has been pretty well demolished.

From the ruins of the economic model has grown
the administrative model as it was nurtured, if not
conceived, at Carnegie-Mellon University and cross-
fertilized by the University of Michigan.

Administrative Model

The characterization of the administrative model
is really a synthesis of two different traditions. The
first has its roots in management theory (Barnard, 1938;
Simon, 1957), the second comes from psychology (e.g.,
Vroom, 1964).

That part of the administrative model derived from
psychology centers on the nature of the outcome probabilities and outcome utilities. It says that it is the
perceived magnitude for each of these variables that is
important, not what the actual probability might be or
what the real value of an outcome would turn out to be
if the individual actually experienced it, which is the
notion of utility used by the classic theory. In other
words, it is his or her perceived world not the "real"
world that controls an individual's choices. This
orients the model towards the future in the form of an
individual's expectations. It's what's in the head that
counts. Obviously, this opens the door to all those
variables that can influence an individual's perceptions
and a certain amount of research has revolved around
these relationships.

Certain management theorists (e.g., March & Simon,
1958) have combined the above notion with some assumptions about the nature of the actual decisions that must
be faced in the real world. Contrary to the assumptions
of the classic theory:

1. Alternatives are frequently not available and
must be created.

2. Information concerning outcomes is very incomplete and must be searched for.

3. Search is costly.

4. Information is ambiguous, which leads to uncertainty as to the expected value of specific outcomes.

According to the March and Simon view, the administrative model tends to deal with the cost and uncertainty of information in the following ways.

Uncertainty is reduced by:

1. Concentrating on outcomes whose expected value
can be expressed in quantitative or quasi-quantitative
terms. It's no fun to wrestle with outcomes that cannot be readily quantified on some familiar scale--best
that we avoid it. Although the decision maker must in
the end judge the outcome's value to him, it's easier
to do that for such things as the number of jobs created
or the size of the tax base than for quality of life or
clarity of water.

2. Dealing with outcomes which can be evaluated in
the short run. Other things being equal, the closer the
outcome to the time the alternative is selected, the less
the uncertainty concerning probability and utility estimates. Dirty air right now seems worth more attention
than a ruined ocean decades from now.

The costs associated with gathering information
and evaluating outcomes are reduced by:

1. Keeping computations and information simple.
Decision makers tend to avoid elaborate research projects or highly complex information systems.

2. *Satisficing* not maximizing. That is, decision
makers will create alternatives and gather information
until they find an alternative that is satisfactory
rather than optimal. This implies that decision makers
have a *stereotype* of what a satisfactory alternative
should look like and once they find it they will quit
searching. Satisficing is not unlike the social psychologist's concept of aspiration level and is meant to
obey the same laws. For example, if decision makers
find it easy to satisfice, they most likely raise their
standards for what they consider to be satisfactory,
and vice versa.

In sum, people who live by the administrative model
are governed by their perceived expectancies concerning
what will happen in the future but they live in a world
that is much too complex to know completely. As a result
people satisfice rather than maximize and gravitate to-

ward outcomes that can be thought about in terms of some familiar quantitative scale and which will become manifest over the relatively short run. Thus, other things being equal, it is usually no contest if the purity of air, clarity of water, or long term sources of energy must be paired against number of jobs, tax base, and profit in the short run.

Skinnerian Model

In psychological jargon, The Carnegie/Michigan administrative model is a cognitive one. That is, we looked inside the head of decision makers and asked how they *thought* about things. We assumed that people have expectations about the consequences of their actions or choices and that these expectations help govern their behavior. The Skinnerian or strict reinforcement view (Bolles, 1967; Skinner, 1971) doesn't deny that people think or have expectancies, but it does argue that trying to find out what people think or expect is *not* a very fruitful way of explaining or controlling behavior. The reinforcement model operates outside the head and says that the way to explain choice behavior is to determine retrospectively the specific rewards that have strengthened particular responses in the past. That is, choices or responses are strengthened if they are followed by outcomes which the individual values highly. This is a simple but powerful idea. If we wish to change the behavior of an individual, then we must provide outcomes (rewards) that will serve as reinforcers for these new behaviors. Thus, the decision to pollute or not to pollute is a function of what outcomes are important reinforcers for a decision maker and who controls them.

At this point, please do not make the mistake of most reviewers of Skinner's books and think of the "controller of rewards" as some new kind of technocrat or diety. Legislators, stockholders, vice presidents, boards of regents, parents, and the like will do quite nicely. We elect state legislators with mandates to write laws with which we hope to control our own behavior through various kinds of positive and negative reinforcement.

Please *do* focus on what are really four main points of the Skinnerian position:

1. The most effective reinforcers are those which are most directly connected to the response, both in terms of the latency between response and reinforcement (the shorter the better) and in terms of getting to the core of the individual's strongest needs.

2. Behavior is maintained at a much stronger level if a particular response is reinforced intermittently rather than each time it occurs.

3. Positive reinforcement is much more effective than negative. Unfortunately, our society seems to operate on the converse.

4. The outcomes which are really reinforcing behavior can only be known through empirical observation.

In sum, to understand choices *vis-a-vis* the environment we must look hard at the reinforcements which are available for each choice.

Controlled Anarchist Model

Certain sociologists and political scientists among us have provided yet a fourth model which might be labeled the *incremental* or *controlled anarchy* model (Lindblom, 1959; Allison, 1969).

The basic tenents of the model are again largely a reaction against the classic theory. Even the administrative model depicts a person who is much too systematic a decision maker. The anarchist model assumes that in the real world outcomes are too numerous and complex and the relationship between alternatives and outcomes too poorly understood to permit *any* systematic comparison of alternatives via their relative utility, even if it's only to satisfice. Attempts to make decisions by evaluating outcomes will *necessarily* miss potential outcomes that will ultimately become extremely important.

The only factor which makes decision making anything but a random walk is that it is possible to compare alternatives one at a time against historical data which specify what in fact did result from very similar courses of action in the past. That is, the alternative actions only differ in small incremental amounts from past practice. Comparing present alternatives to very similar alternatives for which the consequences are already known is considerably different from having to evaluate all potential outcomes for a number of alternatives. Budgets don't change by leaps and bounds, they go up and down rather gradually. We don't make massive attempts to rectify social inequities, we begin with small remedial "programs." Decision makers indulge in this incremental approach because it appears to minimize the risk of big mistakes (that is, a large negative outcome) and allows them to deal with a world that's too complex to really know.

There is a second way which this model says unforeseen outcomes can be identified. First, it is a mistake to think of any business organization, governmental agency, community organization, etc., as a single monolithic decision maker. Almost all organizations are made up of competing power centers which take different views of potential outcomes and the utilities that are assigned to them. Further, most organizations are surrounded by a number of external publics, also with different views, which will be quick to point out their own special interests. Thus, even though any particular decision maker may overlook or try to forget important outcomes there are enough other power centers with different interests to force a concern with all of the important ones. Thus, a highway commission may neglect consideration of freeway noise but certain resident groups and professors of acoustical engineering with research grants do not. The moral is that we should provide ample opportunity for special interest groups to operate.

CHANGING DECISION MAKING BEHAVIOR

It would be a mistake to think of these proposed descriptions as competing explanations of the same well defined process. They obviously are not. If one considers the complexity of even a small domain of human behavior, it becomes obvious that decision making covers too much ground to be dealt with by one descriptive model, or even four. Nevertheless, I would like to throw all of them together, stir gently, and see what comes out in terms of what they say it will take to change decision making of the kind we are discussing.

First, let's go back to the behavior itself for a moment. Saying that decision making is choice behavior among alternatives when there is no algorithm to make the choice for us is a bit too simple. For one thing, a choice can be exercised by an individual, a group, an entire organization, or a political body. So far we have lumped all those under the term decision maker.

Secondly, the value system of the decision maker has a lot to do with choice behavior. There is a fundamental difference between decision making in the context of a relatively homogeneous value system and one in which the alternative selected must reconcile different value systems. The former refers to a single decision maker faced with alternative courses of action that he or she is trying valiantly to evaluate. The problems lie in the decision making process itself. By the latter case, I mean a situation in which there are multiple decision makers with significantly different values for different outcomes and the differences cannot necessarily be explained by faulty communication, misunderstanding, or the like. There are simply real differences that won't go away in the way people value outcomes. Almost all decision making models address themselves exclusively to the former context. The incremental model is the only one that doesn't. For convenience it might be useful to reserve the term deci-

sion making for the former and conflict resolution for the latter. Problems of conflict resolution are then piled on top of the decision making process itself. Both activities are involved in the way decisions relative to the environment get fouled up since there are usually multiple interest groups with conflicting goals.

Let me begin with the decision making side and suggest a simple list of potential methods for altering decision making behavior.

Change Through Information About the Process

A number of possible change efforts tend to focus on providing decision makers with more information about the *process* such that they might alter their behavior if it seems advisable. This assumes that decision makers are not explicitly aware of what they are doing.

For example, first there is the matter of gravitating toward *quantifiable outcomes*. I've always been perplexed by the tendency to use GNP or real income as a measure of our standard of living. It's almost as if we are unwilling to include in the concept such things as grass to walk on, freedom to walk on the street (day or night), and a freedom from constant noise and stinging eyes. Obviously, some people are willing to forgo large incomes and move to small towns to obtain these outcomes. However, we have very little systematic data as to what kinds of utility curves people have for these sorts of things. It is really a psychometric rather than an econometric problem and it is well within our present measurement technology to obtain such information. We need it if we are ever going to supplement the almost exclusive use of aggregate economic indicators.

A second area is the focus on *short run outcomes*. In an informational sense, I'm not sure how the concentration on short run outcomes could be countered. There are powerful incentives in the U. S. for this short term view. Politicans are re-evaluated by the voters every 2, 4, or 6 years and they have to have things to show for their efforts considerably before election time. Corporations must answer to the stockholders every year. The university has its biennium. Few long range planning units exist with real decision making power that could counter this aspect of the decision making process.

Third, I would have somewhat more hope for altering the *incremental strategy*. Simply by making this aspect of the process very explicit we may be able to decrease our reliance on it. Too often this approach *seems* the least risky of any but if we examined it more closely, that may not be the case. The Vietnam War was one example.

Fourth, a process element I would concentrate on to a greater extent is the use of *stereotypes* in the satisficing process. Let me mention two series of research studies. One deals with decisions made by college graduates when job hunting (Solberg, 1966; Vroom, 1966), and the other concerns hiring decisions made by employment interviewers (Webster, 1964; Wright, 1969). These studies show that the decision maker begins with a stereotype of what a good job or good applicant should be like and then proceeds to compare available alternatives against this standard. In no real sense is there a comparison *among* the available alternatives. Once a particular alternative comes "close enough," an implicit, but not yet public, decision is reached. Further information is used as *confirmation* of this implicit decision even at the cost of some perceptual distortion. Thus, if a good job or job applicant came along after the point of implicit decision, the probability is increased that this new and better alternative will not be selected, and in fact, the new job or new applicant's negative features instead of their positive features may be emphasized to reconcile this new alternative with the implicit choice already made.

The moral is that if the stereotype is really inappropriate, we are in trouble. We should be able to examine our stereotypes a bit more fully and overcome some of their negative implications. One rather striking example concerns a study of the stereotypes of accountants held by nonaccountant employment interviewers of the type that visit university campuses as compared to the stereotypes held by the members of the accounting profession itself. Hakel, Hollman, and Dunnette (1970) were able to demonstrate that company representatives interviewing accounting graduates for jobs tended to view a good accountant as being conservative, dependable, compulsive, and accurate; while accountants themselves viewed a good accountant as being innovative, dominant, and willing to take risks. In short, the accountant's accountant is the individual who can continually develop new kinds of information systems to reflect the changing conditions and goals of the organization but the people who make the initial employment screening have an entirely different view. Such a discrepancy in stereotypes could be quite maladaptive.

Change Through Information About Outcomes

A second major avenue of altering decision making behavior involves providing more information about possible *outcomes* and the probability of their occurrence. Business organizations, governmental agencies, and citizens could make better decisions if they had more information at their disposal that was feasible to use. I

earlier made a distinction between matters of fact and matters of value as determinants of decisions. It's a hazy distinction at best and we all realize that values help determine how facts are collected but I have a naive faith that things could really improve.

For years, too much relevant information about important environmental decisions was contained in long technical reports, published only in book form, or not codified at all. It thus becomes the province only of the few people who have time to assimilate it, and most of them probably have the time because the special interest they represent can provide the financial support for it. Search is costly and people will make decisions on very little data rather than spend a lot of time gathering more information.

Where is there a reasonably brief, readily available account of our involvement in Vietnam? Where are there summary accounts of the economic and environmental impact of specific industries? Where would we go to find out how many people work there, what kinds of people they are relative to the structural unemployment endemic to the area? We could dig back through newspaper files, but how many voters or even legislators will do that?

I firmly believe that almost all decision making takes place in a state of relative ignorance brought about because the relevant information is not readily available in a usable form. If you're concerned about violence and sex, the Kerner report and *Lockhart* report (respectively) are possible exceptions, but even here there is a large gap between the report in the form of a book, which must be carefully read, and the two column newspaper articles written about it. There ought to be something inbetween.

Think for a moment of a continuum ranging from pure decision making to pure conflict. If outcome information is really sparse then perhaps we are much closer to the conflict end of the continuum than we need be because the conflicting parties don't know they have any common ground.

Change Through Reinforcement

Certainly the most powerful class of change methods are those dealing with *reinforcement* characteristics. Given a particular technological state, the Skinnerian model says if we really want to change the world we must change the reward systems that operate directly on the decision maker. If one doesn't deal with the crucial reinforcement contingencies in a candid way, there is little hope of changing things. A recent speech by Henry Ford II keeps coming to mind again and again. He remarked that the auto industry would never have moved in the direction of controlling exhaust emissions without the force of governmental regulations. In the absence of outcomes controlled by some broader public, a business organization will respond to the rewards operating on its specific sphere of interest and influences. If military field officers are given good fitness reports (i.e., reinforced) on the basis of body counts then field operations will orient toward body counts.

Unfortunately the outcomes that are reinforcing the decision maker in a particular situation are not always obvious. Much has been written about the Cuban Missile Crisis and the decision to opt for a blockade strategy. Certain people may have argued for that strategy because it seemed like the right thing to do in terms of avoiding nuclear war. Others may have supported it because what they really valued was the approval of Robert S. McNamara (then U. S. Secretary of Defense) and that was the way to get it. Who knows? Teasing out the real reinforcements is a difficult task but one that must be done.

Sometimes it's not so hard. A large fraternal organization in a Minneapolis suburb was recently faced with its liquor license being made contingent on striking the "whites only" membership clause from its by-laws. I think I could have predicted the response beforehand. The whites only clause vanished as if by magic. However, this example illustrates yet another point about the reinforcement model. The behavior actually being reinforced may not be what you think (hope) it is. If the reinforced response was that the whites only clause must disappear from a piece of paper, it's a different matter from reinforcing the absence of complaints by non-whites seeking membership or reinforcing the presence of a 10% non-white membership in 18 months. Thus, when we offer tax incentives to businesses for various things, we must be quite careful as to the actual responses that will be reinforced. It doesn't always work out the way it was anticipated at first glance.

I guess I think of the reinforcement notion as being the most powerful concept one can use to analyze the decision making process but, it is the very power of the reinforcement concept that makes me so pessimistic about the future of the country. Consider the immediate reinforcements felt by a community for attracting industry and increasing both its employment rolls and tax base. These are bread and butter outcomes. The more delayed rewards are harder to quantify and do not strike directly at the pocketbook. It's no mystery that the strongest support for nuclear power plants is usually in the

municipality in which they are to be built. To change the course of events in the U. S. we are going to have to change some very important and potent pellets. As yet, I don't see any institution or mechanism for doing so on any substantial scale.

Individual vs. Group Decision Making

At this point, I would like to take a small side step and reconsider the identity of the decision maker. We have not distinguished between the decision maker as an individual, group, or organization. There is in psychology a fairly sizable literature on individual vs. group problem solving and decision making (e.g., Bouchard, 1969; Hoffman, 1965). The data are overwhelmingly clear. Group decision making is worse than individual decision making in the sense that the quality of the group decision is never as good as would be predicted, given the resources possessed by the individual members. It *always* regresses toward a lower common denominator. The reason for this seems to be that placing people in problem solving groups introduces an additional set of interpersonal processes to compete with the decision making processes described previously. When placed in a group some people feel stronger needs to talk than others. Other people have strong needs to be social facilitators, to keep things going, and to show approval for others. Others want to be the persons whose ideas are accepted, regardless of the issue. As people operate to satisfy these more interpersonal needs tangential to the main issue, the decision making process suffers.

The group solution also tends to accentuate whatever stereotype of a good solution is the most common or central within the group (Dion, Baron, & Miller, 1970). Thus if conservative actions are valued, the group's solution will be more conservative than any single individual's. Likewise, if "being different" is the dominant value, then the group's solution will be even more far out than any individual's. The data are not quite as clear for this finding as for that concerning solution quality but the trend is a strong one, strong enough that I think we must deal with it.

There is, however, one very positive side effect of group decision making. The data are again quite conclusive that commitment to a course of action or decision is greatly enhanced by group participation in making it (Campbell, *et al.*, 1970, Chapter 17). Unfortunately we have no good data to tell us what the tradeoff should be between solution quality and commitment. That research is just getting started (Vroom & Yetton, 1973). An alternative way out of this dilemma is to develop methods of group decision making to preserve both individual contribution and genuine participation. A few such techniques are beginning to appear on the horizon (Delbecq, Van de Ven, & Gustafson, 1975).

Decision Making vs. Conflict Resolution

But what of the conflict end of the continuum? Certainly much of the difficulty surrounding our choice of actions concerning the environment results from real conflicts in goals or the way various outcomes are valued. How are we to deal with these?

A number of people distinguish between *destructive* and *constructive* conflict. Constructive conflict occurs under the superordinate goal of cooperation. That is, the parties have the overriding goal of wanting everyone to gain "something." In this case, conflict may have beneficial side effects such as bringing issues out into the open quickly and heightening motivation to get things done. For example, a quarrel between husband and wife can bring things into the open that were previously left unsaid and heighten motivation to resolve things and get back to what's important. Conflicts between environmentalists and producers could have the same effects.

Destructive conflict is when everyone loses, or at least the gains are far from equitable in some overall societal sense. Labor-management conflicts can be constructive or extremely destructive. It is possible for both the firm and the union to gain or for both of them to lose big.

The most widely used model of destructive conflict (Deutsch, 1969) goes something like this: It's characterized by an overall tendency to expand and escalate; it often becomes independent of its initiating causes and is likely to continue after these have been forgotten or become irrelevant. A Gresham's Law of Conflict seems to operate and the harmful elements drive out those which would keep the conflict within bounds. There is an increasing reliance on the tactics of threat, coercion, and deception and a shift away from strategies of conciliation, persuasion, and minimizing differences. Within each conflicting party, there is an increasing pressure for uniformity of opinion and a tendency for leadership to fall to the hawks rather than doves.

This kind of escalation and expansion can result from a number of antecedents:

A. When cooperation as a superordinate goal is not present, *competition takes over,* and this transition has a number of implications.

1. Communication between the parties decreases

and becomes more unreliable.

2. The norm evolves that a solution to the conflict is for one side to win.

3. The suspicions and lack of communication heighten differences and minimize awareness of similarities among the parties.

B. *Actions are misperceived* in the sense that motives for acts are given a more positive connotation when you do it than when another party does it (i.e., I'm giving advice--you are meddling; my kids are spirited--your's are delinquent). There are good data to show that the U. S. and U. S. S. R. have mirror images of each other. In the absence of information, there seems to be almost a universal tendency when competing to legitimize your own motives but not the other person's motives.

C. Finally, we must point to the phenomena of *cognitive consistency,* or the well documented tendency to bring a wide range of attitudes and beliefs in line with a particular commitment that has been made. Some theorists (Festinger, 1957) postulate the existence of an actual motive for self-consistency such that if an individual makes a commitment to work for civil rights legislation, their attitudes and beliefs concerning minority groups, southern sheriffs, etc. must be made consistent. Likewise an environmentalist or pollutor who takes a strong stand must then reconcile a host of other beliefs and actions with this commitment and this further polarizes the parties and escalates conflict.

Destructive conflict of varying degrees seems to be becoming more prominent as we become more and more sensitized to how our resource allocation decisions affect the environment. I think we have techniques available that could substantially de-escalate much of the conflict we are experiencing and turn it to more constructive purposes. Whether we will ever use it is another question.

CONFLICT RESOLUTION

What are some ways that conflict might be resolved? The answer really depends on yet another distinction that we must make. Conflict among the parties can be either perceived or real, or some combination of the two. That is, the disagreement in the values attached to specific outcomes or courses of action may accurately reflect the real preferences of the parties or it may in part be due to misunderstanding or lack of information. For example, if two opposing political factions could both be given a clear picture of the complete set of consequences of

changing the tax structure, there might be very little
conflict between them. In the absence of information,
they rely on their conflicting ideologies.

The method of conflict resolution which is selected
is in part a function of which of these two types we are
trying to ameliorate. Perceived conflict calls for one
set of strategies while real conflict calls for another.
An overall strategy dictates that we first try to resolve the conflict in the eye of the beholder and expli-
cate as clearly as possible the conflicts that are real.
Only then would it make sense to institute strategies to
resolve the latter. A complete discussion of methods
of conflict resolution is beyond the scope of the present paper but an outline of the possibilities is as
follows.

Resolving Perceived Conflict

Perceived conflict could result from a lack of
information, inaccurate information, poor communication, or attitudinal differences which have been
learned over a relatively long period of time. Thus,
there are really two major methods of perceived conflict resolution.

1. Simply providing more plentiful and accurate
information might do it. One has to worry about the
credibility of the information but there is a large
literature on that topic to guide us.

2. There are a large number of techniques derived
from behavioral science origins that are directed at re-
versing the expansion of destructive conflict primarily
by re-establishing accurate and frequent communication
among the parties (e.g., see Bennis, 1969). One such
method involves getting the parties to sit down with
each other under the guidance of a skilled group leader
who tries to get them past their stereotypes of each
other. It may include such simple but effective exercises as asking each party to:

(a) Describe their picture of themselves

(b) Describe their picture of the opposition

(c) Describe what they think the opposition thinks
    of them.

This usually reveals a lot of severely discrepant stereotypes and provides a springboard for exploring more accurate perceptions.

This kind of technique is being used fairly extensively in corporate circles to deal with conflict within
the firm itself and has also found its way into police
training programs in community relations.

It may be that after a great deal of work increasing
authentic communication, re-examining stereotypes, and
getting to understand opposing points of view there still
may be genuine conflict about alternative courses of
action. However, at least it will be more on the real
issue and in the majority of cases there should be a
significant move from unproductive conflict to productive
problem solving.

Resolving Real Conflict

Once the real conflict becomes accurately described
then a number of additional resolution methods become
relevant.

1. The game theorists have expanded the classic
theory to deal with how individuals or organizations
behave when two of them are both trying to choose alternatives that maximize utility but the actions of one
conflict with the outcomes of the other. For example,
if a firm chooses to maximize returns on its capital, it
may generate so much pollution in the process that counter action of environmentalists may wipe out its profit
margin altogether. Conversely, if environmentalists
attempt to maximize, they may appear so extreme that they
receive no public support at all and everything is lost.
The methods or rules for evaluating alternatives which
the theory says evolve under these conditions go under
the general label of *maximin*. One specific strategy is
to choose alternatives that minimize the probability of
maximum (that is, really big) losses but still provide
acceptable gains. If all parties follow this strategy
and can realize small gains even though they never get
all they want, then conflict can be resolved. If this
strategy cannot converge on one acceptable alternative,
then the theory is silent and may the best man win.

2. It is also true that technological breakthroughs
do change things. They sometimes make it possible to
resolve highly conflicting outcome preferences by substituting a new outcome. Massive solar generation of
electrical power could have this effect. One often
hears the argument that we have the capability for
eliminating pollution, why don't we? However, the
issue is not quite so dichotomous. There are many
factors influencing the selection of an alternative
and some technological changes deal with more factors
than others. Controlling auto emissions is a good example. The individual consumer probably does make some
tradeoff between his evaluation of the seriousness of
air pollutants and the increased cost of a car.

3. Recall that the controlled anarchist model
did say something about conflict resolution; namely,
that we should let the special interests fight it out
according to the rules currently in use in the country.
It's difficult to take this notion seriously. It might

work in such restricted spheres as union-management conflict where there are established mechanisms for bargaining, negotiations, and legal recourse. However, even here the success of the enterprise seems to rest on the way both the product market and labor markets are balanced.

4. One could again turn to Skinner. As consumers and voters, we could remove much of the conflict by mandating a new set of reinforcement contingencies for the developers and producers of goods and services. Let there be powerful incentives for developing lakeshore property the way it should be developed. Let's get rid of the Federal highway trust fund, etc.

5. One method that is sometimes appropriate is to search for some superordinate goal about which there would be no conflict. For example, husbands and wives sometimes forget their differences in favor of pursuing a more important goal for their children.

6. In some sectors, such as labor-management disputes, conflicts are often resolved by bargaining and a formalization of the bargaining outcome results in a written contract. Supposedly the contract reflects the balance of power (e.g., economic power) and the parties agree that the balance should remain at a certain level for a specified length of time.

7. Finally, conflicts are often resolved according to procedures specified in a constitution or set of by-laws. In a democracy one such procedure is a formal vote of all those empowered to vote.

SUMMARY

To sum up once and for all, I would like to re-emphasize that our problem can be one of faulty decision making, faulty conflict resolution, or both—most likely both. We could change things on the *decision making* side by:

1. Making people explicitly aware of the processes involved, some of which may be maladaptive—especially the use of stereotypes of good alternatives which are heightened by group decision making.

2. Generating more usable information for decision makers regarding outcomes, payoffs, and probabilities.

3. Analyzing the reinforcement contingencies to see if they are what we want them to be.

We could attempt to *resolve conflict* by:

1. Using various means to clear up misperceptions and define the real conflict.

2. Use whatever means are appropriate to resolve the actual conflict that is present.

REFERENCES

Allison, G. T. "Conceptual Models and the Cuban Missile Crisis." *The American Political Science Review,* 1969, 63, 689-718.

Barnard, C. I. *Functions of the Executive.* Cambridge, MA: Harvard University Press, 1938.

Bennis, W. *Organization Development: Its Nature, Origins, and Prospects.* Reading, MA: Addison-Wesley, 1969.

Bolles, R. C. *Theory of Motivation.* New York: Harper & Row, 1967.

Bouchard, T. "Personality, Problem Solving Procedure, and Performance in Small Groups." *Journal of Applied Psychology,* 1969, 53 (No. 1, Part 2), 1-29.

Campbell, J. P., Dunnette, M. D., Lawler, E. E., and Weick, K. E. *Managerial Behavior, Performance, and Effectiveness.* New York: McGraw-Hill, 1970.

Delbecq, A. L., Van De Ven, A. H., and Gustafson, D. H. *Graph Techniques for Program Planning.* Chicago: Scott, Foresman, 1975.

Dion, K. L., Baron, R. S., and Miller, N. "Why Do Groups Make Riskier Decisions Than Individuals?" In L. Berkowitz (ed.) *Advances in Experimental Social Psychology* (vol. 5). New York: Academic Press, 1970.

Deutsch, M. "Conflicts: Productive and Destructive." *Journal of Social Issues,* 1969.

Festinger, L. *A Theory of Cognitive Dissonance.* Evanston, IL: Row & Peterson, 1957.

Hakel, M. D., Hollman, T. D., and Dunnette, M. D. "Accuracy of Interviewers, Certified Public Accountants, and Students in Identifying the Interests of Accountants." *Journal of Applied Psychology,* 1970, 54, 115-119.

Hoffman, L. R. "Group Problem Solving." In L. Berkowitz (ed.) *Advances in Experimental Social Psychology* (Vol. 2). New York: Academic Press, 1965.

Lindblom, C. E. "The Science of Muddling Through." *Public Administration Review,* 1959, 19, 78-88.

March, J. D., and Simon, H. A. *Organizations.* New York: Wiley, 1958.

Simon, H. A. *Administrative Behavior* (2nd Ed.). New York: MacMillan, 1957.

Skinner, B. F. *Beyond Freedom and Dignity.* New York: Knopf, 1971.

Solberg, P. O. *A Study of Decision Making: Job Choice.*
    Cambridge, MA: M.I.T. Press, 1966.

Taylor, D. W. "Decision Making and Problem Solving."
    In J. G. March (ed.), *Handbook of Organizations.*
    Chicago: Rand McNally, 1965.

Vroom, V. *Work and Motivation.* New York: Wiley, 1964.

Vroom, V. "Organizational Choice: A Study of Pre and
    Post Decision Processes." *Organizational Behavior
    and Human Performance*, 1966, 1, 212-226.

Vroom, V., and Yetton, P. *Leadership and Decision
    Making,* Pittsburgh: University of Pittsburgh
    Press, 1973.

Webster, E. C. (ed.) *Decision Making in the Employ-
    ment Interview.* Montreal: Eagle, 1964.

Wright, O. R. "Summary of Research on the Selection
    Interview Since 1964." *Personnel Psychology,*
    1969, 22, 391-414.

Roman R. Andrus

"APPROACHES TO INFORMATION EVALUATION"

MSU Business Topics (19:3), 1971 Summer, pages 40-46.

A number of different approaches may be used in determining the value of information. This article describes a method based on utility theory. Professor Andrus reasons that information has form, time, place and possession utilities. He therefore proposes an approach to evaluation of information which judgmentally compares these values with the cost of providing the information. The approach is interesting because it applies existing economic theory; it also diverges from the conventional methods.

READING SUGGESTIONS

After an introduction to the need for considering the value of information, the article summarizes the value of perfect and imperfect information based on expected outcomes. The major theme of the article is that utility theory is useful in understanding and evaluating value of information where the expected outcome analysis is not possible. Note that utility is subjectively determined when used in practice. Figure 2 is a good summary of the main points of the article.

QUESTIONS

1. What are the utilities which apply to information?
2. Are the four types of utilities independent? If not, identify and give examples of some dependencies.
3. What generalizations are made about information utility?
4. What are the conditions of the information utilities which might cause a manager to discard or disregard information?
5. What does Andrus mean by AVI = EVPI - (EI + MU)?
6. What is the proposed checklist approach to evaluation of information?
7. Describe the process necessary to determine value in each of the four types of utilities. Are users able to perform this processing? How can the situation be improved?

ROMAN R. ANDRUS

Approaches to Information Evaluation

Form, time, place, and possession utilities all offer a perspective for examining user benefits.

Missing, delayed, or inaccurate information generally results in erroneous decisions and opportunity losses. Costs of acquiring and processing information are high. The worth of available information must be compared with its cost.

This article suggests that utility theory will supplement the concept of expected value in determining the worth of information. *Utilities* provide a basis for understanding how the nature of information, exclusive of its content, may facilitate or retard its use and value.

Management decision making is a form of information processing. Traditionally, management has focused on the tasks of acquiring, controlling, and allocating scarce human and capital resources (money and the things that money may purchase). Performance of these tasks requires that management process information. Information is itself a resource. It is necessary for successful handling of all of the other resources for which management is responsible.

Information is an expensive resource. It is costly not only in its acquisition and handling, but in its neglect. Information processing — including acquisition, storage, transmission, and delivery to decision makers — requires expenditures of time,

human resources, and facilities. The selection of pertinent information from masses of available data is an additional time and resource absorbing activity. Data processing equipment and the necessary accompanying software and information processing staff are major investments.

Faulty or inadequate information may result in inappropriate decisions with potentially disastrous misallocation costs, time losses, and excessive opportunity cost losses.

It is apparent that a balance must be reached between the costs of information neglect (value of information) and the costs of information acquisition and processing. Prudent management of information resources demands a theory and technique for determining the value of information which will allow comparison with associated costs.

Management is interested in information, not for its own sake but rather for the benefits it may generate. Value is assigned to information according to the expected result of decisions based on that information, as opposed to results received without the information.

A manager must determine whether or not to acquire information. He must also decide what to do with information which is already available.

Roman R. Andrus is Associate Professor of Marketing and Head, Department of Marketing, Insurance, and Transportation, Graduate School of Management and Business, University of Oregon.

Reprinted by permission of the publisher, Division of Research, Graduate School of Business Administration, Michigan State University. from MSU Business Topics (19:3), 1971 Summer, pages 40-46.

Decisions are made regarding which items to discard, which to expedite, which to combine or otherwise process, and so forth. Explicit criteria for determining the value of a given item of information are essential.

A variety of approaches may be used in determining the value of information:[1]

The simple savings method is based on the estimated cost of decision errors which would have been avoided if the information in question has been acquired and used.

The return on investment approach provides an after-the-fact calculation of the returns (through better decisions) resulting from alternative information investments.

The present value method employs a calculation of the estimated returns on alternative information investments, discounted by the marginal cost of capital. It considers the present value of future benefit flows resulting from information.

The Bayesian approach incorporates the essential concepts of the value of savings and investment returns found in the other approaches.[2] Bayesian analysis considers outcomes of alternative activities, with estimates of their associated payoffs and probabilities of occurrence. This approach is especially useful when the nature of forthcoming information may be anticipated in advance of acquisition. Bayesian analysis may be applied, for example, in determining whether to conduct or forego marketing research.

Utilities provide an additional vehicle for evaluating the worth of information.[3] Utilities are characteristics which explain the worth of a product (or service).

Information, like products, possesses form, time, place, and possession utilities. These characteristics may be used in explaining the value of individual bits of information and in identifying inhibitors to information use.

Information Value — Expected Outcome

The value of perfect information: The results of managerial decisions are influenced not only by the manager's manipulation of factors over which he has control, but also by a variety of uncontrollable, and often unknown, factors. Natural, governmental,

competitive, and consumer forces offer little opportunity for manipulation. Yet the success of his decisions is directly influenced by these factors.

If a manager were able to perfectly predict the behavior of uncontrollable factors which influence his success, he would then be able to manipulate controllable factors to achieve optimal results. The value of perfect information is the value of the optimal strategies which would result from perfect understanding and prediction of the behavior of uncontrollable elements. This information would result in minimized losses and maximized gains, regardless of the behavior of competitors, government, or the whims of consumers. It represents the maximum dollar saved or earned by a perfect strategy.

Imperfect information: Obviously little information is perfect. We are seldom completely accurate in our predictions, or in our understanding of the way things are. We may assume that the value of information will increase with increases in the accuracy of that information. Using the value of perfect information (the maximum benefit obtainable through perfectly understanding the way things are and will be) as a bench mark, we may then determine the value of imperfect information by estimating how closely it will approximate perfection.

Bayesian analysis generates subjective evaluations of the probability that information will be right, and it provides for that information to be discounted according to its deviation from perfect accuracy. The natural next step is to use that discounted evaluation to determine the worth of the proposed information, according to its estimated deviation from perfect information (the worth of which we may estimate).

The focus of Bayesian analysis is to value anticipated information in terms of the expected value of perfect information. Information value is determined in terms of expected results. This is, of course, a logical and valid approach. Rarely can we justify the collection of information for information's sake (outside of universities and libraries). Information is gathered and processed to produce a result. For the marketing manager, that result appears in the form of strategies which direct activities to profitable outcomes.

Information Value — Utility Characteristics

In addition to analysis of the value of information in terms of a predicted, expected result, it is often necessary to evaluate information without the advantage of being able to predict its outcome or usage. This is, in part, the problem of the system designer, the librarian, and the accountant.

The Bayesian approach focuses on the accuracy and use of information. But the nature of information and the way it is processed may also influence its value. Assuming similar content, what makes some information more useful than other information? Can processing, exclusive of content, influence information value? Or is accuracy of information the only consideration? Is there anything in the information itself which is indicative of its value? Or may we only evaluate it in terms of expected results? May we modify the end value of information by the manner in which we process it? If so, how may we enhance the value of a bit of data or intelligence or information? Economics has been chiefly concerned with exploring the meaning and source of value. A simple and meaningful model may be extracted which answers some of the above questions. Attempts to assign values to products (and to services which are not encased in tangible products), may examine utilities: form utility, place utility, time utility, and possession utility. The logic follows: utilities are useful in understanding the value of products. Products may be defined as tangible bundles of services. Information is a service to decision makers. We would expect form, time, place, and possession utilities to be useful concepts for understanding information value.

Information, Form, Time, Place, and Possession Utilities

Form utility. As the form of information more closely matches the requirements of the decision maker, its value (or utility) increases. There is a strong likelihood that information which utilizes an unfamiliar format or jargon will not be translated, let alone used. It will probably be ignored. Understandability is an important consideration in evaluating the form utility of information.

Data volume also seems to be a chief concern in the design of information systems. The following complaint of an executive in a newly computerized firm is an example: "When I had my daily reports from the field I knew exactly what was happening. Now, I get a two-inch stack of computer printout daily, and I have no idea what is happening." Russell L. Ackoff argues that a major fallacy in information system design is that there is not enough information.[4] The problem is that frequently too much undigested information reaches the decision maker. Good market researchers long ago learned to overlay their studies with "executive summaries" for busy decision makers.

The form of the information delivered to the decision maker is a major determinant of its value. The format, jargon, symbolic system, and volume of information all contribute to the presence or absence of form utility. Information obviously may be evaluated in terms of form utility.

Time utility. If decisions are to be based on information, the information must be available before the decision is made. This appears obvious, yet insuring that the data are available when they are needed is a significant problem. Missing or tardy information results in costly delays or errors in urgent decisions. They may "derail" a manager's trend of thought or line of reasoning. For these reasons, data processing equipment has been designed to provide instantaneous (real time) delivery and display. The decision process dictates what information is needed and when it is needed. Most decision deadlines are not so short as to demand real time delivery. However, if information is not available, the process is interrupted and perhaps permanently redirected. Availability when needed (time utility) is an expensive component of information value.

Place utility (physical accessibility). Place of availability, like time utility, is a determinant of the value and usage of information. Unless information storage and library facilities provide for access and delivery, the information is useless as well as costly. Many of the developments in display hardware and on-line terminals are designed to maximize the place utility, as well as time utility, of information.

Possession utility (organizational location). Control of information is an important facilitator or inhibitor of managerial performance. The platitude *knowledge is power* has meaning for information management. Internal structure and external effectiveness are functions of the location of information within the firm. Possession is a significant information utility for which men have maneuvered since society's beginnings. The impact which a given piece of information may have on company performance is influenced not only by form and timeliness but also by its organizational location. The possessor of information strongly dictates its value.

Perception of the Value of Information

Value may be placed on information through comparing its outcome with that of perfect information, or by evaluating the presence of the various information utilities. These models provide guidelines, not absolute measures of information value. Whether discounting the value of perfect information or examining utilities, the determination of the value of information is a subjective process dependent upon the evaluator's perception of these features. The way in which the user of information perceives its source, format, focus, and so forth, is the real determinant of the value of information. C. West Churchman has correctly argued that before we may design an information system we need a "user model," a model of the way in which the decision maker selects and applies information.[5] Perhaps the major benefit to be derived from models for examining the value of information lies in understanding of the user of that information. The way in which decision makers differently perceive the individual information utilities will provide a partial basis for an information user model, as will the analysis of managerial style.[6]

Information Utility Generalizations

In spite of differences in the perceptions of users of information it is possible to make some generalizations regarding the value of information.[7]

We may observe that the value of information increases as: (1) the format, language, and degree of detail approach the desires of the user; (2) the ease and right of access increases; and (3) the time of acquisition approaches the time of use (as long as it does not occur after the decision).

We may conversely generalize that information value will decrease as (1) the format and language become less understandable; (2) the volume of detail increases; (3) the physical and organizational access to the information becomes more difficult; and (4) the time of acquisition is further from the time of use (and meaningless after the decision).

The expected value approach and the concept of information utility are obviously complementary. They lead to a symbolic representation of actual value of information: $AVI = EVPI - (EI+MU)$. The Actual Value of Information is equal to the Expected Value of Perfect Information discounted for Expected Inaccuracies and Missing Utilities. This symbolic approach may in turn be visualized by a very simple conceptual flow diagram for structuring the perception of the actual value of information, as shown in Figure 1.

Of course, it is easier to identify utilities by their absence than to measure their presence. A pragmatic approach would be to check for the absence of specific utilities, and then to either redesign the system to provide the utilities or to discount the information for the absence of them. This approach leads to an examination of the parameters and possible actions imposed by incomplete information utilities, as shown in Figure 2 on page 45.

A check list may also be used in examining the utility value of available information. It is equally applicable to marketing information, information generated for other uses within the firm, and to unexpected, unsolicited information. A basic information utility check list might be the following:

● Is the language, format, and presentation of the information easily comprehensible to the user?

● Is all extraneous material removed? Maximum summarization?

● Is the time of information delivery near (but in advance) of the time of need?

● Is there easy access and retrieval of needed information?

● Are there unnecessary organizational barriers to information access and usage?

There is no effort to assign weights to the check list factors, nor to provide a formula for melding the individual items into an index of information value.

FIGURE 1

A Conceptual Approach to the Evaluation of Information

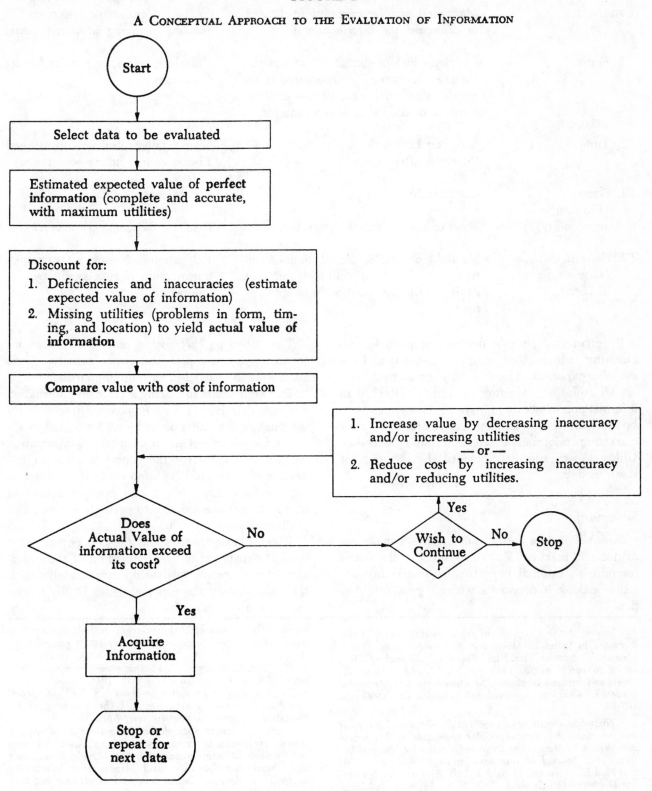

FIGURE 2

UTILITIES:	PARAMETERS (ABSOLUTE LIMITS) *Managers may be expected to discard,* *or disregard the information if:*	POSSIBLE ACTIONS AND CORRECTIVE MEASURES *(usually incurring additional costs)*
I. Form	Language and/or format not understood Volume excessive: Time required to examine information exceeds the intuitive estimate of the value of the contents	Translate, revise, or change format Condense
II. Time	Received before need perceived Received after needed	Store against possible future need Insure against future occurrence
III. Place (Physical accessibility)	Inaccessible Time or cost of access excessive	Create access Relocate data, change access
IV. Possession (Organizational location)	No right of use, or closed communication channels due to conflicting sub-unit goals, authority relationships and so forth.	Relocate information; alter or open transmission channels; change relationships.

Bayesian analysis provides an approach for examining information value. Conceptual flow models, parameter identification, and check lists are all useful in evaluating the utilities attached to information. However, much obviously needs to be done in the development of specific models for marketing information selection and processing. Utility theory suggests some of the elements of these models.

Summary

Information is a costly and essential component of decision making. Since marketing is the firm's response to external opportunities, marketing decision making is disastrous without good information.

The gathering, processing, and delivery of information is a complex and costly activity. Some basis must be used for making comparisons.[8]

Two approaches to placing a value on information are considered: (1) *The Bayesian approach:* By discounting the value of perfect information to account for imperfections in anticipated information we are able to derive the expected value of imperfect information; (2) *Utility analysis:* By examining the form, time, place, and possession utilities of information we are able to partially explain, and perhaps modify, its value.

Since either approach and the concept of value itself is dependent on the perception of the evaluator, it is necessary to develop user models which take into account these perceptions. Utility theory may also assist us in this task.

1. Several of these approaches are enumerated and briefly discussed in James H. Myers and A. Coskun Samli, "Management Control of Marketing Research," *Journal of Marketing Research*, August 1969, pp. 267-77, and in James H. Myers and Richard R. Mead, *The Management of Marketing Research* (Scranton: International Textbook Co., 1969, pp. 107-14.

2. There are a number of excellent discussions of Bayesian analysis available. Two especially applicable to this article are: Frank M. Bass, "The Expected Value of Additional Information," *Journal of Business*, January 1963, pp. 77-90; and Paul E. Green and Donald S. Tull, *Research for Marketing Decisions* (Englewood Cliffs, N. J.: Prentice-Hall, Inc., 1970).

3. The concepts of form utility, time utility, place utility, and possession utility have long been used in describing the functioning of marketing systems.

4. Russell L. Ackoff, "Management Misinformation Systems," *Management Science* (December 1967), pp. B-147 — B-156.

5. C. West Churchman, "On Management Information Systems," *The McKinsey Quarterly*, Fall, 1969, pp. 43-51.

6. This concept is amplified in Donald S. Tull and Gerald S. Albaum, "Decision Processes and the Valuation of Information, *Oregon Business Review*, April 1971.

7. Amstutz's classic discussion of dimensions of information system evaluation is essentially concerned with the same determinants of information value. See Arnold E. Amstutz, "The Marketing Executive and Management Information Systems," in *Science, Technology and Marketing*, ed. Raymond M. Haas (Chicago: American Marketing Association, Fall 1966), pp. 69-86.

8. For another perspective on the worth of information see Adrian M. McDonough, *Information Economics and Management Systems* (New York: McGraw-Hill, Inc., 1963).

John Dearden

"MIS IS A MIRAGE"

Harvard Business Review (50:1), 1972 January-February, pages 90-99

More than anyone else, Professor Dearden has played the role of devil's advocate in MIS. Over the past several years he has effectively caused academicians and practitioners to re-examine their notions and assumptions concerning MIS. Honestly responding to his challenge of MIS thinking is always a fruitful activity for the student of MIS.

The article is not a careful, logical assessment of the MIS concept; rather it is a mixture of valid, invalid, and irrelevant points about the MIS concept. Nevertheless, it is a classic polemic in the field of MIS because of its interesting, controversial style and because of wide readership accorded the article. The article evoked a number of letters to the editor, some of which follow. Many advocates of MIS have promised too much and delivered too little at too great a cost, so the major thrust of Dearden's attack strikes a responsive cord in many organizations.

In this article, Dearden considers it absurd for an organization to try to develop a single, completely integrated management information system. He argues that MIS educational programs are really just teaching about computer-based information systems and that it is impossible to produce an MIS expert with the requisite skills in computer technology, with an understanding of all the functional application areas of business, and with a knowledge of the management process. He contends that coordinated systems for functional areas can be developed without a "total systems approach" and that centralizing the control of a company's information system is simply not feasible.

To rectify the failings of the past, Dearden suggests that an organization place competent people in the information systems area, examine the interfaces between the various systems, examine the logistics system since most early successes were in this area, organize a central computer group for systems control, and establish a position of vice president for administration. The article ends with a set of questions for his critics.

READING SUGGESTIONS

This article should be read thoughtfully and with a sense of challenge to the author. Identify Dearden's specific criticisms of MIS thinking and practice. Also, identify his underlying assumptions. Then try to analyze Dearden's thinking by tracing the criticisms back to some of his definitions, stated and unstated assumptions, and other statements.

The following is a list of some of the major points that Dearden makes. In some cases, there is a slight rearrangement of points for the sake of clarity:
1. An MIS is a computer-based information system. This means it does not include important (especially qualitative) information vital to management, and since the MIS group designs only the computer-based information system it has no impact on the large noncomputer-based information/decision/control system.
2. The MIS approach is based on assumptions that:
   a. Management information is a subject for study and specialization. This is said to mean an MIS consultant can design an MIS system (from the top down, starting with the president) or an MIS staff department can design an MIS system.
   b. The systems approach can and should be used.
   c. The advantages from MIS specialists are:
      1) Better design than from users, 2) unified design, 3) top down design, 4) less costly design, 5) better maintained system.
3. The four fallacies and one misconception.
   a. The fallacies:
      1) Management information is homogeneous enough for specialization. (True MIS expert does not and cannot exist.)
      2) Separately designed functional systems are insufficient. (Coordinated systems for functional areas can be developed without a total systems approach.)
      3) The systems approach is a boon. (The systems approach is merely an elaborate phrase for good management.)
      4) It is practicable to centralize control over the information system. (Centralizing the control of a company's information system in

a staff group creates problems that are
insolvable; therefore, it is simply not
feasible.)

   b. The misconception that information system expertise in one function is transferrable to another.

4. The principal cause of poor information systems is
incompetent or ineffective people in charge.

5. Dearden's approach

   a. Place competent people in each of the formal information systems

   b. Examine the interfaces

   c. Examine the logistics system

   d. Organize a central computer group for systems
control

   e. Create an administrative vice president, if one
does not already exist.

6. Questions for his critics.

QUESTIONS

1. How does Dearden define an MIS? What are the characteristics and direct implications which stem from
this definition?

2. What kind of a system does Dearden envision as the
MIS (e.g., a monolithic total system or a federation
of functional subsystems)?

3. Based on the inital definition of MIS, does Dearden
imply that an MIS must be built all at once?

4. Why does Dearden say management information systems
are not a proper subject for study and specialization?

5. What evidence might suggest that there is a growing
body of knowledge and skills to be imparted in formal
educational programs and from one area of information
systems development to another? List some overall
knowledge and skill areas.

6. What is Dearden's objection to the system's approach?

7. What relationship does Dearden assume between the MIS
specialist and the user?

8. What organizational position does Dearden assume for
the MIS?

9. Dearden suggests that most early successes in information technology occurred in logistics systems. Identify some factors which may have contributed to these
successes. Do these contributing factors exist in
other areas of MIS application?

10. Which of the points in Dearden's approach would be
acceptable to MIS specialists, as you understand it?
Why?

11. What is the effect of this article when read by
those in academia? When read by those in industry?

12. How would you answer the five questions Dearden posed
for his critics at the end of the article?

John Dearden

MIS is a mirage

*Can a single, integrated system be devised
to fill all of management's information needs?
Only if Superman lends a helping hand*

Foreword

Every company of any size has many information systems, both formal and informal. The formal systems it uses cover such a variety of territory that one man cannot possibly comprehend the mass of details and principles required to design a single supersystem that embraces them all. Even a group of systems experts cannot create such a supersystem, the author argues, because the components that must be amalgamated are too different in their natures to be fused

together effectively. After demonstrating the futility of the MIS approach, the author recommends practical steps for reforming defective information systems.

Mr. Dearden is Professor of Business Administration at the Harvard Business School. He is well known to HBR readers, especially for his significant contributions to the theory of divisional control. (A list of Mr. Dearden's previous HBR articles on information systems appears in the ruled insert on page 98.)

Some years ago I expressed the opinion that "of all the ridiculous things that have been foisted on the long-suffering executive in the name of science and progress, the real-time management information system is the silliest."[1]

I no longer believe this statement is true. We now have something even sillier: the current fad for "*the* management information system," whether it is called the Total System, the Total Management Information System, the Management Information System, or simply MIS.

I certainly do not mean to suggest that a company does not need good management information systems—nothing could be further from the truth. But the notion that a company can and ought to have an expert (or a group of experts) create for it a single, completely integrated supersystem—an "MIS"—to help it govern every aspect of its activity is absurd.

For many businessmen, it is probably inconceivable that the lofty phrases and glittering

promises surrounding the MIS conceal a completely unworkable concept. Yet this is exactly what I propose to demonstrate—that a company that pursues an MIS embarks on a wild-goose chase, a search for a will-o'-the-wisp.

Let me first try to explain what I understand by the "MIS concept" and examine its alleged advantages, and then show why the concept is unworkable. Then I shall be in a position to recommend some practical remedies for defective management information systems, which certainly constitute a real problem for executives today.

Confusion between terms

It is difficult even to describe the MIS in a satisfactory way, because this conceptual entity is embedded in a mish-mash of fuzzy thinking and incomprehensible jargon. It is nearly impossible to obtain any agreement on how MIS problems are to be analyzed, what shape their solutions might take, or how these solutions are to be

1. "Myth of Real-Time Management Information," HBR May-June 1966, p. 123.

implemented. This confusion makes it very difficult to attack the concept, because no matter what assumptions a critic makes about the nature of the MIS approach, a proponent can always reply that *his* use of the term is different from others'.

But there is a common thread which runs through the various uses of the term, a thread that at once unifies but also subverts the MIS literature. This thread is the computer-based information system.

Computer-based activity . . .

Wherever the MIS is discussed, it is almost invariably stated that a management information system does not necessarily require a computer and that many forms of management information are not computer-based.

Yet, if one looks at what is actually being discussed, he quickly discovers that the term "MIS" is used, essentially, to stand for "computer-based information systems." For example, a recent article in *Business Week* read as follows:

"[Some], concerned that systems analysts are . . . a 'mixed bag' whose training and knowledge are a hit-or-miss proposition, are convinced that management information systems (MIS) is *the* emerging field in business administration. Both Wharton and MIT have tailored programs especially for systems specialists, but no school has gone further than the University of Minnesota, whose B-school now offers MS and PhD degrees in management information systems and has launched an MIS research center. Since the center's opening three years ago, MIS Director Gordon B. Davis and his staff have worked to develop 12 new systems-related courses—from on-line, real-time systems to a seminar on software. In addition, the program's 50 MS and 22 PhD candidates spend a good portion of their time alone and in teams at work on actual computer problems in industry."[2]

It seems evident to me that MIS education as described here is principally education in computer-based information systems.

It is vital to note, first of all, that the information generated by this kind of system does not include a great deal of the information that is most important to management—especially, important *qualitative* information. Second, a specialist group that develops such a system is usually responsible for implementing only one part of any of a company's individual management information systems—namely, that part that interfaces directly with the computer. For example, such a group has little (if anything) to do with specifying the nature of an accounting and financial control system, although it may be responsible for the computer programming this system employs.

My conclusion, therefore, is that such a group has little impact on most of the information supplied to management, particularly at upper levels. Consequently it is ridiculous to say that it creates (or *can* create) a total management information system.

. . . vs. MIS

To the extent that MIS refers only to company information systems that use a computer base and to the extent that everyone understands this limitation, I have no serious quarrel with the trend to MIS; it is vital that management tightly control its computer-based information systems, and in general the so-called MIS groups seem designed to guarantee a tight rein to management.

In my experience, however, such a limited definition of MIS is *not* what advocates of this approach to information systems mean when they use the term. They intend something novel and far more global, some entity that can provide revolutionary benefits we cannot derive from the traditional approach. Walter Kennevan suggests this definition of the MIS:

"A management information system is an organized method of providing past, present and projection information relating to internal operations and external intelligence. It supports the planning, control and operational function of an organization by furnishing uniform information in the proper time-frame to assist the decision-making process."[3]

This is approximately what I perceive most people to mean by MIS. And if this definition seems grandiose, I can only remark that *"the* management information system" describes a grandiose idea. If the definition were less global in its scope, it would not measure up to the term. If, for example, one were to limit the definition to the context of a company's financial accounting programs, he would have to speak of the *financial* MIS of the company, rather than its general MIS.

2. June 5, 1971, p. 96.

3. "MIS Universe," *Data Management*, September 1970.

However, in practice, no such limitations are intended. Kennevan's inclusive definition of the MIS approach is quite consistent with the nearly universal benefits claimed for it.

The MIS approach

Given this inclusive definition, how is management to apply it? In other words, how should management think about the problem of setting up an MIS?

Fundamental assumptions

First, it appears that if management wishes to subscribe to the theory of the MIS, it must make up its mind to accept two fundamental (if highly questionable) assumptions that are quite different from traditional ones made in this area:

1. Management information is a subject for study and specialization. That is, it is sufficiently homogeneous so that a set of principles and practices can be esablished for evaluating all management's information needs and satisfying them. In short, the MIS approach attacks all the problems of management information as a whole, rather than by individual areas, such as finance and marketing. This homogeneity is a necessary assumption, since without it there is no reason why general solutions to a management's information requirements can be found.

2. The systems approach can and should be used in analyzing management's information requirements. Proponents claim the systems approach is necessary for mastering the sprawl of requirements and for synthesizing the general MIS solution. (I shall have more to say about the systems approach later.)

Diagnosis & development

Once management has accepted these two assumptions, it can begin to develop an MIS program. As the theory goes, there seem to be two techniques for setting to work:

☐ Management can hire an MIS expert to act as a superconsultant to the president of the company. This expert studies the types of problems that the president must solve, the decisions that he must make, and so forth, and recommends methods for satisfying the president's total information requirements. He then drops to lower levels of management and provides the same services there.

In general, the expert depends on others to implement his recommendations. For example, the controller becomes responsible for changing the cost accounting system in the way the consultant recommends.

☐ Management can create a staff department that reports to the top. This group is responsible for the company's computer-based systems but also provides the same type of diagnoses and evaluations as the superconsultant.

The staff group, unlike the consultant, usually has responsibility for implementation.

Its alleged advantages . . .

Under this approach, then, either a single person or a group of persons is responsible for developing and overseeing the construction of the entire management information system. This concentration of authority and responsibility in the hands of systems experts supposedly creates a number of significant advantages:

☐ Experts schooled in the MIS "discipline" can analyze management's information needs more effectively than can the people traditionally responsible for satisfying them. Moreover, these experts can better determine which techniques will best meet these needs.

☐ Because the MIS is developed as a unified, single system, rather than as a number of separate systems, it is completely coordinated and completely consistent.

☐ Information needs are determined from the top down. Hence the top will be in better control; the frequent practice of letting lower management decide what information will pass upward is eliminated.

☐ The company reduces its direct information costs by eliminating systems. Also, the MIS itself is cheaper to run because it has been designed by information experts who know the most economical means for satisfying management's information needs.

☐ Since one expert or group is responsible for the system, management's desire that the system be kept up-to-date can readily be satisfied.

In short, the proponents promise, experts can design an MIS that is more effective, more efficient, more consistent, and more dynamic than the haphazard aggregate of individual systems a company would otherwise employ.

These are impressive advantages that any manager would enjoy, and doubtless this approach was developed to solve the real problems of poor information that have been plaguing management with increasing frequency. The growing complexity and the pace of change of modern business, especially in the last ten years, have surely made many information systems obsolete and many more inadequate for present tasks.

Equally, the last ten years have seen the extensive development of information technology, management science, and systems analysis—a development that has been accompanied by rapid growth in the number of experts working in information systems.

To some—that is, the proponents of MIS—it seemed logical to centralize the development and control of information systems in the hands of these experts. After all, the problems that beset information systems have been the result of change and growth, they reasoned; and these problems could perhaps be solved by using the new information technology that had been developing simultaneously.

Several companies have tried this approach, and many people currently advocate it. In spite of its apparent logic, however, I know of no company in which it has worked out. This fails to surprise me because, as I have already implied, I believe the whole MIS approach is fundamentally fallacious.

. . . & its real fallacies

There are four fallacies and one serious misconception inherent in the MIS approach, as I have described it. The fallacies are these:

◊ Management information is sufficiently homogeneous so that it can be made an area of specialization for an expert.

◊ If the different information systems ordinarily used by a company are developed separately, the resulting management information system will necessarily be uncoordinated and therefore inefficient and unsatisfactory.

◊ The "systems" approach is a new boon to business administration.

◊ It is practicable to centralize the control over a company's entire management information system.

The misconception is this:

◊ The specialist expertise that creates a good logistics system for a company can extend its talents into the broad domain of general com-

pany activity and create a general management information system.

There is no reason to suppose an MIS group can actually do this—in fact, there is good reason to think it cannot.

Let me refute these errors one by one.

1. The true MIS expert does not and cannot exist.

A complete management information system consists of such a huge assortment of different types of activities that no man can possess a broad enough set of special skills to apply to even a small proportion of them. Consider the skills required to build any one of these individual information systems.

The financial accounting and control system: This includes preparation of financial statements, development of budgets and long-range plans, analyses of capital investments, publication of product costs, and so forth.

Traditionally, the controller is responsible for all these financial subsystems; with respect to the financial information systems, he plays the role that the MIS expert is supposed to play in the general management information systems. In complementary fashion, the MIS expert must have a thorough understanding of the controller's systems function.

The logistics information system: This system controls the flow of goods from the purchase of raw materials to the physical distribution of the finished products. Next to the financial control system, it is probably the most comprehensive information system in the typical manufacturing business.

A logistics system normally consists of several subsystems of varying degrees of independence. For example, there could be distinct systems for different product lines. Within each product line, furthermore, there could be subsystems for procurement, production scheduling, finished goods, inventory control, and so forth, and still others for plant utilization and expansion. Depending on its industry, a company has a larger or smaller number of complex, interrelated logistics information subsystems.

The critical point to note here is that the logistics information system is almost completely different from the financial information system. In point of fact, most of the skills needed to develop financial information systems are of no use in developing logistics information systems and vice versa. Even the user relationships are different. In building a financial information system, the controller develops a system that provides information for management outside the finance function, whereas logistics information is normally developed and used by the people directly concerned with logistics.

Furthermore, logistics subsystems frequently have little in common with each other, so that an expert in one type of subsystem might not be able to transfer his expertise to a different type. For example, there may be little or no similarity between a procurement information system and a finished-goods distribution system. Like the financial system, the logistics information system or subsystem is a job for a specialist.

The marketing information systems: Like the two systems just described, the marketing information system can also consist of a number of subsystems. A company may maintain separate subsystems for separate product lines; and within a product line, it may maintain further subsystems for advertising and sales promotion, short-term sales forecasting, long-term sales forecasting, product planning, and so forth.

Again, the critical point is this—a marketing information system is almost completely different from the other two systems. Consequently, expertise in either or both of the other systems would be of limited value in developing a marketing information system and vice versa.

Legal services, industrial relations, and public relations: One of the major purposes of each of these staff functions is to provide top management with specialized information different from that provided by any other staff office and different from that provided by the three information systems previously described.

R&D reporting: The information system management requires in this area is distinct from all others, and expertise in these other areas offers limited help in developing an R&D information system.

In short, except in the small company (which probably needs only simple systems), there are several information systems that have very few similarities and many wide differences. Consequently, it makes no sense to regard the processes of developing and implementing these several management information systems as constituting a single and homogeneous activity.

I conclude that few, if any, individuals have the training to call themselves experts in management information systems. Indeed I believe it is much more practical to teach the new information technology to the functional experts than to teach information technologists functional specialties. After all, the man who could master all the functional specialties—the true MIS expert—would have to be an intellectual superman; and hence he does not and cannot exist except, perhaps, as a very rare exception.

If an MIS can be implemented at all, it can only be implemented by a staff group, and one of considerable size.

2. Coordinated systems for functional areas can be developed without a 'total systems approach.'

"Unless you develop the MIS as a single, integrated system, all you will get is a bunch of unrelated, uncoordinated, ineffective systems." If I have heard this statement once, I have heard it a hundred times; and it still is not true.

I have seen many systems that have intricate interfaces with one another and that are still efficient and effective. In the automobile industry, for example, the development of a new model car involves many functions—styling, engineering, product planning, finance, facility planning, procurement, and production scheduling. Each functional unit develops its internal information system for controlling its part of the operation; in addition, at each interface, the functional units exchange the information necessary to maintain coordination between them.

If an information system is ineffective, the cause is very likely to be the incompetence of the people responsible for it, *not* the absence of the general MIS approach. In this connection I might quote William M. Zani:

"Most companies have not conceived and planned their management information system with any significant amount of attention to their intended function of supporting the manager as he makes his decisions."[4]

Zani goes on to suggest a new approach to developing an MIS as a solution to this situation. My solution would be to make some personnel changes, because anyone who fails to design an information system for its users is incompetent.

Such incompetence is very prevalent. I have seen dozens of companies where management is

4. "Blueprint for MIS," HBR November-December 1970, p. 95.

not receiving half the relevant accounting information that could be made available if the financial information system had been properly designed in the first place. And although I am not sufficiently expert in other types of information systems to know whether the same situation exists there, I have no reason to believe accounting is worse than the others.

To assert that such problems as these result from the independent development of different information systems, rather than from sheer and ordinary incompetence, is simply ridiculous—and to recommend the "MIS cure" is even more ridiculous. To ensure that a company has efficient information systems which are well coordinated with one another, management need only bear down on the personnel in the various functional areas who are responsible.

3. 'The systems approach' is merely an elaborate phrase for 'good management.'

There are many definitions of the systems approach, but the following is representative:

"The systems approach to management is basically a way of thinking. The organization is viewed as an integrated complex of interdependent parts which are capable of sensitive and accurate interaction among themselves and with their environment." [5]

What does this mean? It took me some time to figure it out.

When the systems approach first appeared in the literature, I had a great deal of difficulty understanding the concept; and my confusion increased until I started asking people this question: "What would an executive do differently if he were to adopt the systems approach in place of the traditional one?"

Without exception, the replies I received made assumptions about the traditional approach that simply are not valid. For example, some assumed that the executive perceives his organization as static; others, that he fails to consider the interaction of related variables. In other words, the replies were predicated on an incompetent, even a stupid, executive.

Thus I concluded that the alleged advantages of the systems approach really result from the difference between an adequate and an inadequate manager. If you doubt this, I invite you to ask the question I did the next time you hear

someone champion the systems approach to management.

It is therefore not surprising that good managers follow the systems approach, because this approach is merely the ancient art of management. Would a competent business executive plan a major expansion program without considering the sources and timing of funds, the availability of people, the possible reactions of competitors, and so forth? Certainly not. And he would consider them in relation to one another.

My conclusion, then, is that the systems approach is precisely what every good manager has been using for centuries. The systems approach may be new to science and to weapons acquisition, but it is certainly not new to business administration.

At this point, let me summarize briefly. First, an MIS would have to be developed by a *group* composed of experts in the various types of information systems used by management. This must be so because the possibility that a single individual will be expert in *all* types of information is remote. Second, the approach taken by the MIS group would be approximately the same as that taken by any competent and expert manager working in one of the functional information systems.

How, then, does the MIS approach differ from the traditional approach to information systems?

The only difference I can see is that a company's management information system would be the responsibility of one centralized group; whereas, traditionally, the information systems experts have been located in the various functional areas. This brings me to the last fallacy—that such centralization is practicable.

4. Centralizing the control of a company's information systems in a staff group creates problems that are insoluble; therefore it is simply not feasible.

It is theoretically possible to assemble a staff MIS group that is sufficiently large and diversified to have expertise in all the formal information systems described earlier—marketing, manufacturing (logistics), finance, and so forth. But to organize this group properly, the company should appoint an executive vice president for information to supervise the work of the group—that is to say, the systems of the staff vice presidents, the controller, the logistics information group, the marketing information group, and so

5. Spyros Makridakis, "The Whys and Wherefores of the Systems Approach," *European Business*, Summer 1971.

forth. But what would this accomplish? Let me ignore the fact that no sane manufacturing or marketing executive would delegate the responsibility for his information system.

One result might be that this executive vice president for information would promote better coordination between functional areas. On the other hand, of course, the problems of coordination would drastically increase in the manufacturing and marketing areas because the responsibility for the information systems had been separated from the people who hold the line responsibility. And in any event, simply having all of the information groups, including the MIS group, report to a single executive would hardly change the *approach* to developing information systems. Thus the special value of the MIS approach is still obscure.

In short, it seems to me that if any of the MIS people are competent to tell the functional experts what to do, they should be in the functional area. I see no logical way to centralize the responsibility for all the management information systems.

Significant misconception

If the MIS approach is as fallacious as I believe it to be, how has it been able to maintain even a superficial credibility?

The answer, as I have hinted earlier, is this: the early success of information technology in renovating logistics systems has been so great that there is a natural inclination to try the same methods on the company information systems as a whole.

This misconception has evolved in a natural enough way. Responsibility for a logistics system has traditionally been divided among several executives—e.g., in purchasing, in manufacturing, and in marketing. This divided responsibility has often resulted in poor coordination throughout the system. Furthermore, the people responsible for the system have often been old-fashioned in their methods and relatively unskilled in information techniques. Thus a vacuum has frequently existed with respect to the responsibility for a company's logistics information system into which the burgeoning information technology has moved easily and successfully.

However, as we have seen, there is no reason to suppose that the principles of information technology used so successfully in the logistics area can be generalized to apply to the other

management information systems within a company or to the management information system considered as a whole.

Thus, when a group of experts has completed its overhaul of the logistics system, it will *not* be in a position to attack the financial, marketing, or any other system. First, the group will not have the specialist expertise required. Second, the type of problems the group may have found in the logistics area will almost certainly not exist in other areas if the staffs in these other areas are competent. Third, there will be no responsibility vacuum as in the logistics area; the MIS group will not be in a position to take over by default.

If you have any doubt about the validity of these statements, I suggest that you examine the kinds of things that any MIS group is doing. Outside of the routine computer systems, you will almost certainly find them concerned basically with parts of the *logistics* information system only.

Roots of poor information

So far this article has been quite negative. Now I should like to suggest some positive actions to mitigate the information crisis, if it can be called that. Before I propose these actions, however, it is appropriate to review the causes of management information problems.

As I have pointed out, the principal cause of poor information systems is that we have put incompetent or ineffective people in charge of these systems.

The secondary causes are somewhat more complicated.

Growing use of computers

Computers and computer-related systems activities have been growing very rapidly, and currently the cost of these activities has become very significant in many companies. In spite of large expenditures, however, the quality of the information available to management appears unimproved.

One reason is, of course, that some computer installations are not run effectively. Another is that the computer-based information systems have been oversold; management has been led to expect much more than it has received. In other words, management's dissatisfaction with its information occurs, not from any deterioration in its information systems, but from its inflated expectations.

Interface conditions

Individual systems change and improve at different rates, and this creates problems at the interfaces between them. For example, operations research techniques, used in modern logistics systems, require much more sophisticated cost accounting information than traditional cost accounting techniques can generate. Problems can also occur at the interface between production and marketing, because production-scheduling techniques are frequently much more sophisticated than the techniques ordinarily used in market forecasting.

In general, the benefits of advanced techniques may be largely lost where they are dependent on primitive ones. (To some extent, of course, the problem of proper coordination at the interfaces reflects the competency of the staff involved. Other things being equal, only an incompetent would use an advanced technique whose effectiveness would be undermined by inadequate support.)

Rapidity of change

Many companies are changing very rapidly, and it is necessary that their information systems keep pace. In some companies, information systems are *not* keeping pace. To some extent, this is caused by the inability of the staff personnel traditionally responsible for information systems to react to change. After all, many people who were once perfectly adequate in a relatively static situation become ineffective in a dynamic situation.

Greater management challenge

Management must always operate with insufficient information. And frequently, the more important the decision, the greater the uncertainty. In many areas the truth of these statements is becoming more salient because, while the role of management is becoming more complex, the new information technology is not helping significantly.

For example, I have spent many years working on control systems for decentralized companies. The problems of control in such companies today are much more difficult than they were ten years ago—increases in size, complexity, and geo-

graphical dispersion have made control much more difficult. Yet the new information technology has been of little help in this area, simply because the problems of controlling decentralized divisions do not lend themselves to computerized or mathematical solutions.

Accordingly, it is important to realize that part of our information crisis results from the nature of the present business environment. We shall simply have to live with it. This does not mean, of course, that we should not continue trying to improve the situation.

Toward real solutions

Any company that believes it is facing genuine management information problems and wants to solve them should consider the following measures.

1. Place competent people in each of the formal information systems.

To my mind there is no question that incompetency is the leading cause of problems in many management information systems. Hence the obvious answer is to retrain or replace the incompetents.

2. Examine the interfaces.

This is best done in connection with system evaluation, and the examination should focus on these evaluative questions:

○ Is there adequate communication between individual groups at all important interfaces?

The executive might bear in mind formal techniques such as scheduled meetings and formal agreements.

○ Does each group involved in an interface know enough about the other interfacing systems to do its job effectively?

This is a question of education. For example, cost accountants should know enough about company operations-research models to be sure these models are providing correct information; or, at the very least, they should be able to explain to the OR group the relevant limitations of the information their group can supply. On the other hand, the OR people should know enough about cost accounting to ask for the right type of data and to appreciate the limitations in the data they receive.

But although this is principally a matter of

education, it may well be that some staff members are not intellectually capable of handling interface requirements, and they may have to be replaced.

3. Examine the logistics system.

Originally many logistics systems were organized for manual data processing and have never been changed. Equally, the procurement, production, and distribution functions typically report to different executives, and consequently no one is formally responsible for the logistics information system. Since it is here that computers and information technology are most applicable, management should evaluate its logistics area and,

---

Readers particularly interested in this topic may wish to consult these previous HBR articles by Professor Dearden:

"Can Management Information Be Automated?" March-April 1964, p. 128.

"Computers: No Impact on Divisional Control," January-February 1967, p. 99.

"How to Organize Information Systems," March-April 1965, p. 65.

"Myth of Real-Time Management Information," May-June 1966, p. 123.

For more perspective on the CBIS-MIS controversy, readers may also find these HBR articles helpful:

Warren F. McFarlan, "Problems in Planning the Information System," March-April 1971, p. 75.

William M. Zani, "Blueprint for MIS," November-December 1970, p. 95.

---

where appropriate, reorganize it and make a staff unit, responsible for its logistics information system, report to the company officer who directs the logistic system itself.

4. Organize a central computer group for systems control.

Computer use will continue to expand, and it is vital that management maintain central control over computers and computer-based information systems.[6] Such a group should be responsible for overseeing all computer-related work—for long-range planning, coordination, and control of all computer acquisitions and applications. In addition, it should be responsible for coordinating

6. See Warren F. McFarlan, "Problems in Planning the Information System," HBR March-April 1971, p. 75.

computer-based systems and might even undertake the systems and implementation work in a situation where several organization groups use the same data base.

Most companies already have such groups. Some are even called "MIS groups," although, in reality, they have authority only over computer-related work.

5. Create an administration vice president, if one does not already exist.

I recommend the creation of an office to which the following report:

- O The controller.
- O The treasurer.
- O The computer and systems group.
- O The legal office.
- O The industrial relations office.
- O Other offices for company relations (that is, public and governmental).
- O Organization planning.

The marketing, manufacturing, and R&D groups would continue to be independent.

Such an office has several advantages:

☐ It provides better control over the staff activities. The increasing number of staff operations, together with their increasing specialization, has made it nearly impossible for the president to exercise real control here. An administrative vice president can exercise much more effective control over the size and direction of these activities.

☐ It provides a practical alternative to locating the computer and systems group in the controller's office. An administrative vice president can provide effective supervision and, at the same time, maintain an objectivity that a controller often finds difficult because of his involvement with specific computer applications.

☐ It allows the company to handle miscellaneous projects easily—for example, an evaluation of a functional information system or an analysis of the formal information entering the president's office. To take care of nonrecurring or particularly pressing information systems problems, frequently the best arrangement is to organize temporary task forces that report to the administrative vice president.

☐ It simplifies the process of coordinating staff offices.

However, I would not make the administrative vice president or the offices reporting to him responsible for the *entire* management information system. Marketing, manufacturing, and R&D would all be responsible for their own information systems. Also, the different activities reporting to his office would develop their information systems in relative independence except where interface communications are in question.

Questions for my critics

Inevitably, I shall be accused of setting up a straw issue in this article and then demolishing it.

If the MIS approach really embraces only computer-based information systems or centralized logistics systems, then I *have* set up a straw issue. No harm has been done, however, because I have at least clarified the meaning of "MIS."

But I cannot believe the concept is meant to embrace only this. I have done my best to discover what the MIS approach really is, through talking with its proponents and studying its literature; and this article honestly represents my best understanding.

If I am correct in believing that the approach pretends to embrace more than computerized systems and logistics, then I have *not* set up a straw issue. And those who doubt my conclusions, negative as these may be, would be wise to ask themselves the following questions before they take up the pen of protest:

O Which information systems are to be included in the MIS?

O What kinds of experts are to be included in an MIS group, and what training shall they have?

O Where is this group to fit into the corporate organization? In particular, what will happen to the staff groups from the controller's office, the legal department, the marketing research department and so forth?

O What authority is the MIS group to have? Is it to have authority to design and implement systems, or is it to serve in an advisory function only?

O What can this group accomplish that cannot be better accomplished by placing information specialists under functional groups?

Arguing the viability of the MIS approach is pointless unless answers to these questions are set forth clearly. And the clearer the answers, I believe, the more transparent the MIS mirage.

James C. Emery and Christopher R. Sprague

"MIS: MIRAGE OR MISCONCEPTION"

<u>SMIS Newsletter</u> (3:5), 1972 August, pages 2-6.

Dearden's article "MIS is a Mirage" stimulated considerable response. To some it was a challenge to their area of career dedication; to others it either contradicted or supported their own experience; to still others it was an affront to their intelligence and common sense. As the editor of the <u>Harvard Business Review</u> noted, "A particularly heated debate has been sparked by Mr. Dearden's article on MIS. The controversy centers around the validity of a total systems approach and the qualifications of those responsible for MIS information. For this reason, we have devoted more than the usual amount of space to opinions on this artical and to Mr. Dearden's responses to several of his critics." The letters reproduced here have been selected to sample academic, MIS practitioner, and non-MIS executive comment.

Professors Emery and Sprague, then of the University of Pennsylvania Wharton School, wrote a most thoughtful letter to the editor. Professor Emery is a major figure in the field of MIS and has been a president of the Society for Management Information Systems (SMIS). Emery later became vice-president of EDUCOM concerned with the use of computers in higher education and chairman of the EDUCOM Planning Council. The Emery and Sprague letter was shortened by the Harvard Business Review editor; a full version of the letter is printed here. This includes their comments on the characteristics of a well-designed information system.

Emery and Sprague suggest that when Dearden adopts the definition of MIS as a unified, single system that is completely coordinated and completely consistent, he indeed creates a mirage but it stems from his own misconceptions about the nature of an MIS. They suggest that an MIS cannot be all-encompassing, totally integrated, and centralized. An MIS is a collection of subsystems with varying degrees of integration and whose development is evolutionary. A person who dwells on dissimilarities as Dearden suggests, often fails to exploit what commonness exists. Indeed the degree of commonness is growing and is evidenced in the growing body of knowledge about information systems that can be applied in virtually any organization and can be imparted through professional educational programs.

READING SUGGESTIONS

The letter from Emery and Sprague provides the viewpoint of MIS academicians. It should be read carefully since it includes some extra discussion relating to the important characteristics of an MIS as well as a well-reasoned rebuttal to some comments in Dearden's article.

QUESTIONS

1. How do Emery and Sprague view the notion of integration in MIS?

2. Summarize the six characteristics of a well-designed information system as presented in the Emery and Sprague letter.

3. What are the consequences of focusing on the commonalities of various MIS subsystems?

4. How do Emery and Sprague characterize the formal training required for an MIS professional? Which are important and which are secondary?

MIS: Mirage or Misconception?

James C. Emery
Christopher R. Sprague

Professor Dearden, in his article, *MIS Is a Mirage*, correctly anticipated that his critics would accuse him of setting up a straw issue and then demolishing it. We believe that he has done just that—and thereby marred some otherwise well-conceived advice to management. He quite correctly cautions against wild fancies of MIS advocates. He also raises some provocative questions that help to clarify important issues about information systems and their implementation.

Our quarrel with Dearden stems from his description of an MIS as perceived by practitioners in the field. Dearden states that MIS advocates take the view that the only acceptable MIS is a unified, single system that is completely coordinated and completely consistent. Such an MIS is indeed a mirage—but one created by Dearden's own misconceptions about the nature of an MIS.

Dearden gives us few clues as to the identity of those who still peddle the idea of the totally integrated system. Although such advocates exist, they are hardly worthy opponents: they are few in number and have had little influence on MIS practitioners since the early 1960's. They cannot be long-term practitioners themselves—Darwinian mortality takes its toll too soon for that.

Competent practitioners do not set out to design a totally integrated MIS. They rightly view the MIS—or whatever name one chooses to use—as composed of a collection of subsystems. In some cases a considerable degree of integration exists among these subsystems; but in most cases the subsystems are only loosely coupled or largely independent. The issue is one of degree. The choice in a particular case must take into account such factors as design and operating costs, available technology, system complexity, existing organizational boundaries, management policies and style, and technical risk.

Integration among subsystems is achieved in various ways. An important form of integration is the sharing of data among subsystems—between the logistics and accounting subsystems, for example. To some extent the sharing is accomplished through access to common files; more often it involves the transfer of information from one subsystem to another in the temporary form of some machine-readable storage medium (commonly magnetic tape). Integration is also achieved through the sharing of the computer and other processing resources. The consolidation of functions—such as personnel and payroll functions—provides still another form of integration.

No system is completely integrated; there always exists some duplication of data and data collection, some dedicated processing resources, and a great deal of fragmentation of programs and functions. It is technically, economically, and operationally infeasible to design a completely integrated system. But it is perfectly legitimate, given today's technology and understanding of MIS, to speak of systems that move toward a higher degree of integration than was feasible before.

Thus, a well designed information system is likely to have the following characteristics:

1 *It is based on one or more computers.* Virtually any organization can profit from applying the computer to certain of its functions. The extent to which the computer is applied depends on the tradeoffs involved. For high-volume, routine information processing activities, the computer generally enjoys a great advantage. On the other hand, for infrequent, vague, and ill-defined problems of the sort often faced by high-level managers, the computer is unlikely to provide much direct assistance. However, as advances take place in the technology of decision models and computer science, the boundaries expand within which the computer can prove useful.

2 *It offers a variety of decision aids.* Some (relatively few) decisions are well enough defined to be almost completely programmed in the form of an optimizing model. Others can be partially formalized, and require close cooperation between a human decision maker and the computer (the man, for example, posing "what if . . ." questions, the computer responding—perhaps in real time—with a prediction based on a model of some sort). For still other decisions very little can be formalized; the computer is limited in

this case to providing summarized information or perhaps no role at all. It may well be that this latter category includes some of the organization's most important decisions, but this in no way diminishes the attractiveness of applying the computer to functions for which it is well suited.

3 *The MIS thus cannot be characterized as either exclusively computer-based or all-encompassing.* It should be viewed as a man-machine system, with tasks included according to the comparative advantages currently enjoyed by man and the computer. Its boundaries shift with changes in needs and advances in technology.

4 *The system is composed of a collection of subsystems with varying degrees of integration among the parts.* The extent of data and hardware sharing and the consolidation of functions should be determined through a tradeoff analysis of each specific case.

5 *Implementation of the MIS involves both centralized and decentralized development of systems.* Certain tasks will tend to be handled by a central group—such as hardware and software specification, organization-wide standards (dealing with documentation, for example), maintenance of specialized skills, and the development of systems that cross organizational boundaries or that are used by several departments. Tasks that are largely unique to a particular organizational unit will tend to be handled on a decentralized basis (but normally subject to overall guidelines and standards).

6 *Implementation of the system proceeds over many years, and in fact continues indefinitely.* A well designed system normally gives interim benefits sufficient to justify its cost. It is also designed with flexibility in mind so that it can be adapted to changes in the environment, management needs, and technology. Inevitably, some tradeoffs arise between short-range and long-range benefits.

In short, a good information system embodies a series of complex tradeoffs or compromises—in the extent to which functions are automated; the rapport between man and machine; the integration of files, hardware, and functions; the amount of centralization; and the effort devoted to long-range improvements. There is nothing very profound, radical, or controversial about this view of an MIS. Indeed, a broad majority of MIS practitioners would almost surely subscribe to these concepts.

If this prevailing conception of an MIS differs considerably from that of Prof. Dearden, the prevailing approach to successful implementation does not. Few MIS practitioners would argue against Dearden's guidelines: hire competent MIS personnel, develop functional subsystems, take care of interfaces among subsystems, pay particular attention to the logistics subsystem (or analogous "mainline" functions in non-manufacturing organizations), handle certain functions on a centralized basis, and establish a senior executive in charge of administrative functions. These guidelines are completely compatible with the prevailing view of an MIS; they are, in fact, an essential requirement for its successful implementation.

Despite this seeming agreement between practitioners and Prof. Dearden, we suspect that in practice the approaches to implementation would differ rather substantially. Prof. Dearden emphasizes the dissimilarities that exist among various subsystems of an MIS, while we prefer to focus on their similarities. This rather subtle distinction can lead to major differences in the way one tackles the task of implementation.

A person who dwells on dissimilarities often fails to exploit what commonness exists. He tends to rely on piecemeal implementation carried on in relative isolation. He relies primarily on persons with functional skills rather than persons having generalized MIS skills.

Those of us who take the other viewpoint look for ways to handle the interdependencies and commonness that exist among subsystems. An essential part of this is the development of an overall master plan to guide the development process. Such a plan should only sketch out the system in enough detail to identify (at least provisionally) the boundaries and interfaces of subsystems, their estimated costs and benefits, and the projected sequence of implementation. Planning of this sort generally requires only a few persons, but they must be extremely competent and well versed in the very set of skills that Prof. Dearden claims does not exist.

Reprinted from the SMIS Newsletter (3:5), 1972 August, pages 2-6.

Our differences with Prof. Dearden hinge, then, on the issue of whether or not we can expect an MIS practitioner to acquire generalized skills that allow him to take a relatively global view of the system. Persons having these skills are not in plentiful supply, but they certainly exist—and in growing numbers. An MIS depends heavily, in our view, on an organization's ability to hire and retain at least a few practitioners with such skills.

A person meeting these requirements has a solid background in computer technology and systems design. He understands the nature of systems and how one can best design and implement them. He appreciates the difference between technical sophistication and cost-effectiveness—and opts for the latter if a conflict exists. He understands that a good MIS reflects all manner of tradeoffs. He has an overall view of the major functional areas of management, and is likely to have considerable knowledge of at least one of them. He is neither a superman nor Renaissance Man; he is simply a well-trained and well-seasoned professional who can deal effectively with the exceedingly complex systems that are now evolving.

Obviously, a great deal of other skills are required to implement a successful MIS. These include relatively narrow technical skills, as well as detailed knowledge and experience in each of the various management functions served by the MIS.

Prof. Dearden would not, we suspect, quarrel seriously with our assertion that the implementation of an MIS should be planned, and that competent computer professionals play an important role in such planning. (We make this point lest we, too, be accused of building straw men.) We do part company, however, on the question of the relative importance of the MIS professional versus the functional specialist.

We have been heavily committed over the past dozen years to educating future MIS practitioners. The Wharton School, where we now teach, offers an "information systems option" as part of its MBA program. A student takes four computer-related courses during his two-year stay; the rest of his work is devoted to traditional management subjects (including a major in one of the functional areas). The four systems courses deal with computer technology and general MIS concepts.

With a strong formal background in both management and systems, our students have had no real difficulty in applying their education to a broad range of functional areas, types of organizations (e.g., manufacturing, insurance, public administration, etc.), and countries. We have seen ample evidence that such persons can very soon begin to make substantial contributions to an MIS project. In our own research and consulting we similarly find that lack of detailed knowledge of a particular industry or function rarely constitute a serious barrier to understanding an organization's information system. Indeed, too detailed a knowledge of, and day-to-day involvement with, a particular function is often a hindrance to such understanding.

We draw from this experience two basic conclusions. First, there exists a general body of knowledge about information systems that can be applied in virtually any organization (supplemented, to be sure, by more specialized skills). Second, this body of knowledge can be imparted to talented—but not necessarily brilliant—persons through a professional program of modest length (but, as in all professions, the formal education must be reinforced and extended through experience).

A great deal of nonsense has been written by both the MIS advocates and their debunkers. The issue has been made unnecessarily emotional. We have long ceased looking for that Holy Grail, the MIS Concept. Management Information System is simply a label that has been put on an activity that goes on in every organization—the formalized marshalling of information to support the decision-making process. Every functioning organization already has an MIS—good, bad, or indifferent. The MIS practitioner aims at improving the system in the most cost-effective way, subject to all of the constraints imposed by technology, organizational boundaries, limited resources, and the like. Success in doing this requires continued management support and great professional competence. The investment made in the MIS is likely to yield substantial but not overwhelming benefits; it is, in short, neither an extravagance nor a panacea.

Although a well designed MIS that exploits current technology is likely to differ in many ways from most existing MIS, it will certainly not be entirely computer-based, totally integrated, operating in real-time, and serving all levels of management with equal facility. It is highly misleading to imply that MIS practitioners aim at such gee-whiz systems; it only serves to reinforce the limited prospective of the hairy-chested school of managers who cannot see any significant role of the computer beyond routine data processing.

Robert H. Long, Richard G. Landis, Walter J. Kennevan,   Davis Chapter 8
O. J. Wenzel, and John J. Riccardo

"LETTERS TO THE EDITOR"

Harvard Business Review (50:3), 1972 May-June, pages 23-24, 28, 32.

The following letters in response to Dearden's article were selected to sample academic, MIS practitioner, and non-MIS executive comments.

Robert H. Long was assistant director of research for the Bank Administration Institute.

Richard G. Landis was president of Del Monte Corporation and expresses a non-MIS executive viewpoint.

Walter J. Kennevan was director of the MIS program at American University.

O. J. Wenzel, a manager of Management Information Systems at RCA, represents the views of an MIS executive.

John J. Riccardo was president and later chairman of Chrysler Corporation and represents a second non-MIS executive viewpoint.

READING SUGGESTIONS

The letter from Long provides a good set of answers to the questions Dearden left for his critics. A rejoinder from Dearden follows. The letters from Landis and Riccardo are important for the attitude reflected from the chief executive officers of two large corporations. The non-MIS executives responses are generally supportive of Dearden without considering the weaknesses in the Dearden case. Kennevan responds to what he considers to be a serious misquote Dearden made of his definition of MIS. The letter from Wenzel provides some words in support of Dearden and in support of MIS. All the critics (including the Emery and Sprague response presented separately) commented upon Dearden's incorrect assumption that the MIS is a total, integrated system.

QUESTIONS

1. Do you agree or disagree with the answers Robert Long provides to the questions Dearden left for his critics? Support your answer.
2. Describe the attitude reflected in each of the two papers from Riccardo and Landis, presidents of large corporations. Did they address any significant points in the Dearden article?
3. What significant misinterpretation resulted from the misquote of Walter Kennevan's definition of MIS?
4. Does the validity of the MIS concept depend upon the competence of the practitioners or on the success of past implementation attempts? Explain.

Letters to the editor

Harvard Business Review: May-June 1972

As a goad to stimulate MIS thinking, Mr. Dearden's article is excellent. It also provides a good example of how an apparently conscientious researcher can be led astray when he works within a poorly conceived framework. Since this is exactly the type of error that Dearden places on the MIS designer, it is interesting to note that he himself has fallen into the same trap.

...As for Mr. Dearden's "Questions for my critics," the answers are simple though they are not easily achieved.

What management information systems should be included...?

All information systems should be included in an MIS; if not, we have the ridiculous situation of a sales department whose performance is measured by gross sales, a production department whose performance is measured by units and costs, and a company that is measured by profits. As any executive knows, here we have a case of separate information systems in which both the production and sales departments can be reaching performance highs while the company is going bankrupt. Integration of information systems is a must and, for all of Mr. Dearden's protestations, he should realize the *interfacing* of subsystems is one sign of a total systems approach.

What experts should be included...?

The MIS is in part every manager's job. If there is a special group, its task should be to help the system users define and learn to use the MIS improvements. The "experts" should understand the department they are helping, but, in addition, they should understand decision analysis, the economics of information value, systems theory, and information systems.

Where should the group be located...?

This "group" should not fit into the organization. Its members should infiltrate the organization. Its task is to improve the company's information system and this includes improving the data flow, updating the concept of "what the job or business is all about," creating "games" so that managers can learn new decision making habits and in other ways help coordinate and stimulate the development of the people in the system and the equipment-based data feedback systems.

What authority should the group have...?

The MIS group should work for the CEO and have unlimited authority—but it should never use it. Any information or decision analyst knows that you can move an elephant faster by loosing a mouse than by pulling on his trunk.

Why not place the experts under a functional group...?

If the information and decision analysts are placed *under* functional groups, they will be used to optimize the functional group. It is unlikely that the company will benefit ·from the resulting suboptimization of functional groups. The task is to improve the company—not its respective parts (this...is fully explained in systems theory).

In summary, if Mr. Dearden's MIS article is a mirage or a straw man set up to stimulate discussions about MIS—Bravo! But, if he really believes what he wrote—for shame,

Mr. Dearden, you should know better and, further, you should not blame the MIS concept for the fact that you have discovered that some MIS designers are incompetent.

Robert H. Long,
Assistant Director of Research,
Bank Administration Institute

Author's reply: I would like the HBR reader to examine carefully Long's answers to my five questions. These answers disclose precisely the fuzzy thinking and unworkable concepts that I had in mind when I wrote the article.

First, Long would include *all* information systems in his MIS. Since he places no limit whatsoever on what his MIS includes, I can only conclude that he is talking about all information systems whether formal or informal, whether past or future, whether written, oral, or visual. Such an all-encompassing concept includes just about everything that goes on within a firm. Long is equally global and equally vague about what experts should be included, "The MIS is part of every manager's job." So far he has included about everything and everybody in management in his concept.

Next, in answer to the question "Where should the group be located?" he achieves what must be the ultimate in confusion. His group would "infiltrate" the organization. Since they include all managers who are responsible for all information, one wonders who will be the "infiltrators" and who will be "infiltratees." Finally, Long would give the MIS group (at this point, he seems to have forgotten that it is *all* managers) "unlimited authority" which, of course, they will not use.

This is exactly the type of thinking that my article was aimed at and I thank Long for demonstrating this. If I had quoted anything like this in my article, I certainly would have been accused of setting up straw issues.

John Dearden,
Herman C. Krannert Professor
of Business Administration,
Harvard Business School

Letters to the editor

...Mr. Dearden's main thrust seems perfectly clear and reasonable: there is, as yet, no technology or *technocracy* capable of assimilating, analyzing, and communicating all the information management requires to make effective decisions. I also agree with at least two of his proposed solutions to management information problems: hire competent people (and, I might add, tell them what's expected of them), and encourage communication, not only vertically, but among the interfacing staff groups.

...In my experience, the chief executive, or chief operating officer, benefits from an exposure to a variety of viewpoints (presumably Mr. Dearden does not exclude expert opinions from the management information matrix). The office of staff administrator would, necessarily, screen these various viewpoints and tend to express the natural bias of the administrator, thus suppressing controversy and denying the individual staff member the right to put his case before the decision maker. Perhaps this objection would be cured if the administrative vice president's responsibilities were limited to directing and coordinating staff *services*, and the information function relegated to a planning committee, composed of staff members representing all the important information systems, and chaired by the chief executive officer.

Richard G. Landis,
President,
Del Monte Corporation

...On page 91, in Professor Dearden's interesting article, reference is made to my suggested definition of the term "management information system." However, the definition is incorrectly quoted as "A management information system...supports the planning, control and operational function of an organization by furnishing uniform information in the proper time-frame to assist the decision-maker." The proper quotation should be "A management information system...supports the planning, control and operational

functions of an organization by furnishing uniform information in the proper time-frame to assist the *decision-making process*." (Italics supplied)

...The distinction is not trivial, since to many readers, particularly managerial personnel, the mis-quotation may well imply that an MIS is indeed a total system which relegates their role to that of a superficial adjunct to a machine. As the proponent of the definition, let me assure Mr. Dearden that nothing could be further from the intent; that is why the expression "decision-making process" was carefully selected.

...In summary, rather than concur with the mass firings that Professor Dearden advocates and with his proposal to create an "administration vice president" ("Superman"?) it would appear to be more reasonable and feasible to continue, as many organizations are doing, improving the quality and homogeneity of the information supplied to management.

There are numerous practical illustrations of the success of the MIS approach to management improvement and not all of these are computer-based.

So, despite the prophets of doom and purveyors of gloom, whenever and wherever management wills it, there will continue to be progress in utilizing management information systems for the overall benefit of the entire enterprise.

I would also hope, somewhat wistfully, that the errors on pages 91 and 92 wherein I am referred to as "Walter Kenneron" that "Kenneron" might also be corrected.

Walter J. Kennevan,
Director,
Management Information
Systems Program,
Center for Technology &
Administration,
The American University

Professor John Dearden shows considerable insight into the workings of today's business organizations. Certainly many of us in MIS work will agree that the "total MIS system...determined from the top down" could hardly be sillier. It

would seem better to clarify the title of the article though since it is not MIS that is a mirage, but the single, integrated system devised to fill all of management's information needs.

...I suggest that where information has not improved and costs have not been reduced, perhaps management has insisted that their MIS group attempt impossible tasks (as to develop a total integrated system) or has had them spending time making quick changes to existing systems (enhancing is a perpetual job) and converting present little manual systems. All of us in MIS are deluged with requests, usually from lower level management, to "computerize my records." If there was ever a miserable term, it is "to computerize" something, but in many activities these requests are enforced by higher management. The bitter truth is that in many companies the MIS is required to supply information for the clerks not the management of the company.

...Systems in the operating entity can and should be developed separately to meet the needs of the using activity but the MIS group provides the coordination and integration with other systems for efficient operations. Without this combination, chaos would result. Systems developed at different times and for different users may thus share common data files and will be able to interchange data. It is of utmost importance to place competent people in charge of each of the formal information systems, as Professor Dearden says....

O.J. Wenzel,
Manager,
Management Information
Systems,
RCA

...My reaction to the article can best be summed up by saying that I was pleased to find Mr. Dearden's thinking on the impracticality of a Total Management Information System and his recommendations regarding real solutions to systems problems very closely paralleling our own thinking and actions here at Chrysler Corporation....

John J. Riccardo,
President,
Chrysler Corporation

John Dearden   Davis Chapter 8

"MYTH OF REAL-TIME MANAGEMENT INFORMATION"

Harvard Business Review (44:3), 1966 May-June, pages 123-132.

This second and earlier article by John Dearden attacks a particular facet of MIS. He is a critic of overenthusiastic claims for information systems. This article was published in 1966 following the introduction of the third generation of computers (typified by IBM System/360). These computers had improved capabilities for data entry via user terminals, immediate processing, and immediate response back to the user terminals. These fast response systems are referred to as realtime systems because the processing occurs and response is made while an operation or transaction is being performed. For example, in the case of a realtime airline reservation system, the processing of the reservation is done and the confirmation responses are made while the customer waits (usually a few seconds).

The value of realtime processing is apparent for some applications; the question is the value of realtime processing in support of top management activities. Dearden denies that there is any real need or value in a realtime information system for top management. More than a decade has passed since Dearden raised these questions; the number of realtime systems has grown dramatically, but the management applications have been a relatively small proportion. The Dearden article may help to understand the reason for this slow rate of development. On the other hand, the Dearden article is written in a popular, argumentative style which obscures many alternative views to be considered. Some of these are pointed out by the letter from Head following this article.

Dearden argues that top management has six categories of functions: management control, strategic planning, personnel planning, coordination, operating control, and personal appearances. Examining the role of a realtime computer system in each of these functions, Dearden fails to see any real value to realtime information. Only in the case of logistics systems which control the flow of goods through a company is Dearden willing to admit that fast response systems can be effective. Dearden then examines reasons why realtime systems seem to have an appeal to top management and concludes that they are not sound.

READING SUGGESTIONS

Note the confusion in definition. "Realtime" has a useful operational meaning for airline reservations or control of a missle in flight, but what is "realtime" for a management decision? Note that Dearden defines the system as having a terminal in the manager's office and very fast response to input from the terminal.

The heart of the article consists of the description of the six top management functions and the discussion of how these might be affected by a realtime information system. Some peripheral points are the value of realtime processing for monitoring the logistics system, the value of a terminal to display reports instead of the system printing regular hard copy reports, and some considerations of ecomomics and human reaction to such a system. The last part of the paper examines three reasons top managers adopt realtime systems in spite of the disadvantages perceived by Dearden: the expectation of improved control, the appearance of being a scientific manager, and the expectation tnat success in logistics systems can be transferred to top management functions.

QUESTIONS

1. In what area of a company does Dearden concede realtime processing may have value?
2. How does Dearden define "management" for purposes of the article?
3. Characterize the six functions of management.
4. Explain for each management function the activities that are not assisted by realtime information and those for which realtime information might be useful. Where appropriate for the latter activities explain whether and why realtime information is likely to be cost/effective.
5. Explain why Dearden says realtime information is not useful for management control.
6. Traditional reports could be replaced by a terminal from which the manager could obtain the desired report. Dearden objects. Why?
7. Dearden says "improved control" is a fallacy. Why?

Myth of Real-Time Management Information

By John Dearden

The latest vogue in computer information systems is the so-called real-time management information system. The general idea is to have in each executive's office a remote computer terminal which is connected to a large-scale computer with a data bank containing all of the relevant information in the company. The data bank, updated continuously, can be "interrogated" by the manager at any time. Answers to questions are immediately flashed on a screen in his office. Allegedly, a real-time management information system enables the manager to obtain complete and up-to-the-minute information about everything that is happening within the company.

The purpose of this article — aimed at a time span of the next five to seven years — is to raise some serious questions concerning the utility of a real-time information system for top management. I will try to show that it would not be practicable to operate a real-time *management control* system and, moreover, that such a system would not help to solve any of the critical problems even if it could be implemented. I will also try to show that in other areas of top management concern a real-time system is, at best, of marginal value. It is my personal opinion that, of all the ridiculous things that have been foisted on the long-suffering executive in the name of science and progress, the real-time management information system is the silliest.

Meaning of Real-Time

One of the problems in any new field of endeavor is that there is frequently no universally accepted definition for many of the terms. It therefore becomes nearly impossible to question the validity of the concepts underlying the terms because their meanings are different to different people. The term "real-time" is no exception. In fact, in a single issue of one computer magazine, back-to-back articles defined real-time differently; and one example, cited in the first article as an illustration of what real-time is *not*, appeared in the second article as an illustration of what a real-time system *is*.

Semantic Confusion

One concept of real-time is demonstrated by these two quotations:

• "A real-time management information system — i.e., one that delivers information in time to do something about it." [1]

• "A real-time computer system may be defined as one that controls an environment by receiving data, processing them and returning results sufficiently quickly to affect the functioning of the environment at that time." [2]

---

[1] Gilbert Burck and the Editors of *Fortune, The Computer Age* (New York, Harper & Row, Publishers, 1965), p. 106.

[2] James Martin, *Programming Real-Time Computer Systems* (Englewood Cliffs, New Jersey, Prentice-Hall, Inc., 1965), p. 378.

The problem with both of these definitions is that they are too broad. *All* management control systems must be real-time systems under this concept. It would be a little silly to plan to provide management with budget performance reports, for instance, if they were received too late for management to take any action.

The following is a description of real-time that comes closer to the concept of real-time as it is used by most systems and computer people:

"The delays involved in batch processing are often natural delays, and little advantage can be obtained by reducing them. But elimination of the *necessity* for such delays opens new and relatively unexplored possibilities for changing the entire nature of the data processing system — from a passive recorder of history (which, of course, is valuable for many decisions) to an active participant in the minute-to-minute operations of the organization. It becomes possible to process data in *real-time* — so that the output may be fed back immediately to control current operations. Thus the computer can interact with people on a dynamic basis, obtaining and providing information, recording the decisions of humans, or even making some of these decisions." [3]

System Characteristics

To expand somewhat on this description, the term "real-time system" as used in this article will mean a computer system with the following characteristics.

(1) *Data will be maintained "on-line."* In other words, all data used in the system will be directly available to the computer — that is, they will be stored in the computer memory or in random access files attached to the computer. (This is in contrast to data maintained on magnetic tapes, which must be mounted and searched before information is available to the computer.)

(2) *Data will be updated as events occur.* (In contrast to the "batch" process, where changes are accumulated and periodically updated.)

(3) *The computer can be interrogated from remote terminals.* This means that the information stored in the computer can be obtained on request from a number of locations at a distance from the place where the data are processed and stored.

Perhaps the most widely known example of a real-time system currently in operation is the

[3] E. Wainright Martin, Jr., *Electronic Data Processing* (Homewood, Illinois, Richard D. Irwin, Inc., 1965), p. 381.

American Airlines SABRE system for making plane reservations.

Potential Applications

With the new generation of computers, random access memories have become much less expensive than has been true until now. This fact, coupled with the advances made in data transmission equipment and techniques, will make many real-time applications economically feasible.

Real-time methods will improve those systems where the lack of up-to-the-minute information has in the past resulted in increased costs or loss of revenue. I believe that many companies will employ real-time methods to control all or part of their logistics (the flow of goods through the company) systems. For example:

A manufacturer of major household appliances might have raw material and work-in-process inventories in his manufacturing plants, and finished goods inventories both in company and distributor warehouses and in dealer showrooms. There is a more or less continuous logistics flow all along the route from raw material to retail customer. If all of the data on inventory levels and flows could be maintained centrally and updated and analyzed continuously, this would not only solve many of the problems now faced by such a manufacturer, but would make it possible to provide better all-around service with lower inventory levels and lower costs (particularly in transportation and obsolescence).

There are, of course, many other potential applications for real-time management information systems, and I believe that they will be used extensively in the next few years. However, these applications will take place almost exclusively in logistics, and, as I shall explain later on, techniques that may improve a logistics system will not necessarily improve a management control system. I want to make it clear at this point that I am not opposed to real-time systems per se. I believe they have valuable applications in operating situations. I am only opposed to using real-time information systems where they do not apply. The balance of this article will consider top management's use of real-time systems.

Management Functions

As used here, the term "top management" will apply to the president and executive vice president in centralized companies, plus divisional managers in decentralized companies. In other words, I am considering as top management those people responsible for the full range of a business activity — marketing, production, research, and so forth. I am also assuming that the company or division is sufficiently large and complex so that the executive makes only a limited number of operating decisions, if any. I be-

lieve that this is a reasonable assumption in considering real-time management information systems. A company where the president makes most of the operating decisions could scarcely be considering a sophisticated and expensive computer installation.

Six Categories

This part of the discussion considers, in general terms, the functions of top management. The purpose is to establish how a typical executive might spend his time so that we may later evaluate the extent to which his decision making can or cannot be helped by real-time computer systems. I have divided top management's functions into six general categories — management control, strategic planning, personnel planning, coordination, operating control, and personal appearances. Each is discussed below.

1. *Management Control.* One of the principal tasks of a manager is to exercise control over the people to whom he has delegated responsibility. Ideally, this control consists of coordinating, directing, and motivating subordinates by reviewing and approving an operating plan; by comparing periodically the actual performance against this plan; by evaluating the performance of subordinates; and by taking ac-

tion with respect to subordinates where and when it becomes necessary.

The formal management control system will, of course, vary with the type and size of business as well as with the type and amount of responsibility delegated to the subordinate. Nevertheless, all effective formal management control systems need three things:

(a) A good plan, objective, or standard. The manager and the subordinate must agree as to what will constitute satisfactory performance.

(b) A system for evaluating actual performance periodically against the plan. This would include both a clear explanation of why variances have occurred and a forecast of future performance.

(c) An "early warning" system to notify management in the event that conditions warrant attention between reporting periods.

2. *Strategic Planning.* This consists of determining long-range objectives and making the necessary decisions to implement these objectives. Much of top management's strategic planning activity involves reviewing studies made by staff groups. Capital expenditure programs, acquisition proposals, and new product programs are examples of studies that fall into this area.

Another phase of strategic planning consists of developing ideas for subordinates to study — that is, instead of waiting for staff or line groups to recommend courses of action, the executive develops ideas of his own as to what the company should be doing.

3. *Personnel Planning.* This important function of management deals with making decisions on hiring, discharging, promoting, demoting, compensating, or changing key personnel. In the broadest sense, this consists of organizational planning. Personnel planning is, of course, related both to management control and strategic planning. Nevertheless, there are so many unique problems associated with personnel planning that I believe it is reasonable to consider it as a separate function.

4. *Coordination.* Here management's function is to harmonize the activities of subordinates, especially where it is necessary to solve a problem that cuts across organizational lines. For example, a quality control problem might affect several operating executives, and the solution to this problem might require top management's active participation. In general, this activity tends to be more important at the lower organization levels. The president of a large,

decentralized company would perform less of this coordination function than his divisional managers because interdepartmental problems are more common at the divisional level.

5. *Operating Control.* Almost all top executives perform some operating functions. For example, I know a company president who buys certain major raw materials used by his company. Usually, the operating decisions made by top management are those which are so important to the welfare of the company that the executive believes the responsibility for making them cannot be properly delegated.

6. *Personal Appearances.* Many top executives spend much time in performing functions that require their making a personal appearance. This can vary from entertaining visiting dignitaries to giving out 25-year watches. (I shall assume the activities involving such personal appearances will not be affected by a real-time management information system.)

Real-Time Practicality?

The purpose of this part of the article is to examine, in turn, each of the management functions described above (except #6) to see whether or not it can be improved by a real-time information system.

1. Management Control

I do not see how a real-time system can be *used* in management control. In fact, I believe

that any attempt to use real-time will considerably weaken even a good management control system. (In setting objectives or budgets, it may be useful to have a computer available at the time of the budget review to calculate the effects of various alternatives suggested by management. This, however, is not a real-time system, since a computer console need be installed only for the review sessions.)

Calculating Performance. In the area of performance evaluation, real-time management information systems are particularly ridiculous. When a division manager agrees to earn, say, $360,000 in 1966, he does not agree to earn $1,000 a day or $1,000/24 per hour. The only way actual performance can be compared with a budget is to break down the budget into the time periods against which performance is to be measured. If the smallest period is a month (as it usually is), nothing short of a month's actual performance is significant (with the exception of the events picked up by the early warning system to be described below). Why, then, have a computer system that allows the manager to interrogate a memory bank to show him the hour-to-hour or even day-to-day status of performance against plan?

Even assuming objectives could logically be calendarized by day or hour, we run into worse problems in calculating actual performance, and worse still in making the comparison of actual to standard meaningful. If the performance measures involve accounting data (and they most frequently do), the data will never be up-to-date until they are normalized (adjusted) at the end of the accounting period. I will not bore you with the details. Suffice it to say only that a real-time accounting system which yields meaningful results on even a daily basis would be a horrendous and expensive undertaking.

Let us go one step further. Performance reports, to be meaningful, must include an explanation of the variances. This frequently involves considerable effort and often requires the analyst to spend time at the source of the variance in order to determine the cause. Would this be done every day or oftener? Ridiculous! There is one more thing about performance reports. The important message in many reports is the action being taken and the estimated effect of this action. In other words, the projection of future events is the important top management consideration. Will this be built into the real-time system? Since this involves the considered judgment of the subordinate and his staff, I do not see how this could possibly be done even on a daily basis.

Early Warning. How about real-time for providing an early warning? Here, also, I do not see how it could be of help. Early warning has not been a problem in any top management control system with which I have been acquainted. In most instances, when situations deteriorate to the point where immediate action is required, top management knows about it. As the manager of a division ($100 million a year in sales) said to me, when I asked him how he knew when things might be out of hand in one of his plants, "That's what the telephone is for."

In any case, it is possible to prescribe the situations which management should be apprised of immediately, without even relying on a computer. Furthermore, the important thing is to bring the situation to top management's attention *before* something happens. For example, it is important to inform management of a threatened strike. Yet a real-time management information system would pick it up only *after* the strike had occurred.

In summary, then, early warning systems have been put into operation and have worked satisfactorily without a real-time system. I see nothing in a real-time management information system that would improve the means of early warning, and such a system would certainly be more expensive. (Note that here I am talking about management control systems. The early warning

techniques of many logistical control systems, in contrast, could be greatly improved by real-time systems.)

My conclusion on management control is that real-time information cannot be made meaningful — even at an extremely high cost — and that any attempt to do so cannot help but result in a waste of money and management time. Improvements in most management control systems must come from sources other than real-time information systems.

2. Strategic Planning

Since strategic planning largely involves predicting the long-run future, I fail to see how a real-time management information system will be of appreciable use here. It *is* true that past data are required to forecast future events, but these need hardly be continuously updated and immediately available. Furthermore, much of the preparation of detailed strategic plans is done by staff groups. While these groups may on occasion work with computer models, the models would certainly be stored away, not maintained on line between uses.

Perhaps the most persistent concept of a real-time management information system is the pic-

ture of the manager sitting down at his console and interacting with the computer. For example, as a strategic planning idea comes to him, he calls in a simulation model to test it out, or a regression analysis to help him forecast some event; or, again, he asks for all of the information about a certain subject on which he is required to make a decision.

It seems to me that the typical manager would have neither the time nor the inclination to interact with the computer on a day-to-day basis about strategic planning. Problems requiring computer models are likely to be extremely complex. In most instances, the formulation of these problems can be turned over to staff specialists. Furthermore, I think it would be quite expensive to build a series of models to anticipate the manager's needs.

Under any conditions, strategic planning either by the manager alone or by staff groups does not appear to be improved by a real-time system. Models can be fed into the computer and coefficients can be updated as they are used. Between uses, it seems to me, these models would be most economically stored on magnetic tape.

3. Personnel Planning

A real-time management information system does not help the top manager to solve his problems of personnel planning, although the computer can be useful in certain types of personnel

data analysis. About the only advantage to the manager is that information becomes available somewhat more quickly. Instead of calling for the history of a particular individual and waiting for personnel to deliver it, the manager can request this information directly from the computer. Therefore, while a remote console device

with a visual display unit *could* be used for retrieving personnel information, the question of whether it *should* be used is one of simple economics. Is the additional cost of storing and maintaining the information, plus the cost of the retrieval devices, worth the convenience?

4. Coordination

The coordination function is very similar to the management control function with respect to potential real-time applicability. A manager wants to know right away when there is an interdepartmental problem that will require his attention. As is the case with early warning systems developed for management control, a real-time system is not necessary (or even useful, in most cases) to convey this information. Further, I cannot see how a real-time management information system could be used in the solution of these coordination problems, except in unusual cases.

5. Operating Control

There is no question that real-time methods are useful in certain types of operating systems, particularly in logistics systems.[4] To the extent that a top executive retains certain operating control functions, there is a possibility that he may be able to use a real-time information system. Because of the necessity of doing other things, however, most executives will be able to spend only a limited amount of time on operating functions. This means generally that they must work on the "exception" principle. Under most conditions, therefore, it would seem much more economical for a subordinate to monitor the real-time information and inform the top executives when a decision has to be made.

It is very difficult to generalize about this situation. Here, again, it appears to be one of simple economics. How much is a real-time system worth to the manager in relation to what it is costing? I cannot believe that there would be many instances where a manager would be concerned with operating problems to the extent that a real-time information system operating from his office would be justified.

Reporting by Computer

In recent months, there have been experiments to replace traditional published reports

[4] See Robert E. McGarrah, "Logistics for the International Manufacturer," HBR March–April 1966, p. 157.

by utilizing consoles and display devices to report information directly to management. Although these techniques, strictly speaking, are not real-time, they bear such a close relationship to real-time systems that it will be useful to consider them here.

Modus Operandi

The general idea is that the information contained in the management reports would be stored in the computer memory so that the manager could ask for only the information he needed. This request would be made from the computer console, and the information would be flashed on a screen in his office. For example, a manager could ask for a report on how sales compared with quota. After looking at this, he could then ask for data on the sales of the particular regions that were below quota and, subsequently, for detail of the districts that were out of line.

The benefits claimed for this type of reporting are as follows:

• The manager will receive only the information he wants.

• Each manager can obtain the information in the format in which he wants it. In other words, each manager can design his own reports. One manager may use graphs almost exclusively, while another may use tabulation.

• The information can be assembled in whatever way the manager wants it — that is, one manager may want sales by areas, and another may want it by product line. Furthermore, the manager can have the data processed in any way that he wants.

• The information will be received more quickly.

Important Considerations

Before installing such a system, it seems to me, a number of things should be taken into account.

First, what advantage, if any, does this system have over a well-designed reporting system? Since the storage and retrieval of data in a computer do not add anything that could not be obtained in a traditional reporting system, the benefits must be related to convenience. Is there enough additional convenience to justify the additional cost?

Second, is it possible that for many executives such a system will be more of a nuisance than a convenience? It may be much easier for them to open a notebook and read the information needed, since in a well-designed system the information is reported in levels of details so that only data of interest need be examined.

Finally, will the saving in time be of any value?

It seems to me that the two main considerations in installing such a system are the economics and the desires of the particular executive. There is one further possibility, however, that should be carefully considered. What will be the impact on the lower level executives? If these people do not know the kind of information their superiors are using to measure their performance, will this not create human relations problems?

Without going into the details, I can see many problems being created if this is not handled correctly. With a regular reporting system, the subordinate knows exactly what information his superior is receiving — and when he receives it — concerning his performance. Furthermore, the subordinate receives the information *first*. Any deviations in this relationship can cause problems, and the use of a computer to retrieve varying kinds of information from a data base is a deviation from this relationship.

Three Fallacies

If management information on a real-time basis is so impractical and uneconomic, why are so many people evidently enamored with this concept? I believe that the alleged benefits of real-time management information systems are based on three major fallacies.

1. Improved Control

Just about every manager feels, at some time, that he does not really have control of his company. Many managers feel this way frequently. This is natural, since complete control is just about impossible even with the best management control system. Since most companies have management control systems that are far from optimum, there is little wonder that a feeling of insecurity exists. In the face of this feeling of insecurity, the promise of "knowing everything that is happening as soon as it happens" has an overpowering appeal.

As explained previously, real-time will not improve management control and, consequently, will not help to eliminate the insecurity that exists. What is usually needed is a combination of improved management control systems and better selection and training of personnel. Even at best, however, the executive will have to accept responsibility for what other people do, without having full control over their actions.

2. 'Scientific Management'

There appears to be considerable sentiment to the effect that the scientific way to manage is to use a computer. This fallacy implies that the executive with a computer console in his office is a scientific manager who uses man-machine communication to extend his ability into new, heretofore unavailable, realms of decision making.

I believe that it is nonsense to expect most managers to communicate directly with a computer. Every manager and every business is different. If a manager has the necessary training and wishes to do so, it may be helpful for him to use a computer to test out some of his ideas. To say, however, that *all* managers should do this, or that this is "scientific management," is ridiculous. A manager has to allocate his time so that he spends it on those areas where his contribution is greatest. If a computer is useful for testing out his ideas in a given situation, there is no reason why he should have to do it personally. The assignment can just as easily be turned over to a staff group. In other words, where a computer is helpful in solving some management problems, there is no reason for the manager to have any direct contact with the machine.

In most instances, the computer is of best use where there are complex problems to be solved. The formulation of a solution to these complex problems can generally be done best by a staff group. Not only are staff personnel better qualified (they are selected for these qualifications), but they have the uninterrupted time to do it. It seems to me that there is nothing wrong with a manager spending his time managing and letting others play "Liberace at the console."

3. Logistics Similarity

This fallacy is the belief that management control systems are merely higher manifestations of logistics systems.

The fact is that the typical real-time system, either in operation or being planned, is a *logistics* system. In such a system, for example, a production plan is developed and the degree of allowable variances established in a centralized computer installation. The actual production is constantly compared to plan; and when a deviation exceeds the established norm, this fact is communicated to the appropriate source. On receiving this information, action is always taken. Either the schedules are changed or the deficiency is somehow made up.

Notice that speed in handling and transmitting vast amounts of information is essential. This is the critical problem that limits many manual logistics systems; and the computer, particularly with real-time applications, goes a long way toward solving the speed problem.

In contrast, speed in processing and transmitting large amounts of data is *not* a critical problem in *management control* systems. Consequently, the improvements that real-time techniques may effect in logistics systems cannot be extrapolated into management control systems.

The critical problems in management control are (a) determining the level of objectives, (b) determining when a deviation from the objective requires action, and (c) deciding what particular action should be taken. The higher in the organizational hierarchy the manager is positioned, the more critical these three problems tend to become. For example, they are usually much more difficult in planning divisional profit budgets than plant expense budgets. In some instances the computer can help the manager with these problems, but I do not see how it can solve them for him. Furthermore, the use of computers in solving these problems has nothing to do with real-time.

Short-Term View

While real-time management information systems may be very useful in improving certain kinds of operating systems, particularly complex logistics systems, they will be of little use in improving management control. This is particularly true in the short-range time span of the next five to seven years.

The following is a checklist of questions that I believe the manager should have answers to before letting anyone install a remote computer terminal and a visual display screen in his office:

1. What will the total incremental cost of the equipment and programming be? (Be sure to consider the cost of continuing systems and programming work that the real-time systems will involve.)

2. Exactly how will this equipment be used? (Be sure to obtain a complete description of the proposed uses and the date when each application will become operational.)

3. Exactly how will each of these uses improve the ability to make decisions? In particular, how will the management control system be improved?

With precise answers to these three questions, it seems to me that a manager can decide whether or not a remote terminal and visual display device should be installed. Do not be surprised, however, if the answer is negative.

Long-Range Outlook

What are the prospects of real-time systems; say, 15 or 20 years from now? Some experts believe that, by that time, staff assistance to top management will have largely disappeared. Not only will the staff have disappeared, but so will most of the paper that flows through present organizations. A manager in the year 1985 or so will sit in his paperless, peopleless office with his computer terminal and make decisions based on information and analyses displayed on a screen in his office.

Caution Urged

It seems to me that, at the present time, the long-term potential of real-time management information systems is completely unknown. No one can say with any degree of certainty that the prediction cited above is incorrect. After all, 15 or 20 years is a long time away, and the concept of a manager using a computer to replace his staff is not beyond the realm of theoretical possibility. On the other hand, this concept could be a complete pipedream.

Under any circumstances, many significant changes in technology, organization, and managerial personnel will be required before this prediction could be a reality for business in general. As a result, if such changes do occur, they will come slowly, and there will be ample opportunity for business executives to adjust to them. For example, I believe there is little danger of a company president waking up some morning to find his chief competitor has installed a computer-based, decision-making system so effective that it will run him out of business.

I believe all executives should be open-minded to suggestions for any improvements in management information systems, but they should require evidence that any proposed real-time management information system will actually increase their effectiveness. Above all, no one should rush into this now because of its future potential.

The present state of real-time management information systems has been compared to that of the transportation field at the beginning of the Model-T era. At that time, only visionaries had any idea of how transportation would be revolutionized by the automobile. It would have been foolish, however, for a businessman to get rid of his horse-drawn vehicles just because some visionaries said that trucks would take over completely in 20 years.

It seems to me that this is the identical situation now. Even if the most revolutionary changes will eventually take place in management information systems 20 years hence, it would be silly for business executives to scrap present methods until they are positive the new methods are better.

Robert V. Head   Davis Chapter 8

"REAL-TIME MANAGEMENT INFORMATION? LET'S NOT BE SILLY"

Datamation (12:8), 1966 August, pages 124-125.

        Robert Head is a well-known information systems execu-
tive and consultant. His experience covers the types of
systems which Dearden claims are not viable.* Note that
the letter is published in Datamation, not in the Harvard
Business Review which published the Dearden article. The
comment by Head is polemic and argumentative and matches
the style of the Dearden article.

READING SUGGESTIONS

        There are two streams of argument in the Head letter:
the first is an attack on the Dearden presentation and the
sweeping, inaccurate, or imprecise statements he made, the
second is a point-by-point comment or rebuttal of Dearden's
analysis of the impact of realtime systems on management
functions. Head points out that the variations of real-
time system design make many of Dearden's arguments not
generally applicable.

QUESTIONS

1. What are Head's comments regarding Dearden's three
    characteristics of a realtime system?
2. Head has rebuttal comments on four of the six func-
    tions described by Dearden. What are the Head coun-
    terarguments? Which functions described by Dearden
    are not mentioned by Head?
3. Head says "early warning" is a management funciton in
    Dearden's article. Is this true? Where does it fit
    in the Dearden argument?

_____
*Robert V. Head, Real-Time Business Systems, New York:
 Holt, Rinehart and Winston, Inc., 1964, 368 pages.

the forum

The Forum is offered for readers who want to express their opinion on any aspect of information processing. Your contributions are invited.

REAL-TIME MANAGEMENT INFORMATION? LET'S NOT BE SILLY

Inevitably, as real-time systems assume an increasingly important role in many industries, the general business publications must come to venture into the real-time world. Last year, for instance, there was Fortune's excellent series on "The Computer Age." And now we find the Harvard Business Review, the prestigious elder statesman of these journals, providing commentary on the subject in its pages. The May-June issue of HBR harbors not the genteel and judicious overview that one might have expected, but rather a crude frontal assault by John Dearden on the "Myth of Real-time Management Information."

Professor Dearden, who is a sort of house oracle on information systems at the B School, thinks that real-time management information systems are silly. He says so plainly at the beginning of his polemic and at the end. He even says so in the middle.

Things get off to an interesting start with an assertion that "allegedly, a real-time management information system enables the manager to obtain complete and up-to-the-minute information about everything that is happening within the company." The reader is left to puzzle out for himself who, besides Mr. Dearden, would make such a sweeping allegation. Certainly no responsible real-time system designer, who has learned to be wary of words like "complete" and "everything." Up-to-the-minute information about every-*thing?*

With this for openers, the author proceeds to identify three characteristics of a real-time system, all irrelevant to an evaluation of management's need for timely information. He says first that "data will be maintained 'on-line.' In other words, all data used in the system will be directly available to the computer—that is, they will be stored in the computer memory or in random access files attached to the computer." This statement, of course, blithely ignores the fact that one can provide real-time management information without maintaining all data on line. To the contrary, most system designers contemplate a hierarchy of storage, with only the most critical data stored in main memory or direct access storage and the less critical and more voluminous files maintained on magnetic tape and other less expensive media.

Next, Mr. Dearden asserts that, according to his view of a real-time system, "data will be updated as events occur." He does not perceive that one can do a splendid job of providing real-time management information from a data base which is maintained by off-line techniques. This is, in fact, exactly the method by which the central information files of several real-time commercial banking systems are updated.

Thirdly, Professor Dearden says that real-time systems are characterized by computer-stored information which "can be obtained on request from a number of locations at a distance from the place where the data are processed and stored". He thus singles out one of the most expensive features of certain real-time systems, such as SABRE, but neglects to note that a real-time management information system need not necessarily have remote terminals at all. There are perfectly respectable systems housed entirely under one roof and possessing no more than one or two terminals to provide real-time management information.

The body of Mr. Dearden's paper is devoted to a discussion of several basic managerial functions and to a consideration of the appropriateness of real-time systems in supporting these functions. The first is Management Control. Here, Mr. Dearden somewhat grumpily concedes that "it may be useful to have a computer available at the time of the budget review to calculate the effects of various alternatives suggested by management" but his previously defined view of real-time systems leads him to conclude that usage of tne computer in this fashion "is not a real-time system, since a computer console need be installed only for the review sessions." Seemingly, Mr. Dearden feels that a system cannot qualify as real-time unless it makes information available when it is *not needed*. Actually, the hallmark of a real-time information system is its responsiveness to managerial needs, not how many consoles it drives or how frequently these consoles are connected on line.

Another management function which Mr. Dearden analyzes is that of Early Warning about potentially troublesome managerial problems. Here he expresses the somewhat startling opinion that "early warning has not been a problem in any top management control system with which I have been acquainted." One wonders how many of Mr. Dearden's executive readers would concur in this curious judgment.

In considering the management function of Strategic Planning, the author concedes "that past data are required to forecast future events," but goes on to complain that "these need hardly be continuously updated and immediately available." Absolutely correct, but the information is nonetheless needed in real-time *during* the planning session.

Personnel Planning is another management function identified by Mr. Dearden. In solving problems of personnel planning, "about the only advantage" that he can see to a real-time system "is that information becomes available somewhat more quickly." Perhaps the professor is making progress after all, for one must agree that,

while this may not be the *only* advantage to any real-time system, it is an advantage which is oftentimes of critical importance in personnel or any other kind of planning.

Mr. Dearden concludes his survey of top management functions by discussing the applicability of real-time systems to Operational Control. He says that "it is very difficult to generalize about this situation" before going on to generalize later in the same paragraph that "I cannot believe that there would be many instances where a manager would be concerned with operating problems to the extent that a real-time information system operating from his office would be justified."

Are you beginning to get the idea? Set up some straw men in the form of assertions that no self-respecting system designer would utter, then proceed to demolish them. The notion of the console in the office is perhaps the author's favorite straw man. Either that or he is genuinely unaware that it is a matter of the utmost indifference whether a manager prefers to obtain his real-time information directly or through staff assistants who operate the consoles.

If you stay with him to the end, Professor Dearden offers some fascinating conclusions. He believes that "there is little danger of a company president waking up some morning to find his chief competitor has installed a computer-based, decision-making system so effective that it will run him out of business." There are many systems professionals who hold the opinion that this is a clear and present danger, particularly in the case of company presidents who heed the type of counsel provided by Mr. Dearden.

The author winds things up with what could very well go down as one of the most inappropriately chosen analogies in contemporary business literature when he compares the development of real-time systems to that of the automobile. He says "It would have been foolish for a businessman to get rid of his horse-drawn vehicles just because some visionaries said that trucks would take over completely in 20 years."

ROBERT V. HEAD, Manager
Management Information Technology
Computer Sciences Corporation

"AN EXECUTIVE VIEW OF MIS"

Datamation (18:11), 1972 November, pages 65-71.

This article is significant because it is a well-written, colorful rebuttal to Dearden's "MIS is a Mirage" from a person with a substantial background of experience. Hanold is president of the Pillsbury Corporation where management information systems have penetrated all levels of the organization and proven their effectiveness in helping managers manage. He is also an honorary founder of the Society for Management Information Systems.

Hanold charges Dearden with clothing his prejudices in the guise of reason and engaging in scholastic spurious debate, where he picks an absent opponent, sets all the terms of the argument, imposes all of the assumptions employed, and then demolishes his adversary with considerable ease. Hanold accepts Kennevan's definition as a competent and sufficiently extensive description of an MIS but claims that Dearden gave it a character it does not claim. Dearden attributes to the definition the universal dimension of a total, completely integrated management information system. Hanold sums up his rebuttal by saying that the willful logic of small minds is hardly the proper test of the fact or possibility of an MIS.

With that, Hanold reflects on the nature of information and contrasts it with data in a unique way. Information begins with data that is infused with an organizing and purposeful intelligence. Then he describes and relates the terms information system, business information system, managerial information system, and accounting information system. He uses an extended example to illustrate the transformation of data through accounting and other business information systems to eventually become useful for managerial purposes. After discussing the relationship between accounting and MIS, he explains his idea of the key to MIS.

READING SUGGESTIONS

This article is important for its well-reasoned arguments from two perspectives -- as a rebuttal to the Dearden article, and as a message to the accounting profession. Be sure to grasp Hanold's definitions of data, information, information system, management information system, and accounting system. Read lightly over the middle part of the article picking up an appreciation for the transformation of data into information and an understanding of the relationship between accounting and MIS, particularly why he argues that accounting is outside the management function and thence can no longer serve as an MIS. At the end of the article, find his explanation of the necessity of MIS and of the key to MIS.

QUESTIONS

1. How does Hanold show the absolute necessity of an MIS in the large, complex organization?

2. How does Hanold define data and information and the relationship between the two?

3. When and under what conditions is it acceptable for management to use intuitive information rather than systematic information in decision making?

4. How does he describe an MIS and how does this relate to his definition of information system?

5. What is the importance of integration in MIS?

6. In what sense is an accounting information system not a management information system? Why is accounting necessarily outside of the management function? Why must the MIS be kept separate and distinct from the accounting function?

7. Describe how data gets transformed into information for management.

8. Why does the MIS function report directly to the executive office at the Pillsbury Corporation?

9. What is the key to MIS? the critical problem to the construction of an MIS? the real obstacle to MIS?

10. How does Hanold include the notion of a model bank in his concept of MIS?

Theoreticians may debate the topic fruitlessly, but a management information system has become an absolute necessity for successful operation of a large and complex business enterprise

An Executive View of MIS

by Terrance Hanold

Whether there can be a management information system was once a matter of great debate. And there were signs for a time that exhaustion had settled the issue. The debate had been prolonged but hardly profound, so we were grateful for the respite. But recently the charge that MIS is a mirage has once more been raised in the *Harvard Business Review*.

Truth, it seems, is always on the scaffold and Error on the throne.

Scholars, too, I suppose are human. At least the claims of charity require this assumption. But where the rest of us rely simply on blunt assertion to support our biases, they with greater guile clothe their prejudices in the guise of reason.

The classical and perhaps the deadliest weapon they employ for the subversion of truth is the scholastic debate. Even lower in bad eminence is the scholastic spurious debate, where he picks an absent opponent, often unnamed and always unaware of the contest, sets all the terms of the argument, imposes all of the assumptions employed and, if he is worthy of his PhD, demolishes his adversary with considerable ease. This, of course, is the favorite strategy of those who write business review articles.

It is a despicable, villainous device.

This article is based on an address to the Midwest Conference of the Financial Executives Institute. A portion of the text appeared in the *CPA Journal,* published by the New York State Society of Certified Public Accountants.

Let me advise you in confidence that this is exactly what I now propose to do myself.

As the description of the system he proposes to disprove, my anonymous antagonist (John Dearden, Herman Krannert Professor of Business Administration at Harvard University,

---

. . . how an MIS comes into being, where its direction and control are properly lodged, and why it is essential . . .

"MIS Is a Mirage," *Harvard Business Review,* January-February, 1972, p. 90) quotes the following:

"A management information system is an organized method of providing past, present and projection information related to internal operations and external intelligence. It supports the planning, control and operational function of an organization by furnishing uniform information in the proper time-frame to assist the decision making process." (Walter J. Kennevan, "MIS Universe," *Data Management*, September, 1970)

Whether or not acute analysis might modify it in part, this is a competent and sufficiently extensive description of a management information system.

How does a scholar go about its destruction? His first effort at discreditation is to describe it as "grandiose." Aside from the charge itself, he offers nothing but ridicule to support the de-

scription. Then to give it a character it does not claim, he attributes to the definition the universal dimension of a *total* management information system. Quite clearly, the author of the statement makes no such claim of universal content, and it is certainly not fairly subject to attack on that score. It includes only information capable of systematic collection and of organized processing and presentation in a business environment.

The next means of establishing the proposition that MIS is a phantasmagorical mirage is the attempted demonstration by logic rather than by evidence that the creation of a *total* management information system is beyond the capability of man.

He declares the fact that certain rival business schools now offer MS and PhD degrees in management information systems. Such persons, he says, "must clearly be technicians and would have little impact on most of the information supplied to management, particularly at upper levels." Since the author is engaged in the manufacture of Masters of Science and DBAs, his authority on this point far exceeds mine, and I must accept his estimate of their fundamental incompetence to create a useful product. So this category of potential inventors of an MIS is by concession disqualified.

In order to disqualify the rest of the world, he imposes on us his assumptions that the creator of a management information system must be a specialist, that he must attack the information system as a whole, and that the systems approach must be used in making that attack. This, of course, indulges in the contradictory assumptions (1) that management is incapable of participating effectively in the designation of the content and methodology of an information system and (2) that anyone outside of management would be incompetent to define what management needs. By this system of logic, he attempts to disqualify that part of the world other than doctors of philosophy from competence in this field.

But the only person unequivocally excluded by this misshapen logic is my anonymous antagonist himself. The willful logic of small minds is hardly the proper test of the fact or possibility of an MIS. The best evidence, I think, follows from experience. With this beginning I should like to describe how an MIS comes into being, where its direction and control are properly lodged, and why it is essential to a modern business organization of scale.

Information is at the core of my subject. Hence a few minutes' reflection on the nature of information is an unavoidable inconvenience.

Information has to do with the communication of knowledge inspired by observation—with the interchange of thoughts and ideas proceeding from experience. A more expansive definition embraces knowledge derived from study or instruction as well. So the contributions of the schools are under no ban of exclusion from information if we take a generous view.

Information is different in kind from data. Information has the attribute of communication which data does not have. In the context of business, data is merely the digital shadow of haphazard events indifferently recorded. It enters our data bank in the accidental series of occurrence in time. And even that degree of order is indifferently observed. Each bit is a meaningless fragment in itself, and the mass communicates nothing.

Yet information begins with data. Data is transformed into information through the infusion of purposeful intelligence. Thus information is data refined by intelligence so that it communicates meaning or knowledge, and in the course of communication will inform one or more parties to the interchange with ideas or conclusions.

Further, the quality of the information resulting from this alchemy can be of several degrees, depending upon the sophistication of the intellectual tools applied to the data and to the nature of the actions which the information process must support.

In the ordinary affairs of life, data is transformed into information on an extemporized basis. We make no pretense at a systematic collection of relevant data, nor do we pretend to apply consistent principles, values or methods to its treatment. Thus when eggs are on the breakfast menu, my wife may advise their rejection today because the cholesterol level revealed in my annual physical report is at the top of her consciousness; tomorrow, under the same circumstances, she may insist that I have them because eggs and grapefruit have a tempering effect on my weight.

But in a business context, informa-

Information begins with data, but it is data infused with an organizing and purposeful intelligence.

---

tion must be developed in systematic fashion if it is to merit a confidence level warranting immediate credence and use. Our initial statement of meaning emphasized that information is the *communication* of knowledge. Credibility is at the heart of communication, and the speed with which information is communicated determines its worth.

I neither deny the value nor decry the use of intuitive rather than systematic information in the critical case. It is occasionally an essential exercise of business expertise. Mutations in corporate practice are as necessary as in the realms of nature when environmental adaptation requires it. But it has an infrequent place in the continuing conduct of a business. And it is legitimate for use in the exceptional case only after the systematic information has been examined and found not quite adequate.

Business information, then, requires the systematic collection of data and its systematic processing according to a series of intellectually valid methods. The output of the system will communicate knowledge which will dictate or assist the selection of action decisions in fields to which the data and the methods are relevant.

Managerial Information. Now, let us consider the nature of *managerial* information. Is managerial information a subclass of business information? We may at least assume that to be the case for the purpose of inquiry. And it is certainly true that, as there is a hierarchical difference between data and information, so there are hierarchical differences between the several levels of business information and between the information systems which serve them.

Information Systems. The definition of a management information *system* raises the fiercest disputations vented since the Diet of Worms. As an honorary founder of the Society for Management Information Systems, I follow its proceedings with the closest attention. Since the scope of its function obviously depends upon a definition of such systems, it is an area of principal controversy among certain of our members.

After much informal debate and a few unilateral pronouncements by our more authoritative fellows, a formal colloquium on the subject was arranged. For eight hours the subject was collectively threshed. Each participant assailed every definition proposed, including his own, from id to ibidem. None received acceptance by vote, consensus or extrasensory perception.

So the field is free to each to adopt his own as long as he agrees to impose it on no one else. Perhaps the humanistic approach suggested by Bishop Walton in opening one of our annual sessions is the most appropriate for group therapy. He said, by way of paraphrase, "It is almost impossible to define an information system, but it is easy to recognize one." So I shall describe a managerial information system as I see it.

An information *system* defines the data needed to generate the information required to serve a specific business function. It employs a data collection system; a data transmission system; a data storage system; a data retrieval system; an appropriate array of intelligence infusion systems, which are usually described as software or application programs and which employ the principles and methods of the function or discipline served; and an information/communication system.

MIS Described. As distinguished from an *information* system, I conceive a *management* information system to consist of a *cluster* of business information systems. MIS is a symbol rather than a descriptive name, which designates an integrated complex of information systems of such variety and sophistication and interrelationship as experience qualified by rational assessment determines to be essential or useful to the general or executive management of the business enterprise.

These are ordinarily conceived to be strung on an electronic network with a myriad of mind-boggling devices. For any particular information system, it may be demonstrated that there is no need for a computer or random access files or remote terminals or any of the other electronic gear that decorate our offices and inflate our equipment accounts. The span and effectiveness of the information system justify its name, not the apparatus which serves it.

But the conduct in concert of a complex of information systems is in practical terms impossible without a computer.

The Accounting Information System. Accounting supplied the first business information system, I suppose. Accounting defined the data needed to generate the information required for its purpose as that data relating to the assets and liabilities of the firm and to transactions affecting those assets and liabilities. It collected the data needed by the accounting system through the day book, gave it order by processing it through the journal, and meaning and relationship by transferring these entries to the ledger according to the shifting principles and prejudices of the profession. Accounting communicated the resulting information through the balance sheet, profit and loss statement and supplementary schedules.

From the accountant's viewpoint, only the compulsions of time have made a transfer from manual to mechanical to electronic methods tolerable. As far as he is concerned, no change in the accounting information system has occurred in consequence of this shift in tools. Taken by itself, an accounting system is an accountant's information system and not a managerial information system. Only as it becomes entwined in a complex of several information systems does it become a part of a whole deserving that cachet.

Accounting and MIS. An MIS dealing with numbers of information systems as an integrated complex can

---

. . . this change from skill-centered craftsmen who knew their job to knowledge-centered professionals who knew their world . . .

---

hardly be established or operated or utilized by management unless they are all threaded together on a computer-directed network. And if it is to succeed, the threading must somehow be directed by the management, not by accountants or systems types or other functionaries. Let me try to illustrate this point by a scatter of examples from one of our businesses—our flour milling enterprise.

Each car of wheat received at one of our flour mills results in an entry which discloses the cost per unit, an official classification, an official grade, a total weight, a protein analysis, a bin location in our elevator where it is stored, a freight transit credit in most cases and several other bits of data. All of these pieces of data are collected in our central data bank.

In the course of processing this data, we derive an inventory of our wheat. Since each shipment loses its identity in the bin in which it is placed, the

inventory of each bin is an average of the type, grade, protein, cost and so forth of its contents. We derive accounts payable in favor of the seller. A transit credit account and other fascinating offal of the milling accounting process also result. So by processing this data into like or related classes, we begin its transformation into information.

Concurrently, it is hoped, sales of flour are being made. As orders are received, they are scheduled for production. The central production department allocates orders among the mills by means of a program which employs inventory data, data respecting the location of each mill, the character of wheat supply tributary to each mill, the delivery point of the order, the availability of transit billing suitable for application to its further shipment, the specifications of the flour ordered, the capacity and load balance of our mills and so on. This determination rests on data which have reciprocal as well as consecutive relationships and hence are handled best through computer-administered programs. These programs employ raw data from the data bank, as well as information derived from the accounting system. So information at one level of use is merely data at the next.

On receipt of its production schedule, the wheat committee at the mill uses another computer program to determine the optimum cost and quality of wheat mixes to be used to produce these orders. It is based on data respecting its wheat inventories and the array of orders directed to be placed on the mill. It also uses subjective data in our data bank respecting many functional characteristics of various types of wheat, their several milling qualities, yield and so forth. This program, of course, serves also to indicate the specified order in which these shipments will be manufactured.

The wheat procurement department is advised of the planned depletion of stocks by kind, grade and amount. So having a view both of the kinds and qualities of wheats consumed, of the future orders received or anticipated for milling at that location and the destination points, it makes plans for purchasing wheats in the market of the predicted type, grade, protein, origins, destinations, etc. Again, in making this decision, accounting information is used in combination with a great deal of historical crop and sales data.

Through these processes, an immense amount of market data accumulates respecting the total and seasonal uses of present and potential customers by product and by delivery point. Employing models of several kinds, the marketing department can determine the most profitable mix of products to

sell, to whom and at what destinations and by sales periods. In consequence, it is able to assign specific targets by time period, by customer and by product.

Finally, the general management in flour milling is able to make medium term forecasts, taking into account estimates of wheat supplies by origin, type, cost, estimates of the effect of these elements on prices, margins, volumes and product mix by market area. By varying the data and assumptions, they derive alternative strategies to fit changes in wheat supplies, transportation costs, competitive action and other contingencies. Necessary capital investments, distribution networks, sales force assignments and personnel requirements are also indicated.

What we see here briefly and simplistically is the transformation of data to information for use in immediate departmental actions through the injection of the functional intelligence of that department. As each informational component is successively woven into other data processed through further functional methods and intellectual disciplines, we ultimately reach a system complex and a volume and variety of informational flows which begin to match the needs of the general or executive management. Only at that point do we begin to justify the label of a managerial information system.

The structure begins with the primitive selection and abbreviated classification of data according to the accounting dictate. Accounting is first concerned with an orderly record of every item and movement and transformation of firm assets and of every contract and obligation of the firm which may enhance or diminish those assets.

This is first-level knowledge of critical importance which is not diminished by its position in the managerial scale, but it hardly rationalizes or utilizes all of the data in the bank, nor does it apply all of the talents, such as procurement, production, finance and marketing, that the development of managerial information requires.

Information begins with data, but it is data infused with an organizing and purposeful intelligence. The initial intelligence applied to data is that of accounting, but a whole array of disciplines is introduced into the process as it proceeds to managerial use. The base of the data during these successive processes is perpetually expanding in both detail and extent.

Thus, information is data infused or refined by intelligence so that it communicates meanings not immediately reflected by the data alone. When information is communicated, it informs either or both of the parties involved. But the nature of the information conveyed will differ according to the function of the person informed and according to the point in the informational hierarchy from which he derives his information.

We have arrived at the conclusion that accounting produces an information system almost adequate for accountants. We have found that an accounting system is not an MIS because it is not designed to develop the data or

---

The burden of management is to influence the future favorably, and even predictably.

---

to communicate the information required by the multiplying disciplines which must today feed business management. That system is designed to collect only such data as accountants deem relevant to their function and to put that data in such order, to marinate the data in such values and principles, and to subject the data to such procedures as are embraced in their particular functional philosophy.

These are not conclusions comfortable to accountants. In my defense may I be permitted to say that in my view Karl Marx somewhat overstated the case when he described accountants as "jackals of capitalism."

Disappointment is the product of expectation. As I remember it, 20 years ago the accounting profession felt it had the key to dominance in business decisions. It appeared to sprout from the revelation by our outside auditors of the breakeven chart. From the ranges of results it displayed we could readily select the proper sales and cost levels we ought to obtain, garlanded with an attractive return on investment. And these results could be neatly battened down and guaranteed by a set of controls derived from the DuPont chart room and administered by the accounting department.

Controls could forestall all mishaps and assure a golden future. And obviously the controller would be suitably adorned with dignities and powers and a seat at the right hand of the chairman almighty.

But something unfunny happened on the way to the board room. A number of analyses have since been made, and there are several nominees for the blame. And, of course, there is blame enough so that it may be distributed lavishly among them. Charity forbids that they be singled out. Collectively we may designate them as the inciters

of the knowledge revolution.

Technology made huge additions to the stock of data which could be made into business information. Computers performed its transformation at speeds and costs which made it economically useful. Computers also gave entry into the office of the "science of abstraction —mathematics" in a multitude of applications. This led to the professionalization of the established branches of business and to the invasion of the counting room by a host of new sciences and professions. Both the effect and the cause of this change from skill-centered craftsmen who knew their job to knowledge-centered professionals who knew their world was the transition of the business information base from a transaction record to a data file enormously wider in scope.

So business has advanced to the statistical analysis of the present and the mathematical computation of the future, while the controller was left to this arithmetical accounting of the past. Sic Transit Gloria.

What Now? Fifteen years ago the controller had the only rational and continuing information system in the firm. Today every department in the firm is developing a business information system suited to its function. And the general and executive managements are securing, by accretion if not by design, a management information system which is the composite sum of the lot, plus the contribution made by executive management themselves as required by their own functions.

Can the controller recapture the information monopoly he once embraced? Can he again become the croupier of the only game in town? I think not.

Each information system requires of its governor expertise in the function or discipline it serves. And an information system forms an organic union with those it serves. As Professor Whisler puts it, "Older technologies are extensions of man's hands and muscles and were his tools and servants, while modern information technology is an extension of man's brain and is his partner—or even his master." No manager can afford to tolerate an interloper here. He must establish his own direct, continuing, reciprocal, interacting involvement in the system, subject to no man's leave of hindrance and certainly subject to no man's control.

For these reasons, Pillsbury's corporate policy obliges each of its operating firms "to obtain full utilization and value from Pillsbury's Business Information System." To ensure this result, the policy provides that "the General Manager must assume responsibility for the definition of the information and processing requirements of his" operation. "A senior professional from

the corporate department will be attached to the (firm) to serve as the General Manager sees fit in helping him to define his subsystem's requirements."

This same concept is carried to the corporate level. Our policy states that "Certain affairs of The Pillsbury Company are inseparable from its Executive Office. Among them is the Pillsbury Business Information System. Without immediate control of the design and operations of this system in its entirety, the Executive Office cannot effectively function. It is for this reason that PBIS reports directly to the Executive Office."

What Next? What becomes of "managerial accounting for decision making" in such an environment? How am I to deal with a letter from a young and ambitious member of the controller's group who expresses his point of view by this textbook quotation: ". . . it is felt that an accountant's role should not be confined to merely dealing with historic systems, data and controls. Along with looking at the past and present, he must also look to the future of the company which he serves. Nor should he be narrowly viewed as a corporate policeman, but more as an objective viewer of the corporate reality (performing an evaluative-mirroring function). While he may not be the supplier of answers, he can at least help to raise relevant questions and identify problem areas."

These phrases have a singing quality which appeals without persuading. It is the accountant's instinct to coach the

---

The MIS is the responsibility of the general and executive management.

---

manager respecting the decisions he makes, and at the end of the year, it is his function to sit in judgment on the results of those decisions. You and I understand the game, but the lads who are answerable to the world for the published results do not.

They think it indecorous for a man to urge a decision while uncommitted to its consequences. And they think it indecent, to put the matter in its politest terms, for him later to publish, underline and critique these consequences when they prove unfavorable, while hiding under the flag of neutrality that his accounting title gives him.

The burden of management is to influence the future favorably, and even predictably. A leading partner of one of the principal public auditing firms remarks that in the torment of change which tosses all enterprises today, "Success in committing resources to profitable opportunities is being measured less and less adequately by focusing on profits achieved . . . The concepts proposed in this discussion are based on the firm conviction that generally accepted accounting principles, as they are now constituted, and the management accounting practices that result from them, are inadequate —that they cannot respond to the forces of society which are, today, calling for meaningful information."

As a remedy he proposes a scheme of "entrepreneurial accounting"—a scheme for reflecting the future profitability of a firm—which would alter accounting concepts long in fashion, but would do little to enlarge the basis of judgment or the area of certainty for a manager required to deal with "problems (which) have been exponentially expanded."

We are dealing, of course, with the ancient urge toward aggrandizement of function which is neither foreign nor peculiar to accountants. And the supporting rationale is seductive. Accounting has honorably assisted the decisional processes of management in the past—why not enlarge its dominion so that it embraces the whole information structure on which managers depend?

A computer environment does add a favorable time dimension to accounting information which suits it to use in the arena as well as in the postmortem parlor. This new dimension offers accountants the temptation to float widely over the whole informational range. But they enlarge their span of activity at the peril of loss of stature and effectiveness which depends on their respectful obedience to the limits of their professional domain.

Accountants have the capacity to convert accounting data into accounting information because their professional training qualified them to infuse that data with accounting intelligence. Outside their field they become mere data gatherers, for their training gives them no special competence to convert data into the marketing, production, procurement or other information systems which ultimately fuse into an MIS. If they attempt an indiscriminate power of dictation in areas outside their own field, they lose their professional identity and become simply computer systems technicians.

Worse, they become a well-meaning but formidable obstruction to the creation of the end they say they desire—a true MIS—for they deter the entry of the variety of talents, disciplines and intelligences necessary to that end. The fact is that no single function or discipline can furnish a sufficient information base for management. That is why we have kept our information systems free of the grasp of any one function. Thus, we have enabled our managers to draw the informational output of

every function freely into its channel. Each functional information system is the responsibility of the functional manager in matters of design, structure and purpose. The MIS is the responsibility of the general and executive management.

Also at the heart of the matter is the distinctive character of the accounting function. Here we come to the point of division. MIS is essentially an operative system completely enmeshed in the management function. Accounting, control and audit are essentially an evaluative system—a system for evaluating management's performance *and hence necessarily outside of the management function.*

Accounting's prime concern was once with the form of the entry. Today its first test must be with the clarity of the disclosure. Its function was once private and procedural. It is now professional, charged with a public trust. Recognition of this obligation will be a business landmark in the 1970s. The primacy of their fiduciary duty will preclude conflicting postures, such as are implied by "managerial accounting," or entangling alliances with management which their dominance over MIS would create.

The accounting fraternity is under a fiduciary obligation to the board of directors, to the owners, and to the public to furnish such performance evaluations of the firm and its management. The success of an accounting information system is measured by the support it furnishes to the discharge of this mission. Happily, the better the accounting information system serves this end, the more useful are its inputs to the MIS, because they more faithfully reflect professional accounting intelligence.

Not only must these evaluative judgments be made free of bias, they must be free of the suspicion of bias which comes from a compromising involvement in the operative management function. The fiduciary obligation must rest on the internal staff as well as on the outside auditors. For I cannot conceive, looking to the future, how an outside auditor can certify financial statements prepared by a staff whose interests are conflicting and whose loyalties are divided.

It has been argued that thus limited the accountant's role is simply demeaning. In my opinion, the inputs we get from men who maintain a position of professional integrity are of the ultimate value in the heat of time-pressed indecision. In my opinion the counsel of those who rightly maintain the posture of counselor will be of highest

worth to those who have the burden of management in this decade. Those who counsel on the basis of professional principles profoundly understood and respected have a value beyond measure. And their value is the greater because they counsel rather than control, because they reason rather than rule.

A great profession is one whose practitioners think greatly of their calling. Perhaps the privilege of a prideful self regard, justly entertained, is the greatest reward that any future employment can offer.

The Financial Officer. One of my associates has pointed out an uncomfortable omission in my argument which requires a further point to be made. In an accountant's working day role, accounting may be "merely a subset of the substance of his function." It does not recognize "the double identity of a controller, as chief accountant and as finance officer." And my friend puts into place the proper recognition of the critical leadership and contributions which our divisional controllers have made to the development of our MIS, not only in the areas dealing with the hard facts of the past, but in the systems designed to "record, process and evaluate the *uncertain future* of an *uncertain world."*

He also establishes the interesting proposition that certain of our accountants took the initiative in developing tools for *decision* making in the managerial world of *uncertainty,* and that their example finally led to the "emancipation" of these "managerial functions from the traditional controller's control." So we attain again unto the revealed truth that decisions pertaining

---

As in all cases where an absolute line of division is wished for, there is a band of overlap.

---

to the uncertain present and the unseen future are the prerogatives of management, not the controller.

But there are some decisional areas often managed by accountants which are beyond the areas of transaction records, control mechanisms, and evaluative measurements and judgments of management. These are the functions of the finance officer.

To adopt my associate's conclusions, "A clear distinction is needed between the controller as an accountant and the controller as a finance officer. The function of finance is distinctly a managerial function dealing with uncertainty, as much as the other functions (marketing, production, etc.). The finance officer has to deal with the timing of finance decisions, the choice of sources of financing, the control of liquidity, the estimation of future shortages or surpluses, and predicting future interest rates. His information system is distinguishable and separate from the accounting system. However, there is a tendency for finance officers and chief accountants to be identical and drawn from the accounting profession."

As in all cases where an absolute line of division is wished for, there is a band of overlap. At the operational levels in the firm these may be both necessary and extensive. But at the senior policy levels it is undesirable and in my judgment will not long be tolerable.

Theoretically, as my friend supposes, the fiduciary character of the controller has always existed. But the focus of responsibility continually shifts with the scale and mission of our institutions and with the ideals and objectives of our society. So the fiduciary nature of the controller's function has advanced from an occasional aspect to the dominant character of his function. (Walter F. Frese and Robert K. Mautz, "Financial Reporting By Whom?" *Harvard Business Review,* March-April, 1972.)

Hence, while the financial office is derived from the accounting function, it has attained a status and character distinct from that of the controller. Prediction is the dominant contribution of the financial officer, who is preoccupied with the acquisition and allocation of resources by the firm; while designation and measurement is the prime concern of the controller who accounts for the inventory and evaluates the benefits of the corporate resources.

Finance by its nature adheres to management. The controller by his function must be allied to ownership and its representatives, the board of directors.

The Imperative Necessity for MIS. I must now return for a closing session with my anonymous adversary. He contends that a series of business information systems, each oriented to a particular function or operation, must result in an MIS which is "uncoordinated, and therefore inefficient and unsatisfactory." Because of the vast differences which necessarily exist between these several systems created for accounting and control, for production and distribution, for marketing, etc., he contends that expertise in one area is of little value in another. It follows he thinks that since one man cannot master the design of every system, there can be no single homogeneous MIS embracing them all.

If we followed the same logic we must also conclude that there cannot be a firm of size or complexity because no one man has the talent to master every function and operation necessary to the accomplishment of its mission.

Consequently, according to his test, no one is qualified to manage it in total. Perhaps we have inadvertently stumbled upon the flaw in the system! But the fact is that we do have the executive office, and it is required to oversee the total effort of the firm. And it must have an MIS to get the job done.

The key to MIS is an integrated data base, not a universal genius expert and omniscient in everything. As we have noted, each of the functional systems utilizes data and output from other systems as well as data inputs from sources peculiar to its function. From these materials it generates information suited to the performance of its

---

. . . executive management considers a different opportunity horizon and a different time span than does operating management.

---

particular function. And this information also feeds back into the data base where it is available as data for all of the other business systems.

It follows that if our functional information systems cover the operations of the firm with reasonable sufficiency, there is information in the data base adequate to support an executive management information system. Some further data will be needed, of course, because executive management considers a different opportunity horizon and a different time span than does operating management. But with this modest qualification the material is at hand to do the job.

And the job is no more complex—indeed, it is less so—than the problem of creating the several operating systems. The critical problem to the construction of an MIS is the integrated data base itself. This requires first a unified communication system through which the system data must flow, it requires rapidly expanding data file facilities, and it demands a data coding and addressing scheme which makes all the data in the bank reasonably available (hopefully randomly and instantly available) to every system in the firm.

The real obstacle to MIS in most firms is the structure of the data files themselves, and the means in hand for accessing them. Without adequate methods and structures here the problem of system interfaces—which means people interfaces—becomes the condition precedent to performance. And a guarantee of unsatisfactory performance. My anonymous antagonist says that this is a matter to be solved by education, but as you will recall he disqualified B school products as a solution much earlier in the game. So he is bucking the problem to some other branch of learning when he takes this

exit. And indeed he closes his article in a state of hopelessness.

"Management must always operate with insufficient information . . . In many areas the truth of these statements is becoming more salient because while the role of management is becoming more complex, the new information technology is not helping significantly . . . The problems of control in decentralized companies are much more difficult than they were ten years ago—increases in size, complexity, and geographical dispersion have made control much more difficult. Yet the new information technology has been of little help in this area, simply because the problems of controlling decentralized decisions do not lend themselves to computerized or mathematical solutions . . . part of our information crisis results from the nature of the present business environment. We shall simply have to live with it."

This is a perfect demonstration of the absolute necessity of MIS, and a complete admission of the impossibility of reaching it through his approach. He has discredited people interfaces as a means of establishing data flows between related information systems. He has failed to see either the necessity or feasibility of avoiding this impediment by an integrated data base.

For we shall not reach the MIS we need for the management of the enterprises we have created through the scholastic logic bequeathed us by a medieval heritage. We shall reach it by the perceptive application of the information technology which daily experience teaches us, if we are disposed to learn.   □

Mr. Hanold has been president of The Pillsbury Company since 1967 and a member of its board of directors since 1961. He joined the company in 1946 as an attorney, held a succession of financial posts, and before becoming president was executive vice president of finance and international operations. Among other activities, he is a director of the First National Bank of Minneapolis and a trustee of the Committee for Economic Development. He has BA and BLL degrees from the Univ. of Minnesota.

"NEW LOOK AT COMPUTER DATA ENTRY"

Journal of Systems Management (24:2), 1973 February, pages 24-33.

Data entry is the process by which input data for a processing application is made available in machine readable form. The traditional method has been keypunching of data into cards. Beginning in the period 1969-70, technology changes have provided several cost effective alternatives to punched cards. Data entry changes are essentially important because they tend to impact the procedures of personnel who capture and record the data. The article surveys the significant developments in data entry technology. Although the article is now somewhat dated, it clearly lays out the alternatives and their characteristics.

READING SUGGESTIONS

The article has two major parts: discussion of major data entry alternatives and discussion of an approach to evaluation of alternatives. The discussion of major data entry alternatives contains the following elements:

1. Keypunch and keypunch replacement equipment
    a. Buffered keypunch
    b. Keytape
    c. Keydisk
2. Character recognition systems
    a. Optical character (OCR)
    b. Optical mark (OMR)
    c. Bar code
    d. Magnetic ink character recognition (MICR)
3. Terminal systems
    a. Integrated terminal systems
       (1) Online from CRT or typewriter
       (2) Offline from keydisk, point of sale, and data collection equipment.
    b. Composite terminal systems
       (1) Online using batch terminal
       (2) Offline using paper tape

In reading the article, note the alternatives and the major considerations affecting their adoption. The reader should recognize that the conclusions of the article are generally true but that technology advances have not occurred exactly as expected. For example, keydisk systems are replacing keytape units and are a stronger competitor for data entry than indicated by the article. Bar codes are now encoded on almost all grocery products; checkout systems to read the codes are in limited use and substantial use is expected.

The evaluation model is traditional. It considers monthly fixed costs, monthly variable costs, and conversion costs (fixed and variable) for each major data entry application.

QUESTIONS

1. How significant is data entry as an item of EDP expenditure?
2. What are the authors' estimates of trends in keypunch replacement devices?
3. Why is a buffered keypunch superior? What causes an increase in operator productivity?
4. What are the advantages of keydisk over keytape?
5. What are the difficulties with OCR? How are rejects handled?
6. What is the major condition suggesting the need for online terminal entry?
7. What are the measurable factors in productivity increases in keypunch replacement equipment?

This special report details the many alternatives and factors that management must consider before choosing or updating data entry equipment.

■ The technology of most aspects of computing has changed so rapidly as to be barely recognizable from the technology of a mere seven years ago. We have seen several hundredfold improvements in internal processing speeds and on-line mass storage. Software operating systems have allowed a more efficient utilization of increasingly more powerful computers. Communications capability has added an entirely new dimension to the scope of computer applications. Most companies have quickly assimilated computing advancements and have benefited from the performance improvements. Business, especially big business, would

Are the keypunch and the punched card, like the wheel, designs that cannot be fundamentally improved? The punch card does have some obvious advantages: it can be read by both man and machine; it is largely resistant to environmental conditions, and, like the keypunch, it is relatively inexpensive. But the disadvantages are just as apparent. The information able to be contained on any one card is limited, leading to troublesome multiple-card records. The speed at which cards can be input to the computer is 10 to 100 times slower than with other recording media such as magnetic tape; and, most im-

NEW LOOK AT COMPUTER DATA ENTRY

By RAYMOND FERRARA
and RICHARD L. NOLAN

find it difficult to operate if it weren't for these advancements. The volume of work would simply be too great to handle manually or with first or even second-generation computers.

However, there is one notable exception to business' rapid assimilation of new computer technology: data entry. Broadly defined, data entry is the process by which information is generated in a form suitable to be read by the computer. Here, we will be concerned primarily with volume data entry—how an organization's standardized, repetitive information can be captured as opposed to, say, textual data entry (word-processing) or program data entry.

Until the mid-60's, volume data entry was nearly synonymous with keypunching. Although a much wider range of alternative methods now is available, keypunching still accounts for the large majority of computer data requirements. Considering the performance progress in other areas of the technology, it is rather surprising to note that this vast bulk of data is being prepared on equipment initially designed for the 1890 U. S. Census. The keypunch's standard medium, the 80-column, 12-row punch card, was developed more recently, in 1924, but its origins extend even further back to the card-controlled weaving machines of the 1850's.

portant, card preparation is time-consuming and highly labor-intensive.

The design of better data entry systems has been approached from two basic directions. *Keypunch replacement* focuses on improving or replacing the keypunch, yet still retaining an operator dedicated to keying data from source documents to a computer-readable medium. Data entry systems utilizing the buffered keypunch, key-tape units, or key-disk systems fall into this category. *Source data entry*, on the other hand, implies eliminating the intermediate operators necessary in a keypunch or keypunch replacement system. Optical character recognition equipment, for example, translates handwritten, typed, or printed information directly from a source document.

Most terminal systems, even keyboard terminal systems, are used as source data entry systems. An airline reservation agent, although he may often key from a prepared document just like a keypunch operator, isn't employed solely to type into a terminal. He would be there, terminal or not; the terminal is simply a device allowing him to obtain rapid con-

---

The research for this article was supported by the Associates of the Harvard Business School. Working drafts were reviewed as CBIS (Computer-Based Information Systems) Working Paper #3.

Reprinted from the Journal of Systems Management, 1973 February.

148

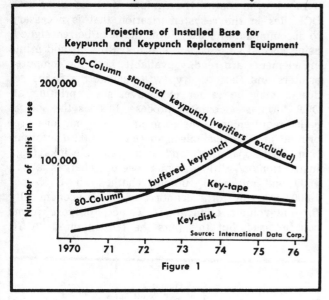

Projections of Installed Base for Keypunch and Keypunch Replacement Equipment

80-Column standard keypunch (verifiers excluded)

buffered keypunch

Key-tape

80-Column

Key-disk

Number of units in use

200,000

100,000

1970 71 72 73 74 75 76

Source: International Data Corp.

Figure 1

key-tape unit to off-line tape station). Response capability is also possible through a batch or off-line network provided immediate response is not required. Finally, cost-effective source data entry can be achieved through a wide variety of devices, from flexowriters to industrial data collection systems, without the heavy central computer utilization and communications line charges which continuously on-line terminals incur.

Major Data Entry Alternatives

The major data entry alternatives can be grouped into (1) keypunch and keypunch replacement, (2) optical character recognition and related equipment, and (3) terminal systems. Figure 1 shows the projected trends in installed units for the keypunch and the three major types of keypunch replacement equipment: buffered keypunch, key-tape, and key-disk.

All three types of replacement equipment share some fundamental advantages over the standard keypunch. Each unit can function in both data entry and verify[1] modes, eliminating the necessity for separate verification equipment. Another common feature is the electronically buffered keyboard. Because characters are imprinted *after* a record is complete, the operator does not have to "wait" on formerly mechanically-constrained actions like card registration, skipping, and duplicating. Nor does the operator have to rekey the whole record upon detecting an error. The operator simply backspaces and rekeys the correction. Though individual operators may have trouble becoming accustomed to a buffered keyboard, most users have experienced productivity increases from 10-25 percent over standard keypunchers and verifiers.[2]

Aside from the keyboard, the buffered keypunch is basically equivalent to standard models. Univac, the originators, had the market entirely to themselves from 1968 to 1971, until IBM announced a buffered keypunch for standard 80-column cards and another for the newer System/3 96-column cards.[3] IBM's entrance is expected to give a tremendous boost to buffered keypunch sales; chances are the buffered models will outnumber standard models by late 1974.

With key-tape, the operator keys directly onto magnetic tape, bypassing the card entirely. With tape, records lengths can be variable, thus avoiding multiple card records. Tape is also a faster, more accurate medium than cards for computer input. In practice, however, tape has proved cumbersome for the installation that is characterized by a large variety of data entry jobs. The operator must mount new tapes frequently or key different batches on the same tape. The latter method requires pooling,[4] or separating appropriate records onto appropriate tapes. Pooling has proved a time-consuming and expensive process in installations with a large job mix.

Key-tape manufacturers, the pioneers of keypunch replacement, are facing a semi-saturated market. Some

firmation of passenger requests. A byproduct of this activity is that the information he keys is obtained in computer readable form.

Basis for Reviewing Alternatives

Data entry typically accounts for 20-40 percent of EDP expenditures. Consequently, the decisions concerning the types of data entry to be used in an organization are likely to have major cost ramifications. Equally important, these decisions can affect the timeliness and accuracy of the organization's information flow. But keypunch replacement and especially source data entry may never be investigated without some co-operation and prodding by top management.

Even if there is an awareness of the potential savings to be gained in data entry, there is little incentive for change. Performance is not always measured in financial terms. The premium can be on maximizing the quality and reliability of service rather than minimizing cost. Source data entry methods are also especially hard to implement, since these require commitment and cooperation across departmental boundaries.

But, with computer manufacturers leading the way, managers at all levels are becoming aware of the benefits of on-line keyboard terminals. On-line keyboard terminals probably will be the general purpose data entry devices of the future, but it is also clear that we are in a transition stage, with most companies possessing neither the resources nor the need to convert all their data entry workloads to on-line systems. Moreover, it would be misleading to associate the benefits of on-line keyboard terminals *only* with on-line keyboard terminals. Rapid communication with a central computer can be achieved through remote batch terminals or even an off-line network (e.g., of the more recent models offer communications options for users desiring an off-line data entry network, but with many former key-tape installations converting to key-disk or on-line terminal entry, retirements are expected to exceed sales, leading to the projected decline in the installed base.

Key-disk systems avoid the pooling problem and offer other positive advantages. The basic concept of a key-disk system is to link several buffered keystations to a small controller or minicomputer. Data records can be keyed, extensively checked and validated using the minicomputer, and stored on its disk. When complete batches are accumulated, the data can be automatically re-recorded on magnetic tape for input to a central computer.

The first key-disk system was introduced in 1969, followed by at least 10 other introductions within a year. Many of these "early" systems were large 16 to 64 keystation systems. But several companies are now providing smaller-scale, reasonably priced key-disk systems.[5] Over 80 percent of the present keypunch population is located at sites with less than 16 machines,[6] so key-disk should penetrate quite deeply.

In the past year, there have been several announcements of small computer systems which are functionally very similar to key-disk. Each can support a number of keystations, and also peripherals such as line printers, card reader/punches, and communications interfaces allowing disk-accumulated data to be transmitted directly to a host computer. These systems, although they may be more expensive on a per-keystation basis, combine the advantages of key-disk and remote batch processing.

Optical Character Recognition

Optical Character Recognition (OCR), heralded during the 60's as the coming solution for data entry problems, has yet to fulfill its promise. All but a few of the OCR systems produced to date have been sophisticated and expensive. They have been attractive primarily in high-volume, specialized applications but of little use to smaller installations.

Besides the cost of the equipment, a difficulty with OCR lies in the resystematization that is necessary to accommodate its use. Forms have to be redesigned, using special OCR papers and ink. Ribbons and printing elements are readily available, both for computer printers and Selectric typewriters, but the forms redesign may be rather expensive, since printing an OCR form is a complex process. Besides the special paper requirements, the form may have portions preprinted in OCR-readable inks (e.g., standard information, field separation) and in nonreadable inks (e.g., instructions). With minimum setup charges above $500 and minimum running charges above $5 per 1,000, an OCR form cannot be printed economically for low-volume applications. General-purpose forms can be used, but this puts the burden on the OCR

Figure 2 Typical OCR Reject Rates			
	Typed input	Handprinted input	Computer-printed input
Supervised preparation	Less than 1%	1—3%	negligible
Unsupervised but familiar with OCR rules	Less than 5%	Less than 10%	negligible

typist. For example, she would be required to locate information such as field and record separation. Efficient OCR typing requires training equivalent to that of a keypunch operator.

The principal features of OCR equipment which affect potential users are reject handling and operating flexibility. Some scanning units can read only selected portions of an input document (e.g., one or two lines) and thus restrict potential applications.[7] The ease with which new forms can be accommodated is also important. Machine specific higher-level languages exist, but their complexity and flexibility vary. Usually the manufacturer will provide support in this area, helping the user design and accommodate new forms.

Raymond Ferrara

Raymond Ferrara is employed with Raytheon Company, Equipment Division, where he is working on an Integrated Data Entry project. Mr. Ferrara has had several years experience in data processing, including EDP consulting in the Boston area and as a resident technical advisor to the government of Barbados, West Indies. He holds an M.B.A. degree from the Harvard Business School and a B.S. in Industrial Management from M.I.T.

Richard L. Nolan

Richard Nolan is an Associate Professor at the Graduate School of Business Administration, Harvard University. At the Harvard Business School, he teaches and does research in the Computer-Based Systems area. Professor Nolan has published a number of articles and books. His latest book is co-authored with F. Warren McFarlan, and David P. Norton: **Information Systems Administration** (Holt, Rinehart, and Winston). Professor Nolan also consults with several major companies on their computer-based system activities.

OCR readers differ in how they handle rejects or unreadable data. Some have a rescan feature which may help to cut down the incidence of rejects. An increasing number of readers are being equipped with one or more graphic displays and keyboards. Unreadable characters are projected on the display; the operator keys in his interpretation. This technique can reduce the reject rate enormously, but may result in significant lower OCR throughput speeds because the reader must pause until the reject is processed. Whatever the methods for handling rejects, the critical features are that clear, convenient techniques exist for (1) identifying the rejected data, (2) correcting it, and (3) maintaining batch integrity while avoiding data duplication.

Some manufacturers also emphasize reading speed and multifont capability as important features. Neither of these is likely to warrant a price premium for most potential users. Reading speeds should be checked to ensure that the projected workload can be handled in a reasonable time, but most users will find there is time to spare. Multifont capability (e.g., reading more than one type of OCR font) is becoming less important with OCR "A" emerging as American industry's standard font.

The ability to read handprinted numeric characters is available. Provided some fairly basic rules are followed, character-substitution error rates of less than one-tenth of one percent are achievable.[8] Except on two lower-priced OCR terminals, however, the handprint feature can be found only on equipment costing over $100,000. There are also at least two machines with alphanumeric handprint options.

As a source data entry system, OCR has been most successful where much of the information to be captured can be pre-printed (e.g., the return stub on a computer printed utility bill), or where some degree of control can be exercised in preparing the form. A high reject rate will offset the advantages of OCR, since rejected documents will have to be retyped or even cycled back to the source for correction. Providing that reasonable care is exercised to separate out folded or mutilated documents beforehand, the following reject rates are typical of users' experiences.[9]

As a keypunch replacement, OCR is feasible where the cost of OCR equipment can be offset by a reduction in keypunch and EAM equipment rentals and by the increased productivity of typists. Wages for typists are generally lower than for keypunch operators, but productivity will be much higher when sight-verification can be substituted for key-verification.[10]

Figure 3 shows the projected trends for OCR equipment. The steadily upward trend is expected to accelerate with the introduction of lower cost, minicomputer based OCR units. Four systems now on the market sell for less than $50,000. Given a limited number of source data entry jobs, this lower cost OCR equipment could be a cost effective replacement for as few as five or six keypunches. Several OCR

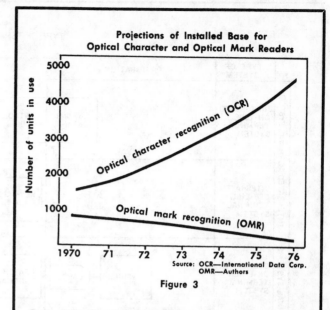

Figure 3

Optical mark readers (OMR) cannot "read" characters as true OCR units do; they can only detect the presence or absence of marks on a paper form. Because of OMR's inherently simpler recognition logic, the price of these units is substantially lower than OCR. Some sell for as low as $2,000 but the average is closer to $25,000.

manufacturers have announced combined OCR disk systems. Data read through the OCR unit is stored on disk; corrections to this data as well as entirely new batches of data may be entered through the keyboards.

As a data entry method, OMR has limited applicability. It can be useful on documents where responses are limited to "yes-no" or multiple choice answers, but it is an inaccurate, clumsy way of handling alphanumeric data. OMR's present installed base is less than half of the OCR's on a per-unit basis. Many OMR installations are now switching to OCR with numeric handprint capability, so OMR's installed base is probably on a permanent decline, despite several new product announcements.

Bar code and Magnetic Ink Character Recognition (MICR) are even less common data entry methods. Except for its entrenched position in the banking industry, MICR is unsuited for volume data entry. Document control is at least as difficult as with conventional OCR, the machines are just as expensive, and most MICR readers can translate only the numeric font used by the banking industry.

Bar code readers have alphanumeric capability,[11] but require mechanical devices (e.g., embossers, modified typewriters) for source document generation. Bar code has not been extensively promoted as a general purpose data entry method. A further decline is probable as OCR becomes less expensive, since bar code offers no other advantages over conventional OCR.

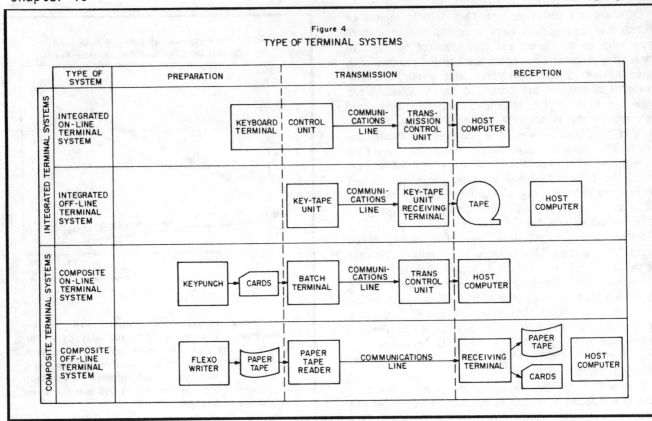

Figure 4
TYPE OF TERMINAL SYSTEMS

Terminal Systems

In comparing terminals to the other data entry alternatives, more is involved than just data preparation; transmission and reception can be equally important considerations. Figure 4 helps clarify these lines of comparison as well as provide a basic classification scheme for terminal data entry systems.

In an integrated terminal system, terminal equipment is used for both data preparation and transmission. In a composite system, the terminal equipment is used only for data transmission; virtually any stand-alone data entry equipment can be used for data preparation. In practice, paper tape and cards are the most popular preparation media, since reliable inexpensive transmission terminals for these are readily available.

All the terminal systems in Figure 4 can transmit information to a central site more rapidly than we would expect with a non-terminal system. However, transmission will be a major expense with any remote terminal system.[12] If terminal lines extend more than, say, 2000 feet from the host computer or cross a public right-of-way, then communications must be by way of telephone or slower speed telegraph lines. Large-scale alternative communications methods (i.e. via independent companies with microwave or satellite relays) will appear 3-5 years from now, at best.

Some costs for transmission via telephone lines are: (1) line charges. Leased line: $5 mile/month plus conditioning charges. Dial-up line: same rates as normal business telephone. One line can support several terminal units. Transmission speeds may vary from 300 to 1600 characters per second. Higher-capacity lines are available. (2) modems ($75/mo. up) or acoustic couplers ($10/mo. up). These must be connected at both ends of the communications line. Prices vary widely depending on transmission speed and error correction ability.

Other things being equal, rapid entry to a central computer should be an established need before considering a terminal data entry system. Then even if a terminal data entry is needed, there should be additional justifications for an on-line entry. For an installation to go on-line, several prerequisites will have to be satisfied. Physically, it needs a relatively large, fast computer with an operating system and teleprocessing monitor compatible to terminal operation. Then a frontend transmission control unit will be necessary to interface communications lines with the main computer.[13] Finally, the process of designing, programming, and maintaining on-line applications is considerably more complex than with batch applications. Consequently skilled technical personnel will assume a much greater importance.

On-line updating of data bases and error checking are two frequently mentioned justifications for on-line operation. Neither of these is usually a sufficient justification in itself. With off-line terminal systems, data can be entered quickly enough for most applications, and there are alternative methods for controlling errors (e.g. verification, check digits, batch totals, etc.) which can be employed regardless of the type of equipment used.

Response capability is the only characteristic of a terminal system that really requires on-line operation. By response, we mean the ability to obtain additional data and return it for display or printing within a relatively short time. This is in contrast to "echoes" of the data just entered. Several key-tape and key-disk systems are quite sophisticated in their echo capability—displaying the full record, performing error checks and minor calculations, or allowing limited retrieval of previously keyed information. Nevertheless, echoing is still a long way from the variety of response capable with an on-line system.

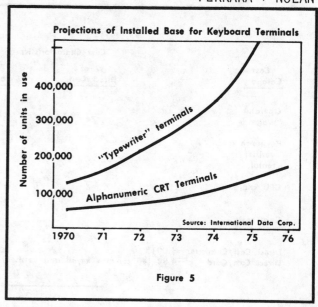

Figure 5

Integrated On-Line Systems

Of the two major types of keyboard terminals used in integrated on-line systems, alphanumeric cathode ray tube (CRT) terminals are by far the more popular for volume data entry applications.[14, 15] Typewriter terminals (e.g. Teletypes) are used by those desiring hard copy with data entry, but the projected growth for this type of terminal will come largely through time-sharing and remote job entry applications rather than data entry.

Alphanumeric CRT terminals are included in the product lines of all the major computer manufacturers. In addition, there are over 30 independent manufacturers of CRT terminals. Prices range from below $2,000 to over $10,000 per unit.[16] Price, however, is not usually a major selection criterion, since the terminal by itself usually represents a relatively minor cost in an on-line system. Terminal design considerations such as screen size and clarity, editing capability, and especially transmission methods are likely to assume important roles.

There is a definite trend towards increasing the terminal's local editing and processing power, thereby cutting down the load on the host computer and reducing communications line charges. Some terminals include this power in the terminal itself, while others depend on local minicomputer control units. The latter may be able to support peripherals (e.g. line printers), provide intermediate storage, and even operate off-line, although transmission is performed on-line.

Key-tape or key-disk equipment can form the basis for an integrated off-line terminal system. The only other terminal equipment which generally fit into this category are industrial data collection systems and point-of-sale systems. Both of these terminal systems are designed for specific applications: industrial data collection for the factory floor and point-of-sale for the retail store. In their own applications, they deserve close consideration, since their specialized design—resulting in source data entry—may prove more economical than any generalized form of data entry.

After some initial set-backs, the point-of-sale con-

cept seems set for rapid growth. Singer, the principal vendor already claims over a $100 million order backlog, and at least four other major companies are now involved in producing modified cash registers for data entry. Industrial data collection represents a more mature but still underdeveloped market. These systems generally incorporate badge or card readers, time clocks, and simple keyboards for gathering data from the production floor. There are now six vendors sharing an installed base close to $150 million.

Framework for Evaluating Alternatives

With the large array of data entry equipment and methods, selecting the reasonable, cost-effective system can be a complex process. Here we will focus mainly on the economics of equipment selection—the operating and conversion costs for each alternative. Of course, non-economic factors should enter into any selection process. Reliability, operator convenience, and ease of conversion may not find their way into the numbers, but are very real considerations nonetheless. What a cost comparison of alternatives can do is provide the background against which these non-economic factors can be assessed.

Examining the keypunch replacement decision first provides a sense for the basic economics of data entry. Then we will develop a more general framework, a "top-down" approach suitable for evaluating a wider variety of data entry alternatives.

Figure 6 summarizes the cost characteristics of a typical keypunch operation. Only those costs which are likely to vary with the keypunch replacement decision are included. Occupancy, supervisory expenses, etc. are excluded for this reason.

Card costs are a real though minor savings with key-tape and key-disk, but reduced CPU utilization may not be. Unless the installation can get rid of the computer's card reader or rents computer time on

Figure 6
Cost Characteristics of Typical Keypunch Operation

Cost Catagory	% of Direct Cost	Potential Source of Cost Savings	Assumptions
Operator wages	74	Productivity increases	$500/mo., 22 days/mo., 8,000 keystrokes/hr., 7 productive hrs./day.
Keypunch and verifier rental	17	—	keypunch—$125/mo. verifier—$100/mo.
CPU charges	7	Reduced CPU charges	200 cards/minute processing speed, $40/CPU hour
Card costs	2	No cards With tape input	$1 per 1000 cards

Direct Cost/Character = $.0012
Direct Cost/Card   = 4.8¢ (40 columns keyed and verified)

Figure 7
Monthly Rentals for Keypunch and Keypunch Replacement Equipment (Options excluded)

Standard Equipment	Buffered Keypunch	Key-Tape	Key-Disk
Keypunch: $44-110 Verifier: $80-85	Units: $69-150	Units: $120-240 PLUS Pooler(s) and Pooler Operating Personnel	Units: $50-125 Controller: $560 up

the outside, CPU savings are more apparent than real. The exception is the conversion of former unit record machine applications (e.g., sorting) to the main computer. Although computer utilization might actually increase, the reduction in unit record equipment rental could more than balance this, and be included as a cost savings in this category.

Productivity increases are potentially the most important source of savings. Does keypunch replacement result in productivity increases? Yes, almost invariably. Productivity increases can result from four separate factors, three of which are susceptible to some degree of measurement and prediction.

The first measurable factor is the reduction in operator "idle" time. The standard keypunch duplicates at 18 card columns per second, skips up to 80 columns/second, and takes approximately a quarter of a second for card registration. For an operator keying, say, 1400 cards per day with an average of 20 columns skipped and 20 columns duplicated per card, this means 12% of the time (50 minutes) is spent waiting on the machine. With a buffered keyboard, the operator can spend virtually all this time actively keying.

Improved accuracy and verification procedures also affect productivity, albeit indirectly. A typical keypunch installation might spend 5% of its time on error correction. All of the sources we have referenced

indicate 10% to 90% first-pass error reduction with keypunch replacement.[17] Usually this reduction is not significant enough to bypass the need for verification, but it does make for easier verification. And the verification step itself is simplified, since the verifier operator can make corrections on the spot without recycling the record back to be re-keyed.

The third "measurable" factor, applicable to most key-tape and key-disk systems, results from reformatting card records for tape input. Extraneous columns with blank fill or, in multiple card records, card identifiers and repetitive information can all be eliminated. Essentially, operators can prepare the same information with less keystrokes.

The unpredictable factor is operator acceptance. In general, most trained operators seem to react favorably to keypunch replacement equipment,[18] particularly if the keyboard arrangement and audible keystroke "click" remain much the same as on the standard keypunch. Due to the intangible "operator image enhancement" features of keypunch replacement, it is not at all unusual to see productivity increase more than one would expect from a consideration of the three measurable factors. However, any intangible factors leading to abnormally high productivity may not be persistent, as many early key-tape users have noted.

Any savings from productivity increases must be

Figure 8
Sample Calculation of Monthly Savings
Before Equipment Rental

Cost Category	Cost Category Percent of Direct Cost	Buffered Keypunch		Key-Tape		Key-Disk	
		Source of Savings	Savings as Percent of Direct Cost	Source of Savings	Savings as Percent of Direct Cost	Source of Savings	Savings as Percent of Direct Cost
	A	B	A X B	C	A X C	D	A X D
Operator Wages	74	10% from buffered keyboard	7.4	10% from buffered keyboard and 10% from formatting	14.8	10% from buffered keyboard and 10% from reformatting	14.8
Keypunch and Verifier Rental	17	100%, new equipment costs will be taken into account later	17	100%, new equipment costs will be taken into account later	17	100%, new equipment costs will be taken into account later	17
CPU Charges	7	None	0	None	0	None	0
Punch Cards	2	None	0	approximately 100% no cards, tapes are reusable	2	approximately 100% no cards, tapes are reusable	2
Totals	100		24.4		33.8		33.8

realized indirectly through decreased personnel and machine requirements. This is common sense. If the same number of operators are kept working on the same number of machines as before, the net result will be a jump in direct costs—keypunch replacement equipment is always more expensive on an equivalent unit basis than standard keypunches and verifiers.

Determining whether keypunch replacement equipment will pay off overall is relatively straightforward *if* productivity increases are predicted with a reasonable degree of accuracy. In an installation with cost characteristics similar to those in Figure 6, one can expect a 10 percent productivity increase with buffered keyboards, and another 10 percent from reformatting some multiple card records to tape. Before conversion costs and rental charges for replacement equipment are taken into account, monthly savings as a percentage of direct costs can be calculated as shown in Figure 8.

Suppose the sample installation is presently employing 15 operators on 15 keypunch/verifier machines and incurring $10,000 per month in direct costs. The bottom line of figure 8 tells us that the installation could spend up to $2,440 for monthly rental of buffered keypunches or up to $3,380 for key-disk or key-tape and still realize a net savings. How much the savings would be depends on the rental for the equipment actually selected. If we chose, say, 14 buffered keypunches with an aggregate monthly rental of $1,750 (Avg. unit rental = $125) (see Figure 7), net direct cost savings would be on the order of $700 per month. If we choose a 12-station key-disk system renting for $1,800, savings should approximate $3,380 minus $1,800, or $1,580 per month.

Factors other than rental cost may be taken into

consideration at this point. With the buffered keypunch, there are no conversion problems other than some minimal operator training. With key-type and key-disk, operator training may be slightly more complicated, but still not a major problem. Any manufacturer will provide help in this respect with short on-site training sessions. Because operator productivity should be the critical factor in determining whether keypunch replacement is economical, a trial period of several weeks duration is usually justified. But even if this cannot be arranged, potential customers will benefit by taking a close look at the projected workload. If most jobs cannot take advantage of reformatting or the increased skipping and duplicating speeds, then there may be no justification for keypunch replacement.

Converting computer programs to accept tape input can be a difficulty, though certainly not an insurmountable one. Another tape-oriented consideration is how errors detected during the computer validation run will be corrected. If the device does not have a full-record display (only a few key-disk systems do) and search capability, post-validation correction can be a recurring headache. In general, tape loses its attractiveness as an input medium if the installation processes many small jobs.

Finally, help in judging factors like system reliability, vendor maintenance policies, and vendor stability should be sought wherever possible. Comments from other users usually prove invaluable.

Generalizing the Framework

A large organization's data entry workload usually consists of different input streams which run the gamut for volume, accuracy requirements, and time-

Figure 9

EVALUATING DATA ENTRY ALTERNATIVES

ALTERNATIVE	TYPE OF COST	MONTHLY FIXED COST	CONVERSION FIXED COST	JOB TYPE "A" MONTHLY VARIABLE COST	JOB TYPE "A" CONVERSION VARIABLE COST	JOB TYPE "B" MONTHLY VARIABLE COST	JOB TYPE "B" CONVERSION VARIABLE COST
PRESENT KEYPUNCHING	OPERATORS	0	0	ACTUAL DIRECT EXP.	0		
	EQUIPMENT	0	0	ACTUAL DIRECT EXP.	0		
	CPU CHARGES	0	0	ACTUAL DIRECT EXP.	0		
	SUPPLIES	0	0	ACTUAL DIRECT EXP.	0		
	OTHER	SUPERVISORY AND OCCUPANCY EXPENSE	0	INDIRECT EXP. PREPARATION AND MAILING TO CENTRAL SITE	0		
OCR	OPERATORS	OCR OPERATORS	TRAINING	OCR TYPISTS*	TRAINING		
	EQUIPMENT	OCR EQUIPMENT	0	TYPEWRITERS*	0		
	CPU CHARGES	0	0	CPU OVERHEAD	TESTING		
	SUPPLIES	0	0	FORMS	FORMS DESIGN		
	OTHER	0	ADD. CORE?	INDIRECT EXP. AND REJECT HANDLING*	REPROGRAMMING FOR OCR DIRECT OR TAPE INPUT		
INTEGRATED ON-LINE SYSTEM	OPERATORS	0	0	TERMINAL OPERATORS KEYBOARD TERMINALS, CONTROL UNITS, MODEMS*	TRAINING		
	EQUIPMENT	TRANSMISSION CONTROL EQUIPMENT	0	CPU OVERHEAD	0		
	CPU CHARGES	0	0	0	TESTING		
	SUPPLIES	0	0	0	0		
	OTHER	OS CONVERSION TP MONITOR	EDUCATION FOR PROGRAMMING STAFF	COMMUNICATIONS CHARGES	REPROGRAMMING		
COMPOSITE ON-LINE SYSTEM (REMOTE BATCH TERMINALS WITH KEYPUNCH)	OPERATORS	BATCH TERMINAL OPERATORS	0	OPERATOR WAGES AND KEYPUNCHES AT REMOTE LOCATION	0		
	EQUIPMENT	TRANSMISSION CONTROL EQUIPMENT BATCH TERMINALS	0	0	0		
	CPU CHARGES	0	0	CPU OVERHEAD	TESTING		
	SUPPLIES	0	0	CARDS	0		
	OTHER	OS CONVERSION TP MONITOR LEASED LINES	EDUCATION FOR PROGRAMMING STAFF	0	REPROGRAMMING		

* MOST OF THE COST ASSOCIATED WITH THIS ITEM WOULD NOT APPLY IF THE JOB IS SUSCEPTIBLE TO SOURCE DATA ENTRY.

liness of entry and response. By tracing through each of the major input streams, we are likely to find most of it is not time-critical. As a general rule, it will not be worthwhile to enter this data through an integrated on-line system. This is not so much because of the cost of terminal equipment—most keyboard terminals are less expensive than keypunches—but because of the conversion and operating expense for an on-line system.

However, if on-line applications are already up and running, the point at which it is desirable to cross over to on-line entry may not be so clear-cut, especially if true source data entry can be achieved. Most of the costs for hardware/software conversion, and the technical expertise necessary to accommodate on-line operation will have been incurred. Intermediate operator wages account for up to 75 percent of the direct cost of keypunching. The elimination of these costs can go a long way toward financing communications charges and modern terminal equipment rental. There may be other desirable alternatives to process some or all of this workload. In a large organization, OCR might be feasible, or perhaps some data entry might remain keypunch-oriented but decentralized to branch office locations with existing batch terminals.

Figure 9 shows a worksheet method for analyzing the economic implications of this and similar decisions. Three types of costs are considered: one-time conversion costs, monthly variable costs, and monthly fixed costs. Meaningful comparisons *between* alternatives can be made by defining these as follows:

1. *Monthly Fixed Costs.* Those costs which will be continuously incurred if the data entry alternative is used regardless of the number and type of jobs processed using that alternative (e.g. OCR equipment rental).

2. *Monthly Variable Costs.* Those costs which will be continuously incurred, over and above any fixed costs, if a particular alternative is used on a particular type of job.

3. *Conversion Costs.* A. Fixed: One-time costs which will be incurred if an alternative is used, regardless of the number and type of jobs processed. B. Variable: One-time costs which will be incurred, over and above any fixed conversion costs, if a particular alternative is used on a particular type of job.

Some of the major items which would be included in each cost category are identified in Figure 9. In this case we assume comparisons are being made relative to a central-site keypunch operation.

Four major alternatives are listed in this example. In practice, we would list only the particular alternatives being considered and eventually include specific manufacturers' data entry equipment. Since monthly and conversion variable costs are dependent on the type of job for which the alternative is used, these would have to be listed separately for each type of job included in the evaluation.

Some care must be taken in determining the relevant job classification for that portion of data entry workload being analyzed. If job classifications are defined too broadly, or include separate rate input streams, one may not be able to obtain meaningful cost estimates on, say, reject rates for OCR forms or productivity increases. Jobs should be classified so that one can estimate costs by alternative and by job.

Getting reasonable cost estimates should be the most difficult part of all, especially for large on-line networks. As with any cost analysis some common sense rules must be observed. Any cost items which vary across the set of alternatives and jobs being considered should be included. Those which do not vary should not be included and may bias the results if they are. For example, in a department with existing batch terminal expenses for transmission, equipment and software teleprocessing monitors should be included in evaluating new applications only to the extent additional charges for these items would be incurred.

Setting cost estimates in this framework may not make economic implications immediately obvious. But once the framework is established, the mechanics of estimating total costs are straight forward. The way in which the cost structure has been defined permits the evaluation and comparison of total costs for any single alternative or mix of alternatives over any given time span.

Summary

An organization's data entry system is an area for potential cost savings, and provides an opportunity to improve the performance of the overall computer activity. For a variety of industry and organizational reasons, the data entry system of the organization may not have been reassessed recently. Nevertheless, within the past few years data entry technology has undergone considerable improvement.

Evaluating both the tangible and intangible factors of data entry system alternatives within the context of an organization can get quite complex. An approach is to start with a consideration of the tangible economic factors benchmarked on the existing data entry system. Within the background of the economic factors, the less tangible factors such as training and data integrity improvements can be successively considered. The worksheet approach is a useful technique for getting into the analysis.   •jsm

---

References

1. Verification is a step employed in most keypunch installations to reduce errors. Basically, each card is re-keyed by another operator on another machine. If there are any discrepancies, the card is returned for correction.

2. The June 1970 *Datamation* includes seven articles on the keypunch replacement. A descriptive article on key-tape can be seen in September-October 1968 *Data Processing Magazine*. Three user experiences with key-disk are reported in August-September 1971, *Data Dynamics*.

3. 96-column buffered keypunches are not included in Figure 1. Except for installations with System/3 computers, 96-column keypunches will rarely be used as standard keypunch replacements.

4. If the key-tape unit records on computer-compatible tape, then pooling may be performed on a host computer or on a specialized off-line device called a pooler. If the unit records are on noncompatible tape (e.g., cassette or cartridge), then pooling must be performed on an off-line device which also produces computer-compatible tapes.

5. See Figure 7 for representative price ranges for keypunch and keypunch replacement equipment.

6. *Data Entry Equipment*, International Data Corporation, 1972.

7. Within the OCR industry, there has been a distinction between page and document readers. Page readers typically handle larger forms (e.g., 8½" by 11" or more), and operate faster than document readers. The price differential between the two types of readers exists mainly within the vendors' product lines, not so much across the industry. Several manufacturers produce combined document/page readers.

8. A character-substitution error occurs when the machine processes a character but reads it incorrectly. Rejects, on the other hand, occur when the machine will not process the character(s) at all. Many manufacturers will quote character-substitution error rates for their machines, but very few will quote on the reject rate since this depends heavily on the particular application.

9. *AUERBACH On Optical Character Recognition* (Philadelphia: AUERBACH Publishers, Inc., 1971).

10. "Improvements in Data Entry," *EDP Analyzer* (September-October 1971).

11. Bar code readers read characters encoded as vertical lines. Some devices print normal typed characters above or below the bar code.

12. For a further discussion, see *The Future of Telecommunications*, by James Martin. (Prentice-Hall, 1971).

13. See the August, 1972 *Datamation* or the February, 1972 *Computer Decision* for an explanation and market survey for this type of equipment.

14. Alphanumeric CRT terminals possess a keyboard and cathode ray tube capable of producing only character images. Graphic CRT terminals, on the other hand, can produce and manipulate curves and lines as well as characters, but because of the expense and CPU overhead required for graphic CRT's, they are not normally considered appropriate for volume data entry.

15. Several companies have developed inexpensive line printers or photographic display reproduction techniques for use with alphanumeric CRT terminals.

16. For price/performance information on all types of terminal equipment see *AUERBACH Terminal Equipment Digest* (Philadelphia, AUERBACH Publishers, 1971).

17. The degree of error reduction will depend upon the error prevention checks built into the equipment (e.g. field-length checks, numeric only checks, etc.) and the operator incentive system.

18. See "The Human Side of Data Input", April 1971, *Data Dynamics*; "Improvements to Data Entry", Sept.-Oct., *EDP Analyzer*, and footnote 2.

John W. Luke   Davis Chapter 11

"DATA BASE SYSTEMS: PUTTING MANAGEMENT BACK IN THE PICTURE"

CSC Report (9:1), 1975 May, pages 8-12.

Although still suffering from a little oversell, this article provides an excellent overview of database management systems. The article is written from a broad perspective recognizing the pragmatic organizational concerns of management. It covers many of the central concepts of database management systems such as the database concept, database administrator, motivation for database management, and the conversion to database management.

Luke suggests that the ability to bring together the data relating to various functions of an organization enables top management to obtain an overall perspective on the organization. The new technologies associated with database management systems improve the feasibility of integrating data and making it more readily available. The historical, fragmented, applications-oriented approach to management information systems development is set in bold contrast to the database management system approach. Luke provides several useful insights for an organization contemplating adopting the database approach and converting to a database management system.

READING SUGGESTIONS

The reader should grasp the central facts in the paper. Do not be misled by such overstatements as (italics added):

- "*on-demand* information service known as the data base management system,"
- "DBMS makes information vital to corporate decision making *immediately* available from a centralized data resource,"
- "the data base is a *flexible* community of data from which information can be retrieved in *any* desired format or classification,"
- "*any* program can be *extensively* modified or new applications added *without affecting* the physical organization of the data. Even the structure of the data base and the logical relationships among the data elements are *easily* changed," and
- "providing managers at *all* levels with consistent summary data from *all* functions of their organization."

Many of these statements are merely absolute expressions of desirable goals to be achieved using database management systems but not completely achievable. The real importance of these statements rests in the contrast with the more traditional methods of management information systems development. For example, to say a database management system makes information available immediately depends upon the interpretation of immediate -- the real significance is that it will be quicker than with traditional methods. Nevertheless, it may be extremely costly to further reduce a response delay which has already been changed to minutes or seconds.

QUESTIONS

1. How does Luke characterize the historical approach to the development of management information systems? What was the result of such an approach?

2. What is meant by the three layer approach of database management systems? What are the three layers? Are all three always used?

3. What does Luke mean by the phrase "DBMS processing depends on a central resource of references"?

4. What is the data dictionary and why is it an important part of a DBMS?

5. How does Luke characterize the position of database administrator in an organization? What are his responsibilities?

6. List several factors mentioned by Luke which motivate an organization to use a database management system. What are some compelling reasons? What are the expected benefits?

7. Why does Luke argue against the inhouse development and maintenance of a database management system? One answer can be found in the article, the other stems from his job responsibility.

8. How should an organization convert to and effectively utilize a database management system?

9. How does the field of telecommunications relate to database management systems?

Data Base Systems: Putting Management Back in the Picture

John Luke
President, Information Network Division
Computer Sciences Corporation

The rapid growth in business over the past few years has created an urgent need for more — and better — management visibility and control. As companies have expanded and broadened their product lines, management has had to delegate more and more of its authority. Production, sales, finance, administration, and other aspects of a business have become separate functional entities, each collecting, processing, and disseminating information for its own operations. As these functional operations proliferate, overall management visibility tends to diminish. Now, new concepts are needed to put management back in the picture.

One of the most significant concepts to emerge to meet this challenge is the on-demand information service known as the data base management system (DBMS). Made possible through the introduction of third-generation computers with large-capacity direct-access storage devices and the parallel development of intelligent remote terminals and teleprocessing networks, DBMS provides a heightened level of control over disparate applications. Essentially, DBMS makes information vital to corporate decision-making immediately available from a centralized data resource.

A retrospective look at information systems development will help highlight the advantages of data base management.

historical perspectives

The applications-oriented approach, used as a basis for many early "management information systems", was developed during the first and second generations of computers, and reflected many of the limitations inherent in those machines and their operating systems.

In early computer systems, a new program was designed for each individual information requirement. The requirement could be a sales transaction, the number of hours worked, hourly rates, charge numbers, and so forth. Even though the same data often was used in more than one application, it had to be entered separately each time. For instance, time cards entered for payroll were processed again for production control, and sales orders were entered separately into the systems for production control, material requirements, and sales analysis.

The real shortcoming of this approach was that it failed to recognize that true management information systems cannot be based solely on reports from discrete functional areas. Nor could certain information external to the system (forecasts of product demand, competitor's profiles, and outside economic factors, etc.) be reflected. Although the input, such as sales volumes, costs, production status, backlogs and schedules, might be extracted from individual functional application programs, the output — to be meaningful to management — must appear in a significantly revised format with different emphases and perspectives, and cross-related in a multitude of ways.

With individual applications programs, it was difficult — and sometimes impossible — to combine multiple processed information into a single comprehensive report. Thus, when non-data processing management asked the so-called "simple question" — one not anticipated by the designers of the original system — the data processing manager had two choices: he could tell management that the answer to their simple question was next-to-impossible to get, or he could divert the time and skills of the application programmers from other productive efforts to this special-purpose, one-time-only job.

The "fragmented" applications approach also gave rise to a considerable amount of duplication and inconsistency. Many systems were based on automation of existing manual systems, which were designed more as labor-saving devices than as information systems. They solved paper handling problems and were selected for automation without thought to relationships or effectiveness. Standardization within related application areas received low priority or was neglected altogether.

Centralized file management systems provided the first automated solution to relating and interlinking data from several different applications. Today's versions usually provide a powerful retrieval and reporting capability, easy-to-use updating procedures, and a programming language interface. When used to process a large number of similar transactions against a large file, they have proved ideal. Perhaps the best known examples of large centralized systems are airline reservation systems and securities pricing information systems. In these two instances, the files are typically large, containing millions of records, and the number of transactions processed daily runs into the hundreds of thousands.

However, like their fragmentary counterparts, large file management systems suffer from inflexibility when tasked to do anything beyond the job they were originally designed to do. The mechanical processes of sorting, creating external indices, or maintaining internal indices to relate, say, the payroll file to the production control file, are simply too cumbersome.

The shortcomings of the fragmented applications-oriented approach and file management approach helped to clarify managements' real objectives: information systems, it was learned, should be able to respond quickly and effectively to changing information requirements and technology; be capable of satisfying both standard, anticipated information needs, as well as unpredictable, ad hoc requests, and above all, they should provide information that is accurate, timely, relevant, and complete.

the data base concept

The DBMS approach stands in bold contrast to the earlier approaches. In effect, it puts all the eggs in one basket, instead of spreading them all over the place.

The data base, by its very nature, employs an elaborate system of access via multiple retrieval paths to each item of data. Communication lines cross traditional company and functional boundaries to serve the needs of the total organization.

Second-and third-generation file management techniques using master files specifically designed for one application may be compared to a two-layer sandwich — the top layer being the application and the bottom layer the data sets, data files, and master files that go with the application.

In contrast, DBMS is a three-layer sandwich — the top and bottom the same but with a middle layer that interfaces the two. This middle layer is the DBMS, and it's structured in such a way that the application program does not physically retrieve data from the data base but issues calls to the DBMS which does the storing and retrieving.

The data base is a flexible community of data from which information can be retrieved in any desired format or classification. Data is easily associated with other logically relevant information and available to any user with an established need to know wherever and whenever needed. Data management software performs the functions of associating logically related data elements (for example, employees' names are logically associated with job skills, classifications, hourly pay rates, co-workers, department supervisors, etc.) regardless of the physical organization or location of the individual data elements in the data base. The user can concentrate on the information need rather than the complexities of language programming. No knowledge of physical storage is required since the DBMS has this information and does the actual retrieval.

DBMS processing depends on a central resource of references. For instance, a customer's address need only appear once in the data base — a feature that produces a consistent response every time the data is used. A further advantage of the data base approach is its flexibility. Since the user accesses the management systems, rather than the actual data, any program can be extensively modified or new applications added without affecting the physical organization of the data. New data elements can be added and old ones deleted without affecting all the application programs that use the data base. Even the structure of the data base and the logical relationships among the data elements are easily changed.

The most common DBMS storage medium is disk which satisfies the need for relatively uniform access speeds to the data base. Use of disk storage allows the computer, rather than an operator, to control much of the internal processing. Storage costs are slightly higher, but the use of this medium makes it possible to retain several billion characters on-line at any one time, with an access time of less than one-tenth of a second.

The essential tool in any DBMS is the data dictionary. Serving as the standard of nomenclature and a cross-reference between users and applications, the dictionary organizes and classifies data by type, frequency of occurrence, storage structure, relationship to other data, and usage by application. By pinpointing redundancies in data usage, the dictionary actually helps justify the role of the data base in an organization's edp system. Reports that contain common data items become candidates for elimination or combination, without affecting end results in any way. The data directory is an extension of the dictionary in that it records the physical location of data by means of internal tables and indexes.

The dictionary also plays an important part in recovery situations. With several programs accessing the data base at the same time, extra precautions have to be taken to enable the reconstruction of the system if an unforeseen breakdown occurs. This entails continual journaling of transactions and the use of these lists for backup and restore operations. Recovery itself is a two-step operation: first to reconstitute the data and, second, to reestablish the relationships between the various records of the data base so as to include all changes made up to the time of failure.

data base administrator

Some one has to shoulder the responsibility of managing the data base throughout its life cycle — the data base administrator. One of the DBA's rare qualities is that of diplomat charged with keeping communication lines open between the various user departments. He is also something of a superstar, with a strong technical background and better than average managerial skills. His position and lines of command vary, depending upon the size and organizational structure of the company, but his chief mandate is always the same: guide, coordinate, administer, and control the data base and the programs that use it.

Throughout the lifetime of the data base, the DBA is the focal point for maintaining the data dictionary and directory, and upgrading procedures and recovery routines. He reviews audits, monitors operating statistics, and generally keeps the data base working efficiently.

The DBA is also educator for other staff members and system users, and ensures compliance with the established standards and documentation guidelines. In a data base system, emphasis on dictionary and directory standardization is close to a full-time job.

what everyone should know about converting to a data base system

Faced with the obvious advantages of timeliness, accuracy, and flexibility, most businesses agree that a data base system would be nice (or at any rate fashionable) — but is it worth the time and expense of converting from existing information systems?

Implementation and maintenance costs are usually higher than for conventional storage systems because of the greater software and systems expertise required. As an intricate piece of software, a data base system probably ranks second only to an operating system in complexity.

Data bases also incur increased expense in terms of computer storage and CPU time, allowing much of the programming effort to be shifted from the applications programmer to the computer itself. As a result, information applications can be designed, installed, and put into operation in days or weeks as opposed to the traditional experience of months or years to develop and debug a new application.

One of the compelling reasons for DBMS is the savings in programming and debugging time for new business applications. Once DBMS has been installed, studies show that all factors being equal, a programmer using DBMS is two to four times faster than one using Cobol to develop his own master files. Since the cost of software, according to most accepted standards is four to five times that of hardware, any plan that saves programming costs is a persuasive argument.

The ease with which new applications are developed on a DBMS is most significant, since the hardest part of business data processing is building and maintaining the master files. Freeing the programmer of day-to-day maintenance of the master files allows time for more productive activities.

Determining the right system for each company's needs and supervising its implementation is a job for data processing specialists — those who know not only computer architecture and software systems but which areas to automate for best return on investment.

Business must go on as usual while the conversion effort is taking place, making added demands on the sophisticated skills that are needed to retain the existing system as this new system takes shape. One user of a data base management system summed up his experience in the following words: "My biggest recommendation to anyone who goes to a data base system is: don't shortchange it. If you're going to spend those bucks, and it's going to have a real impact on your organization, worrying about overhead is foolish."

Rarely are a company's systems merely converted into a DBMS. The resourceful company will use the conversion as an opportunity for complete redesign and as a springboard for a more versatile product; one, for example, that will generate ad hoc summary reports instead of grinding out masses of paper from which the requester must extract information by hand.

A go-it-alone approach tends to suffer from the limitations of in-bred viewpoints and inexperience with similar efforts. It is a truism that no matter how experienced the in-house edp manager may be, he's bound to encounter the new and unexpected in massive conversion efforts like these. Because of the complicated nature of data base systems, a DBMS developed and monitored by an independent software house is usually preferable in terms of cost control and state-of-the-art effectiveness. Developments in data base procedures are coming at such a fast pace, it is almost impossible for the average in-house edp specialist to keep up with the field.

decision to convert to a data base system

Once management makes the decision to take the plunge and become data-base oriented, they must be prepared to commit a considerable amount of their own time and personnel resources to the development process. While design and development is the responsibility of the information system specialists, the requirements decisions must be balanced, with equal contributions from data specialists, corporate management, and functional managers. Management's participation assures a system that really delivers what management needs to support critical decisions.

Even with the best definition of data base structure, implementation should proceed cautiously, one module at a time. Converting and integrating all application areas simultaneously is risky for two reasons: first, it exposes the entire operation to any number of initial technical problems; second, a significant number of major simultaneous changes often meets with resistance from the people the system is designed to serve. This resistance may continue even after the initial shock of installation, resulting in less than optimal use of the system. Modifications and tradeoffs to the original plan often occur along the way. Therefore, a flexible planning approach significantly reduces the trauma and allows the developers time to adjust for mistakes made during the installation of the first functions.

Each application must be value-analyzed individually to determine if the benefits of computerization merit the costs of developing and maintaining the function. Past experience has shown that about twenty percent of the candidate functions are eliminated because they are not cost-effective, not practical, or simply because they are inappropriate to a data base environment.

computer/communications symbiosis

Developing the teleprocessing systems needed to permit on-line inquiries to the corporate data base is an ambitious undertaking for any organization. Costs of modeling and performing statistical analyses of the communications interfaces, evaluating alternative approaches, and designing and installing often add up to one of the biggest expenditures in the DBMS conversion.

Network services fall into the once-in-a-lifetime category. Few individuals can accumulate the extensive range of experiences required to build a data network. The demand is for a combination of backgrounds: both software and communications. Demonstrated reliability with a variety of add-on options is critical, plus the knowledge of data communication media, values, and services. Established networks obviously relieve the user of the entire problem of maintaining the communications gear that is often the key to effective DBMS operations. Teleprocessing networks such as CSC's INFONET also take the responsibility of maintaining the DBMS as well.

The very essence of a data base system — putting all data in one integrated location, publishing its definition, and making it generally accessible — can be one of its biggest problems. Early establishment of a security system is an important step in guarding against unauthorized access to the data base. Security procedures must protect the system against copying, removal, disclosure, or destruction of any of its contents.

Access control is primary to security. Methods range from the simple and basic user identification and password authentication to the storage of security tables defining the privilege of individual users. Other measures include read and write protect features for main memory, use of parity checks, and built-in detection of all undefined coding that might be used to create a "trapdoor" into the system.

A key point in any security system is assignment of responsibility. Someone must be made responsible for monitoring the security of each and every sensitive file. Such a person — usually the DBA — oversees the whole security system.

INFONET's data management system*

A prepackaged data management system usually consists of the tools necessary for building the data base, support programs for querying, indexing, and managing the data, a file organization capability, and data communications network. In selecting the appropriate data management system, a company has two basic choices: to select a "black box" off-the-shelf system or to choose a modular system that requires a certain amount of tailoring before it is ready to use. The advantages of the "black box" are essentially cost and availability.

INFONET offers three distinct systems to meet the requirements of data management environments ranging from small data bases supporting simple retrieval activities to very large complex data bases supporting many functional requirements:

ALADIN — A Language for Decision Information — A powerful, language-oriented system developed by CSC

IGIM — INFONET's Generalized Information Management system, licensed from TRW

SYSTEM 2000 — A well-known data management system, licensed from MRI Systems Corporation.

This family of flexible tools gives INFONET users a unique advantage. Because of the wide spectrum of capabilities afforded by the three systems, INFONET can analyze each data management requirement objectively from the viewpoint of the best system to solve the problem rather than bending user needs to fit the system.

ALADIN is a flexible and extremely easy-to-learn tool for the definition, creation maintenance, and querying of data bases.

As a language-oriented system, ALADIN conforms to the many requirements of data management and affords many advantages to the user.

Retrieval capabilities range from simple keyed retrievals to selection based on complex logical conditions. Output generation can range from simple unformatted data lists to complex reports and applications requiring a great deal of data

manipulation in terms of numeric computation and character string handling. The variety of logical structures permits the user to define his data bases in the best possible manner to meet his needs.

The IGIM data management system was developed by TRW Systems Group and CSC. All the software facilities required to create, maintain, and interrogate a large, complex data base are provided by IGIM and are designed to be used by persons without prior data processing experience. Because the powerful facilities are self-contained, requiring no additional computer programs to adapt them to particular applications, an information system based on IGIM can be implemented in a very short time.

Special instructions, such as security codes, conversion, maximum/minimum size, storage method, and data associations for handling each user's data are specified and stored in IGIM dictionaries at the time a data base is created. These instructions may be modified at any time with minimal impact on system performance.

System 2000, general-purpose data management system developed by MRI Systems Corporation, supports hierarchically structured data bases. Elements, named with terms appropriate for the application, are used to store data. Since there are no restrictions as to which data base elements become key fields, System 2000 is ideally suited to data retrieval problems. The user, therefore, is free to focus only on the data of interest. Additional capabilities include provisions for data base definition and creation, interactive update and retrieval languages, interfaces to host languages, and report generation.

will the real MIS stand up?

Data base management systems make it easier to analyze financial, production marketing, and other operational data. In general, they increase operating efficiency by eliminating redundancies in data files; they speed responsiveness to every information need; slash the time required to get new applications working; and afford greater flexibility and control in the use of data.

Data base management has proved to be the most successful way of arresting the drift away from management control in the last few years. By providing managers at all levels with consistent summary data from all functions of their organization, corporate decisions can be made in the interest of the organization as a whole.

Equally important is the fact that data base systems are open-ended. Their potential is limited only by the imagination, time, and budget of the user. In the hands of progressive management, a carefully designed and implemented data base system can have a dramatic impact on a company's future growth and profitability.

It is anticipated that the greatest potential for growth in computer systems will be in data bases network operations, more descriptively known as on-demand information services. According to one authority,* "By 1985 or 1987 the degree of automation of information will affect at least one-fourth and perhaps even one-third of all information transfers." On-demand information services delivered by "information utilities" is gaining in usage and soon will be required by larger segments of the general public. On-demand information is foreseen as a rich resource for home and community activities; professionals in law, medicine, education, research and similar information intensive fields; and even broader categories, such as employment opportunities, news, and entertainment.

---

*Data Management Systems, Computer Sciences Corporation, Publication No. 380A, 1975.

---

*George Anderla, "Information in 1985," Organization for Economic Cooperation and Development, Paris, 1973.

"DATABASE MANAGEMENT SYSTEMS TUTORIAL"

Fifth Annual Midwest AIDS Conference Proceedings, Vol. 1, Minneapolis, Minnesota, 1974 May 10-11, edited by Norman L. Chervany, Minneapolis: University of Minnesota, College of Business Administration, 1974, pages A1-A12.

The database concept and the related database management systems represent essential ingredients for a management information system. The Everest tutorial is a description of the fundamental concepts and functions of a database management system and should especially help in clarifying definitions and terminology.

The tutorial article starts by defining major terms and describing the motivation and objectives of a database management system. It then explains the database administrator function before proceeding with a classification of users, a classification of current systems, and a taxonomy of functions found in database management systems.

READING SUGGESTIONS

In reading the article, special attention should be paid to the definitions and taxonomies. There are definitions for the following:

data	database manager
database	generalized nonprogramming user
database concept	parametric user
evolvability	host language system
integrity	self-contained system

The role of database administration and the user of the data are defined. Note especially the place of the database administrator in the organization and the functions assigned to that position. User roles are divided between nonprogramming users and programming users.

The database systems are classified as host language systems or self-contained systems. Note the taxonomy of DBM functions -- the two major sets of functions -- direct availability functions (database establishment and use) and underlying support functions (integrity control, performance monitoring and usage statistics). The programming user facilities embodied in the use of the schema and subschema are also explained.

QUESTIONS

1. What is the database concept?
2. What is the motivation for a database?
3. What are the major objectives of a DMS?
4. What are the functions of a database administrator?
5. What is the difference between a generalized non-programming user and a parametric user?
6. What is the difference between a host language system and a self-contained system?
7. List database functions.
8. What are the integrity control functions?
9. What is the relationship between the schema and subschema?

DATABASE MANAGEMENT SYSTEMS TUTORIAL

Gordon C. Everest, University of Minnesota

This paper describes the organizational and functional aspects of generalized database management systems. A database management system (DMS) is a computer-based system used to establish, make available for use, and maintain the integrity of, a mechanized, formally-defined, and centrally-controlled collection of data.

DATA

The objects of the management activity are the data resources in an organization. Grammatically, data is a collective noun taking either a singular or a plural verb depending on the context of its usage [38, page 161]. As an organizational resource, data comes in many forms: from financial and quantitative data to qualitative and subjective data; internal and external data; and historical and forecast data. Organizational data resources include financial and managerial accounting data, production data, sales data, payroll and personnel data, planning data, etc.

Data is not considered to be information. Information is derived from data. Data becomes information when evaluated in a specific situation or when applied to the solution of a particular problem. Data becomes information when used in the context of making a decision. The value of information derives from the problem or decision context; data per se only represents a cost.

DATABASE

In a broad sense, organizational data resources extend to include informal, private, and manual data. Data resources which are public (shared) and mechanized constitute the database of an organization. A DMS deals with the databases within an organization. As an organization matures, a greater proportion of its data resources are formally defined and placed into databases. The corporate database may consist of several databases centrally controlled with respect to some organizational unit. There could be a large, single integrated database for the whole organization; several separate databases maintained on a central computer facility; or separate databases maintained on separate computer facilities within organizational divisions.

DATABASE MANAGEMENT SYSTEM

Within a computer system there may exist various degrees of control over the mechanized data resources. At one extreme, control, if any, would reside with the diverse

collection of application programs. Even though there may
be external administrative procedures to control the cata-
loguing and initiation of programs, once in execution, they
are free to arbitrarily access and change the database.
The ideal DMS represents a high degree of control over the
database within a computer system. All program access as
well as direct human access to the database is funnelled
through the DMS.

THE DATABASE CONCEPT

Independent of the mechanisms surrounding the database,
an organization must recognize and embrace the database concept. The database concept is rooted in an attitude of

- sharing common data resources,
- releasing control of those data resources to
  a common responsible authority, and
- cooperating in the maintenance of those shared
  data resources.

If data is a valued, shared resource in the organization, it
must be managed like any other asset such as men, materials,
machines, and money. Management in its fullest sense involves
the establishment of appropriate organizational arrangements
(giving rise to the database administrator) and the institution of system-based tools and procedures (giving rise to
the database management system).

MOTIVATION FOR DATABASE MANAGEMENT SYSTEMS

The need to effect the management of organizational data
resources is the prime motivator for database management
systems. Some specific conditions which may cause an organization to consider acquiring a DMS include:

- need to get quick answers to "simple" questions; to
  respond to ad hoc questions in a timely and economical
  fashion; to make data resources available on demand
  whether to a person, or to a decision or simulation
  model.
- need to reduce long lead times and high development
  costs in the design, implementation, maintenance,
  and revision of data-oriented applications.
- need to improve the quality of, and control access
  to, data resources.
- desire for greater sophistication and completeness
  in modeling data structures.

The first need is satisfied by a powerful, generalized query
language and reporting facility. The second requires a
collection of generalized tools with which to define, create,
revise, interrogate, and update a database. The third
requires some underlying mechanism to service and control the
access to the database. These represent the fundamental
facilities of a database management system. Most currently

available systems, however, do not meet all these needs and
they vary in their degree of satisfaction.

Both human and machine resources are used in data processing systems. Application system development and modification depend primarily on human resources, while application
system operation depends primarily on machine resources. More
effective utilization of human resources reduces the effort
required for systems development and modification. Human
resources can be better utilized by:

- having the data readily available, or by providing an
  established mechanism for the definition and acquisition of data, and
- providing generalized (software) tools to access the
  database, or pooling talent to develop such tools.

OBJECTIVES OF DATABASE MANAGEMENT

Management connotes both using a resource and controlling
the resource. This leads to the dual objectives of availability and integrity, respectively. Availability functions
in a DMS include database definition, creation, revision,
interrogation, and update, the latter two being provided for
both direct human use and indirect human use through application processes and decision systems. These functions may
be made available in various forms including batch processing
mode for efficiency and online-interactive mode for immediacy,
and language styles ranging from narrative to fixed form.

Evolvability, or future availability, refers to the
capacity of a database system to respond to changing technology and changing user demands. Evolvability is accomplished
through generalization, data independence, and programming
user facilities.

Database integrity is used in its broadest sense to
imply the completeness, soundness, purity, veracity, and
confidentiality of data. Database integrity involves:

- protecting the existence of the database through
  physical security, and backup and recovery measures.
- maintaining the quality of the database through input
  validation, diagnostic routines to ensure that the
  data always conforms to its definition (a definition
  which includes validation criteria on the stored
  data), and controlling processes which update the
  database.
- maintaining the privacy of the stored data through
  isolation, access regulation, encryption, and
  monitoring.

More detailed discussion of the objectives of database
management can be found in [17].

DATABASE ADMINISTRATOR

The satisfaction of database management objectives
entails both human and machine components. The human component of the solution is embodied in the database administrator.
Historically, the functions relating to database administration were performed by programmers, system analysts, and
machine operators. Without appropriate organizational
arrangements and without establishing a clear locus of
administrative responsibility, the quality of service and
level of integrity diminishes with respect to the data
resources.

Several recent expressions of the role of database
administrator have appeared in the literature [33, 23, 7, 8,
12, 28, 5, 22, 16]. From these it is possible to gain a
synthesis.

Database administration focuses primarily on the management of corporate database resources. Within the corporate
information systems organization, database administration
should eventually reside on a par with systems development,
and with operations or job administration [1], as shown in
Figure 1.

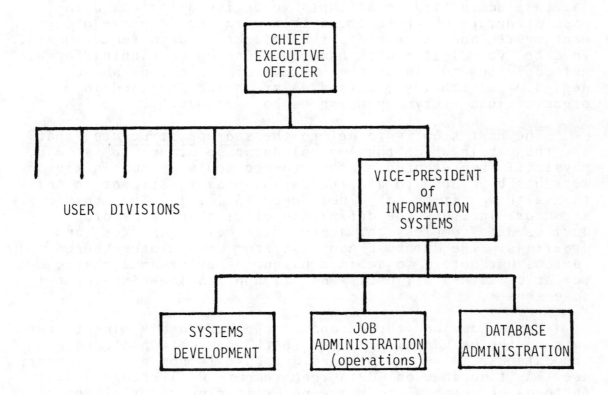

Figure 1.   Database Administration within the Organization.

Database administration is fundamentally a people-
oriented function, attempting to meet the data needs of all
the users in an organization.

SHARING
produces CONFLICT
necessitating MEDIATION
resulting in COMPROMISE for one,
but yielding GLOBAL OPTIMA for all.

Since common data resources are shared, any individual user
or any individual application must be prepared to accept a
compromise solution in the satisfaction of data requirements.
The database administrator must gather together all the data
requirements and performance response requirements and attempt
to provide a database structure which will satisfy the collective needs of the community of users.

FUNCTIONS OF DATABASE ADMINISTRATION

Several functions are unique to the role of database
administrator.

Define, Create, and Retire Data

The process of defining data begins in response to
stated data requirements from the using environment. The
database administrator attempts to define a logical database structure which is compatible with the database management system and which meets the collective data requirements.
To date, very little work has been done on developing formal
methodologies to aid in the process of logical database
design. Nevertheless, databases are being designed in
organizations every day using ad hoc methods.

The next step is to define the storage structure, that
is, the way in which the logical database structure is to be
physically represented on the storage media. Some initial
work has been done to aid the database administrator in this
task although it is not widely used [36, 11]. The storage
structure includes the definition of block size, storage
devices data compression, access strategies, indexes, and
orderings. The database administrator manipulates these
various parameters to achieve balanced performance characteristics across all users and all applications (at least in
some sense).

Having defined the database, the database administrator
sets up the mechanisms to acquire the new data and create
the database. The established database is now available for
use. As time goes on, data requirements will change and
patterns of usage will change necessitating redefinition of
the database structure and its storage structure. Finally,
the database administrator is responsible for setting policies
for the retention of data and the retirement of old data
to archival storage.

Provide Availability Tools

The database administrator is responsible for providing the tools with which various types of users operating in various modes can interrogate and update an established database. This responsibility is increasingly met today through the use of commercially-available database management systems. It is the database administrator's responsibility to select, acquire, install, and maintain all database management system software.

Inform and Service Users

Having established a database and provided tools with which the users can access the database, the database administrator must inform, educate, and assist users in the use of the database and the DMS tool. He provides user manuals, reference manuals, and current documentation on the operation of the system, and the definition and status of the database. For new application systems under development, he provides assistance and direction concerning the feasibility of meeting data requirements, the suitability of the database to the application, and the expected economy and performance characteristics in using the database.

Maintain Database Integrity

The goal of implementing integrity control procedures is reduction in the incidence of degradation or failure and reduction in the cost of recovering from or repairing a loss of integrity. Complete integrity protection is impossible, but if deemed important enough (and the level of importance can usually be reflected in cost consequences), substantial resources can be applied to enhance and maintain a high level of integrity. Several integrity control measures can be implemented to varying degrees. The database administrator must set the parameters and policies for integrity control according to a cost-benefit analysis. Such analysis is most difficult and not often done today. Consequently many organizations are maintaining a database at an alarmingly low level of integrity. Database integrity control mechanisms consist of the following:

- existence protection - frequency and extent of dumping and logging for backup and the provision of recovery procedures.
- quality control - control over all updating actions; controlling the interaction of concurrent update processes; validation parameters for input data transactions; validation criteria applied to stored data.
- access regulation - setting up authorizations for what certain identified individuals and processes can do to certain data in the database.

Monitoring Operations

Finally, the database administrator is responsible for monitoring the operation of the database, including performance monitoring, security threat monitoring, logging all interactions with the database to form an audit trail, and control over the mounting and demounting of offline files.

DATABASE MANAGEMENT SYSTEM MODEL

A database management system is the machine component for meeting the database management objectives. The system acts as the internal agent of the database administrator carrying out the policies and procedures he specifies. Figure 2 illustrates the overall DMS model. It is predominantly a functional view with the functions grouped according to different types of users. The database is shown in the upper right along with its stored database definition. The contents of the database and its logically-separate definition are available through, and controlled internally by, the database manager.

The Database Manager

The database manager is the single, controlling door through which all access to the database is accomplished. It is the run-time module providing data services for programs while they are in execution; it is the module which responds to all requests to access and manipulate data in the database; it is the security guard which intercepts and checks all such requests for proper authorization as well as syntactic and semantic legality; and it is the auditor who keeps a log of all events and changes affecting the database. Providing a single door for the availability functions is desirable for improved performance, but it is mandatory for integrity control.

DATABASE MANAGEMENT SYSTEM USERS

In the database management system environment there is one administrative role, the database administrator, and four user roles. As shown in Figure 2, the database administrator (DBA) has exclusive control of the database definition and creation functions as well as other functions related to redefinition, restructure, storage structure, device-media control, and integrity control.

Nonprogramming Users

The two basic types or users of a database management system are programmers and nonprogrammers. The nonprogramming users are so called because they do not have to write a procedural program in a conventional programming language in order to access the database. The system provides its own

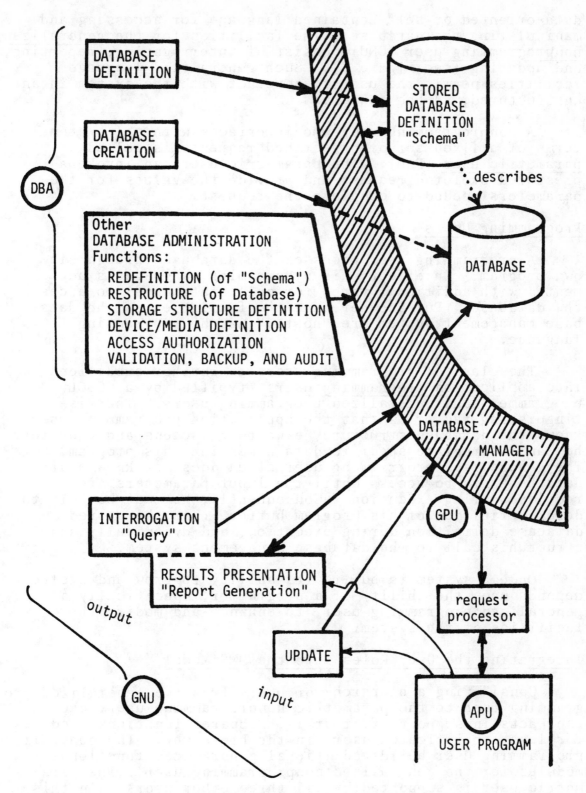

Figure 2.   Overall Conceptual Model of a Database Management System.

data-oriented or self-contained language for accessing and manipulating the database. The facilities for the generalized nonprogramming user (GNU) consist of interrogating, reporting, and updating (see Figure 2). Such generalized language facilities permit the user to interact with the system in an unstructured, ad hoc manner.

A nonprogramming user who interfaces with the system in terms of a fixed set of prescribed requests is called a parametric user (PNU). The parametric user can invoke a prestored skeleton request and provide the values for the parameters needed to complete the request.

Programming Users

A programming user accesses the database through his own program. In effect, his programming language is augmented with additional verbs (or call statements) to access the database. Put another way, the facilities of the database management system are "hosted" in the programming language.

The class of programming users is further subdivided into application programming users (typified by a COBOL programmer) and generalized programming users. The distinguishing factor is that the application programming user knows the database structure he wants to access and therefore he can incorporate specific data names into his program. The generalized programming user often does not know what data he wants to access until the input parameters are received during execution. Consequently, he must be able to defer definition of his program buffer, read the stored database definition during execution, and dynamically construct his call to the database management system.

Once a system is built, its ability to grow and evolve depends upon the ability of a programmer, specifically a generalized programming user, to enhance and modify the facilities of the system.

Integrating the User Roles into the DMS Model

Considering a hierarchy of users from the generalized programming user to the parametric nonprogramming user, each user acts in support of, that is, prepares functional modules for less sophisticated users in the hierarchy. The generalized programming user builds additional generalized functional modules for the generalized nonprogramming user. The parametric user is supported by all three other users. In this way a system is able to reach out and evolve to better meet the needs of all types of users in the environment.

THE DICHOTOMY IN CURRENT SYSTEMS

A review of the taxonomies of database management systems suggested in the literature (see Figure 3) [19, 16, 21, 33, 32, 18, 24] leads to the following synthesis:

A. access methods, the most primitive form of database management capability.
B. database management facilities embedded in a host programming language.
C. retrieval systems oriented to sequential file processing and including little, if any, file maintenance capability.
D. self-contained database management systems providing no access to the database through an application program.
E. database management systems providing access capabilities to both the nonprogrammer and the programmer.

A close examination reveals that B. is an extension of A., that D. is an extension of C., and that E. is a combination of B. and D.

Practically all systems up to the present fall into one of the two categories, popularly called host language systems (B.) or self-contained systems (C. or D.). Notice that the basis for the dichotomy is the type of user served -- programmer or nonprogrammer. If the same organizational data resources are to be shared by all types of users the dichotomy must disappear. Fortunately, a few commercially * available systems in category E. are beginning to appear. An alternative is to acquire one system of each type where an appropriate interface has been constructed. In many cases, this can be a dangerous strategy to follow from the standpoint of database integrity.

A TAXONOMY OF DATABASE MANAGEMENT FUNCTIONS

Several authors have put forth a taxonomy of database management functions [31, 14, 15, 13, 34, 21, 29, 9, 8]. The chart in Figure 4 shows the various taxonomies and relates them to each other using a common vertical scale.

---

*MARS III from CDC; QWIK-SCAN from Applied Systems Associates (on IBM); UAIMS from United Aircraft (on IBM); MARS VI/2 from CDC; SYSTEM 2000 from MRI Systems (on IBM, Univac, and CDC); METABASE from Programming Methods Inc. (on IBM); NIMMS from ICL, England; and FORIMS-1 from Nippon Univac, Japan.

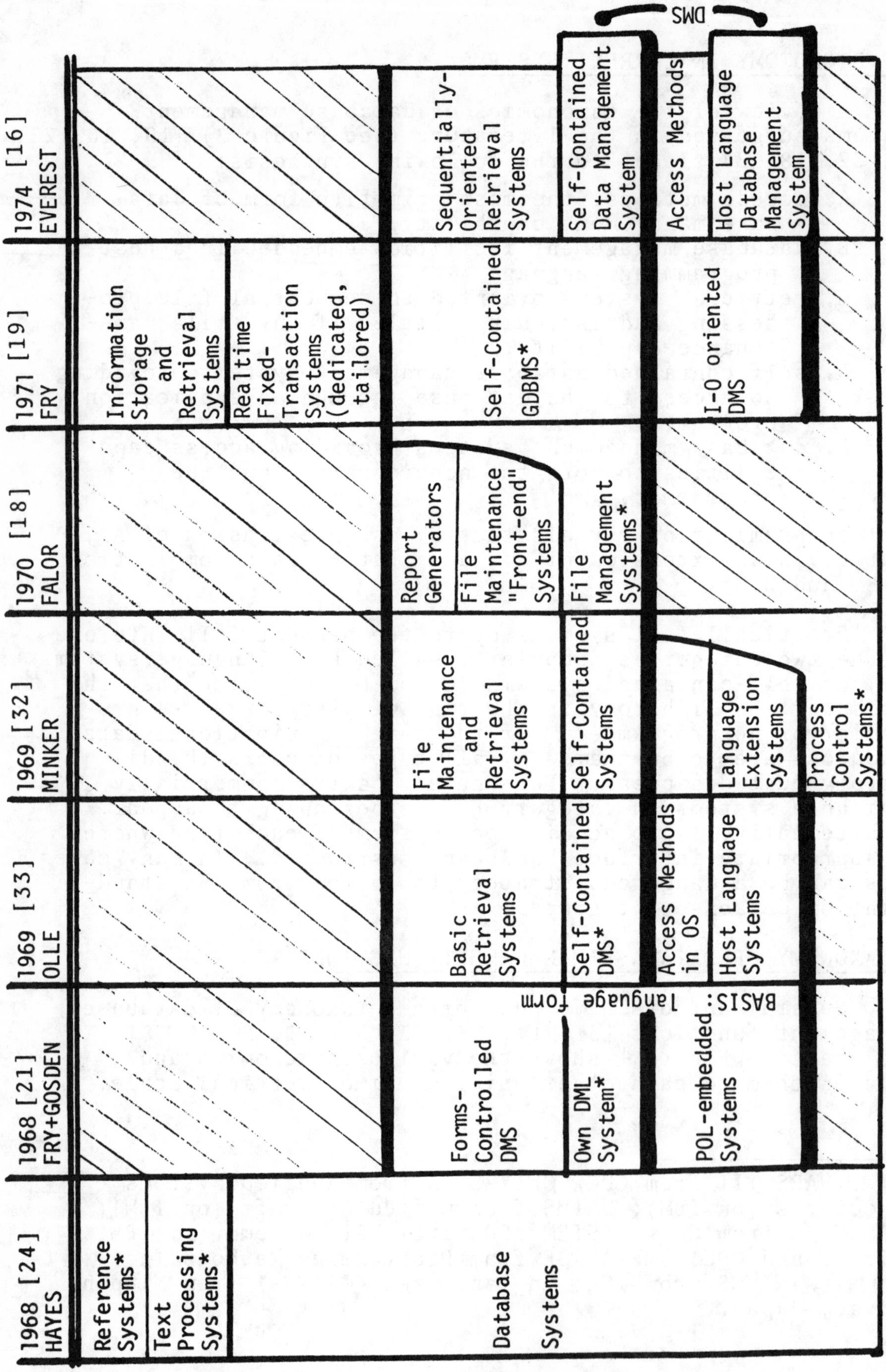

*author's focus or bias

Figure 3. Taxonomies of Database Management Systems.

1959 [31] McGee	1965 [14] Dobbs	1967 [15] Dowkont	1968 [13] Dixon	1968 [34] Olle	1968 [21] Fry	1969 [29] McGee	1969 [9] CODASYL Systems Committee	1971 [8]
	Definition	Definition	Definition	Establishment	File Generation	File Definition	Data Structure Definition	Data Definition
							Storage Structure Definition	Storage Structure Definition
	File Creation	Creation			File "Creation"	File Creation	File Creation	File Creation
			Maintenance	Revision		File Redefinition		
	Maintenance	Maintenance		Update	File Updating	File Updating	Update	Update
File Maintenance					Retrieval			
Report Generation	Retrieval	Retrieval Processing	Use	Interrogation	Output Presentation	Report Writing	Interrogation	Interrogation
	Presentation	Output						
Record Generation					File Creation	File Writing		
								Programming Facilities
								Data Administration Functions

Figure 4. Summary Chart of Functional Taxonomies.

A synthesis yields the following taxonomy of functions [16]:

    Direct Availability Functions
        Database Establishment and Structural Evolution
            Definition
            Creation
            Revision
        Database Use
            Interrogation
            Update
            Programming User Facilities
    Underlying Support Functions
        Integrity Control
        Performance Monitoring and Usage Statistics

Database Establishment

Establishment includes the functions of database definition and database creation, as shown in Figure 5. A full database definition includes:

- structural information relating to data items, groups, and relationships.
- storage structure information.
- device-media control information.
- nonstructural information such as output labels and format, and validation criteria.
- data dictionary information, if any.

Database creation is the process of taking new data and storing it in the database according to its definition. If the creation function requires data in a standard format, it may be necessary to write a special conversion program to allow the input of existing mechanized files.

Revision

Revision is the process of changing the structure of a previously established database. Redefinition may lead to the necessity to restructure the stored data so that it conforms to its new definition. This can be a very difficult and time-consuming process and is handled very inadequately in most database management systems. At the same time, as an organization establishes a greater proportion of its data resources in the database management system, the process of revision begins to dominate with the development of new applications. Reorganization is a special case of revision wherein the physical storage structure is changed while the logical database structure remains constant.

Interrogation

Interrogation is the process of query and response, of asking a question and obtaining an answer in terms of the

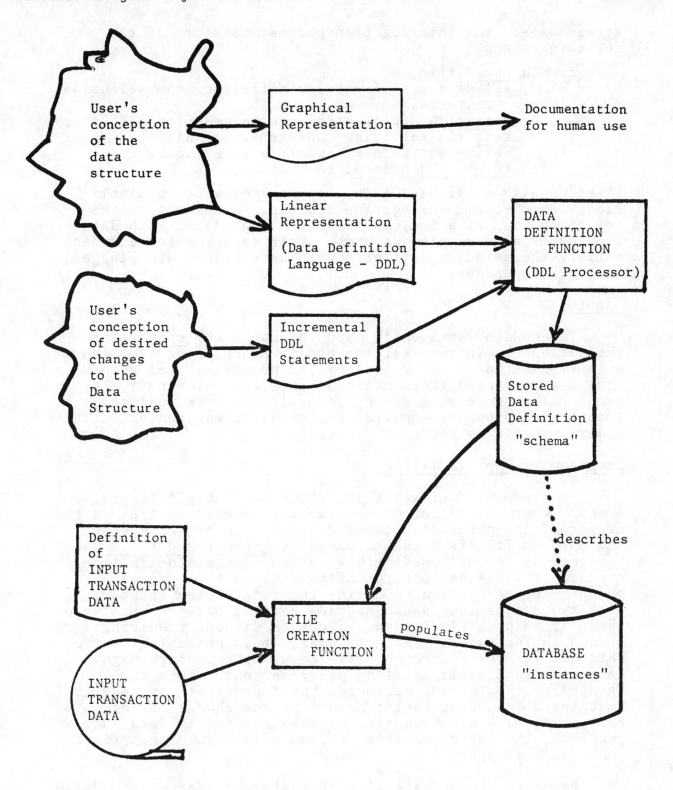

Figure 5. Data Definition and File Creation Functions.

stored data.   The interrogation process consists of the
following steps:

> from a <u>named file</u>,
> > <u>select</u> a set of entries satisfying the selection
> > > criteria,
> > <u>extract</u> a set of attribute values from each entry,
> > <u>sort</u> the resulting subfile (optional),
> > <u>derive</u> entry-level and file level data,
> and <u>format and present</u> the results.

Starting with a "simple" file, Figure 6 provides a simplified view of the interrogation process.   The input to the
selection step is a Boolean selection expression with data
item names as variable operands.   Entries are selected which
satisfy the selection criteria when data values are plugged
in to the operands.

Update

The update function is used to change the <u>content</u> of
the database.   In general, the update process receives input
data transactions, and validates and processes them according to a prestored transaction definition.   Alternatively,
transaction processing may be accomplished with tailored
transaction programs supplied by the using environment.   The
update process is shown in Figure 7.

Programming User Facilities

Programming facilities are those available to a program.
A most important aspect of programming user facilities is the
degree of independence between data as seen by the program
and data as it exists in the database.   <u>Program data inde-
pendence</u> is accomplished by having two separate definitions
<u>of data</u> -- the subschema to define data in the program
buffer, and the schema to define the data in the database.
With two definitions and a mapping defined between the two of
them, it is possible for one to change without requiring a
change in the other.   In particular, it is possible for the
database to evolve through revision without having to go
back and rewrite all existing programs that access the
changed portion of the database.   Some programs may have to
be changed depending on the nature of the change to the database, but, with a substantial measure of program data independence, the day of massive program maintenance and program
conversion is gone.

Programs communicate with the database management system
in terms of six types of information:

- the action to be performed, e.g., OPEN, READ, WRITE,
  CLOSE.
- names of the data attributes or groups to be
  extracted.

Simple File: EMPLOYEES

Attributes

EMPL. NO.	NAME	UNIT	JOB CODE	LEVEL	POSITION TITLE
45584	PETERSON, N. M.	2000	0110	HEAD	DIVISION MANAGER
32579	LYNN, K. R.	2000	5210	EMPL	SECRETARY
57060	CARR, P. I.	2100	1110	HEAD	MANAGER, DEVELOPMENT DEPT.
15324	CALLAGAN, R. F.	2100	5210	EMPL	SECRETARY
10261	GUTTMAN, G. J.	2110	1110	HEAD	MANAGER, SYST. ENGR. GROUP
72556	HARRIS, D. L.	2110	5210	EMPL	SECRETARY
24188	WALTERS, R. J.	2111	1110	HEAD	CHIEF, PROPOSAL SECTION
21675	SCARBOROUGH, J. B.	2111	1120	EMPL	MECH ENGR
18130	HENDERSON, R. G.	2111	1130	EMPL	ELEC ENGR
91152	GARBER, R. E.	2111	1330	EMPL	DRAFTSMAN
30793	COMPTON, D. R.	2111	1550	EMPL	COST ESTIMATOR
81599	FRIEDMAN, J. M.	2113	1110	HEAD	CHIEF, ADV. SYSTEMS SECTION
21777	FRANCIS, G. C.	2113	1110	EMPL	SYSTEMS ENGR
24749	FAULKNER, W. H.	2113	1120	EMPL	MECH ENGR
13581	FITINGER, G. J.	2113	1130	EMPL	ELEC ENGR
22959	BRIGGS, G. R.	2115	1113	HEAD	CHIEF, PROD. SPEC. SECTION
29414	ARTHUR, P. J.	2115	1120	EMPL	MECH ENGR
82802	APGAR, A. J.	2115	1130	EMPL	ELEC ENGR
37113	ARNETTE, L. J.	2115	1130	EMPL	ELEC ENGR
63633	BLANK, L. F.	2115	1330	EMPL	DRAFTSMAN

Entries

Question:

PRINT NAME, UNIT OF EMPLOYEES WHERE POSITION TITLE EQ ELEC ENGR.

Selection:

POSITION TITLE
    EQ   ELEC ENGR

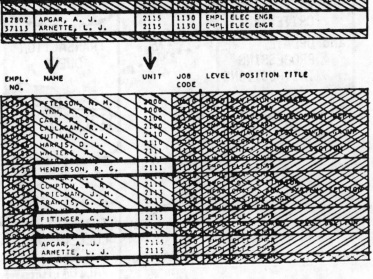

Extraction:

NAME, UNIT

Presentation of Answer:

NAME	UNIT
HENDERSON, R. G.	2111
FITINGER, G. J.	2113
APGAR, A. J.	2115
ARNETTE, L. J.	2115

Figure 6. A Simplified View of the Interrogation Process.

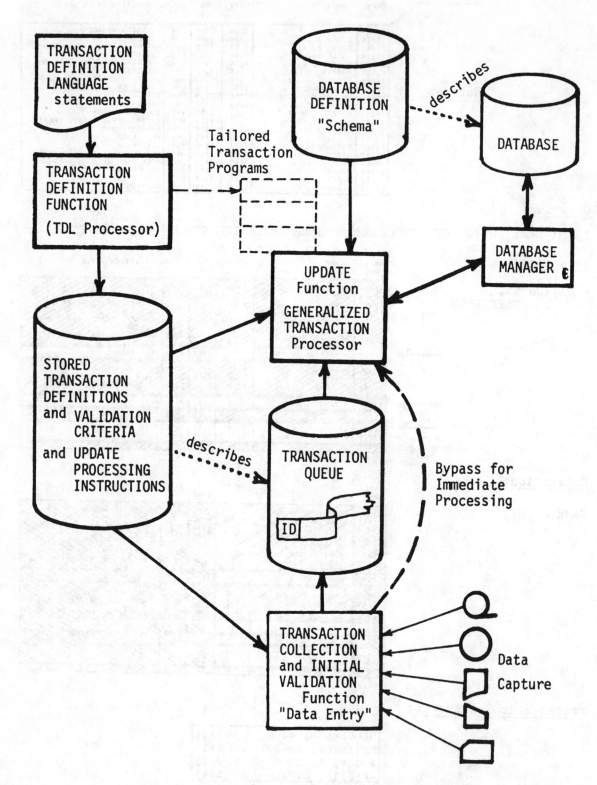

Figure 7.   The Process of Database Update.

- selection criteria in the form of positional
  criteria or a Boolean selection expression.
- subschema definition and the buffer location.
- response on detection of an error or exception
  condition.
- access authorization to confidential or controlled
  data.

Comparison with the steps in the interrogation process
reveals substantial similarity. Whereas the nonprogramming
user generally thinks in terms of a whole file, the programming user tends to think in terms of accessing and
manipulating individual records. He thinks of stepping
through the database from one record to the next along certain
hierarchical or network path relationships. The context of
the programming user interface is illustrated in Figure 8.

Underlying Integrity Control Functions

The underlying integrity control functions reside in the
database manager shown in Figure 2. All the direct availability functions must go through the integrity control
functions in accessing the database. The integrity control
functions include:

- validation of stored data.
- backup and recovery -- logging changes to the database and periodically dumping portions of the
  database.
- data access regulation which involves initially
  storing the authorizations associated with users
  of the database, identifying users when they are
  asking to do with what they are permitted to do,
  and finally, permitting or denying execution of the
  request.
- encryption, any form of transformation performed on
  data prior to transmission or storage which makes
  it difficult for an unauthorized person to interpret the data.
- controlling concurrent update processes through some
  form of lockout mechanism while also avoiding a
  deadlock situation.
- monitoring for threats to database integrity, and
  keeping an audit trail to permit a post analysis
  or investigation.

Considerable literature has appeared recently on some of
these aspects of database integrity [4, 37, 25, 10, 26].

Performance Monitoring and Usage Statistics

Monitoring the performance of the database system by
gathering usage statistics is essential to improved performance and enhanced availability. A wide variety of
statistics can be gathered depending on the specific

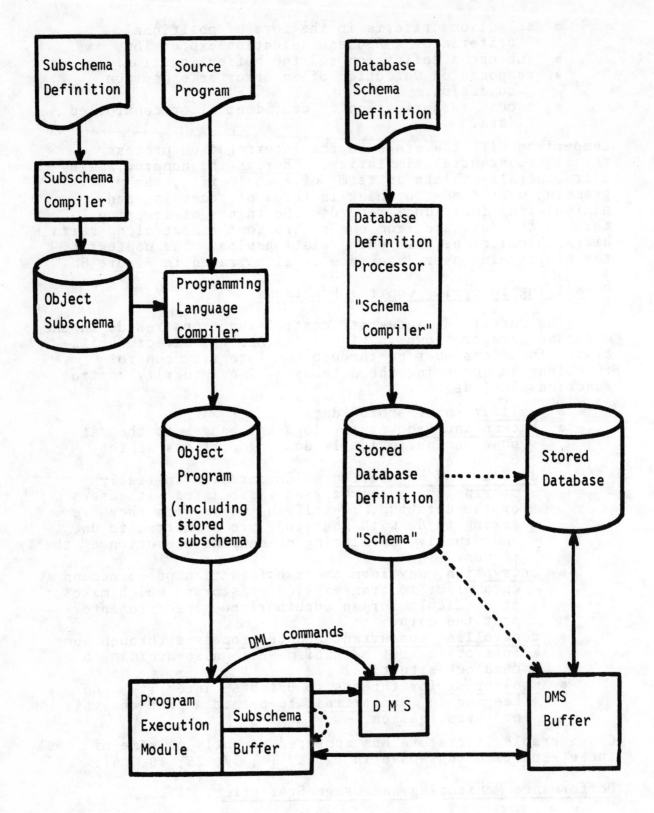

Figure 8. <u>Compromise Approach to Binding of Program and Data.</u>

objectives, problem areas, or bottlenecks of concern to users and management. Changing patterns of usage, as revealed in performance statistics, may signal the need for reorganization of the storage structure and perhaps revision of the database structure. Krinos has reported one attempt to gather usage statistics in a database management system environment [27].

DMS SUPPORT OF MANAGEMENT INFORMATION-DECISION SYSTEMS

One of the problems in building a management information system to support management decision making is the lack of an adequate, managed base of data. It is difficult to forecast and model decision processes without an explicit and formal _image_ of the organization and its environment. The behaviour of an organism is heavily determined by its image, increasingly so for social systems at the higher end of the levels of organizations [3]. It is imperative that organizations set about to establish a well-managed base of timely, accurate, and available data.

This tutorial provides a brief coverage of the organizational arrangements and system functions relating to database management. As such it should aid in the selection (or construction) of a viable and reasonably complete database management system (or at least provide an indication of what is not included in a selected system). It should also aid in setting up appropriate organizational arrangements to be able to effectively use a database management system to manage data resources.

This paper is based upon the author's doctoral dissertation [16] which will soon be published in book form.

References

[1] BACHMAN, Charles W., "Data Base Management: The
     Keystone of Applied Systems Architecture," in
     Critical Factors in Data Management, edited by
     Fred Gruenberger, Englewood Cliffs, NJ: Prentice-
     Hall, 1969, pages 33-40.

[2] BACHMAN, Charles W., "Data Structure Diagrams," Data
     Base (1:2), 1969 Summer, pages 4-10

[3] BOULDING, Kenneth E., The Image: Knowledge in Life and
     Society, Ann Arbor, MI: University of Michigan
     Press, 1956 (Ann Arbor paperback AA47, 1961), 175
     pages.

[4] BROWNE, Peter S., "Computer Security -- a Survey,"
     Data Base (4:3), 1972 Fall, pages 1-12.

[5] CANNING, Richard G., "The 'Data Administrator' Function,"
     EDP Analyzer (10:11), 1972 November, 14 pages.

[6] CANNING, Richard G., "The Debate on Data Base Management,"
     EDP Analyzer (10:3), 1972 March, 16 pages.

[7] CODASYL Programming Language Committee, Data Base Task
     Group Report, New York: Association for Computing
     Machinery, 1971 April, 273 pages, (in Europe:
     British Computer Society, London, England, or
     IFIP Administrative Data Processing Group, Amster-
     dam, Netherlands).

[8] CODASYL Systems Committee, Feature Analysis of Gener-
     alized Data Base Management Systems, New York:
     Association for Computing Machinery, 1971 May, 520
     pages, (in Europe: British Computer Society,
     London, England, or IFIP Administrative Data
     Processing Group, Amsterdam, Netherlands).

[9] CODASYL Systems Committee, A Survey of Generalized
     Data Base Management Systems, New York: Associ-
     ation for Computing Machinery, 1969 May,
     (PB 203 142), 398 pages.

[10] CONWAY, Richard W., William L. MAXWELL and Howard L.
     MORGAN, "On the Implementation of Security Measures
     in Information Systems," Communications of the ACM
     (15:4), 1972 April, pages 211-220.

[11] CURTICE, R. M., "Data Base Design Using IMS/360," AFIPS
     Fall Joint Computer Conference Proceedings, (volume
     41, part II), 1972, pages 1105-1110.

[12]   Diebold Research Program, Organizing for Data Base
       Management, New York: The Diebold Group, Inc.,
       Document Number S16, 1971 December, 94 pages.

[13]   DIXON, Paul J., "Generalized Data Management --
       Functional Requirements," File Organisation,
       selected papers from "FILE 68" - an IAG Conference,
       Denmark, 1968 November 20, Amsterdam: Swets and
       Zeitlinger N.V., 1969, IAG Occasional Publication
       No. 3, pages 302-309.

[14]   DOBBS, Guy H., "State-of-the-Art Survey of Data Base
       Systems," Proceedings of the Second Symposium on
       Computer-Centered Data Base Systems, Santa Monica,
       1965 September 20-21, edited by Claude Baum and L.
       Gorsuch, Santa Monica, California: System Develop-
       ment Corporation, TM-2624, (AD 625 417), 1965
       December 1, pages 2-3 to 2-10.

[15]   DOWKONT, Anthony J., William MORRIS and T. Dwight
       BUETTELL, A Methodology for Comparison of Genera-
       lized Data Management Systems: PEGS (Parametric
       Evaluation of Generalized Systems), Sherman Oaks,
       CA: Informatics, Inc., (for United States Air
       Force, Electronic Systems Division, Hanscom Field,
       Bedford, MA, ESD-TR-67-2), (AD 811 682), 1967 March,
       286 pages.

[16]   EVEREST, Gordon C., "Managing Corporate Data Resources:
       Objectives and a Conceptual Model of Database
       Management Systems," unpublished doctoral disser-
       tation, Wharton School, University of Pennsylvania,
       Philadelphia, 1974 May, 602 pages (publication
       forthcoming)

[17]   EVEREST, Gordon C., "The Objectives of Database Manage-
       ment," in Information Systems, Proceedings of Fourth
       International Symposium on Computer and Information
       Science (COINS-72), Miami Beach, Florida, 1972
       December 14-16, edited by Julius Tou, New York:
       Plenum Publishing Corporation, 1974, pages 1-35.

[18]   FALOR, Ken, "Survey of Program Packages -- Report Gener-
       ators and File Management Systems," Modern Data
       (3:8), 1970 August, pages 48-59.

[19]   FRY, James P., "Managing Data is the Key to MIS,"
       Computer Decisions (3:1), 1971 January, pages 6-10.

[20]   FRY, James P., et al., A Survey of Data Management
       Systems, Washington, DC: The MITRE Corporation,
       (for the United States Defense Communications
       Agency), (AD 684 707), 1969 January, 206 pages.

[21] FRY, James P. and John GOSDEN, "Survey of Management
      Information Systems and their Languages,"
      Washington, DC: MITRE Corporation, MTP-313, 1968
      May, AD 684 706, (reprinted in Critical Factors in
      Data Management, edited by Fred Gruenberger,
      Englewood Cliffs, NJ: Prentice-Hall, 1969, pages
      41-55).

[22] GUIDE Data Base Administration Project, "The Data Base
      Administrator," Chicago, IL: GUIDE International,
      Information Systems Division, 1972 November 3, 76
      pages.

[23] GUIDE-SHARE Data Base Requirements Group, Data Base
      Management System Requirements, New York: SHARE,
      Inc., 1970 November 11, 132 pages.

[24] HAYES, Robert M., "Information Retrieval: An Intro-
      duction," Datamation (14:3), 1968 March, pages 22-
      26.

[25] HOFFMAN, Lance J., "Computers and Privacy: A Survey,"
      Computing Surveys (1:2), 1969 June, (Stanford
      University, California, 1968 August, PB 184 332),
      pages 85-103.

[26] KING, Paul F. and Arthur J. COLLMEYER, "Database Sharing--
      An Efficient Mechanism for Supporting Concurrent
      Processes," AFIPS National Computer Conference
      Proceedings, 1973, pages 271-275.

[27] KRINOS, John D., "Interaction Statistics from a Database
      Management System," AFIPS National Computer Confer-
      ence Proceedings, 1973, pages 283-290.

[28] LYON, John K., "The Role of the Data Base Administrator:
      Excerpts from a talk given to ACM-SIGBDP, Chicago,
      1971 August 4," Data Base (3:4), 1971 Winter, pages
      11-12.

[29] McGEE, William C., "Generalized File Processing," in
      Annual Review in Automatic Programming, Volume 5,
      edited by Mark I. Halpern and Christopher J. Shaw,
      Oxford, England: Pergamon Press, 1969, pages 77-
      149.

[30] McGee, William C., "File Structures for Generalized
      Data Management," in Information Processing 68,
      Proceedings of IFIP Congress, Edinburgh, 1968
      August 5-10, volume 2, edited by A. J. H. Morrell,
      Amsterdam: North-Holland Publishing Co., 1969,
      pages 1233-1239.

[31] McGEE, William C., "Generalization: Key to Successful
        Electronic Data Processing," Journal of the ACM
        (6:1), 1959 January, pages 1-23.

[32] MINKER, Jack, Generalized Data Management Systems --
        Some Perspectives, College Park, MD: University
        of Maryland, Computer Science Center, Technical
        Report 69-101, 1969 December.

[33] OLLE, T. William, "An Analysis of Generalized Data Base
        Management Systems," Proceedings of the Founding
        Conference of the Society for Management Information
        Systems, Minneapolis, Minnesota, 1969 September 8-9.

[34] OLLE, T. William, "UL/1: A Non-Procedural Language for
        Retrieving Information from Data Bases," Information
        Processing 68, Volume 1, Proceedings of IFIP Congress,
        Edinburgh, 1968 August 5-10, edited by A. J. H.
        Morrell, Amsterdam: North-Holland Publishing Co.,
        1969, pages 572-578.

[35] PLAGMAN, Bernard K. and Gene P. ALTSHULER, "A Data
        Dictionary/Directory System Within the Context of
        an Integrated Corporate Data Base," AFIPS Fall
        Joint Computer Conference Proceedings (volume 41),
        1972, pages 572-578.

[36] SENKO, M. E., "Details of a Scientific Approach to
        Information Systems," in Data Base Systems, Courant
        Computer Science Symposium 6, 1971 May 24-25,
        edited by Randall Rustin, Englewood Cliffs, NJ:
        Prentice-Hall, 1972, pages 143-174.

[37] TURN, Rein and Norman Z. SHAPIRO, "Privacy and Security
        in Database Systems -- Measures of Effectiveness,
        Costs, and Protector-Intruder Interactions," AFIPS
        Fall Joint Computer Conference Proceedings (volume
        41), 1972, pages 435-444.

[38] ULMAN, Joseph N., Jr., and Jay R. GOULD, Technical
        Reporting, Rev. ed., New York: Holt Rinehart,
        and Winston, 1959, 382 pages.

"THE PROCESS OF PROBLEM FINDING"

Industrial Management Review (11:1), 1969 Fall, pages 1-19.

William F. Pounds is Dean of the Sloan School of Management at Massachusetts Institute of Technology.

Models of decision making generally assume that the problem is recognized or known. This article is an excellent exploration into the process of finding the problem to be solved. It surveys the small amount of progress that has been made in terms of problem identification and notes research on chess as a related development. The paper is conceptual but many of the problems are supported by data drawn from an empirical study of managerial problem finding by 50 executives of a large company.

A problem is defined as the difference between some existing situation and some desired situation. The problem finding model is one of choosing what is desired, comparing this to reality, identifying differences, and selecting a difference which is perceived to be a problem. "The problem of understanding problem finding is eventually reduced to the problem of understanding the models which the manager uses to define differences."

Pounds discusses four models which produce expectations:
1. Historical models in which the manager's expectation is based on an extrapolation of past experience.
2. Planning models in which the plan is the expectation.
3. Other people's models, in which the expectation comes from others inside the organization, such as superiors or subordinates.
4. Extra-organizational models in which expectations are derived from competitors, customers, and professional organizations.

The differences between the situation at hand and the expectations from the model generate a variety of stimuli which compete for management attention. Whether or not a problem will then be identified and worked on depends on the priority used by the manager.

READING SUGGESTIONS

The reader should focus on how the author characterizes a problem. The theoretical structure of problem finding as illustrated in flowchart 1 is the central idea of the article. Understand and distinguish carefully the four models and their level of importance for problem finding. The discussion presents the consequences of the manager's use of simple decision models as they relate to inadequate problem finding. If a decision making model is very simple the problem finding model is likely also to be very simple and naive. This suggests that there is an iterative relationship between model selection and problem identification. The use of the problem finding procedures generate more stimuli than managers can utilize, necessitating a selection of problems to work on. The evidence suggests that the stimuli selected for problem finding processes are conditioned by the priority rules used by the manager.

QUESTIONS

1. How does Pounds characterize a problem?
2. Explain briefly the theory of problem finding.
3. Describe the four models used in problem finding. Identify the differences in the nature of the input data to each of these four models.
4. Under historical and planning models, what is the nature of the responses to a positive difference? a negative difference? no significant difference?
5. How powerful is each type of model at identifying problems and thereby demanding a decision maker's time?
6. Identify the weaknesses of each type of model.
7. How do executives decide on the stimulus which will cause them to enter into a problem finding process?

The Process of Problem Finding*

William F. Pounds
Massachusetts Institute of Technology

Today's manager is confronted with a greater number and variety of problems than ever before. In the growing body of knowledge on the profession of management, the focus has almost exclusively been on the structuring and solution of these problems. Rarely, if ever, do managers analyze or understand the sources of their problems. This article provides an insight into the origins of every manager's problems and may be a key to the efficient use of managerial time. *Ed.*

Introduction

As a result of research efforts over the past twenty years, a number of extremely effective analytical techniques are currently available for the solution of management problems. Linear programming is used routinely in the specification of optimum cattle feeds and fertilizers. Decision rules based on inventory models form the basis for production and inventory control systems in a wide variety of manufacturing companies. Simulation is evolving from a means for doing research on complex managerial problems to a process which can provide useful information to managers on a real-time basis.

Like other technological changes, these methods raise a number of social and organizational issues within the organizations which use them, but their net contribution is no longer seriously in doubt. As a result, in most large organizations and in many smaller ones, operating managers either are aware of these methods or have ready access to help and advice in their application.

But the manager's job is not only to solve well-defined problems. He must also identify the problems to be solved. He must somehow assess the cost of analysis and its potential return. He must allocate resources to questions before he knows their answers. To many managers and students of management, the availibility of formal problem solving procedures serves only to highlight those parts of the manager's job with which these procedures do *not* deal: problem identification, the assignment of problem priority, and the allocation of scarce resources to problems. These tasks, which must be performed without the benefit of a well-defined body of theory, may be among the most critical of the manager's decision making responsibilities.

This paper is concerned primarily with the first of these tasks — problem identification. It reviews some research relevant to understanding decisions of this type, presents a theoretical structure, and reports some results of an empirical study of the process by which managers in a successful industrial organization define their problems. Because this research was stimulated in part by an interest in the relationship between the so-called new techniques of management and what might be called traditional managerial behavior, similarities between these two modes of management which are suggested both by the theory and the empirical evidence are briefly noted.

Background

Prior to 1945, our understanding of most cognitive tasks within industrial organizations was not much better than our understanding of the process of problem finding is today. Inventory levels were maintained, production schedules were determined, and distribution systems were designed by individuals who, through years of experience, had learned ways to get these jobs done. With few exceptions these individuals were not explicit about how they performed these tasks and, as a result, training for these jobs was a slow process and the development and testing of new procedures was difficult indeed.

So it is with the process of problem finding today. All managers have discovered ways to maintain a list of problems that can occupy their working hours — and other hours as well. They frequently find it difficult, however, to be explicit about the process by which their problems are selected. Consequently, the development of improved problem finding procedures is difficult.

Since 1945, however, some progress has been made in understanding certain cognitive tasks in the areas of production and inventory control. Decisions rules have been derived from mathematical models of particular tasks, and in a number of cases these rules have performed as well as or better than the complex intuitive process they have replaced. The significant fact about these developments for this discussion is not, however, the economic impact of such rules, although it has been significant. Rather, it is the implication that the essential processes by which important decisions are made may be carried out satisfactorily by simple explicit decision rules which are easy to teach and execute and easy to improve through analysis, simulation, or experimentation.

Of course it is possible to discount these accomplishments by saying that inventory decisions were always rather simple ones to make. The validity of such arguments, however, seems suspiciously dependent on knowledge of what has been accomplished and on a lack of knowledge of inventory systems.

It is true, however, that mathematical analysis has been able only to suggest decision rules for a wide variety of managerial tasks. These tasks, including the definition of problems, seem to require symbols and analytical procedures not readily represented by standard mathematical forms. Some other means for discovering the decision rules by which such tasks are performed is clearly required.

Some progress in this direction has already been made. Encouraged both by the success of the analytical approach to decision problems, and by the availability of large digital computers, Newell, Simon, and others have been studying human decision behavior since the early 1950's. They have focused their attention primarily on tasks which would facilitate the development of a methodology for approaching decision situations not readily describable in mathematical terms. They have considered the decision processes involved in proving theorems in symbolic logic[1] and plane geometry.[2] They have considered decision processes involved in playing games like chess[3] and checkers.[4] They have worked on the assembly line balancing problem[5] and on trust investment.[6] The relevance of this research to problem finding can perhaps best be illustrated by considering the work on chess.

Research on Chess Chess is a game with rules simple enough for almost anyone to learn and yet complex enough that even the largest computer cannot play it by working out the consequences of all possible moves. Chess is a game of strategy in which individual moves can not always be evaluated without considering future moves. Chess moves are inconvenient to describe in mathematical terms and few people can be explicit about how they play chess. For these reasons and several others, chess was an attractive medium in which to attempt to unravel human decision processes that could not be modeled mathematically.

Three aspects of the work on chess playing behavior are relevant to this discussion. First, simple explicit decision rules were discovered which make for very good chess play. This result has been tested by programming computers with such rules and observing the quality of play which resulted in response to the play of human experts. Second, the decision rules for chess playing were derived from observations, interviews, and the writings of chess masters. Thus, it is not necessary that simple, explicit decision rules be derived from mathematical or theoretical considerations. They can be abstracted from humans who have themselves never systematically considered the process of their own decision making. And, third, the decision rules by which humans play chess appear to be separable into three rather distinct classes: rules for defining alternative moves, rules for evaluating alternative moves, and rules for choosing a move from among evaluated alternatives. H.A. Simon has called these three classes of behavior intelligence, design, and choice, respectively,[7] and on the basis of his work both on chess and other decision making situations has concluded that the process of intelligence or alternative definition is the key to effective behavior.

The work on chess and other complex tasks does not directly suggest how managers go about finding and defining the problems to which they devote their time. It does suggest, however, that tasks of this same order of complexity may be understood through careful observation of and abstraction from the behavior of human experts. It further suggests that, if useful insights into managerial problem finding can be gained, they may contribute significantly to managerial effectiveness.

* Research for this paper was supported in part by a grant from NASA. The author gratefully acknowledges the many contributions of Professor E.H. Bowman to all phases of this study and particularly those he made to the planning and execution of the company study.

[1] Newell, Shaw, and Simon [6].   [2] Gelernter [3].   [3] Newell, Shaw, and Simon [5].
[4] Samuel [8].   [5] Tonge [10].   [6] Clarkson [2].   [7] Simon [9].

An Empirical Study of Managerial Problem Finding

Since it was possible to gain useful insights into the process by which humans play chess by observing experts, it seemed likely that insights into the process of managerial problem finding might be derived from careful observation of successful managers. Arrangements were made therefore to interview, observe, and interrogate about 50 executives in a decentralized operating division of a large technically based corporation, which will be referred to as the Southern Company.

The study consisted of four relatively distinct activities. First, interviews were conducted during which executives were asked to describe the problems they faced and the processes by which they had become aware of these problems. Second, observations were made of meetings during which problems were identified, discussed, and sometimes solved. Third, investigations were made of the source and disposition of several specific problems. And, fourth, a questionnaire was devised and administered to each executive who participated in the study.

As data began to accumulate from each of these activities, it became clear that a major objective of the study would be to discover some level of abstraction which would preserve what seemed to be essential details of the managerial situations being observed and at the same time provide a structure which would convert isolated anecdotes into data from which some generalizations might be drawn. This structure will be described in the following pages together with some of the observations it explains. Observations made outside this particular study will also be reported.

Theoretical Structure   Like any number of other industrial tasks, the process of management can be viewed as the sequential execution of elementary activities. In describing their own work, executives find it easy to think and talk in terms of elementary activities like making out the production schedule, reading the quality control report, visiting a customer, etc. The attractive feature of this view of managerial work is that elementary tasks can be defined at almost any level of detail. Clearly the task of preparing a production schedule is itself made up of more elementary tasks like collecting data on orders and labor availability, which are themselves made up of even more elementary activities. On the other hand, one can aggregate elements like production scheduling into larger units of analysis like managing production.

A choice of some level of abstraction cannot be avoided. For purposes of this study, the level chosen was that which the managers themselves used in describing their activities. Thus, even at the theoretical level, advantage was taken of the fact that the managers' language had evolved as a useful means for processing information about their jobs.

Elements of managerial activity will be referred to as *operators*. An operator transforms a set of input variables into a set of output variables according to some predetermined plan. For example, the operator "lay out a production schedule" takes machine capacities, labor productivities, product requirements, and other input variables and yields man, product, machine, and time associations covering some appropriate period of time. Since the action of an operator produces an effect which is more or less predictable, operators are frequently named for their effect on the environment. The operator "lay out production schedule" changes the production organization from one with no schedule to one with a schedule. The operator "hire qualified lathe operator" changes the size of the work force.

The word "problem" is associated with the difference between some existing situation and some desired situation. The problem of reducing material cost, for example, indicates a difference between the existing material cost and some desired level of material cost. The problems of hiring qualified engineers and of reducing finished goods inventories similarly define differences to be reduced. Because problems are defined by differences and operators can be executed to reduce differences, strong associations are formed between problems and operators. The problem of devising a production schedule can ordinarily be "solved" by applying the operator "lay out production schedule." The problem of "increasing sales volume" can sometimes be "solved" by applying the operator "revise advertising budget." Since operator selection is triggered by the difference to be reduced, the process of problem finding is the process of defining differences. Problem solving, on the other hand, is the process of selecting operators which will reduce differences.

The manager defines differences by comparing what he perceives to the output of a *model* which predicts the same variables. A difference might be defined by comparing an idle machine to a production schedule which implies high machine utilization. In this case, the production schedule is the model used to define a difference. A difference might be defined by comparing a 10 percent reject rate in a department to a budgeted rate of two percent. In this case, the budget is the model. A difference might be defined by comparing available data to those required for a special report. The problem of understanding problem finding is therefore eventually reduced to the problem of understanding the models which managers use to define differences.

It should be noted that the theoretical framework proposed here has drawn on ideas discussed by Miller, Galanter, and Pribram,[9] who in turn refer to some basic work by Newell, Shaw, and Simon.[10] Figure I presents a flow chart of the process described in this section and, for comparison, the structures proposed by others.

Miller, Galanter, and Pribram:

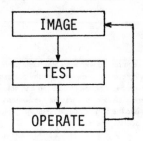

Simon:

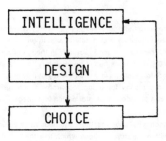

Pounds:

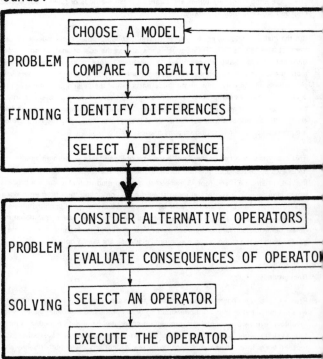

1. Flow Chart of Managerial Behavior

K Because this paper is concerned primarily with problem finding, the process of operator selection and execution will not be discussed. The definitions are included only to complete the description of the theoretical structure.
9 Miller, Galanter, and Pribram [4].
10 Newell, Shaw, and Simon [7].

Managerial Models for Problem Finding

Historical Models On the assumption that recent past experience is the best estimate of the short term future, managers maintain a wide variety of models based on the continuity of historical relationships: April sales exceed March sales by 10 percent; Department X runs five percent defective product; the cost of making item Y is $10.50 per thousand; the lead time on that raw material is three weeks, etc. Because the manager's world is complex and these models tend to be simple, discrepancies frequently arise between the models' predictions and what actually takes place. Such discrepancies are a major source of problems to which managers devote their time. Why is our inventory account drifting out of line? Why is our reject rate so high this week? What has happened to make so many deliveries late? What can be done to reverse this trend in absenteeism? Why is our safety record suddenly so good? All these problems and a host of others like them are triggered by discrepancies from historical models and can keep a manager and his organization busy all day every day.

For the most part these models are non-explicit. The manager "carries them in his head" or "just knows." In a number of cases, however, these models are strongly supported by routine reports. Pieces of paper on which are printed monthly P & L statements, weekly reports of sales totals, daily reports of orders behind schedule, semi-annual inventories, and many other items of interest flow across the manager's desk in a steady stream and, except in its historical context, each one has little meaning to the manager or anyone else.[11]

Recognizing this fact, most management reports in the Southern Company were prepared in such a way that current figures and recent reports of the same variables appeared side by side. Trends or sharp variations in any variable could be easily noted. The confidence placed in such analysis was clearly indicated by the fact that a large number of variables were added to routine reports following an unanticipated fluctuation in corporate profits. After several months, managers could review their history of "Return on Sales," "Return on Investment," and many other variables in addition to those previously reported.

The importance of routine reports as well as the use of an historical model to identify a problem were both illustrated when the rejection rate of one department moved past an historic high and thereby attracted attention to the Quality Assurance organization. A number of other examples could be cited. Out of 52 managers, 42 agreed with the statement that "most improvements come from correcting unsatisfactory situations," and, for the most part, unsatisfactory situations were defined by departures from historically established models of performance.

Departures of performance in a favorable direction — lower than historical cost or higher than historical sales, for example — were used to modify the historical model not to define a problem *per se*. Several managers reported that better-than-average performance was frequently used as evidence of what could be accomplished when reduced cost allowances or increased profit expectations were being discussed. At the time of this study, the Southern Company was doing very well relative to its own past performance and a number of managers shared the sentiments of one who reported, "This year is going too well." They were clearly concerned about their ability to continue to meet what would become a new historical standard. Several were already working on that problem-to-be.

Besides serving as triggers for corrective and innovative problem solving, historical models are used extensively in the process of devising plans for future operations. These plans are in turn converted into budget objectives, and the budget objectives can sometimes serve as models which trigger managerial problem solving. Because of the complex process by which they are devised, managerial planning models will be discussed separately from the more straightforward historical ones.

Planning Models Managers in the Southern Company devoted substantial amounts of time to planning future operations. Detailed projections of operating variables for the coming year and less detailed projections for the coming five years were presented annually to corporate officers by each product department manager. When approved, perhaps after some modification, these projections were used periodically to evaluate managerial performance, and for other purposes as well.

In view of the importance attributed to planning by the Southern Company, it might be expected that planning models would constitute an important part of the problem finding process. In fact they did not. Historical models were more influential on managerial behavior than planning models. To understand why, it is necessary to examine both the function of planning models and the process by which they were devised.

Among other things, plans are organizationally defined limits of managerial independence. So long as the manager is able to perform at least as well as his plan requires, he expects, and is normally granted, the right to define his problems as he sees fit. That is to say, as long as meeting his plan does not itself constitute a problem, the manager can use other criteria for defining his problems. If, however, he is unable to perform as well as he planned, he can expect to attract the attention of higher levels of management and to receive substantial assistance in problem identification. In other words, he will lose, perhaps only temporarily, the right to manage. One product manager put the matter this way, "The best way to remain in charge is to be successful." Other managers strongly supported this position. Success was defined relative to the predictions of the planning model.

In view of the fact that unfavorable deviations in performance were far more undesirable to managers than favorable deviations, it is not surprising that planning models were not simple descriptions of what the managers expected would happen. On the contrary, planning models represented the minimum performance the manager could reasonably expect if several of his plans failed or were based on the minimum organizational expectations of managerial performance, whichever was higher. Planning models were in general very conservatively biased historical models. For the most part these biases in plans were not injected surreptitiously. After approving a manager's plan, upper level managers always inquired about how he would deal with various contingencies. At this point the manager would reveal some but usually not all of his "hedges" against uncertainty. If he could report a number of conservative estimates and contingent plans to back up the plan being proposed, this was viewed as highly desirable.

In aggregating departmental plans, further "adjustments" were made which led the plan to depart from expectations. In some cases, these adjustments shifted expected profits from one department to another to "make the package look OK." In other cases, already conservative departmental estimates were "rounded down" to cover contingencies further. Some of these adjustments were made explicit at higher levels.

Even with all its conservative biases, the Division's plan still exceeded the Corporation's minimum profit and volume expectations. It is not surprising, therefore, that the planning model was a far less important source of management problems than historical models. Extrapolations of past performance simply implied much higher levels of performance than the planning model called for. Only in those cases (not observed) where the corporate expectations required improvements over historical trends would one expect planning models to be important in the process of problem finding.

Other Peoples' Models Some models which define problems for the manager are maintained by other people. A customer whose model of product quality is violated by the product he receives may notify the manager of the producing organization of this fact and thereby define a problem for him. A higher level manager may lack information to complete an analysis and this discrepancy can define a problem for a lower level manager. An employee may need a decision on vacation policy and his request will define a problem for his supervisor. A basic function of an organization structure is to channel problems which are identified by its various members to individuals especially qualified to solve them. Managers as well as other members of the organization do not always work on problems defined by their own models.

In the Southern Company, invitations to attend meetings, requests to prepare reports, and requests for projects of various kinds whether made by superiors, subordinates, or peers were rarely questioned by managers as appropriate ways to spend their time. While it was sometimes easy to get vehement testimony as to the uselessness of many of these activities, the behavior of managers clearly indicated the strong influence of other people's models. One reason for the influence of these models may be the cost to the manager of doubting them. Any attempt to validate each request made on him could easily imply a heavier workload on the manager than the simple execution of the work requested. In addition, by providing "good service" the manager builds (or at least many managers believe they build) a store of goodwill among other managers toward his own requests.

During the course of the company study, several clear examples of the influence of these models were observed. In a series of interviews, managers were asked to specify the problems currently faced by them and their organizations. Most of them mentioned from five to eight problems. Later in the same interview, each manager was asked to describe in broad terms his own activities for the previous week. In reviewing the data from these interviews as they were collected, it was noted that no manager had reported any activity which could be directly associated with the problems he had described.

---

[11] Budgets, which can also provide context for such data, are discussed in the next section.

In order to be sure that this result was not due to some semantic problem, this point was discussed with several managers — in some cases during the first interview with them and in other cases as a follow-up question. One manager found the point both accurate and amusing. He smiled as he replied, "That's right. I don't have time to work on *my* problems — I'm too busy." Another manager took a different tack in agreeing with the general conclusion. He replied rather confidentially, "I don't really make decisions. I just work here." In further discussion with a number of managers, the power of other peoples' models was repeatedly indicated. The influence of these models was also noted in the case of a rather involved project which was observed in some detail.

The Plant Engineering Department, using a quite different model, decided to look at the desirability of revising the management of the company's 21 fork trucks. Besides scheduling and other operating questions which were investigated by people within the Engineering Department, studies of the contract under which the trucks were leased and an economic evaluation of leasing versus buying trucks were also felt to be required. The Manager of Plant Engineering called representatives of the Comptroller's organization and the Legal Department to a meeting in which the project was discussed in some detail. This discussion clearly indicated that the project was risky both from the point of view of economic payoff and political considerations. The representatives accepted their tasks, however, and in due course their studies were completed. In neither case did the studies take much time, but the assumption that it was the job of the Accounting Department and the Legal Department to serve the Plant Engineering Department was clear. A problem found by someone in the organization carries with it substantial influence over the problems on which other parts of the organization will work.

Even clearer evidence of the power of other peoples' models was the time devoted by all the managers in the Southern Company to the preparation of reports "required" by higher management. These reports ranged in their demands on managerial time from a few minutes in the case of a request for routine information to several man months of work on the preparation of a plan for the coming year's operations. In reply to the question, "If you were responsible for the whole company's operations would you require more, the same, or less planning?" four managers responded that they would require more planning, 32 said the same amount of planning, and 16 replied less. For many managers the expectations of the organization were consistent with their own ideas of the time required for effective planning. For a number of others, however, the influence of other people was clear.

In discussing these models as a source of problems, it is difficult to avoid a negative connotation due to the widely held ethic which values individual problem definition. Two points are worth emphasizing. First, the study was conducted to find out how managers do define their problems — not how they should do so — although that, of course, may be a long-term objective of this work. Second, both the organization and the individuals described here would, by almost any standards, be judged to be highly successful and this fact should be included in any attempt to evaluate their behavior.

Because historical, planning, and other peoples' models require almost no generalization to make them relevant to particular events of interest to the manager, and because these three types of models can easily generate more problems than the manager can reasonably hope to deal with, it is not surprising, perhaps, that models requiring somewhat more generalization are less important elements of the process of problem finding. It is true, however, that on occasion managers draw on experiences other than their own to define problems for themselves and their organizations.

Extra-Organizational Models

Trade journals which report new practices and their effects in other organizations can sometimes define useful areas for managerial analysis. Customers frequently serve the same function by reporting the accomplishments of competitors in the area of price, service, and/or product quality. General Motors is known for its practice of ranking the performance measures of a number of plants producing the same or similar products and making this information available to the managers of these facilities. The implication is strong in these comparisons that problems exist in plants where performance is poor relative to other plants.

In using all such extra-organizational models to define intra-organizational problems, the manager must resolve the difficult question of model validity. "Is the fact that our West Coast plant has lower maintenance costs relevant to our operations? After all, they have newer equipment." "Is the fact that our competitor is lowering its price relevant to our pricing policy? After all, our quality is better." There are enough attributes in any industrial situation to make it unlikely indeed that any extra-organizational model will fit the manager's situation perfectly. Judgments on the question of model validity must frequently be made by operating managers.

In the Southern Company one clear case was observed where two extra-organizational models were employed in an attempt to define a problem. A member of the Plant Engineering Department attended a meeting of an engineering society at which a technique called "work sampling" was discussed in the context of several successful applications in other plants. This model of a current engineering practice, which had not been employed by his department, led this man to consider the problem of finding an application for work sampling in the Southern Company. Clearly if this technique could be successfully applied, it would reduce the difference between his department and his extra-organizational model. A few days later this engineer noticed an idle, unattended fork truck in one of the manufacturing shops and he immediately thought that an analysis of fork truck operations might be the application he was looking for. He discussed this idea with his supervisors and they agreed that the project should be undertaken.

Because of the lack of direct responsibility for fork trucks, Plant Engineering was aware from the beginning of the project that its primary task would be to convince the product departments that their fork trucks indeed constituted a problem. To provide the department managers with evidence on this point, in addition to the internal work sampling study, a survey of fork truck operations was made in six nearby plants engaged in similar manufacturing operations. The explicit purpose of the survey was to define a basis (an extra-organizational model) on which internal fork truck operations could be evaluated.

The six company survey yielded in part the following results:

1   The number of trucks operated ranged from six to 50, with an average of 21 — same as Southern Company;

2   Utilizations ranged from 50 percent to 71 percent, with an average of 63 percent — 18.5 percent higher than Southern Company;

3   Responsibility for trucks was centralized in all six companies — contrary to Southern Company;

4   Trucks were controlled through dispatching or scheduling in five of the six companies (some used radio control) — contrary to Southern Company;

5   All companies owned rather than leased their trucks — contrary to Southern Company;

6   All companies performed their own maintenance of their trucks — contrary to Southern Company;

7   Three companies licensed their drivers, and assigned them full time to driving — contrary to Southern Company.

The fact that the surveyed companies on the average operated the same number of trucks as the Southern Company was clearly cited as evidence supporting the validity of this extra-organizational model.

Because the six company survey and the work sampling study had defined the problem in aggregate terms, the analysis and recommendations proceeded at this level. The Plant Engineering Department decided to make their recommendation on the basis of an overall utilization of 60 percent (the average utilization found in the six company survey) which implied a reduction of five trucks. They then looked at their work sampling data and re-allocated trucks among departments to bring individual truck utilization figures as close to 60 percent as possible. The recommended re-allocation in fact supplied a saving of five trucks. The recommendation went on to suggest that Product Departments "compensate [for this reduction in trucks] by establishing sharing arrangements between departments."

The recommendation also proposed "permanent [full time] licensed drivers" instead of production workers operating the trucks on an *ad hoc* basis as part of their regular duties. As a result of a study which had indicated that leasing was preferable to buying the fork trucks, no change in ownership or maintenance was proposed. The annual savings anticipated from the recommended changes amounted to $7,250.

It is interesting to note that the recommendations themselves constituted problems for the Product Department Managers. The task of "establishing sharing arrangements among departments" had not been resolved by the study and remained a thorny problem. The task of transferring qualified production workers to full-time truck driving duties involved not only complex problems of morale and labor relations but also economic trade-offs not evaluated by the study. The task of redefining departmental work procedures to relate to centrally controlled truck services was similarly unresolved. In return for these problems, the seven product department managers could expect to share in an annual saving of $7,250. Their response to the recommendation was less than enthusiastic. They agreed; after some bargaining, to return one truck to the leasing company but were not willing to pursue the matter any further.

Despite this rather negative conclusion, it is interesting to note that most managers considered the fork truck study a success. The validity of using the extra-organizational model derived from the survey as a means of defining the problem was never questioned and an evaluation of the existing policy on this basis was considered well-justified.

A more complicated use of extra-organizational models occurred in the case of several managers who had had personal experience in other organizations. In several situations they used this experience to define intra-organizational problems by emphasizing the personal element of this experience as evidence of its validity and by de-emphasizing (or not mentioning) where this experience was gained.

Extra-organizational models have a natural disadvantage as sources of problems because of the question of model validity which can always be raised against them. When extra-organizational experience agrees with local experience (historical model), it is seen as valid, but since it agrees with the local experience, it defines no problem. When extra-organizational experience disagrees with local experience and might therefore define a problem, the discrepancy itself raises the question of model validity. This attribute of extra-organizational models may serve to explain the fact that they were a relatively weak source of management problems in the Southern Company. Out of 52 managers, 47 agreed with the statement: "Most of our new ideas are generated within the company."

In the case of new organizations, of course, historical models are not available and extra-organizational models become more influential. One such situation was observed in the Southern Company. A promising new product was moving from the latter stages of development into the early stages of production and sales. A new product department was formed on an informal basis and the standard procedures of accounting data collection and reporting were instituted. No one expected the new department to be profitable immediately but after some months an executive at the product group level used a model not based on the history of the new department but one based on the performance of other departments to define a problem. He described the process this way:

"The numbers [on the monthly reports] were horrifying. I asked for a report and I got fuzzy answers that I didn't believe so I said, 'Fellows, I'm taking over the right to ask questions.

"In asking questions I found I could pick holes in their analysis of the situation. Everything was loose.

"I analyzed their orders and found that with their overhead they couldn't make money.

"The department was reorganized."

In new organizations, extra-organizational models can be powerful sources of management problems.

Some Normative Questions

The principal objective of this study was to find a relatively simple theoretical structure to explain the process of problem finding used by the managers at the Southern Company, and the set of four models just described represents that structure. These models, which range from ones maintained by other members of the organization, through simple historical and planning models, to those which apply the experience of other organizations to local situations, have been tested against the rather massive sample of data collected at the Southern Company and have been found sufficient to explain all these observations. That is to say, it is possible to trace all the observed behavior back to differences defined by one of these four classes of models. To this extent the study was successful.

But observations like these, even after abstraction into a theoretical structure, are only observations. They do not suggest the consequences of using other kinds of models or using these same models with different frequencies. They do not suggest how managers might behave more effectively than they do. Isolated observations cannot define differences. Observations must be compared to a model before normative questions can be answered.

One way to generate such comparisons would be to conduct comparative studies within and among a number of organizations. One could then answer such questions as: "Are these same models used by unsuccessful managers? If so, how can the difference in performance be explained? If not, what models are used? Do managers in other organizations use these models with different frequencies or under different circumstances? Are there systematic differences in the use of these models at different levels of the organization?" All such questions could be answered by careful study of several organizations or several levels of the same organization and these extra-organizational models might serve to suggest management improvements. Until such studies are completed, however, the only models which can be used to evaluate the behavior observed in the Southern Company are some which were not used there.

Scientific Models When compared to models used in the physical and social sciences for quite similar purposes, the models used by the managers in the Southern Company (and elsewhere) are almost startling in their naivete. In the same company, electrical engineers explicitly used quite complex theoretical models to help them define problems associated with the design of a relatively simple electronic control system. Similarly, mechanical engineers employed a variety of quite general theories in the design of new high speed production equipment. In neither of these cases did the engineers base their predictions on their own experience except in a very general sense. They quite confidently applied theories derived from the observations of others and the equipment which resulted from their work required relatively little redesign after construction. Managers, on the other hand, based their expectations on relatively small samples of their own experience. Their rather simple theories, as has already been noted, yielded rather poor predictions, and managers therefore spent a substantial amount of time solving either their own problems or those defined by others.

The behavior of scientists (an extra-organizational model) suggests that there is an alternative to this rather frantic approach to a complex world. When discrepancies arise between a model and the environment, one can undertake to improve the model rather than change the environment. In fact, a scientist might even go so far as to suggest that, until one has a fairly reliable model of the environment, it is not only foolish but perhaps even dangerous to take action when its effect cannot be predicted.

If carried to an extreme, of course, the scientist's tendency to search for better models of the world as it is would leave no time for taking action to change it, and it seems unlikely that this allocation of time and talent would be an appropriate one for the operating manager. In the Southern Company, it must be remembered, those managers who based their actions on very simple models which took very little time to construct were judged to be quite successful by their organization.

On the other hand, the increasing use by managers of more sophisticated modeling techniques like those mentioned earlier in this paper may suggest that the balance between model building and action taking is shifting. A number of companies now base changes in distribution systems, production and inventory control systems, quality control systems, advertising allocation systems, etc., on the predictions of relatively complex models which are based on substantial bodies of theory and empirical evidence. To the extent that these models fail to describe events which take place, they, like the simpler models they replace, can serve to define problems. To the extent that these more complete models take into account events which the manager cannot, or prefers not to, control, these models can serve to protect the manager from problems on which he might otherwise waste his energy.

While it may be true that these more explicit scientific models will gradually replace simple intuitive models, several reasons suggest that the change will take some time. First, many operating managers today find the language of the new techniques foreign, despite increasing attempts to change this situation through training. Second, the new techniques often involve even more generalization than extra-organizational models, and honest questions of model validity will tend to delay their widespread use. And third, the process of problem finding currently used will perpetuate itself simply by keeping managers so busy that they will find little time to learn about and try these new methods of problem finding.

More important than any of these reasons, however, may be one which, curiously, has been created by the advocates of management science. In most, if not all, of the literature describing them, model building techniques are described as means for solving management problems. In their now classical book on operations research, Churchman, Ackoff and Arnoff, for example, suggest model building as a step which should follow "formulating the problem."[12] The process by which the problem should be formulated, however, is left totally unspecified — and this is where managers as well as students of management frequently report their greatest difficulty. They can see the process by which these techniques can solve problems but they cannot see how to define the problems.

---

[12] Churchman, Ackoff, and Arnoff [1].

The theory which has been proposed here suggests that problem definition cannot precede model construction. It is impossible to know, for example, that a cost is too high unless one has some basis (a model) which suggests it might be lower. This basis might be one's own experience, the experience of a competitor, or the output of a scientific model. Similarly, one cannot be sure that his distribution costs will be reduced by linear programming until a model is constructed and solved which suggests that rescheduling will lower costs. The imperfections of an inventory system are revealed only by comparing it to some theoretical model; they cannot be defined until after the model has been built. The logical inconsistency which suggests that problems must be clearly defined in order to justify model construction is very likely an important reason that scientific models will only slowly be recognized by operating managers as important aids in the definition of their problems.

Despite their current disadvantages, the so-called new techniques of model building are, as has already been noted, making significant contributions to management effectiveness. They represent, therefore, not only a means for evaluating current managerial behavior but also a new class of models which can be used by managers to define their problems.

The Problem of Model Selection

The study of managers in the Southern Company indicates that concepts like image and intelligence which have been proposed to explain the process of problem finding can be made somewhat more operational. A rather small set of model classes has been defined which constitutes sufficient stimuli to trigger a fairly large sample of managerial behavior. This is not to say that future observations may not indicate the need for additional model classes or that future work is not required to make the process of managerial model building even more operational and testable. The study of the Southern Company represents perhaps only an encouraging start at understanding an important and little understood area of management.

Even with these initial insights, however, it is possible to see where major theoretical gaps still exist. Chief among these is the problem of model selection. As has already been noted, the requests of other people are sufficient to define a full time job for many managers. The problem of investigating and taking corrective action on discrepancies from historical trends can keep any manager busy all the time. The construction of extra-organizational and/or scientific models and the actions which they trigger are similarly time-consuming. Even after the manager has constructed the models he will use to define his problems, he must somehow select from among the differences which are simultaneously defined by these models. Personal requests, historical discrepancies, extra-organizational ideas, and the stimuli of scientific models do not in general define differences one at a time. The choice of the discrepancy to attend to next may be as important a process as the construction of the models which define them. It seems clear, however, that we must understand the process by which differences are defined before we can worry seriously about understanding the process of selecting from among them. The study in the Southern Company, therefore, largely ignored the priority problem and concentrated on difference definitions only.

It is impossible, however, to observe managers at work without getting some rough ideas about how they deal with the priority problem. Telephone calls for example are very high priority stimuli. A ringing telephone will interrupt work of virtually every kind. This priority rule is complicated sometimes by an intervening secretary but many managers pride themselves on always answering their own phone. One manager reported that he always worked on problems which would "get worse" before he worked on static problems. Thus, he dealt with a problem involving a conflict between a foreman and a troublesome employee before pressing forward on a cost reduction program.

Perhaps the most explicit priorities in the Southern Company were established by means of deadlines. Most problems defined by other members of the organization carried with them a time at which, or by which, the request should be satisfied. Certain reports were due monthly, a fixed number of working days after the end of the preceding month. Meetings were scheduled at stated times. Annual plans were required on a specified date. While a number of such requests might face a manager simultaneously, they almost never would have the same deadline and by this means the manager could decide which to do when. The fact that most problems triggered by other people's models carried deadlines may explain why these problems seemed to be given so much attention. When asked to indicate "Which problems do you usually get to first, time deadline, big payoff or personal interest?" 43 out of 52 managers indicated time deadline.

From a theoritical point of view, one could consider the flow of problems through an organization as analogous to the flow of jobs through a job shop and perhaps apply some of the theories which have been developed there to understand and perhaps prescribe the process of priority assignment. Managers, for example, must trade off relative lateness of their tasks with the duration of the tasks just as a foreman loading machines in a machine shop. Once the problem of problem definition is well understood it would appear that some theory is already available to structure the process of assigning problem priorities. The array of models used by and available to managers suggests that an understanding of the process by which problems are defined will not constitute a complete theory of problem finding. A process which assigns priorities to a set of simultaneously defined problems remains to be specified.

References

[1] Churchman, C.W., Ackoff, R.L., and Arnoff, E.L. *Introduction to Operations Research.* New York, John Wiley & Sons, 1957.

[2] Clarkson, G.P. *Portfolio Selection: A Simulation of Trust Investment.* Englewood Cliffs, N.J., Prentice-Hall, 1962.

[3] Gelernter, H.L. "Realization of a Geometry Theorem Proving Machine," *UNESCO Conference on Information Processing Proceedings* (1959).

[4] Miller, G.A., Galanter, E., and Pribram, K.H. *Plans and the Structure of Behavior.* New York, Henry Holt & Co., 1960.

[5] Newell, A., Shaw, J.C., and Simon, H.A. "Chess-Playing Programs and the Problem of Complexity," *IBM Journal of Research and Development* (October 1958), pp. 320-335.

[6] Newell, A., Shaw, J.C., and Simon, H.A. "Empirical Explorations of the Logic Theory Machine," *Proceedings of the Western Joint Computer Conference* (February 1957), pp. 218-230.

[7] Newell, A., Shaw, J.C., and Simon, H.A. "Report on a General Problem-Solving Program," *Proceedings of the ICIP* (June 1960). Reprinted in: *Computers and Automation* (July 1960), as "A General Problem-Solving Program for a Computer."

[8] Samuel, A.L. "Some Studies in Machine Learning, Using the Game of Checkers," *IBM Journal of Research and Development*, Vol. 3, no. 3 (July 1959), pp. 210-230.

[9] Simon, H.A. *The New Science of Management Decision.* New York, Harper and Brothers, 1960.

[10] Tonge, F.M. *A Heuristic Program for Assembly-Line Balancing.* Englewood Cliffs, N.J., Prentice-Hall, 1962.

William F. Pounds, Ph.D., Professor of Management and Dean, Alfred P. Sloan School of Management, Massachusetts Institute of Technology. Formerly: Ford Foundation Fellow, Carnegie Institute of Technology; Assistant to the General Manager of Forbes Finishes Division, Pittsburgh Plate Glass Company; Industrial Engineer, Eastman Kodak Company. Co-author of "Statistical Scheduling of a Highly Mechanized Production Facility," *Journal of Industrial Engineering* (1959); "The Scheduling Environment" in *Industrial Scheduling,* Prentice-Hall (1963); "Theory and Method in the Exploration of Human Decision Behavior," *Industrial Management Review* (1963).

Charles H. Kriebel   Davis Chapter 12

"THE FUTURE MIS"

Business Automation (19:6), 1972 June, pages 18-19, 42ff.

This article is from a leading academic spokesman in the field of MIS. Kriebel discusses management information systems in relationship to a four stage characterization of the decision process. He also discusses the evolutionary development of management information systems with a critical look at the next ten years.

Kriebel first defines MIS as information processing activities in support of management, taking a decision-making view of management. Next he describes the decision process in terms of four stages of activity: observation, inference, evaluation, and choice. Getting into the substance of the article, he uses this view of the decision process to characterize four levels of the relative maturity achieved by an information system. Figures further characterize each of the four levels. With this background, Kriebel explores and analyzes the evolutionary development of management information systems through four generations, dwelling on the future, fourth generation.

READING SUGGESTIONS

Read this article carefully to identify, characterize, and distinguish the four stages of the decision process, four corresponding levels of information systems, and four generations of MIS. In the four levels of MIS, note what parts correspond to each stage of the decision process. Seek to understand how we get to the fourth generation of MIS.

QUESTIONS

1. What are the four stages of the decision process as suggested by Kriebel?
2. Contrast Kriebel's four stage decision process with the three stage decision process of Simon (Intelligence, Design, Choice).
3. How does Kriebel characterize the nature of each level of MIS developed in support of each stage of the decision process?
4. What is the shortcoming of the first level MIS developed in support of only the first stage of the decision process?
5. What are the required inputs for both development and operation of information systems at each level?

6. At what level of MIS does a model come into play? Characterize the basic nature of the model at each higher level.
7. At what level does the information system completely take over from management? What becomes the role of the decision-making manager?
8. To what does Kriebel attribute the lack of success in MIS to date?
9. What are the two basic components of design in any information system?
10. Kriebel identifies four steps in the evolutionary development of management information systems. Each is discussed in terms of the two basic components of design. A focus on the input of accounting transactions to build a data bank characterized the first generation of MIS. Identify the other three generations of MIS and describe the shift in focus from the prior generation.
11. What does Kriebel predict for the next ten years of evolutionary MIS development? That is, what will be the nature of the fourth generation of management information systems? What skills will dominate their development?
12. What does Kriebel mean by the "distributed data processing approach"?
13. Discuss some of the economic implications of MIS brought out in this reading.

The Future MIS*

Charles H. Kriebel presented these ideas to last month's Spring Joint Computer Conference. He's professor of Industrial Administration, Graduate School of Industrial Administration, Carnegie-Mellon Univ.—and a successful consultant outside the walls of ivy.

After providing us with a conceptual framework (we drew some sketches to give you a graphic notion of his meaning), Charlie predicts (1) the decline of today's orientation of management infosystems to data bases, (2) the rise of personalized infosystems for decision-makers, (3) the emergence of distributed data processing using minicomputers, and (4) the increasing importance of the make-or-buy decision in building a "portfolio" of user infosystems.

The continuing exponential growth in raw computing power prompted Art Buchwald recently to editorialize on "The Great Data Famine" of the 1970's. According to Buchwald's expert source, by January 12, 1976 "... every last bit of data in the world will have been fed into a machine and an information famine will follow." To cope with this impending disaster, a crash program is urged in which (1) "no computer can be plugged in more than three hours a day;" (2) the government will spend $50 billion to set up data manufacturing plants and their output will be mixed with soy bean production; and finally, (3) a

birth control program will be advocated for all computers—provided, "the Vatican's computer gives us its blessing."

Instead of a "data famine" the technological issue today is that computers haven't been able to do all that was expected of them. In stronger language, Isaac Auerbach has said that the performance obtained by users of computers for business data processing shows: 20% are successful, 40% are marginal, and 40% are failures. Reviews by others of computers in management information systems also sharply criticize the notable lack of results in spite of great expectations. If true, this is a dismal return for a $40 billion investment in equipment. What went wrong? Who is at fault?

We can gain perspective on the problem by briefly probing the issues involved. A conceptual framework is particularly important in this case because the broad connotation of MIS and misunderstanding are the source of most of today's difficulties.

The phrase "management information systems," or "MIS," has gained popularity as a descriptor for information processing activities in support of management. If one explores the environment of management it is soon apparent that decision-making is the primary function that distinguishes managerial activity from other behaviors. In fact, management decision occupies a singular role in management literature, since other behavior—such as planning and control—is often defined in terms of decision activity. Thus, an understanding of the central issues in MIS might logically begin with the concept of management decision.

A parsimonious description of the decision process would include four identifiable stages of activity: observation, inference, evaluation and choice. The process begins with *observing* states of the environment; measurements are taken, and data are collected, encoded and stored. The second stage in the process involves analysis of the recorded data as a base for *inference* and prediction. Stage three is initiated by the need for a decision. Inferences and projections are analyzed to identify action alternatives and these in turn are *evaluated* with respect to goals, constraints and efficiency. Finally, an alternative is selected which is preferred (or "best") under the criterion of choice, the action is communicated, resources are

committed, and the *decision* is implemented. The process actually perpetuates itself through cycling and feedback, since upon implementation the decision becomes a source for new observations, and so on.

Consider the development of information structures in support of this process. The simplistic decision model can serve to characterize four levels of the relative maturity (or sophistication) achieved by an information system. In its most elemental form an information system is simply a repository or data bank, encompassing only the "observation" activities of the model. The raw data has been organized in some convenient manner and is stored, say, in a computer file; upon interrogation, the computer gives a report to the manager, who performs all subsequent analyses from inference to decision. Most accounting systems

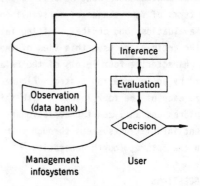

Management infosystems   User

FIRST LEVEL

are of this elementary form. Simplicity, *per se*, is not a criticism of such systems; their shortcoming in application is that typically they do not discriminate between vital information and trivia. Thus, managers interacting with an elementary data bank system often become frustrated by the lack of relevancy in large volumes of data.

At the second level of maturity in development the data bank system has been expanded to include most of the activities of inference as part of the formal system. In addition to exception reporting, the system now includes the capacity to forecast and to artificially test the consequences of implicit decisions. Here the manager can interrogate the system with "What if ..." questions, and receive an array

*The author presented a longer version of this article at last month's Spring Joint Computer Conference—and gave us permission to edit his remarks for BA. The longer version can be found in AFIPS Conference Proceedings Vol. 40, AFIPS Press.

of consequences in response for his evaluation. The hidden danger in this dialogue is that the manager is usually insulated from factual data in the system by a host of assumptions imbedded in the model which provides the inferences. It is surprising how readily individuals are lulled into believing that "realistic-looking" output is fact.

At level three, evaluation activities

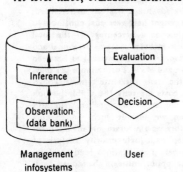

Management   User
infosystems

SECOND LEVEL

have been programmed into the selective-inference structures so that the information system now encompasses action recommendation. Here the need for a decision is triggered within the formal system on the basis of monitored observations and predetermined rules of a time-scheduled event. Procedures are programed to evaluate alternatives against assigned goals as the situation requires, the "best" course of action is chosen and the recommendation is communicated to the manager. At that point the manager either implements a decision based on the recommendation or he rejects the alternative and further analysis may be initiated. The most common form of this action-recommending information system in organizations today is the advisory staff group or committee. In this case line management delegates authority for a certain area of responsibility to a staff department, but retains final control for decision through review and certification. Another variant of this system has appeared in the form of large-scale optimization models, particularly linear programing applications in industrial scheduling. In many of these cases, systems originally designed for "action recommendation" have reverted back to "selective-inference" systems as limitations of the model became apparent.

In the final stage of maturity the entire decision process has been automated within the information system.

All activities from observation to choice and the ability to initiate action, commit resources and monitor results have been programed. In effect the manager is now outside the structure, having fully delegated his authority, although he retains the power to revoke the delegation at some future time. The simplest form of the automated decision system is the "standard operating procedure" in organizations; a more sophisticated example would be a computerized process control system in a petroleum refinery. Modern factory inventory control systems are another common example. Obviously, automated decision systems require extensive knowledge of the decision process for the given application and consequently their development has been limited to well-defined environments.

The MIS in a modern organization today is not one of these information structures; it is a composite of all four types. Said differently, the two basic

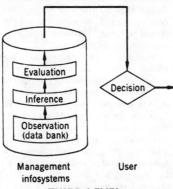

Management   User
infosystems

THIRD LEVEL

components of design in any information system are (1) a model of the user, and (2) a data store. The former defines the output interface of system application, and the latter constitutes the environmental image or system input. For MIS, the user model reference is management decision processes. In the evolution from "data bank" to "automated decision" the user model becomes technologically more sophisticated as more activities of the process are formalized and programed into the system.

But decision processes exist at all management levels in an organization hierarchy. Thus, one finds information structures of different maturity at different management levels. The most mature computer automated information structures in MIS today are still confined to lower management levels. The lackluster results vis-a-vis expecta-

tions realized in MIS to date can be attributed in part to the fact that the implicit model of the user has remained naive.

As total costs increased in spite of gains in computer hardware efficiencies, the third generation systems of the mid-to-late 1960's saw a shift in emphasis toward consolidation—though not necessarily of the "total systems" variety. The output-oriented, management function user models in large measure were abandoned for an input-oriented data base model with the goal of data processing efficiency. The development orientation in MIS focused on a corporate data bank which stressed input data format, flows, and files with little attention to the specific output requirements of end users. Working applications programs in the system were de-coupled from data files through the imposition of file management software. Most formal information systems today are still in this stage of evolution.

This raises several questions concerning future developments in the user model dimension of MIS technology. For example, the profit center organization is a move toward the information utility concept; but is "information processing" a homogeneous commodity? Divorcing the system design from specific user needs is an attempt to make the technology independent; but is MIS technology inert? The contemporary orientation on data input and EDP technology implies that resource efficiency is a major bottleneck; but has EDP utilization been the key barrier in MIS implementation? The data base model development of an MIS seeks to establish a corporate data bank, often building from the bottom up; but do information structures for managers draw upon common data?

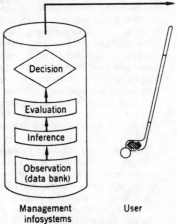

Management   User
infosystems

FOURTH LEVEL

In anticipating the next ten years, my first prediction is the demise of the present-day data base orientation as the dominant user model image in MIS development. Instead, the development focus will shift back to an output orientation that is user dependent. The emphasis will be on basic decision processes and problems of the specific organization and manager without regard to the functional environment. Information structures will be developed to solve a particular manager's problems; some of the structures will be generally applicable to other situations in broad outline.

The user model image that focuses on *critical decision* processes for MIS development, however, is only one aspect of the new technology. Allied with the change in orientation will be a rise in the application of operations research and behavioral science in developing and implementing these information structures. It is common knowledge that many of the basic methods and known results in operations research are not being used by managers today, even though many of the techniques have considerable potential as decision aids. This issue has been labeled a "communications gap."

The empirical evidence on MIS implementation suggests: (1) except for the most routine activities, managers actively resist attempts (real or perceived) to erode their authority base; (2) the executive's orientation is toward the "people" in the organization, his self-concept is as an individual who directs the activities of others; (3) there is relatively little understanding of upper management decision processes.

Emerging information structures in the next decade will increasingly incorporate behavioral parameters in their design which reflect organizational associations, leadership style, and management attitudes as a means toward improving acceptance and effectiveness at the user/system interface. Before the end of the decade I anticipate appearance of more "personalized" information structures which better match the users' needs. Within the data processing industry the emerging trend toward companies which provide "information services" will continue; they will be the developers of the new technology which solves the user's problems.

EDP technology encompasses a broad domain beyond "the computer," from firmware to peripheral devices and communications, from POLS (Procedure Oriented Languages) to data management software and supervisors, from system configuration to systems analysis and people. The most distinguishing characteristic of third-generation EDP system operations was the emergence of teleprocessing, facilitated by multi-programing and data communications

technology. This development is significant for at least two reasons. First, it provided the basic framework for distributed data processing; second, it turned the centralized vs. decentralized operations debate into an academic issue to be decided on a relative basis by organizational philosophy.

The distributed data processing (DDP) approach employs a hierarchy of EDP centers, ordered on the dimension of capacity and interconnected through direct communication lines. (Increasingly in the future these lines will be used for data transmission rather than modifications of voice networks.) At the lowest level in the DDP grid the point-of-origin device for data capture and interaction will be an "intelligent terminal," ranging from a Picturephone-like device to a minicomputer with local data processing capacity. Where on-line access and speed are not important, data cassettes will provide communication linkages. In more sophisticated applications computer networking will be employed for direct communication between computers and multiprocessor centers. Although thus far the DDP concept has been employed primarily in experimental systems, I believe it will be commonplace in the future.

The distributed data processing approach in one sense is a natural outgrowth of the time-sharing principle to extend system utilization while capturing some of the economies-of-scale in hardware technology. However, experience has shown that the massive "universal" system approach rapidly leads to substantial diseconomies in software overhead and administration. By analogy, the computer is not a universal machine; "a truck, a motorcycle or a racing car–each has a different engine which is designed for high performance and in the specific use intended." The computer system and MIS that seeks to be all things to all people in one package is doomed to failure at the outset. The cost balance in configuration is between operating control over a fragmentation of diverse specialized systems which may be locally optimal but globally expensive, and the universal system "dinosaur."

The basic difference under DDP is not to integrate but, instead, to provide a well-defined interface for relatively independent subsystems. Data managers have been a first step, and in the future these systems will be dedicated to sub-set applications as required. What emerges then is a portfolio of technology (packages) optimized with respect to the portfolio of user information structures. Some of the elements in the overall portfolio will interact, some will not; however, all elements will be highly modular. That is, one application may periodically require augmented computer capacity from the sector or

regional centers in "competition" with other applications, others may share certain master files for data and still others may be locally self-sufficient.

The economic rationale by management in making the commitment to EDP and MIS was essentially to replace labor with capital and improve productivity. What has happened, however, is that total costs have increased. Even if one examines only the apparent costs of systems operations and development, the capital/labor ratio advantage has not materialized; equipment hardware cost continues to decline as a percentage of the total which includes systems personnel and administration–today ranging between 35% and 45%. Furthermore, as most of the trade literature reports, apparent costs are only the visible portion of the economic "iceberg" in MIS when we include such hidden cost factors as the drain on management time, inadequate priority analysis of competing applications (and the foregone opportunities), abandoned projects due to vacillating support, security in the EDP department, inefficient software, etc. The constant advance in the sophistication of the new technology will continue to raise the economic stakes for payoff in MIS as this total cost base expands. Sunk cost notwithstanding, the decision many companies are beginning to face is whether or not they literally can afford to be in the MIS business.

This economic crossroad in MIS is not to suggest that management is contemplating a nostalgic return to the Dark Ages. More realistically, they are weighing the practicality of making it themselves or buying it on the outside. Today information services companies sell pieces of an MIS; you can buy information problem solutions as a complete package and for a price contracted in advance. Often this opportunity does not exist in-house and cost estimates are notoriously biased. The large corporations with the requisite capital base and absolute system constraints will retain in-house technology for their MIS. Increasing numbers of companies in the $50 million annual sales or less category, however, are going to buy their MIS technology over the next ten years. Few companies today generate their own electrical power requirements; many companies buy their legal services as needed; most small companies buy their accounting services. The distributed data processing approach will facilitate a comparable opportunity for EDP technology. Management will decide how much of it to "buy" and how much to "make" in establishing an economically viable MIS. For the data processing industry, establishing the centers, developing the technology, and regulating operations will be determined in the marketplace by the user, or the government, or both. ∎

Ralph H. Sprague, Jr.   Davis Chapter 13

"SYSTEM SUPPORT FOR A FINANCIAL PLANNING MODEL"

<u>Management Accounting</u> (53:12), 1972 June, pages 29-34.

This article describes the operation of a computer-based planning model for financial planning in commercial banks. Although the planning model is reasonably complex, the description in this article is readily understandable.

Sprague describes and diagrams the planning process in terms of the set of inputs needed to make tentative planning decisions, and the running of the simulation model of the firm under a given set of assumptions, forecasts, and decisions. The projected performance of the firm expressed in terms of proforma financial statements is compared with the objectives. The manager can modify his prior planning decisions or his prior forecasts and rerun the model. The supporting database contains historical and resulting projected data by time periods for each of the accounts normally making up the balance sheet and income statement for a bank. The system also supports management in making forecasts of the market, the competitive conditions, and the economic and political environment. An interface system enables managers and analysts to access the database, analyze it, and enter changes for a rerun of the planning model. At the end of each month, the database for the model is updated to reflect the actual current status of the banking enterprise. During the month, the managers and analysts have access to the planning system through remote terminals located throughout the bank. They can examine and print out the historical data in a variety of ways or they can run a projection based upon the input of forecasts and planning decisions.

READING SUGGESTIONS

A careful reading of this article can provide the reader with an understanding of how a computer-based planning model can support the planning process in a commercial bank. It can assist the manager or analyst to retrieve and analyze historical data, develop projections of forecasts and exogenous variables, and experiment with various planning alternatives to see what the outcome might be if certain actions are taken in the future. The article is written to enable the reader to focus on the general elements of the planning process and the supporting system.

QUESTIONS

1. How does the financial planning model described in the article operate?
2. How does the model interface with the manager doing the planning?
3. What general input information is needed to make tentative planning decisions? Classify the information as either internal or external to the bank.
4. Distinguish exogenous and endogenous variables in a planning model. How are the values of each type of variable established?
5. Describe the iterative nature of the planning process.
6. Describe how the planning model in this article was used to support the manager in asking "What if . . .?" questions.
7. Was the model plugged directly into the corporate database or did all the historical data in the matrix of the model have to be specifically derived in order to use the model? What are the implications of this?
8. Reflecting on the general model of a database management system from Chapter 11, what functions within the financial planning model would normally be included in a DMS? How would the use of a DMS enhance the capabilities and usefulness of the planning model?
9. In contrast to a bank, what type of planning decisions would be made in a manufacturing enterprise?

SYSTEM SUPPORT FOR A FINANCIAL PLANNING MODEL

It Is Better To Give The Manager A Suggestion To Which He Can React Than To Merely Expect Him To Submit A Projection

By Ralph H. Sprague, Jr.

In 1967, the development of a computer-oriented financial planning model was begun for a commercial bank on the east coast. It soon became apparent that the model must be resident in a system which would make its use convenient for the members of top management who were responsible for planning. This article describes the system which supports the financial planning model.

The General Planning Process

The planning process might be represented as shown in Exhibit 1. The planner, located in the center, gathers information in the process of making decisions. From right to left, he must first identify the goals and objectives which will guide the operation of his firm. He must assess his competition and what they are likely to do. He must make market forecasts and establish an expected product demand. He must also develop a description of the market environment in which the firm will operate, by making economic and political forecasts. Finally, he must assess the internal strengths and weaknesses of his organization in order to identify potential opportunities and challenges for the future.

Once the information describing the future conditions in each of these areas is collected, the planner submits tentative planning decisions to a planning model. The model may merely be a mental process from which evolves a set of decisions; or the model may require a staff of financial analysts and a computer which combines the collective forecasts and the tentative decisions into a set of pro-forma financial statements. The output of the model is a simulated performance of the firm under a given set of assumptions, forecasts, guidelines, and decisions. The simulated performance is summarized in the same terms as the goals and objectives so that the adequacy of the firm's performance can be compared with those goals and objectives. If simulated performance falls short, the input assumptions must be examined or the decisions must be revised.

Eventually the model's projections would show that a set of decisions interacting with the assumed forecasts would satisfy the firm's goals and objectives. These decisions would then become the approved plans and implementation would begin. The integrity of the planning process and its usefulness must be monitored over time by comparing actual developments with those forecasted by the model. The feedback is then used to refine the model and the forecasting techniques.

The Bank's Financial Planning System

The concepts outlined above were implemented at a commercial bank, as shown in Exhibit 2. The goals and objectives, and the various forecasts, were phrased in specific terms. These inputs, together with the tentative managerial decisions, were then entered directly into the planning model for an initial compilation. The output of the model, as a projected performance of the bank, was in the form of a set of financial statements for each period. These included the balance sheet and income statement, plus a specialized report of particular interest to bankers which depicts liquidity, cash flow, and various operating ratios.[1]

In response to this initial simulation of the bank's performance, the managers can now exercise their creative judgement in assessing the appropriateness of the forecast information and their initial set of decisions. They may "override" previously developed forecasts in the light of more recent developments. Comparison of the pro-forma performance of the bank with objectives may dictate changes in the initial decisions. With appropriate system support, the managers may utilize the planning model in an interactive and creative manner to test the potential results of changes in decisions or forecasts.

---

[1] For a conceptual and mathematical description of the model which the system uses, see: Ralph H. Sprague, "A Conceptual Description of a Financial Planning Model For Commercial Banks," *Decision Sciences*, January-March 1971.

R. H. SPRAGUE, JR.

is an Associate Professor in the College of Business Administration, University of Hawaii. Professor Sprague holds the B.A. degree in Mathematics from Anderson College and M.B.A. and D.B.A. degrees in Quantitative Business Analysis from Indiana University.

"The purpose of the financial simulator is to depict the performance of the bank . . ."

For example, after the initial simulation, a manager may wish to see what effect a change in the savings account interest rate would have on after-tax earnings. He might also ask other questions that involve complex interrelationships in the financial structure of the bank. "When will we need additional capital?" "How much should we be willing to pay for new funds?" "How much is it costing us to maintain a safe level of liquidity?"

The Structure of The System

The structure of the system can be best defined by describing the nature and interaction of: (a) the data matrix, (b) the financial simulator, and (c) the executive access system. The data matrix holds nearly all of the input and output variables handled by the system. The financial simulator and the executive access system are sets of computer programs which operate on the data in the matrix.

THE DATA MATRIX

The data array which holds the input and output variables can be visualized as a two dimensional matrix, as shown in Exhibit 3. A row is reserved for each variable contained in the model and a column is used for each time period. The data items listed along the left side include the major and intermediate accounts

which normally comprise the balance sheet and income statement for a bank. In addition to the financial statement report items, there is a set of parameters which define the interrelationships inherent in the bank's operations. Included here, for example, are the interest rates for each type of loan and security, and parameters defining the relationship between service charges and demand deposits. Each cell of the matrix holds a value for a given report item or parameter for a given time period.

The time dimension is divided into two major parts, (a) a historical section, and (b) a future section. The historical section is analyzed by various statistical routines to generate projections used in the simulation process. The future time periods, filled in by the projection routines and the simulator, provide the basis for forecasting or simulating the performance of the bank in the future.

The planning horizon is a "constant horizon," because it always contains the same number of future periods. At the beginning of each period (for instance, a month) the actual results of the most recently completed month are recorded in the historical section, and a projection is developed for the most distant future month. This procedure avoids the troublesome case of decision making in November without benefit of a forecast for next year.

THE FINANCIAL SIMULATOR

The purpose of the financial simulator is to depict the performance of the bank under a given set of assumptions and projections throughout the planning horizon. The exogenous variables (supplied from the outside) are those data items which are defined by management or are projected by some external means. The endogenous variables (from the inside) are generated by the simulation model using the exogenous variables and the internal relationships between variables within the bank. Finally, the exogenous and endogenous variables are combined to produce the expected performance of the bank. Thus, the simulation process can be divided into three parts, each of which is handled by a separate module or subsystem.

THE PROJECTION MODULE. The projection module consists of a set of statistical routines for forecasting future values of a data series given a set of historical values. The strongest program in this set is a generalized time series analysis program which fits a historical data series to each of ten different curve forms, automatically chooses the curve which best fits the data, and generates a seasonally adjusted projection for the future periods. This projection procedure is used on all exogenous variables, even though the bank's managers and analysts may feel that certain data streams are not susceptible to time series projection. The automated projection is then subjected to management scrutiny and "override" for those projections in which a manager's judgment is more appropriate than statistical projection. The philosophy of this approach asserts that it is better to give the manager a suggestion to which he can react than to merely expect him to submit a projection. We shall see in the final section how his reaction and any modifications to the suggested projections can be easily and quickly accom-

Exhibit 1
THE PLANNING PROCESS

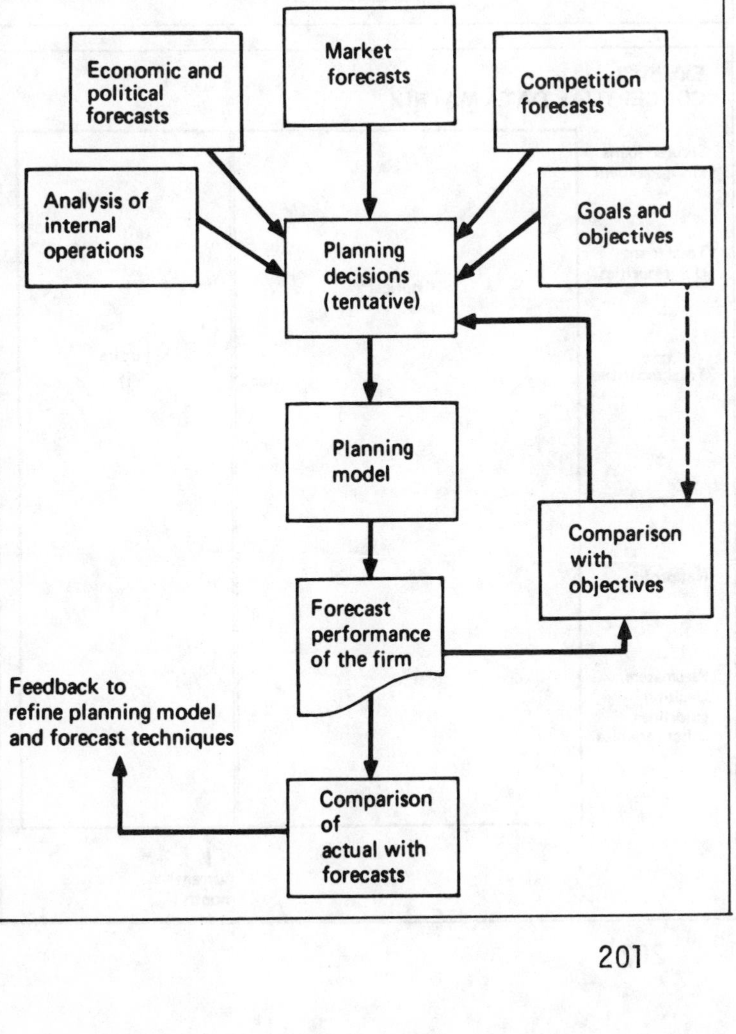

modated and incorporated in the operation of the simulation model.

THE ASSET ALLOCATION MODULE. The simulation procedure of a bank is somewhat different than for an industrial firm. An industrial firm's operation and eventual financial performance is dictated primarily by a production-distribution-sales process. In a bank, the driving set of decisions is that which determines the way the bank allocates its resources among a set of earning assets. The allocation process is subject to a great many constraints and restrictions, some imposed by the supervisory authorities, some by "good banking practice," some by the structure of the market for banking services. The decisions are guided by the nature of the resources and the desire to maximize income while observing these constraints. Much conceptual work in the last few years has gone into defining interrelationships between the objectives, constraints, and the maximization approach.[2]

THE REPORT GENERATOR MODULE. The final step in the simulation process is the development of a balance sheet, income statement, and operating analysis report for each of the planning periods in the planning horizon. The report generator draws together those variables which are statistically projected, those which are supplied by management, and those developed by the asset allocation module, combining them according to the parameters which define the internal interrelationships of the bank.

THE EXECUTIVE ACCESS SYSTEM

The final major element is the Executive Access System (EXAC), as shown in Exhibit 4, which enables managers and analysts to access the data base, analyze it, and enter changes. Through the use of a time-sharing approach, managers and analysts throughout the bank can have immediate and simultaneous access to the data base for analysis, inquiry, and repetitive interactive testing of alternative plans. The EXAC system consists of a set of computer programs which enable managers and analysts to perform the following basic operations over the entire time span, both historical and future:

1. Print any data item (PR)
2. Graph any data item (GR)
3. Divide any data item by another (DV) and print or graph the result
4. Full print of the financial statements for a given time period (FP)

Implementation and Operation

The entire system is implemented on a commercial time-sharing service which provides access to the data files and programs either on a "conversational" basis or a "batch" basis. The former approach, which typically uses a terminal such as a teletype with low input-output speeds, is appropriate for interrogating the data base and performing short analyses. The batch approach, which is usually implemented with a higher

[2] A landmark paper in this area is: K. J. Cohen, and F. S. Hammer, "Applications of Financial Theory, Linear Programming and Optimal Bank Asset Management Decisions," *The Journal of Finance*, May 1967.

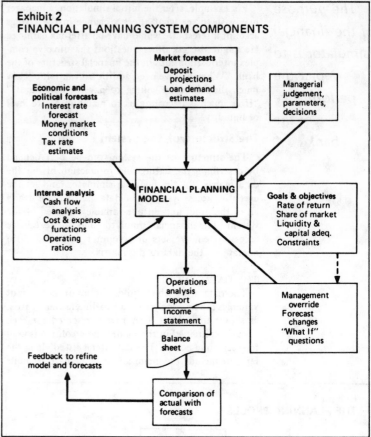

Exhibit 2
FINANCIAL PLANNING SYSTEM COMPONENTS

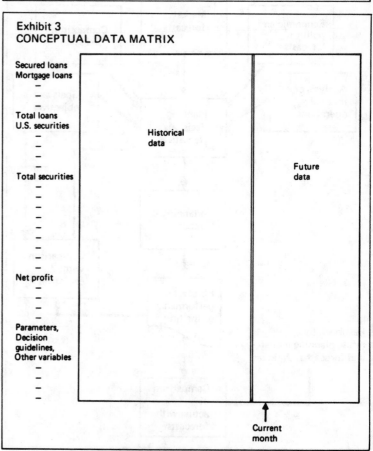

Exhibit 3
CONCEPTUAL DATA MATRIX

"The computer program accepts the most recently completed month and eliminates the oldest month from the data matrix."

speed terminal or a small satellite computer, is more appropriate for large analyses and the printing of many reports.

SYSTEM OPERATION

Planners may wish to operate the system according to a regular periodic schedule, or they may want it available "on call," whenever questions arise. Obviously, the use of the system for inquiry and special purpose analysis is best handled on demand. However, there is a periodic schedule to the planning process which infers that some parts of the system need to be operated regularly. In this system, the two modes of use (batch and conversational) interact with the two time frequencies (demand and periodic) to provide a great deal of flexibility in the use of the system.

THE REGULAR MONTHLY RUN. Let us assume for convenience that the planning process is repeated monthly and that each time period in the data base represents one month. (See Exhibit 5.) The operation of the system begins in Block 0 with the posting of the actual historical data for the most recently completed month. The monthly run is submitted in batch mode because the volume of data to be input and output is too great to be economically done in conversational mode. The computer program accepts the most recently completed month and eliminates the oldest month from the data matrix. At the same time, the space for a new month is added at the end of the future planning horizon. In effect, the data matrix is shifted forward one time period (Block 1).

To illustrate the shift, suppose the data matrix consists of twenty-four months of historical data and twelve months of data which represent the future. During the month of January 1972, the data matrix contains historical data for January 1970, through December 1971, and future data for the months of January 1972, through December 1972. Notice that during January (the current month) the data matrix

---

Exhibit 4
EXECUTIVE ACCESS SYSTEM

PLEASE ENTER DESIRED INSTRUCTION: PR, DV, GR, FP —   ! PR

ENTER VARIABLE TO BE PRINTED —   ! TD

ENTER THE STARTING MONTH NUMBER, YEAR AND NUMBER
OF PERIODS DESIRED. I.E. — 08, 69, 06 · · ·   ! 01, 70, 06

```
*************************************************
************TIME DEPOSITS************
*************************************************
```

JAN–70	FEB–70	MAR–70	APR–70	MAY–70	JUN–70
121666.	122092.	122666.	126507.	133683.	137958.

DO YOU WISH TO DO ANYTHING ELSE?
ENTER –1– IF YES, –2– IF NO · · · ·! 1

PLEASE ENTER DESIRED INSTRUCTION: PR, DV, GR, FP – ! DV

TO DETERMINE THE RATIO DESIRED, YOU MUST ENTER
THE MNEMONIC NAMES FOR THE TWO DATA STREAMS.
FIRST – ENTER THE NUMERATOR –   ! TD

SECOND – ENTER THE DENOMINATOR – ! TT

ENTER THE STARTING MONTH NUMBER, YEAR, AND NUMBER
OF PERIODS DESIRED. I.E. – 08, 69, 06 · · ·   ! 01,70,06

ENTER A NAME FOR THE RATIO YOU HAVE JUST CREATED
! TIME / TOTAL DEPOSITS

```
*************************************
********TIME / TOTAL DEPOSITS********
*************************************
```

JAN–70	FEB–70	MAR–70	APR–70	MAY–70	JUN–70
0.3706	0.3757	0.3662	0.3644	0.3730	0.3855

----

contains projected data for January since actual figures are not yet in. At the beginning of February, the data matrix is shifted. January 1970, is eliminated and February 1970, becomes the oldest month in the data base. Actual data for January 1972, replaces the previous projected data, and space is created at the end of the data matrix for January 1973. Thus, there is always a twelve-month future horizon and twenty-four months of history.

The next step in the procedure (Block 2) is the automatic projection of all the exogenous variables, which are then posted to the future section of the data matrix. Notice that the system does not merely add a figure for the most distant month. It regenerates the entire future period projections based on the data in the historical section. In this way, the future projections are responsive to recent changes in actual conditions, thus eliminating the problem of an annual forecast which becomes progressively further out of date as conditions change.

Once the exogenous variables are projected, the asset allocation algorithm draws together these variables and the decision rules and guidelines to generate the optimum asset allocation (Block 3). The recommended allocation, in the form of asset balances, is also posted to the future section of the data matrix.

Finally, the program develops the remaining report items, which are also posted to the data matrix. The output reports are printed (Blocks 4, 5), and become the topic of discussion at a regularly scheduled planning session at the beginning of each month. Managers examine the initial set of reports, compare them with previous plans, and with goals and objectives for the

coming twelve months (Block 6). If they wish to submit some modifications to the projections or decision guidelines, the program is re-entered at Block 2, and a new set of reports is prepared. Recycling from Blocks 2 through 6 ultimately produces a current "approved" plan for the coming twelve months. This approved plan is stored in the future section of the data matrix.

CONVERSATIONAL MODE. During the month, the managers and analysts have access to the planning system through remote terminals located throughout the bank. They may use the system to answer two kinds of questions as depicted in Exhibit 6. If they merely wish to display the figures in the data base, they do so by using the four basic instructions in the Executive Access System described earlier. EXAC prints or graphs any data item or the quotient from the division of two data items on the terminal immediately after request. It is also able to print the balance sheet and the income statement for any given period or across any time interval. This capability gives the manager the option of accessing much of the information which is contained in the full set of reports without waiting for the output from the batch run.

Rather than accessing and analyzing the history and existing plans, the manager may wish to "experiment" with new plans and forecasts. To accommodate this experimentation without destroying the approved plans, a duplicate data base is created for experimental purposes. It has the same structure and characteristics as the original data base, but it acts as a "scratch pad" for the manager's experimentation. In order to answer "what if" questions, the manager may direct the pro-

". . . the manager may wish to 'experiment' with new plans and forecasts."

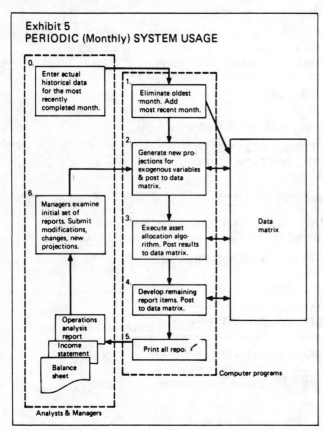

**Exhibit 5
PERIODIC (Monthly) SYSTEM USAGE**

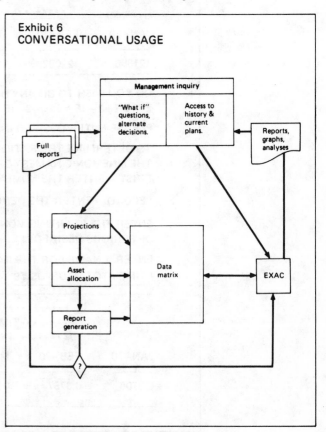

**Exhibit 6
CONVERSATIONAL USAGE**

"EXAC can access all of the information contained on the full reports . . ."

gram to generate new projections, rerun the asset allocation algorithm, and redevelop the remaining entries in the experimental data base. At this point the manager can decide whether he wishes to have a full set of printed reports to fully illustrate the results of his experimental run, or whether he prefers to use EXAC to interrogate the experimental base. The choice of requesting full reports or using EXAC depends on the time requirements. EXAC can access all of the information contained on the full reports, but reproduction is a time-consuming process on a terminal with relatively low output speed. Generally, the full reports are prepared at the computer site on high speed printers and delivered the following day.

This iterative, experimental approach is quite similar to the procedure used for developing the plans at the beginning of the month as illustrated in Exhibit 5. The only difference is the use of an experimental data base instead of the "approved" data base. In fact, the conversational approach can even be used during the monthly planning session. Several "what if" questions could be postulated and answered in the process

of developing the standard plan. When the managers in the planning meeting are satisfied with the result, the future section of the experimental data base can be transferred to the approved matrix.

Conclusion

We have seen that the planning model, especially if it is based on sophisticated concepts and implemented on a computer, must be contained within a system which supports and encourages its use in the planning process. The central concept is the necessity for providing interaction between the decision maker and the model. In this example, the interactive capability is provided by a generalized data matrix to which both the simulation model and the planner have direct access. The planner can run the model to test alternative decisions and plans of action, and have immediate access to the expected results of those plans. Thus, the system and the model support the manager in his decision making, giving him a potent tool with which to confront the increasing complexity of today's business environment.   □

Bernard P. Dzielinski

"ABSTRACTS OF FINANCIAL PLANNING PROGRAMS"

IBM Systems Journal (12:2), 1973, pages 140-143.

It is sometimes difficult for students to visualize the range of software that is available to assist in planning. This appendix describes five IBM financial planning programs. These help to illustrate planning software. Other manufacturers and software vendors have similar products.

READING SUGGESTIONS

It is not necessary to read all parts of the program descriptions in detail. The description of each package is the most significant and provides a survey of the variety of routines which are available to support the planning process. The operating system data and documentation is important, but not for a survey reading. The programming language and mode of operation (batch or time sharing) are also of interest.

QUESTIONS

1. Which of the program products will calculate rate of return or net present value?
2. Which programs will generate data using a growth rate?
3. Which programs are interactive?
4. Which programs do depreciation calculations?

ABSTRACTS OF FINANCIAL PLANNING PROGRAMS

Bernard P. Dzielinski

BA / BASIC

Business Analysis/BASIC

- **Availability: Program Product**

- **Description**
  Business Analysis/BASIC is a comprehensive set of interactive tools written in the BASIC language, that can assist the business analyst in preparing financial plans and in analyzing investment opportunities. Interactive features include instructional messages, flexible control of calculations, extensive error checking, and data editing. The program contains three general functions: data file management, spread-sheet analysis, and quantitative economic analysis. The financial planning routines include:

  Time-series analysis calculations using moving average, seasonal analysis, cyclical analysis, autocovariance/autocorrelation, crosscovariance/cross-correlation, exponential smoothing, and simple regression.

  Depreciation of assets using straight-line, double-declining-balance, sum-of-the-years'-digits, and equipment units methods.

  Break-even analysis under certainty and uncertainty.

  Return on investment using payback method, duPont method, accounting method, and discounted cash-flow methods (NPV and IRR).

  Multiple and single loan analysis.

  Lease versus purchase analysis.

  Make versus buy analysis.

- **Programming systems**
  Operating systems: System/360 of System/370 configurations with the Interactive Terminal Facility (ITF) under DOS, OS (MFT or MVT), or MVT with Time Sharing Operation (TSO). System/370 configurations with ITF under OS/VS1 or OS/VS2 in Virtual-Real Mode; or under OS/VS2 with TSO in Virtual Mode; or OS/MFT, OS/MVT, OS/VS1, or OS/VS2 in Virtual-Real Mode under VM/370: or DOS/VS in Virtual-Real Mode: or DOS or DOS/VS in Virtual-Real Mode under VM/370. This program also operates on a System/3 Model 6.

  Programming language: BASIC
  Mode of operation: Terminal-oriented, time sharing using IBM 2741

- **Documentation**
  Program identification numbers: 5734-XMB (OS and DOS) and 5703-XM3 (System/3 Model 6)
  General Information Manual: GH20-1175
  Program Reference Manual: SH20-1264

Bernard P. Dzielinski

Data Processing Division, White Plains, New York.

Mathematics and economics (M.S., University of Connecticut, 1952). Prior to joining IBM in 1957, he was engaged in operations research analysis at U.S. Time Corporation for five years. He has since participated in the development of manufacturing control methods and presently is an Advisory Industry Development Analyst, developing business planning systems.

BUDPLAN

Budgets and Plans Generator

- **Availability: Program Product**

- **Description**
  BUDPLAN is an application program that processes logic statements, print specifications, and data cards supplied by the user producing plans such as budgets, operating plans, and strategic plans. These plans are two-dimensional reports where, for example, lines represent balance sheet items and columns represent time periods.

  BUDPLAN consists of three phases. Phase 1 analyzes the logic statements and generates PL/I statements used as input to Phase 3. Phase 2 analyzes the print specifications and generates print commands that are also used as an input to Phase 3. Phase 3 is the budgets and plans generator, processing the planning data and producing reports as required.

  Planning concepts:
  Subset concept. A particular part of a business plan, such as a department, product line, or market, is called a subset. A subset may also be related to a group of departments. For example, if the company sells products A, B, C and D, and if subsets 01, 02, 03, and 04 are the respective marketing plans of these products, subset 05 can be the consolidated marketing plan for all these products. To produce the marketing plan for product A, the user specifies the data to be processed, the calculation to be executed, and the report to be printed. The planner can use the same planning logic and, therefore, the same program, for several subsets. He can also produce the output reports with the same print specifications for several subsets.
  View concept. An iteration or view is the processing of one or several subsets. It is the development of a plan by the user's model of one hypothesis concerning company development, sales forecasting, and so forth. One or several views can be processed within one computer run. BUDPLAN provides the capability to summarize or consolidate data. Therefore, the user can transfer data from one subset to other subsets during the same view. Through several views and by modifying some of his input data, the user can text several cases or hypotheses about company plans. Data can be transferred between two subsets that do not belong to the same view, thus permitting the differences on the most significant figures to be printed when several plans are compared.

  Subroutines that perform specialized calculations include the following:

  Simple and compound growth rates.

  Marginal analysis calculations between the increments of two data lines.

  Extrapolation using continuation, simple, or yearly growth rates.

  Extrapolation of a previous result given the growth amounts and/or the growth rate for the forecast periods.

  Interpolation using linear, sum-of-the-years'-digits, or compound growth rates methods.

  Average production cost as a function of the volume of production.

  Net present-value calculation of revenues or expenses.

  Internal rate-of-return calculation of an investment.

  Ratios and percentages.

  Spreading a value into partial amounts by a specific distribution pattern.

  Interest and the repayment of a loan for each period.

  Normally distributed random number generation for given mean and standard deviation.

- **Programming systems**
  Operating systems: System/360 and System/370 configurations of OS/MFT and OS/MVT; System/370 configurations of OS/VS1 and OS/VS2; or any of the previous operating systems executing under VM/370.
  Programming language: PL/I
  Mode of operation: batch

- **Documentation**
  Program identification number: 5734-F51
  General Information Manual: GH19-1038
  Program Reference Manual: SH19-1040

FAMS

Forecasting And Modeling System

- Availability: Program Product

- Description
  FAMS is a collection of statistical and data handling routines used for forecasting. FAMS can be used for time-series or cross-section models and also for single- or simultaneous-equation models. The forecasting techniques include the following:

  Plotting data series.

  Transformations such as square root, multiply, add, reciprocal, and logorithm.

  Simple correlation.

  Exponential smoothing.

  Polynomial regression.

  Seasonal decomposition.

  Ordinary least squares.

  Stepwise least squares.

  Two-stage least squares.

  Statistical measurements such as t-value, F-value, and Durbin-Watson d statistic.

  Growth rate and growth amount.

- Programming systems
  Operating systems: System/360 configurations under DOS, OS/MFT and OS/MVT. System/370 configurations under DOS, DOS/VS, OS/MFT, OS/MVT, OS/VS1, and OS/VS2; or under the control of any of the six latter operating systems executing under VM/370.
  Programming language: FORTRAN IV
  Model of operation: batch

- Documentation
  Program identification numbers: 5736-XS4(DOS) and 5734-XS7(OS)
  General Information Manual: GH19-4000
  Program Reference Manual: SH19-4001

MINI-PLAN

Business Planning for System/3, Model 10[6]

- Availability: Field Developed Program

- Description
  MINI-PLAN is designed to provide for the financial planner and analyst a framework within which financial planning models may be developed. The user is provided with methods for planning-data file creation and maintenance; for using standard planning functions to perform certain commonly used calculations and for printing multiple standard reports including input worksheets, single column, and double column reports to display original input data and results of any computations. MINI-PLAN provides subset facilities similar to those in PSG II and BUDPLAN. The techniques available include:

  Extrapolation using compound growth rate or continuation methods.

  Interpolation using the linear method.

  Percentage calculations.

- Programming systems
  Operating systems: MINI-PLAN operates under the System Control Program (SCP) for disk System/3 (5702-SC1) Version 5. Program products required are FORTRAN III (5702-FO1).
  Programming language: FORTRAN III

- Documentation
  Program identification number: 5798-AKB
  Program Description/Operations Manual: SB21-0590

PSG II

Planning Systems Generator II[7]

- Availability: Program Product

- Description
  PSG II contains the same subset and view concepts previously described in the BUDPLAN abstract. It provides the means to produce and evaluate a variety of financial plans. The user builds financial models within the framework of PSG II. Methods are provided for organizing planning data, for establishing computational logic to be applied to the data, and for generating data displays and reports. The user writes the logic in FORTRAN and, to aid in the development of models, he can use the PSG II library of planning functions to perform certain commonly used calculations. Using the PSG II print specfications, the planner can have input worksheets, single and double column reports, and three types of charts produced to display selected data. Transfer of planning data from one model to another and consolidation of the results of detail models into more comprehensive models are additional facilities provided. Financial planning techniques include:

  Simple and compound growth rates.

  Marginal analysis calculation between the increments of two data lines.

  Extrapolation using continuation, simple, or yearly growth rate methods.

  Extrapolation of a previous result given the growth amounts and/or the growth rate for the forecasted periods.

  Interpolation using linear, sum-of-the-years'-digits, or compound growth rate methods.

  Depreciation of assets (straight-line, sum-of-the-years'-digits, and double-declining-balance methods).

  Average production cost as a function of the volume of production.

  Discounted cash-flow calculation using the internal rate-of-return method.

  Ratios and percentages.

  Spreading a value into partial amounts by a specific distribution pattern.

  Year-to-date accumulation.

  Retirement of assets

  Tax carry-forward and carry-back calculation.

- Programming systems
  Operating systems: System/360 configurations under DOS, OS/MFT, and OS/MVT; System/370 configurations under DOS, DOS/VS, OS/MFT, OS/MVT, OS/VS1, and OS/VS2; or under the control of any of the six preceding operating systems executing under VM/370.
  Programming language: FORTRAN and Assembler Language
  Mode of operation: batch

- Documentation

	DOS	OS
Program identification numbers:	5736-XT1	5734-XT1
General Information Manual:	GH20-1035	GH20-1035
Program Reference Manual:	SH20-1174	SH20-1042

E. Drake Lundell, Jr.   Davis Chapter 14

"DP TITLES STANDARDIZED BY NEW GSA GUIDELINES"

Computerworld (6:16), 1972 April 19, pages 1-2.

This newspaper article reports on another expression of position titles and their description as related to computers and data processing. It is particularly important since it comes from the General Services Administration, the central purchasing agent for the United States government.

In seeking price quotations for personnel services from software firms, the General Services Administration defined standardized job descriptions of ten positions. Each software firm is to quote a price for personnel services in each of the ten positions. The position titles include project manager, system analyst, senior programmer, programmer, computer hardware specialist, computer software specialist (system engineer), technical information specialist, technical automation specialist, communications specialist, and coder or programmer aide. Each of these positions is described in terms of what the person in the position does, what special areas of knowledge and skill are needed, and the prerequisite job requirements in terms of years of experience and educational level (or equivalent experience). The article reports 50 firms responding with hourly price quotations for each job classification.

READING SUGGESTIONS

Standard job descriptions and position titles do not yet exist in the field of management information systems. Considerable diversity and even confusion exists within and between organizations. Any attempt at standardization would be welcome. This report of the GSA expression of standard titles and job descriptions should be read as one such attempt for purposes of contracting for personnel services by the United States government. There is nothing absolute about such an expression. The reader should contemplate the description of ten positions, focusing particularly on what differentiates the various positions described.

QUESTIONS

1. Why is this particular expression of position titles and their job descriptions important?
2. Make a table listing each of the ten positions down the side and then across the top for each position

record:
   - what is done
   - how it is done (who work with and who interface with)
   - areas of specialized knowledge or skill
   - requirements in terms of years of experience and level of education

3. Draw a transition diagram showing how a person might advance (be promoted) from one position to another.
4. What data processing positions are missing from the list?
5. How useful would these descriptions be to a MIS manager in a computer-using organization?

COMPUTERWORLD,   April 19, 1972   Vol. VI, No. 16

DP Titles Standardized By New GSA Guidelines

By E. Drake Lundell Jr.
Of the CW Staff

WASHINGTON, D.C. – Federal officials here may have solved a problem that has plagued computer users for years by standardizing job descriptions for data processing personnel services.

Region 3 of the General Services Administration (GSA) issued the standards as part of a Basic Ordering Agreement (BOA) which requires software firms to post standard prices for the various services.

10 Software Categories

Presently, the BOA defines 10 separate categories of software personnel, but it will probably be extended to other job categories and experience levels after a six-month trial period, according to T. Fred Nobel, chief of the federal ADP resources staff of the Automated Data Management Division in GSA's Region 3.

The definitions in their present state are "not perfect," Nobel said, and GSA is working with both industry and government users to develop better standards. Comments from other interested users are also welcome, he added.

The 10 categories and their definitions are:

● **Systems Management Engineer/Project Manager:** "He formulates statements of management, scientific and business problems by use of electronic data processing systems, and acts as project manager in the implementation. He must be an individual capable of meeting in conference with programs managers, and other cognizant officials and to state problems in a form capable of being solved. He must be able to prepare plans, charts, tables and diagrams to assist in analyzing and displaying problems, working with a variety of scientific, business or engineering tables and formulas requiring a sound knowledge of mathematics.

"He evaluates proposed computer systems to determine technical feasibility, costs for implementation and operation as well as functional adequacy. He must have demonstrated capability for managing a team composed of analyst/programmers and specialists in implementing computer systems."

Such a person must have five years' experience as an analyst/programmer and a college degree or equivalent (with nine months' experience equaling a year of college), according to the definition.

● **System Analyst:** "He devises and prepares layouts for computer systems requirements and develops procedures to process data by means of ADP/EDP. He confers with other technical personnel to determine problems and type of data to be processed. He analyzes the problem in terms of equipment capability to determine techniques and formulates computer system requirements most feasible for processing data.

"He is adept in preparing a definition of the problems, together with recommendations for equipment needed for its solution, from which the programmer prepares flowchart and computer instructions. He writes specifications to the exact requirements for each program which will be written by the programmer within the system. The detailed written specifications for each program shall be supplied as a part of his function as an analyst, before any effort is applied to actually begin the program effort. He may be required to supervise the preparation and implementation of individual programs."

He must have a minimum of four years' experience as an analyst or programmer and a college degree or equivalent.

● **Senior Programmer:** "A senior computer programmer develops and prepares diagrammatic plans for solution of business, scientific and technical problems . . . He analyzes programs outlined by a systems analyst in terms of such factors as type and extent of information to be transferred from storage units, variety of times to be processed, extent of sorting and format of the final printed results. Additionally, he designs detailed programs, flowcharts and diagrams indicating mathematical computations and sequence of machine operations necessary . . .

"The senior programmer also verifies accuracy and completeness of programs by preparing sample data and testing them by means of systems acceptance test runs made by operating personnel.

He corrects program errors by revising instructions or altering sequence of operations. He is responsible for system documentation and operating runs procedures documented according to established . . . operations standards.

"He evaluates and modifies existing programs to take into account changes in procedures or type of reports desired. He translates detailed flowcharts into coded machine instructions, confers with technical personnel in planning programs and works in programs within the system. He may be required to use concepts generally associated with third-generation equipment. Mathematical programming techniques may also be required."

This position calls for a minimum of three years' experience and a college degree or its equivalent (which is equal to three years' experience as a programmer.)

● **Programmer:** "A programmer is an individual who is capable, under general supervision, of analyzing and defining systems requirements and of developing programs for automatic data processing. This programmer conducts detailed analysis, studies all systems requirements and develops all levels of block diagrams and logic flowcharts. He must translate the details into a program of coded instructions used by a computer.

"He tests, checks, debugs, revises and refines the computer program as required to produce the product required by the written specifications. Additionally, the programmer documents all procedures used throughout the program to allow the program to be run as a part of the systems by operating computer personnel and completes system documentation to enable a subsequent programmer to make changes as may be required. The programmer should also be able to revise existing programs to make refinements, reduce operating time or improve present techniques."

The programmer job calls for one year of experience and a college degree or the equivalent (three additional years of programming experience).

● **Computer Hardware Specialist:** "He reviews computer software systems and data requirements as well as communications and response needs and devises computer hardware configurations to support them. He analyzes computer programs in terms of computer and communications hardware and develops techniques to improve systems throughput and optimizes hardware utilizations. He evaluates computer hardware systems relative to their ability to support specified requirements, and, by determining potential and actual bottlenecks, improves systems capacity through recommended hardware changes.

"He is well versed in hardware compatibility. He has participated in the design of real-time or remote access systems and has working knowledge of process control and/or large time-sharing hardware systems."

He must have a minimum of four years' experience as an analyst or programmer, college degree or equivalent, and he must have a minimum of two years' experience as either a computer hardware specialist or as an analyst where specific duties can be demonstrated to include hardware specialities.

● **Computer Software Specialist/System Engineer:** "He reviews computer software systems and data requirements as well as communication and response needs and determines operating systems and languages to support them. He analyzes computer programs in terms of hardware and operating system compatibility and utilization. He is familiar with compilers and other language translators and can determine costs for converting computer programs from one language or machine to another.

"Given the constraints of the operating system and the hardware, he can structure software programs to operate within the environment. He improves software systems efficiency through recommending better utilization of operating system capabilities. Minimally, he has participated in the design of one operating system and had working knowledge of the systems of three manufacturers. He has acted as a systems analyst and programmer and has programmed in assembly language as well as several higher-level languages. He is familiar with queuing techniques and job sequencing controls within a multi-programming environment.

He has a minimum of four years' experience, college degree or equivalent, and a minimum of two years' experience as a software specialist or as an analyst working in that area.

● **Technical Information Specialist:** "He specializes in the application of computer technology to bibliographic and other textual information. He analyzes and develops indexing and abstracting techniques. He can evaluate retrieval methodologies. . . . He has worked in the library field and participated in the design of large computer-supported technical information systems."

This job calls for four years' experience as a programmer or analyst and a college degree or equivalent.

● **Technical Automation Specialist:** "He reviews laboratory experimentation equipment needs and determines computer hardware and software support. He has working technical knowledge of laboratory equipment as well as analog-to-digital converters and small real-time computers. He has conducted research in automated laboratory environments or has designed and implemented process control systems."

The job calls for a minimum of four years' experience and a college degree or equivalent.

● **Communications Specialist:** "He is technically experienced in the area of data communications and transmission and analyzes computer software systems, data requirements response times and computer hardware configurations relative to the communications and data transmission requirements.

"He reviews communication networks as to their ability to support data processing requirements. He recommends changes to transmission networks, both in terms of hardware devices and switching points required to improve network performance . . . He has working knowledge of coding and error detection methodologies. He has participated in the analysis, design and implementation of communication networks including data processing transmissions.

"He must have a college degree or the equivalent and four years' experience as a communications specialist or in an allied area where specific duties can be demonstrated to include communications applications."

● **Coder/Programmer Aide:** "The coder or programmer aide is capable of translating detail program flowcharts into program-coded instructions used by the computer. He must have a minimum of one-year's experience as a trainee or junior-level programmer."

List Hourly Rates

Firms agreeing to the Basic Ordering Agreement must list the hourly rate for each job classification. When the governmetn needs to go outside of its in-house capability, then Region 3 can recommend the user agency contract with one of the firms on the BOA.

The hourly rate charged must be applied evenly to all government users, that is, if a firm charges one agency $10/hr for a programmer, that price must be available to all other user agencies.

Since the list of prices is public knowledge for the 50 firms that have signed the Basic Ordering Agreement, several sources have suggested the individual users could check with the list to make sure that their software service suppliers were not charging them more than they are charging the government for the same work.

"THE CENTRALIZATION VS. DECENTRALIZATION ISSUE:
ARGUMENTS, ALTERNATIVES, AND GUIDELINES"

Data Base (2:3), 1970 Fall/Winter, pages 1-7.

This relatively short yet comprehensive article provides a thorough analysis of the issues and alternatives relating to the organization of MIS activities. George Glaser is well known as an MIS consultant. In 1973, he was elected president of the American Federation of Information Processing Societies.

Centralization or decentralization is a major organizational issue facing management today in the use of computers and management information systems. After briefly reviewing the general arguments for centralization, Glaser focuses on the particular issues with respect to data processing. Large data processing costs suggest centralization to gain the advantages of economies of scale while considerations of effective service to users suggests decentralization. Unfortunately, these two objectives -- efficient utilization of corporate computer assets and a high level of service to users -- are often in direct conflict. The organizational resolution of the issue often depends upon the relative strengths of the corporate data processing staff and users in the political climate of the organization. Glaser summarizes the arguments for centralization as company-wide consolidation of operating results, economies of scale, shortage of qualified data processing personnel, and ease of control. Similarly, the arguments for decentralization are familiarity with local problems, rapid response to local processing needs, and profit and loss responsibility.

Glaser further analyzes these arguments by separately considering equipment, staff, and decision authorities. His analysis brings into question some of the principles which have often previously been accepted without question. The alternatives range from centralization of both development and operations, through decentralized development with centralized operation, to decentralized development and operation with some measure of central coordination. The article concludes with some guidelines for the allocation of tasks to a centralized corporate staff versus decentralized staffs.

READING SUGGESTIONS

This article must be read more carefully toward the end, therefore, start out reading rapidly and slow down as you progress through the article. The reader should seek to go beyond the simplistic rules of thumb which have too long been used to govern the centralization or decentralization of data processing activities. This article provides the basis to understand the issues of centralization versus decentralization by considering separately the elements of equipment, staff, and decision authorities. Note how Glaser deals with the general pro and con arguments under each element. Note also the trends he observes in the availability of equipment and staff. Finally, note his underlying principle under guidelines for allocating tasks.

QUESTIONS

1. Under what conditions should an organization even consider a change in the existing status of its data processing activities, whether centralized or decentralized?

2. What kind of recommendation is likely to come from the corporate data processing staff concerning centralization or decentralization? Why?

3. Why might new developments in minicomputers and telecommunications result in greater decentralization of data processing personnel and equipment?

4. What is the major argument for centralizing computer facilities and what does that usually mean in terms of effectiveness in servicing users and achieving organizational goals?

5. What is the most compelling argument for centralization of staff? Will this argument become stronger or weaker in the future? Why?

6. Why does Glaser suggest that arguments based on staff considerations are the most important?

7. What should be the default, centralization or decentralization when faced with the performance of a data-processing-related task? Any deviation from the default would have to be justified by compelling reasons to do otherwise.

8. What does Glaser suggest is the ultimate justification for the use of computers? Do you agree?

9. Does decentralization affect our basic definition and conceptual model of management information systems?

THE CENTRALIZATION VS. DECENTRALIZATION ISSUE: ARGUMENTS, ALTERNATIVES, AND GUIDELINES

by George Glaser

The major organizational issues facing industrial management today in its use of computers are four:

1. Centralization versus decentralization of staff, equipment and authorities
2. Reporting relationship of the data processing manager
3. Internal organization of the data processing department
4. Procedures to be used for charging (or absorbing) data processing costs.

This paper deals only with the first—the most controversial—of these issues: centralization versus decentralization—an issue arising from disagreements about the degree (and form) of control that a company should exercise over data processing in its operating divisions* and staff functions.

The Centralization vs. Decentralization Issue

The centralization issue is not a new one; it has been widely discussed and hotly debated in academic institutions, management literature, and in less formal arenas for years—long before those particular aspects relating to the use of computers in industry came to the fore. It is an issue of great importance for governments—particularly those that do extensive economic planning at the state or industry level for multiple dispersed production units.

Obviously, many of the traditional arguments for or against centralization boil down to matters of management style. Even though it is rather difficult to *prove* whether, for example, a centralized purchasing function is intrinsically superior to a decentralized one, both alternatives have strong proponents. And to add to the confusion, styles change as the pendulum of management philosophy swings to and fro—it may be quite fashionable to be highly decentralized in one era and equally unfashionable only a few years later. Furthermore, at any one time, individual management styles inevitably will differ within an organization.

---

*The term "division(s)" will be used throughout to refer to an operating unit located at a distance from corporate headquarters.

GEORGE GLASER *is a principal in the San Francisco office of McKinsey & Company, Inc. He is Treasurer of ACM and previously was Chairman of SIGBDP. This paper was presented at the SIGBDP Breakfast Meeting at the 1970 Fall Joint Computer Conference, Houston, Texas.*

As a result, arguments often are charged with emotion, leading to incomplete or misleading analyses of the alleged economics of the alternatives. And because organizations (and the individuals who make them up) are characterized by a variety of styles, abilities, and needs, it is not possible to propose a "solution" that will apply in all situations. One can only suggest alternatives—and the questions that must be answered in deciding among them.

General rules are always dangerous (and often trite), but these seem to apply:

- The organizational approach to data processing should be consistent with the overall organizational approach of the company in which it functions. For example, a company that operates multiple manufacturing units, each in a separate geographic location, and that imposes strict profit and loss accountability on local managers would be expected to lean strongly toward decentralized data processing. Very few economies—and perhaps many difficulties—would await it if it attempted to centralize data processing in a single corporate location.
- It will be expensive (at least in the short term) and possibly disruptive to make any organizational change; therefore, no change should be introduced unless the projected benefits of transition are both large and concrete. In other words, a centralized organization that is functioning well should probably remain centralized (and vice versa).
- Reorganization may be a good idea, but only competent people and hard work can produce consistently good performance. If hiring practices have been sloppy and training programs nonexistent, then staff qualifications most likely are weak as a result—and, regardless of how a staff is organized, weak qualifications tend to lead to poorly designed systems.

Perhaps the most challenging "rule" of all: No organizational structure or policy will work unless accepted by the majority of people affected by it as logical, satisfactory, and workable.

The Issue in Data Processing

When the issue of centralization versus decentralization of data processing arises, those who argue for centralization point out that the costs of data processing are large and that the economies of scale are very important. Those who argue for decentralization express primary concern for the level of data processing service available to users; they believe that the additional out-of-pocket costs typically associated with a decentralized operation are justified.

The issue is a serious one for most industrial enterprises. And it becomes critical (and particularly difficult to resolve) for organizations that manufacture products in multiple operating divisions in diverse locations. Additional complications arise when lines of control cross international boundaries because of differences in national practices and laws, and poor cross-boundary communications, both human and electrical. Still further complications—and some of the most difficult to deal with—are caused by acquisitions and mergers that result in the need to manage incompatible equipment, programming languages, data structures, systems, and people; these may complicate (or even preclude) the interchange of data and limit sharing of technical accomplishments.

Most industrial data processing departments would claim these two objectives: (1) the desire to utilize corporate computer assets efficiently and effectively, and (2) the desire to offer a high level of service at low cost in solving a wide range of user problems.

Unfortunately, these two objectives often are in direct conflict, for increased efficiency of computer hardware nearly always leads to reduced accessibility and degraded service for individual users. For example, consider the "efficiencies" bestowed upon users of data processing by developments in operating systems: operating systems have been designed to allow highly efficient use of very powerful computers; but this "efficiency" has made it necessary for all users (or their agents) to master a difficult job control language that contributes nothing directly to the solution of their problems.

Analyzing the Pros and Cons

When an analysis of the pros and cons of centralization (or decentralization) is undertaken, said analysis typically is performed by a corporate data processing staff whose sensitivity to the needs of individual users is dulled by its passion for working with the most exotic hardware available—a strong economic motive for resume-conscious technicians. And typical users are no more rational in their counter-arguments—they embrace the concepts of autonomy and economy with considerable fervor—perhaps, in the process, rejecting badly needed assistance from well-qualified professionals in the central organization. And although the users outnumber the central staff, the former usually are geographically dispersed, poorly organized, and poorly qualified (in a technical sense) to ensure themselves of an equal hearing in the debate. As a result, more often than not, the corporate staff wins and centralized control results. Let's examine the arguments used by both sides.

ARGUMENTS FOR CENTRALIZATION

Proponents of centralization cite the following grounds for their point:

1. *Company-wide consolidation of operating results.* Divisional financial and operating data must be consolidated at the corporate level. Compatibility of systems design, coding schemes, and data formats facilitate this consolidation. And such compatibility can be achieved only by close centralized direction of hardware/software procurement and development efforts.

2. *Economies of scale.* Economies of scale—as measured by purchase or rental costs—result when several small computers are replaced by a single large one. Other economies of scale result from consolidation of development staffs and reduction of duplicate development efforts. Because rental and personnel costs appear as identifiable expenditures on accounting reports, they present obvious targets for those charged with the responsibility for keeping costs low.

3. *Shortage of qualified data processing personnel.* Qualified data processing personnel are scarce and, from all evidence at hand and the present economy notwithstanding, will continue to be so. They show less allegiance to their employer than to their technology. Turnover is high, as individuals move from company to company, boosting their salaries substantially in the process. Centralization reduces the impact of this phenomenon by permitting fewer staffs of larger size, thus reducing dependence on individuals and enhancing the company's ability to recruit and retain a well-qualified staff.

4. *Ease of control.* It is easier for corporate executives to control individual divisions when reporting systems are uniform. Unique systems in operating divisions are regarded as an impediment to adequate control. Through centralization, the arguments run, uniformity can be enforced.

ARGUMENTS FOR DECENTRALIZATION

Proponents of decentralization argue the following points:

1. *Familiarity with local problems.* To apply the computer intelligently to the solution of complex problems in complex environments, systems analysts and programmers must be thoroughly familiar with the problems in detail. This level of familiarity can best be achieved by individuals who are close (both physically and organizationally) to the problem to be solved and to those who want solutions, i.e., by locating development staffs at the site of the manufacturing plant, warehouse, or other functional operation.

2. *Rapid response to local processing needs.* The need of local management for rapid processing turnaround on large volumes of data often requires that computers be located in their immediate vicinity. This is particularly true in manufacturing operations, where production schedules, order booking, and shipping papers must be prepared and returned rapidly to the user organization for action. Currently available communications facilities are inadequate to allow dependence on a remote computer for such applications.

3. *Profit and loss responsibility.* Many industrial organizations have adopted a principle of decentralized

responsibility for operating results; because the selection and implementation of computer application can play a vital role in actual profits and losses, these tasks should be decentralized as well.

Needless to say, a great many more arguments are heard on both sides, and heatedly defended.[1]

Elements of the Issue

The approach to centralization/decentralization can be made somewhat rational if the major elements of the issue are considered separately; these elements are:

1. Equipment
2. Staff
3. Decision authorities.

EQUIPMENT

The most obvious element of the centralization versus decentralization issue is the location and custody of computing and communications equipment. Because the range of equipment, size, and power is so great, many options are available. Individual manufacturing plants might have small computers, often dedicated to a particular process or product line. Large powerful computers might be located in corporate offices to serve a multitude of corporate needs and home-office-based users; medium-sized machines might be placed in one or more regional centers to serve a number of smaller users in a local area.

Uniformity of equipment configuration, compatibility of languages, and interchangeability of data and storage media are other aspects of the centralization/decentralization issue that are closely related to equipment. For example, to what extent must equipment configurations be identical so that common applications programs may be used in multiple locations?

Equipment issues are further complicated when more than one vendor has manufactured the equipment installed in various locations throughout a single company. This situation may have resulted from independent equipment selection decisions made at an earlier date; or from acquisitions or mergers where uniformity requirements did not exist or could not be foreseen; or when individual applications requirements lead to a deliberate choice of non-compatible equipment.

In most cases, there will be some requirement for the interchange of data and programs within the corporation. The requirements may be continuous or occasional; the cost of meeting them may be high or trivial.

Several trends in equipment design are well established —the cost of electronics assembly has gone down dramatically in recent years, making large-scale integration attractive economically. This, in turn, has led to the minicomputer—now introduced on a broad scale in a number of interesting applications. At the same time, telecommunications capability has improved dramatically, from both a device and a network point of view—although the latter

seems to be lagging badly in some geographical areas. The net result of these developments will be even further decentralization of data processing personnel and widespread dispersion of equipment.

Why? First, the incentive to build very large machines because of manufacturing economies will no longer be present. Second, as equipment becomes smaller and more powerful, fewer economies of scale (based on physical factors such as space and air conditioning) will be available through consolidation of several small machines into one or more larger ones. Third, improved communications will facilitate consolidation of operating results between small machines at remote locations and a larger machine at corporation headquarters without requiring that large volumes of data be moved over long distances.

Large corporations are unlikely to centralize their data in a single file (or small group of files)—although they may very well have highly developed data management standards and explicit controls over the content of data files throughout the corporation.

Unfortunately, the majority of centralization arguments are based on improving the *efficiency* of the equipment used in computer installation; but efficient installations do not necessarily house effective computers.

An efficient steam engine may indeed be a source of great pride to the thermodynamicist who designed it and to the caretaker who maintains it; but if it is impractical to move the mechanical energy from the steam engine to the location where it is needed, then the efficiency of the engine is of little value. Today, there are too many highly efficient computers that bring great satisfaction to *their* caretakers but do so at considerable cost to the organization that pays the rent for both. Furthermore, efficient use of equipment isn't as important (in the United States) as it once was; computer rental costs now comprise only 35 percent of the total costs of data processing.[2] This is certainly not a trivial amount but, in most cases, it is less than the percentage of costs spent on data processing staff salaries.

STAFF

Many people possessing a variety of skills are required to support a corporate data processing effort.[3] Some of these individuals, by definition, must be located in the immediate vicinity of the machines, e.g., operators and maintenance personnel. Keypunch clerks and data preparation clerks have in the past been located near the computer room also, particularly when the volume of data to be handled was high. However, the introduction of keyboard-to-tape and keyboard-to-disc units has relieved the need for close proximity of these personnel to processing equipment.

Other developments in equipment have provided increased latitude in the location of systems analysts and programmers who no longer must be located in the immediate vicinity of major equipment. Conversational programming and remote job entry techniques now allow both analysts and programmers to be at a considerable distance from the computers on which their programs will be run.

Several arguments have been presented above that are used by either centralists or decentralists to influence the location of the technical development staff. One of these —the economies of scale expected from consolidation of development staffs—is based on an alleged synergistic effect.[4] But a single large development staff is *not* necessarily more effective than several smaller ones. Manpower management and project assignments might be facilitated in the larger group, but any economies of direct labor may easily be offset by additional administrative (indirect) labor.

Parties arguing either side of the issue would no doubt agree that it is worthwhile to avoid duplication of effort. But it is not obvious that consolidation of development staffs is the best way to do so; bootleg developments are easy to disguise *if* that is the intent of the developer, whether developments are officially centralized or not. On the other hand, if he is motivated to disclose what he is doing and share his results, he can do so equally well in a decentralized organization.

Perhaps one of the more compelling arguments for staff centralization is that larger staffs are less susceptible to damage from high turnover. True—the loss of even one person who is a key man on a small staff can hurt badly. But turnover rates often are considerably lower in small installations, particularly when these are located in rural or semirural areas. Typically, it is the major cities and densely populated areas that have high turnover rates— primarily because of the multiple opportunities offered without relocating one's family. The counterargument is that large staffs with powerful centralized equipment and extensive training programs are alleged to be more attractive to recruits than are smaller staffs in remote locations. Fortunately, turnover rates (and their causes) and recruiting results can be analyzed quantitatively; they are among the few variables for which this is so.

The decentralist's argument that physical proximity to a problem may ease its solution assumes that qualified people are available. This assumption may not be justified—in fact, it is likely that a larger number of more highly qualified individuals would be members of a central staff than of any one (or all) local staffs. But the tradeoff between technical qualifications and familiarity with a problem can be a tough one to evaluate. A "local" analyst who is familiar with a problem but who lacks certain specialized knowledge may need to ask for help; and a highly qualified specialist who is not familiar with a problem may need to take particular pains to develop the knowledge and rapport at the local level that he will need eventually to solve it. But given the choice between the two, the local an-

alyst often will be more successful because most of the *tough* problems are so defined for other than technical reasons.

A different kind of "problem knowledge" often is important—that knowledge bearing on the operational feasibility* of a particular application. Operational impediments to a successful implementation often are subtle and are never easy to overcome; but familiarity with "how things really work around here," i.e., with local personalities, politics, and mores, may be the key to doing so.

———————
*Operational feasibility is a measure of how well the system will function within the operating policies, organization, and economic environment of the corporation.[5]

Whenever comparisons are being made between the advantages of a centralized versus decentralized staff, it is important (and difficult) to keep the comparisons equitable. If a poorly organized and poorly trained central staff is compared to small but elite decentralized staffs, the latter would surely win. Conversely, decentralization is not a very realistic alternative for the near term if there are only six analysts and programmers in the entire company.

What of the future? Two trends are working in favor of decentralized data processing staffs. First, the problem of scarcity of personnel—recently so severe—will not last indefinitely. Within 5 years, work loads in data processing will be much more stable and the influx of competent individuals from year to year will provide an adequate and stable work force. Companies will no longer centralize as a defensive measure. Second, as the use of data processing becomes more accepted and better understood by middle- and upper-level managers of operating units, they will insist that local data processing talent be available (and responsible) to them; systems analysis and programming will be as routine as plant maintenance and accounting.

In summary, the arguments based on staff—not equipment—considerations are the most important in nearly every case.[6] Failure to recognize this can lead to organizational recommendations that, while intended to *cut* data processing costs, may lead to *higher* costs in the long run.

DECISION AUTHORITIES

The third and most complex aspect of the centralization versus decentralization issue is the assignment of decision authorities. Decision authorities can be grouped under five major headings:

1. *Direction setting.* Who establishes long-range data processing objectives and sets the level of effort?, e.g., funds.

2. *Project evaluation and selection.* On whose authority will projects be approved? Can approval authorities realistically be delegated, allowing lower level organization units to approve certain projects, while reserving control of large projects for higher authorities?

3. *Hardware and software selection.* Who approves new expansion of EDP hardware? On what basis are programming languages selected? To what extent should the use of multiple languages be restricted? Should responsibility for approving the *need* for equipment be separated from responsiblity for approving the type and manufacturer? Should file structures and data definitions be standardized? Coding Systems? Programming and documentation standards?

4. *Personnel assignment.* Who approves staffing levels? How will major interfunctional or interdivisional projects be staffed? Who will lead such projects? How will development costs of such projects be allocated? How will salary levels be administered and career opportunities be provided?

5. *Use of outside services.* Do users have the option when choosing the "source" of manpower for their development and operating needs? If so, under what circumstances will an individual user or department be allowed to contract for outside data processing services? Only for peak loads? Only where special expertise is required?

Questions like these arise every day in large corporations. It is impossible to provide answers that will apply in all situations; but it is imperative that responsibility for answering them be assigned unambiguously and that they be answered clearly and consistently when they arise.

Criteria for the Decision

In attempting to decide between a centralized or decentralized policy (or some combination of the two), seven criteria should be considered:

1. *Minimum total cost.* The total cost of system development, operations, and maintenance is one of the major selection criteria. But it is important to remember that not all costs are reported by the accounting system. For example, late inventory status reports may lead to poor purchasing decisions, or to the loss of a customer order; both have high costs but neither is likely to effect short-term accounting results.

2. *User satisfaction.* Because this criterion is so difficult to quantify, it often receives inadequate consideration. Yet, it represents a fundamental issue in selecting a policy. Efficient computer operations that render poor service have a very high ratio of costs to benefits. This criterion is often difficult to quantify, but not that difficult to evaluate quantitatively. Dissatisfied users usually are quite vocal in their criticism; whether that criticism is fully justified in every case is a moot point. If users are generally unhappy, then odds are that their attitude is based on a real problem.

3. *Effective utilization of personnel.* Because technical talents are scarce, their effective utilization is an im-

portant consideration. But it must not be assumed that effective utilization of personnel calls for consolidated development staffs; quite often, the reverse is true.

4. *The ability to attract and retain personnel.* Certain technical personnel are attracted by installations of large complex computer equipment. Others, equally skilled, prefer the independence that a smaller installation may offer. Some may prefer to work in a big city; others, in the country.

5. *Rational selection of development projects.* Where a number of projects are competing for limited resources, there must be a procedure that will allow rational selection among them. In some cases, this will have to be carried out at the corporate staff level; in others, selection might be the responsibility of the local plant manager or of a functional, e.g., manufacturing, executive.

6. *The opportunity to share common systems.* Companies with fairly uniform products and processes have attractive opportunities to share common systems, facilities, and staffs. Companies characterized by diversity may offer few such opportunities except for certain administrative applications such as personnel and asset accounting.

7. *Adaptability to changes in the technical and economic environment.* Since no one can anticipate all significant changes in technology or developments in industry or company structure, the organization must be sufficiently flexible to accommodate a variety of unforeseen future developments. At no time is this more evident than after a successful merger that results in two programming staffs—one of PL/1 (only) programmers and another of COBOL (only) programmers.

Additional Factors Influencing the Decision

Additional factors—some of which may be unique to the situation—and many of which will be subjective—may play an important role in determining the appropriate degree of centralization.

One of these is the nature of the information flow among sub-units in the organization. If the volume of information is low and infrequent, manual consolidation of operating results may be best, thus reducing the need for centralized processing. If, on the other hand, large volumes of data must be consolidated quickly and frequently, then a centralized approach is indicated. Good examples of the latter case are airline reservations systems that rely completely on a single inventory of available seats.

The need of operating managers for rapid turnaround of operating information may transcend any economies that might be provided by sharing data processing facilities located at some distance (and time) from the local area.

The availability of reliable and inexpensive data communications will often dictate the degree of centralization possible. If communications are poor, the cost of moving data to (and results from) a major installation may be prohibitive. And even when the economics are favorable, provisions must be made for correcting data input errors. If it is necessary to contact the source of the original data, the resulting delays and costs may be unacceptable.

The current "state of the DP art" will heavily influence the centralization decision. A company that is introducing data processing for the first time may wisely elect to begin with a small group in a single location under tight managerial control. As the group expands and matures, it then may be desirable gradually to spin off (decentralize) small subgroups that, in time, will become selfsustaining and will operate independently of the parent organization.

To centralize, i.e., to collapse a number of existing decentralized operations into a single centralized one, is very difficult unless the work load in the decentralized units is heavily concentrated on a few applications that are identical from unit to unit. For example, successful consolidation of credit card processing centers is both possible and (often) attractive economically. But attempts to achieve economies by centralizing heterogeneous applications, currently running on different machines, programmed and operated by independent groups of people, will frequently meet with disastrous results. Unfortunately, there is a seductive but inevitably costly urge to "pull everything together, get it on a single machine, eliminate our operating problems, and cut our costs." The results often are disappointing.

Finally, the degree of uniformity of coding systems, managerial practices, and operating policies within the corporation can be a constraint. If there is little uniformity, centralization will produce relatively marginal benefits; in fact, centralization may be impractical *until* uniformity is achieved—usually a long and difficult process.

The Alternatives

Although there are an infinite number of possible organizational structures that might be offered to deal with the issues discussed above, most existing structures are variations on four major alternatives:

1. *Centralized development and operations.* All development efforts are performed by a centralized development staff; all computing and communications equipment is operated by a centralized organization. Neither staffs nor computers need be in a single location; for example, regional centers might be established under centralized control.
2. *Independent development and centralized operations.* Individual users, based on their individual needs, employ development staffs; a centralized authority operates all computing and communications equipment.

3. *Independent development and operations under central coordination.* Independent users employ their own development *and* operations staffs and operate their own equipment. Those that are too small to justify either staffs or equipment obtain services from other operating units within the company or from outside service bureaus. Central coordination is provided in terms of programming and documentation standards; authority over configuration, types and manufacturers of equipment; establishment of internal training programs, salary administration and career path planning; and responsibility for consistent and rational project evaluation and selection. In short, the central group controls the methods and processes by which data processing is used, but is not responsible for the design and implementation of individual systems.
4. *Independent development and operations.* All aspects of data processing enjoy complete autonomy within the constraints of divisional accountability. If a corporate data processing staff and/or installation exists, its only function is to serve users at the corporate level in the same sense that divisional staffs serve divisional users.

In most situations, industrial companies choose alternatives 2 or 3 above, or compromise between them. Neither the completely centralized nor the completely decentralized mode of operation is found often in practice. Where complete centralization has been attempted, clandestine staffs and equipment installations are likely to develop. The reasons are simple: If a user has a problem and is determined to solve it, and if he cannot get an acceptable solution to his problem from the "legal" source of help, he will seek (and find) illegal sources.

Guidelines for Allocating the Tasks

Although no single set of rules will apply in all cases, the following general guidelines may be useful in deciding when to allocate tasks to a centralized staff as opposed to allocating them to divisions.

The *centralized* staff should be responsible for the following:

1. The work of the corporate office. These needs are "local" at the corporate level in the same sense that production scheduling is a local need in a manufacturing plant.
2. Company-wide functions, e.g., personnel, payroll, and certain other routine accounting applications.
3. Divisional work that does not require rapid turnaround and that can be done more economically on a centralized basis.
4. Work for small divisions that cannot justify facilities or staffs of their own. In this role, the central facility functions as a service bureau; geographically far-flung enterprises may find it appropriate to delegate some

central "bureau" functions to one or more regional outposts.

5. Interdivision and interplant applications that are part of an integrated system where, for technical reasons, a single computer must process all data within the system. Certain order entry and inventory applications are of this nature.

Decentralized staffs should be responsible for:

1. Applications that depend on rapid turnaround, e.g., production scheduling.
2. *All* work for which there are no *compelling* reasons to centralize.

The underlying principle is that *work should be done locally whenever possible;* it should be done centrally only when the economics or some other performance requirement dictates so. This is the converse of the principle frequently applied that presumes that work should be done centrally unless special circumstances dictate otherwise.

*   *   *

In all cases there is a risk of spending too much money and of spending it unwisely; there is the threat of missed opportunities and of duplicated efforts; there is the danger of inappropriate equipment and unqualified staff. All must be considered in designing the organization that is appropriate for each environment.

In the long run, the computer's existence is justified only by its usefulness in solving problems—quickly, with min-

imum disruption to the fundamental operations of the business, and at the lowest feasible costs. To do so depends heavily on close working relationships with those who face the problems and whose valuable insight into their solution, whose ability to generate enthusiasm for the results, and whose dedication to make systems work are the *sine qua non* of success.

REFERENCES

1. For a debate on this subject, see Martin B. Solomon, "Economies of Scale and Computer Personnel," *Datamation,* March 1970, pp. 107-110; Peter Berman, "A Vote Against Centralized Staff," *Datamation,* May 1970, pp. 289-290; Solomon, "Economies of Scale Defended," *Datamation,* June 1970, pp. 293-294; and Berman, "Decentralization Again," *Datamation,* October 15, 1970, pp. 141-142.

2. McKinsey & Company, Inc., *Unlocking the Computer's Profit Potential* (New York, 1968), pp. 7-10.

3. Enid Mumford and T. B. Ward, *Computers: Planning for People* (London, B. T. Batsford Ltd., 1968), pp. 70-78.

4. Solomon, "Economies of Scale and Computer Personnel," *Datamation,* March 1970, pp. 107-110.

5. George Glaser, "Are You Working on the Right Problem?", *Datamation,* June 1967, pp. 22-25.

6. *Joseph Orlicky, The Successful Computer System* (McGraw-Hill Book Company, 1969), p. 179.

William M. Zani   Davis Chapter 14

"BLUEPRINT FOR MIS"

Harvard Business Review (48:6), 1970 November-December, pages 95-100.

Zani's article is one of the best available expressions of the top-down approach to MIS design. He argues that most management information systems have spun off as by-products of operational and automated clerical systems rather than being designed specifically to support the manager in his decision making activity. He puts forth a comprehensive framework for designing and implementing management information systems from the top down.

The top-down approach to MIS design consists of focusing on the critical tasks and major decisions managers make at various levels within an organization to achieve the corporate objectives. A system is initiated by management and conceived from the viewpoint of management. The manager must play a prominent role in the design process. An expression of information requirements derives from the major decision areas of management and the MIS is designed to support these decisions. At the same time, Zani cautions that new systems cannot and should not be developed in the abstract but in the light of the limitations and constraints of existing systems and practices.

READING SUGGESTIONS

Seek to obtain an understanding of what constitutes a top-down approach to MIS development -- the orientation, the important variables, what to look at first, etc. Start out by reading carefully. As you read, key the text into the diagram, that is, keep in mind which box, funnel, or barrel he is talking about and continue to observe how it relates to the other parts of the framework. Do not attempt to memorize the precise details of the framework. An exclusively top-down approach is not universally accepted. Challenge the ideas and evaluate them in terms of:
 * an overall information systems master plan,
 * the integration and coordination of information systems,
 * the evolution of systems in response to a changing environment and to changing managers, and
 * the development of a corporate database.

QUESTIONS

1. Put into your own words a concise statement of the top-down approach to MIS development.

2. How does Zani characterize the bottom-up design approach? What is the danger of designing a system from the bottom up?

3. What are or should be the major determinants of MIS design? Describe the main sequence of steps in a top-down design approach.

4. What input ingredient is vital to the success of an MIS built from the top down?

5. Should an MIS be designed for the position in the organization or for the manager occupying the position? Why?

6. In terms of the input, how does Zani differentiate the three levels of decision making: strategic planning, management control, and operational control?

7. How does Zani's approach relate to the notion of a total, integrated MIS?

8. How does Zani's top-down approach to MIS development influence the development of an integrated corporate database? Which comes first?

William M. Zani

Blueprint for MIS

A general scheme for relating systems
to the jobs they are really supposed to do

Foreword

Most companies have not conceived and planned their management information systems with any significant amount of attention to their intended function—supporting the manager as he makes his decisions. As a result, companies have been disappointed with their systems, and have tended (quite unfairly) to discount the value of the MIS concept in general. Here is a framework for designing any system so that it will fulfill both its function and management's expectations of the potential of information systems at large. The key to good design, as the author explains, is a thorough understanding of the major decisions managers make at various levels in a company, because it is these decisions that define the kinds of information required, and hence define the basic design parameters of the system itself.

Mr. Zani is Assistant Professor of Business Administration at the Harvard Business School. He has taught at l'Institut pour l'Etude des Methodes de Direction de l'Entreprise in Lausanne, Switzerland, and he has worked both in designing and in managing computation centers. His current area of research is managerial implications of time-shared computer systems, a field in which he has published extensively.

Traditionally, management information systems have not really been designed at all. They have been spun off as by-products of the process of automating or improving existing systems within a company.

When a company's information system comes into existence in this second-hand manner, it is largely fortuitous whether the information the system provides is exactly the sort of information the managers in the company need to help them make their decisions. If it does turn out to be exactly what they need, then, well and good. If it does *not*—and this is much more likely to be the case—then clearly the so-called "management information system" is merely a mechanism for cluttering managers' desks with costly, voluminous, and probably irrelevant printouts.

No tool has ever aroused so much hope at its creation as MIS, and no tool has proved so disappointing in use. I trace this disappointment to the fact that most MISs have been developed in the "bottom up" fashion that I have just described. An effective system, under normal conditions, can only be born of a carefully planned, rational design that looks down from the top, the natural vantage point of the managers who will use it.

Rather than mirroring existing procedures, in other words, an information system should be designed to focus on the critical tasks and decisions made within an organization and to provide the kind of information that the manager needs to perform those tasks and make those decisions.

This obvious truth has largely escaped the at-

221

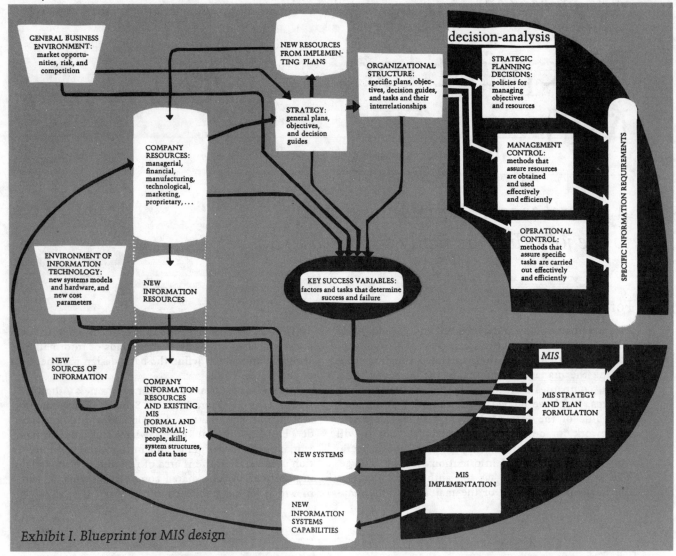

Exhibit I. Blueprint for MIS design

tention of businessmen, information specialists, and computer specialists alike. In this article I should like to present an approach to MIS design that is oriented squarely to decision making. I have presented this approach in the framework shown in *Exhibit I*, which diagrams out the major determinants of MIS design and their relationships to one another. These determinants are:

    ○ Opportunities and risks.
    ○ Company strategy.
    ○ Company structure.
    ○ Management and decision-making
       processes.
    ○ Available technology.
    ○ Available information sources.

These are the factors that should structure the characteristics of information provided to management, and therefore the design of the system itself.

From the top down

By exhibiting the relationships between these factors, the framework helps establish goals and priorities for MIS development, and hence fo-

cuses information technology where it will do the most good. If management sees to it that this framework is used when an information system is being designed, then the resulting system will be smartly tailored to the company from the top down, and not merely patched together from the bottom up in a crazy quilt of residues from automated clerical procedures.

The system, in other words, is likely to support the critical areas of decision making in the company effectively, as it should.

To ensure that the framework will actually be used, however, top management must take a more prominent role in the design process than it has hitherto. Most experts agree that top-management support and participation are necessary for effective system design, but they generally state that this support is necessary only for budget control and control of the data-processing group.

The framework I am presenting, however, implies a much more extensive participation than this. It assumes that top management itself must start the design process—i.e., must first delineate the organization's strategy, structure, and decision-making processes for the specialists in the design group, and then make sure that the specialist designers integrate these elements fully into the basic system design.

An ideal, not a recipe

I do not offer this framework as a panacea that will solve all of a company's information problems, nor as a step-by-step procedure for the whole design process. I offer it as a concept—an ideal, if you will—of how top management should think about the whole question of the management information system.

Its application does not guarantee that managers at all levels will be fully informed at all times about all matters important to the organization. This is obviously impossible. Further, there is nothing about the framework that implies that management can create a finished system by a single masterstroke of planning and development. Quite the contrary—the framework is only a guide to be used in the ongoing process of creating useful systems large or small, simple or complex, for immediate purposes or purposes farther away in the future. But, as such, it has enormous value.

Framework of MIS design

The upper left quadrant of *Exhibit I* indicates that a company strategy is a blend of internal company resources with external forces—market opportunities, risks, and competitive activities. The general strategy then determines organizational structure and also the practical strategy for augmenting the company's resources with new ones via short- and long-range planning.

The study of corporate strategy has occupied many books and journals, but the implication of corporate strategy for MIS design has largely escaped attention. Strategy should exercise a critical influence on information system design, to ensure that the resulting system is on the same "wave length" as the company as a whole. If, for example, a company changes its strategy so that its MIS focuses on factors no longer relevant—if it now urgently needs cash-flow data, say, where it formerly needed sales data—then the system is no longer valuable. Strategy dictates firm, explicit objectives for system design.

Key success variables

Opportunities, risks, competences, and resources, plus the strategy derived from them, yield the company's organizational structure. This structure subdivides the essential tasks to be performed, assigns them to individuals, and spells out the interrelationships of these tasks. These tasks, and the organizational structure they compose, determine the various information needs of the company.

Internal resources, external forces, strategy, and organizational structure define the key success variables of a company. These variables are activities on which the company must score high if it is to succeed. For example:

◇ For a consumer goods company manufacturing nondifferentiated products, the key success areas might be product promotion and understanding customer responses to product, marketing, and competitive changes.

◇ For a manufacturer of commodity products, manufacturing and distribution cost control and efficiency might be the major determinants of success.

The key success variables name the key tasks of the company and thus help identify the priorities for information system development. The system must provide information that makes the individual managers' performance of these tasks easier and better.

Decision analysis

The only way to isolate the specific information requirements of individual managers is to isolate the nature, frequency, and interrelationships of the major decisions made in the company.

One can ask a series of questions which will help isolate the specific information requirements for these decisions:

○ What decisions are made?

○ What decisions need to be made?

○ What factors are important in making these decisions?

○ How and when should these decisions be made?

○ What information is useful in making these decisions?

It is obviously not possible to answer all these questions for every decision made, in even the smallest organizations. But the key success variables help identify the *major decision areas* for detailed analysis.

The decision-analysis section of the framework is divided into three segments—*Strategic planning decisions, Management control,* and *Operational control.* Examples of activities falling under these headings are given in *Exhibit II.*

It is particularly important and useful to recognize these three distinct subprocesses of management in information system design because each requires different types of information and

Exhibit II. The characteristics of input into the three decision-analysis processes

Strategic planning process
   "External" data
      Market analyses
      Technological developments
      Government actions
      Economic data
   Trends
   Predictions

Management control process
   Control
      Internal formation
      Historical summaries
      Goal/performance comparisons
      Monetary reports
      Rhythmic reports
   Decision making
      Future trends & past trends
      Monetary & nonmonetary reports
      Special studies
      Rhythmic reports
      Product & market data
         Market share/potential market share
         Customer & product profiles
         Production-process efficiencies, etc.

Operational control process
   Precise logistic and product data
      Inventory reports
      Production schedules
      Product costs
   Nonmonetary reports

analysis. Within the operational control area, for example, many decisions can be programmed—that is, one can build a program that identifies the time at which a decision is needed, the alternatives available, and the criteria for selecting the best alternative under different circumstances.

Within strategic planning, on the other hand, it is frequently extremely difficult to determine when a decision is needed; and developing alternative solutions to a problem of strategic planning is a creative process that cannot be predefined or prescribed. Hence, the kinds of information and analyses needed for strategic planning are quite different from the kinds

needed for operational control. *Exhibit III* displays the informational characteristics required by each of these subprocesses.

Systems designers who fail to understand the differences between these subprocesses and fail to take them into account may make the mistake of applying to all of them a system that is applicable to only one subprocess and not to the others. Decision analysis should filter information requirements for the appropriate management subprocess. Thus far, then, the framework makes explicit:

   ○ Objectives dictated by strategy.
   ○ Specific tasks and their interrelationships, displayed via organizational structure.
   ○ Key success variables.

Using these elements as a base, an analysis of a company's decision-making patterns in strategy, managerial control, and operational control draws out the specific information requirements for the critical areas of company operations. It is by identifying these factors and guiding their analyses that managers make their contribution to MIS development.

To fulfill their roles properly, managers must be aware of the major sources of information, of alternative methods of supplying data, and of the impact of the major changes of information technology. The major contribution to information systems in these areas, of course, must come from the information and data-processing specialists.

Information technology

The field of information technology has undergone and will continue to undergo rapid change. One funnel in *Exhibit I* symbolizes the influence of change in information technology, and also of information sources, on the development of information systems. Through this funnel are added new methods of processing and storing data, new models, changes in computer and peripheral equipment, and changes in the costs of hardware and software development to the design process. These generate new system ideas and make them feasible.

The barrel labeled "Company information resources . . ." is a reminder that new systems cannot and should not be developed in the abstract. Existing systems and practices cannot be changed overnight, and many times it is too costly and risky to change the existing systems

Exhibit III. Examples of activities in the three decision-analysis processes

Strategic planning	Management control	Operational control
Choosing company objectives	Formulating budgets	
Planning the organization	Planning staff levels	Controlling hiring
Setting personnel policies	Planning working capital	Controlling credit extension
Setting marketing policies	Formulating advertising programs	Controlling placement of advertisements
Setting research policies	Selecting research projects	
Choosing new product lines	Choosing product improvements	
Acquiring new divisions	Deciding on plant rearrangement	Scheduling production
Deciding on nonroutine capital expenditures	Deciding on routine capital expenditures	
	Formulating decision rules for operational control	Controlling inventory
	Measuring, appraising, and improving management performance	Measuring, appraising, and improving workers' efficiency

Source: Adapted from Robert N. Anthony, *Planning and Control
Systems: A Framework for Analysis* (Boston, Division of Research,
Harvard Business School, 1965), p. 19.

radically. Proposals for system changes must also consider the level, quality, and kinds of skills present in the data-processing group. And finally, of course, the computer configuration is fixed in the short term and may be difficult and expensive to alter. New systems must therefore be designed and developed with the limitations and constraints of the old systems clearly in mind.

Using the framework, then, encourages understanding of the critical areas of operations, identification of specific information requirements, and recognition of the technological, economic, and personnel constraints within which an MIS develops. As important as anything else, perhaps, is the fact that systems are of necessity dynamic, changing with the environment and the organization.

In essence, the difference between my viewpoint on MIS design and what I call the bottom-up viewpoint is analogous to the difference between the new, customer-oriented concept of marketing and the old marketing concept. Philip Kotler has spelled out the latter difference as follows:

"The new marketing concept replaces and to some extent reverses the logic of the old one. . . . The old concept starts with the firm's existing products and considers marketing to be the use of selling and promotion to attain sales at a profit. The new concept starts with the firm's existing and potential customers; it seeks profits through the creation of customer satisfaction; and it seeks to achieve this through an integrated, corporate wide marketing program." [1]

The old MIS design approach begins with existing systems, and produces benefits by chance. The approach I advocate focuses on key tasks and decisions leading to more effective decisions, and then attacks the problem of designing information systems to support those tasks.

The framework I have proposed helps management structure MIS so that it can and will influence the decision-making processes in the critical areas of the company, and thus focuses information technology and resources where they do the most good. It also demonstrates that general and operating management must be directly involved in the design of systems. Only management's understanding can delineate the organization's critical success factors for the information specialist or systems designer.

If the design of management information systems begins on a high conceptual level and on a high managerial level as well, a company can avoid the unfortunate "bottom up" design phenomenon of recent history and begin to develop the real, and very great, potential of MIS as a tool for modern management.

1. *Marketing Management* (Englewood Cliffs, New Jersey, Prentice-Hall, Inc., 1967), p. 6.

"MIS PLANNING"

Datamation (16:10), 1970 September 1, pages 28-31.

Herb Schwartz, an MIS executive, has been a leader in
the development of management information systems in industry. His article reflects operating experience and advocates a highly systematic approach to MIS planning.
Schwartz views an MIS as a federation of systems rather
than a single system. His development approach is evolutionary within the context of a long-term plan.

READING SUGGESTIONS

The ESSO six types of business systems are significant
because this is the basic structural framework. The six
systems are: environment, transactions, management information, planning and control systems, management systems,
and operating systems (physical facilities). Each of these
is defined in the article.

The ideal planning system is described in 12 points.
Essentially, Schwartz is describing the development of a
master plan for MIS development. Note the sequence of
steps which start from broad mission statements through
to project selection and preparation of a five-year specific plan.

QUESTIONS

1. How does Schwartz define an MIS?
2. What are the ESSO six types of business systems?
    Which are not generally applicable?
3. What is meant by a federation of subsystems?
4. Why does Schwartz reject a top-down development
    approach?
5. Explain the Schwartz evolutionary approach to develop-
    ment.
6. How does the Schwartz approach handle
    a. current systems
    b. potential systems
7. What are the Schwartz criteria for project selection?
8. How often does Schwartz suggest the five-year plan be
    reviewed?
9. Attempt to relate the twelve steps of Schwartz with
    the blueprint for MIS design described by Zani in the
    previous article.

**It's tough and costly,
but systematic planning
is the only hope**

MIS Planning

by M. H. Schwartz

The crucial purpose of planning in any sphere of life is, in my view, to be as sensible as we can in deciding what to do, how to do it (in terms of methods and resources), and when to do it. There are important relationships and feedbacks among these three objectives: for example, we are practically always constrained in what we decide to do at any given time by limitations in capabilities or resources. Oftentimes we simply do some of those things that we happen to know how to do and that we have resources for without consciously and conscientiously weighing alternatives.

Designing and executing a large scale management information system is a costly and difficult undertaking—far more costly and difficult than early proponents recognized—in reward for which is offered a number of highly desirable potential opportunities for the improvement of management and organization performance. These cost and benefit magnitudes and the complicated relationships among planning objectives demand that MIS management establish a *highly systematic and analytic approach* for short-range and long-range planning. There is no better approach for deciding what to do, how to do it, and when to do it—and these are the most perplexing and most meaningful questions for management to decide.

This article describes the particular systematic and analytic approach to MIS planning that we are experimenting with in the further development of the U.S. Atomic Energy Commission's agency-wide management information system. We could call our approach a "system for MIS planning." In setting forth the planning system, I shall (a) define "MIS" according to my view, (b) place MIS into the context of the major systems of an organization (with the help of material developed at ESSO Standard of New Jersey), (c) take a stand on the overall strategy of MIS development (emphasizing the need for an evolutionary approach), and (d) set forth the planning system we are experimenting with at the AEC.

In my view, an MIS is a system of people, equipment, procedures, documents, and communications that collects, validates, operates on, transforms, stores, retrieves, and presents data for use in planning, budgeting, accounting, controlling, and other management processes for various management purposes. The data concern people, money, physical assets (materials, equipment, and plant), and other resources that are employed in the fulfillment of the organization's objectives. The operations and transformations include recording, comparing, reconciling, tabulating, summarizing, and mathematically analyzing. Information processing systems become management information systems as their purpose transcends a transactions processing orientation in favor of a management decison-making orientation.

This is a pragmatic definition deliberately scaled down from the over-blown, over-sold, all-encompassing definitions of MIS that I believe have hurt the MIS field in the eyes of executive and general management.

Management Information Systems live within a context; they no more stand on their own than do modern communities; they depend upon other, lower level, activities on the one hand, and, on the other hand, are themselves depended upon by other, higher level activities. One of the best descriptions and analyses of which I am aware of the framework within which MIS's exist has been compiled by ESSO Standard of New Jersey. I present the substantial quotation below partly to illuminate my definition of MIS and partly to illuminate the crucial second step of the planning system set forth later in this article. I do not present the quotation as a literal blueprint for immediate application in all organizations; as noted later in the article, local adaptation of the "model" is generally necessary.

The ESSO document defines six types of systems that they believe exist in any kind of business. The document also identifies three organizational levels:

1. Central (Parent Company)
2. Regional (Humble, Esso Europe, Esso Standard Eastern, etc.)
3. Operational (Refinery, Chemical Plant, etc.)

The positions taken in this article are the author's; they should not be considered as a definitive official statement of the U.S. Atomic Energy Commission at this time, pending availability of the results of the planning experience. The article draws very heavily upon presentations made by the author at the Finance and Budget Directors' Conference, U.S. Atomic Energy Commission, April 2, 1970; and at the Sixth Annual International Computer Conference, Amsterdam, Holland, April 8, 1970.

ESSO'S SIX TYPES OF BUSINESS SYSTEMS

1. BUSINESS ENVIRONMENT—These so-called systems represent the environment in which the Jersey organization utilizes its resources to obtain a return on the stockholders' investment. The Business Environment, as opposed to the Jersey Resources System, is not—by definition—controllable by Jersey management. The Business Environment includes the following subunits:

   a. Customers
   b. Vendors
   c. Governments
   d. Public
   e. Stockholders
   f. Manpower Market
   g. Competition (existing and potential)
   h. Opportunity Areas
   i. Financial Community
   j. Contractors

2. BUSINESS TRANSACTION SYSTEM—This major information systems classification includes the following interrelated subsystems:

   a. Data Acquisition and Validation
   b. Order Entry and Processing
   c. Invoicing and Price Checking
   d. Trade Accounts Receivable
   e. Stock Control and Replenishment
   f. Yield and Material Balance Accounting
   g. Materials and Supplies Accounting
   h. Personnel (Payroll, Benefits, Personnel Records)
   i. Retail Business Accounting (Credit Card)
   j. General Accounting
   k. Fixed Assets
   l. Inventory Evaluation
   m. Etc.

   These subsystems are required to process Business Transactions and Operating Results but do not provide the information required for resource management without further processing.

3. MANAGEMENT INFORMATION SYSTEMS—This major information systems classification includes the following interrelated subsystems:

   a. Sales Statistics
   b. Supply/Demand
   c. Manpower
   d. Facilities and Capacities
   e. Costs (Allocation and Statistics)
   f. Prices
   g. Operating Statistics
   h. P/L Statement
   i. Balance Sheets
   j. Budgets
   k. A&O Report
   l. Corporate Outlook
   m. Consolidations
   n. Environmental Information
   o. Planning and Control Data for Math Models
   p. Etc.

   Both historical and forecast information are processed by these subsystems. The resulting output from processing serves to provide mainstream management with the information required for resource management. Business Transaction Systems are one source of input data for Management Information Systems.

4. PLANNING AND CONTROL SYSTEMS—This major information systems classification includes mathematical models and statistical techniques for planning and control, as well as quantitative methods for the design of physical facilities:

   a. Opportunity Indentification and Evaluation
   b. Objectives Development and Evaluation
   c. Investment Planning and Evaluation
   d. Resources Development and Evaluation (including Physical Systems)
   e. Logistics Planning and Evaluation
   f. Operations Scheduling and Evaluation
   g. Operations Control and Evaluation

   These systems are usually developed by Operations Research/Management Sciences specialists.

5. MANAGEMENT SYSTEMS—This classification is intended to represent the oil/chemical management of the business at all organizational levels.

6. OPERATING SYSTEMS—These are the physical facilities of the business (e.g., refineries, pipelines, tankers, oil fields, chemical plants, bulk plants, etc.).

It further notes that business transactions systems, management information systems, and planning and control systems must be planned and coordinated on a unified corporate-wide basis so that long-range plans may be developed and so that individual implementation projects may be effectively identified, scheduled and performed.[1]

The significance of the word "system" in the expression "Management Information System" is that the people, equipment, and other elements of the system are interrelated parts of a coordinated whole. A special word for "coordinated whole" is "integrated." The latter word has no more absolute meaning than does the word "coordinated." Neither word is like the word "pregnant," which a woman cannot be partly or nearly—it's all or nothing at all. Integrated, like coordinated, is a word that embraces a continuum. An information system increases in integration as it flows more smoothly and more automatically, and as the interfaces between the parts become efficient and effective. *Each* management information system within an organization should be as nearly fully integrated as economy dictates.

"The" management information system for an entire organization, however, must be visualized, I maintain, as a supersystem of systems, as a *federation of management information systems*. Only the most monolithic of organizations can build and gain strength from a single total system. The federation is necessary to provide coherence in architecture, design, standards, documentation, operating procedures and other *achievable commonalities,* and to *provide economy* in implementation and operation. The federation should be structured as a set of systems, each

system tightly integrated internally, but loosely integrated when taken together. There must be some integration among all of the systems, for they all contribute to the management and organizational performance of the one enterprise. They are all parts of a whole. But only loosely. The wider the range of activities of the enterprise, the looser must the integration be.

Take the case of a large chemical corporation: can its highly contingent research be managed with the same management system as its large volume, highly deterministic production? Can a single information system serve the needs of the pluralistic management systems?

Development strategy

My view that an MIS should be visualized as a federation of systems, rather than as a "single" system, involves a strategic decision that precedes specific planning. The late Sherman Blumenthal put the issue into the sharpest terms that I know:

"Management information systems whose perspective is 'top-down' are much in vogue, altogether too frequently because of the recklessly drawn analogy between management control in industry and military command and control. The rigid hierarchy of command in the military, and the need for instant, accurate, and coordinated response in singular tactical situations, almost unavoidably entail a monolothic, all at once approach to military command and control

---

[1] From a document (dated 9-11-69) furnished me in 1967 by Mr. Mel H. Grosz, a Vice President of ESSO Mathematics and Systems, Inc.

systems development. This is technologically very risky, financially very expensive, and the resulting problems of systems management are enormous. . . . To postulate and then pursue . . . 'a total, integrated management information system' as the appropriate target of systems planning and development efforts . . . is not only.to court technical disaster, but to lose sight of the basically economic objectives of systems planning. . ."[2]

The second strategic decision that I believe we should make is to adopt an evolutionary approach to planning, design and implementation. The evolutionary approach stands in contrast to the strategy of designing a total blueprint for an entire MIS and then setting out to implement it. "The" evolutionary approach is not a narrowly defined way, however; there are a variety of evolutionary ways. At one extreme, closest to the one-time blueprint, is the decision to *evolve towards a highly specified objective*. That is, the designer really knows exactly where he wants to go. He is not sure, however, how to get there. In this "how" sense, the strategy is evolutionary; but the evolutionary approach in the example is limited to the techniques of implementation. At the other extreme of evolutionary approaches is accidental evolution—haphazard, sprawling growth.

Evolutionary planning

We want evolutionary perspectives, but we want neither of the extremes. As for evolving towards a given specification, modern organizations are too varied and too complex for designers to understand except over a long learning, living, period. For most of us, the planning process must be concurrent with the implementation process. Plans for the future made in the past must be sharply modified by the lessons of experience. Planning must be constantly updated. Planning for information systems for an organization with a wide scope of activities can only be iterative. Planning and learning go hand-in-hand. Indeed, the planning *methodology* is itself evolutionary. That is, we learn how to plan as well as what to plan. As for the extreme of accidental evolution—well, we certainly do not want to end up with an unmanageable hodgepodge of duplicating applications that not only waste resources but that, perhaps more significantly, waste the large opportunity that continuous study of the organization and its problems will surely reveal.

We should stand in the middle, then, not because of the ease of "muddling through" but rather because we believe that both extremes are wide of the mark. We want to know where we are going, but we honestly must recognize that the further ahead we try to look, the less sharp the focus.

To "know" where we are going, we must consciously decide where to go and how to get there. We must establish a long range plan and we must keep that plan up to date. Long range planning of a large-scale information system, however, is a formidable task; it should itself be systematic. There are enormous pragmatic problems in systematic planning. One must begin with an ideal planning system and then—in the

same evolutionary spirit that should dominate MIS design and development—shape the planning methodology to fit living realities. In my present view, an "ideal" planning system for MIS embraces the following steps:

1. Working closely with management, line, and staff people of the organization at large, identify—in terms of management and user needs and apsirations—the broad missions of the MIS effort and the specific objectives whose achievement will fulfill the missions. (N.B. Great effort should be made to encourage management, line, and staff people throughout the organization to participate as actively as possible in the entire planning process. Their ideas at many points are likely to be more valuable than those generated by systems technical experts. The real planning roles of the expert are (a) to bring discipline, structure and articulation to user expressions of problems, needs, and objectives and (b) to provide for reasonable consideration of technological potentials and problems.)

2. Map the framework structure of (a) the external systems that affect and are affected by the organization and (b) the internal systems—present and potential—that comprise the organization.[3]

3. Delineate as fully as possible the purposes, structures, contents, and interrelationships of the management information systems, distinguishing between present and potential systems.

4. Identify those current systems and applications that are working reasonably well, in the understanding that they will enter subsequent phases of the planning process only in connection with relationships to possible systems development efforts.

5. Identify those *current* systems and applications for which highly preliminary priority considerations (rough cuts through step 8 below) suggest that either thoroughly revised implementation or substantially improved implementation is desirable.

6. Identify those *potential* systems and applications for which highly preliminary priority considerations (rough cuts through step 8 below) suggest that initial implementation is desirable.

7. Consider alternative approaches to developing, and alternative ways of operating, the various identified opportunities for current and potential systems and applications.

8. Perform a critical priority analysis of the set of grossly screened possible projects in order that we may be as sensible as we can in deciding what to do, how to do it, and when to do it.
   a. Process of Analysis
     (1) Describe the expected direct and indirect

[2]Sherman C. Blumenthal, **Management Information Systems,** Prentice-Hall, Inc., 1969, page 89.

[3]At the AEC Headquarters, we began with the ESSO framework mentioned above, and it turned out to be a most helpful starting place. Each organization has its own character and its own circumstances, however, and we believe that we shall need to modify the ESSO framework to fit our situation. Mr. W. R. Mitchell, who is in charge of our Financial Information System Development Group, has, for example, proposed that we need to recognize a class of systems called "Indexes and References." Within this class would be, for example, a classified document control system. Such a system fits none of the ESSO classes very neatly, reflecting the relative importance of the class to the two very different organizations. It should be emphasized that I make this comparison not to criticize the ESSO approach—hardly that, for without it we would have had to reinvent a costly wheel—but rather to emphasize the need for MIS and computer applications generally to be shaped to the local and particular situation. Whenever possible, of course, adaptions to existing models like the ESSO model should be preferred to reinvention. We all should avoid the near-fatal NIH disease (not invented here).

benefits of each alternative.

(2) State the grounds for the expectations.

(3) Evaluate the merits of each alternative.

(4) Estimate the resources needed for development, conversion, and operation of each alternative, including resource commitments of users as well as developers and operators.

(5) State the grounds for the estimates.

(6) Measure the costs of the resources.

(7) Allow for the influence of undesirable side effects on the merits of each alternative.

(8) Choose the alternatives that appear to yield the greatest net value from the investment of resources.

b. Criteria for Evaluating the Merits of Alternative Projects[4]

(*Note:* All criteria are constrained by certain influences. For example, no matter how high a potential payoff, there is a limit to the scope of any project, owing to absolute limits on possible expenditures.)

(1) Explicit dollar estimates of the (discounted) value of returns where feasible, like clerical savings (which are not the major goal of the MIS).

(2) Qualitative factors (like the value of faster information where it is needed—a real value exists even if we cannot put dollar figures down).

(3) Institutional factors (like a "fair" sharing of total MIS resources among divisions and other entities of the organization).

(4) Systems management factors (like the probability of success).

(5) Systems technical factors (like implementing "adjacent" applications sequentially).

9. Prepare a five-year proposed implementation and operating plan.

a. Show for each priority project:

(1) the purposes to be served and the implications of implementation—and of delay in implementation,

(2) the justification revealed by the priority analysis, and

(3) broad plans for development, conversion, and operation including resource requirements and schedules.

b. Specify and justify nonproject resource requirements

(1) Management and administration.

(2) Planning.

(3) Resource development.

(4) Standards.

(5) Production operations.

10. Present the proposed plan to management for approval, in the context of missions, objectives, and the framework of systems.

11. Continuously review, test, and refresh the statement of missions and objectives of the MIS effort, and the contents of the priority analysis.

12. Each year recycle

a. mapping of the framework structure of systems,

b. delineating possible management information systems,

[4]A detailed analysis of criteria for project selection appears in the author's "Computer Project Selection in the Business Enterprise," **Journal of Accountancy,** April 1969 and **Datamation,** June 1969.

c. identifying desirable tasks and approaches,

d. performing a priority analysis,

e. improving upon and extending the five-year plan another year, and

f. presenting the five-year plan to management.

Summary

Running through the planning-executing-learning-planning cycle annually is, in my opinion, the heart of the fulfillment of an evolutionary strategy for MIS. The need for interaction with managers and users can hardly be overemphasized. The whole planning-development process should be done in concert with management, line, and staff persons throughout the organization.

Indeed, stimulating effective user involvement creates major challenges for the systems architect. Achieving balance is very hard. At one extreme are the overly dynamic users—applications tweakers—who would never permit any really solid accomplishment to be attained. We know them in all walks of life. At the other extreme are potential users who doggedly turn their backs and dig in their heels. Planning and implementing for either of these extremes is impossible. There is a wide range of responsive, responsible users, however, who—when coupled to responsive, responsible systems developers—not only permit and support but in fact share massively in planning and implementing. In these circumstances, genuine planning is feasible and rewarding.

The systematic approach to planning that I have laid out is clearly a difficult affair. Translating project benefits into comparable value terms is particularly difficult, and while theoretically appealing is in practice a most elusive task. There is no easy way to perform a conscientious priority analysis and this means that there is no easy way to determine how to be as sensible as we can in deciding what to do, how to do it, and when to do it. The system presented must be reckoned, therefore, as an ideal towards which one strives. In the end, its most imperative requirement is give and take among the three parties mostly concerned: management, users, and systems developers. ∎

Mr. Schwartz is assistant controller for Information systems with the Atomic Energy Commission. Previously he was with the First National City Bank of New York following 18 years with the Federal Reserve System, initially as an economist, then as a computer specialist. His degree is in economics from the University of Illinois. He has written about a wide variety of EDP topics and is vice president and founding co-chairman of the new Society for Management Information Systems.

Cyrus F. Gibson and Richard L. Nolan   Davis Chapter 14

"MANAGING THE FOUR STAGES OF EDP GROWTH"

Harvard Business Review (52:1), 1974 January-February, pages 76-88.

Nolan has had a continuing research effort to explain organizational responses to the introduction of computer data processing. His early research concentrated on computer department expenditure patterns beginning when organizations introduced computers and continuing through time as usage and sophistication increased. The expenditure pattern over time has an S-shaped appearance similar to a growth curve or to a learning curve. The current article summarizes the research results to date and ties these to organizational behavior. This explanation is assisted by Gibson, a professor in organizational behavior.

The stage hypothesis is still unproved, but there is evidence which supports the Nolan thesis that organizational response to the use of computers (in terms of expenditures, management, applications, etc.) goes through at least four stages. If true, the hypothesis is useful for organizational management and for information system personnel in understanding the current status of their organization and the likely course of future developments. Such understanding can be useful in evaluating and controlling the growth of EDP in the organization.

READING SUGGESTIONS

There are four stages of growth which are termed:
1. Initiation
2. Expansion (and contagion)
3. Formalization (and control)
4. Maturity (and integration)

The four stages are described in terms of three different measures of the growth. These three measures are reflected in Exhibits I, II, and III.
1. Growth of applications
2. Growth of personnel specialization
3. Changes in techniques for management of EDP

The three exhibits are essentially a summary of the stage hypothesis. Study them before reading the remainder of the article. While reading, keep in mind that there are three measures for each stage in the growth of EDP. In other words, stage 1 is described in terms of typical applications, personnel specialization, and management techniques for control. Stage 2 and stage 3 are similarly explained.

A major idea in the article is that management control practices are different (and need to be different) at the different stages of growth. In stage 1, the major decision is to assign departmental responsibility for the computer. The organizational problem of stage 2 is to acquire or develop middle-management skills and to acquire diverse computer personnel. In stage 3, there is a need for establishing control over the computer resource through such mechanisms as centralization, a steering committee, and system analysts made part of functional or user areas. The last stage is characterized by integration of the EDP resource into the organization. There is emphasis on user participation in design and ongoing review.

QUESTIONS

1. Name the four stages of EDP growth.
2. Describe the changes in types of applications as an organization goes through the four stages of growth.
3. In stage 1, there are operators, programmers, and analysts. How do the personnel job requirements change over the stages of growth?
4. How do the following change for the four stages?
   a. Type of management
   b. Organization of EDP
   c. Type of controls for projects and operations
   d. Type of budgetary control
5. What are some of the dynamics which create the explosive growth of stage 2?
6. What causes the change from informal control to formalized control mechanisms?
7. What three steps are proposed in order to establish necessary control in stage 3?
8. How does the MIS department work with users in stage 4?
9. What new technological development is likely to initiate another S-shaped growth curve emerging from the maturing of hardware technology in an organization?

Cyrus F. Gibson and Richard L. Nolan

Managing the four stages of EDP growth

*Running a new business is a different task
from running a middle-aged one or an old one;
the same is true of the EDP department*

In all that has been said about the computer in business, there are few clues as to how the EDP department ought to grow or what management ought to be doing about the department at each stage of its growth. Here is a convenient categorization for placing the life crises of the EDP department in perspective, for developing the management techniques necessary or useful at various points, and for managing the human issues involved. These human issues, as a matter of fact, complicate the problems of growth at least as much as the hardware and software questions, which have been so well massaged in the literature; the authors show how these issues change shape as a company moves through the four stages of development. This article will be particularly helpful to the new

business that is about to buy its first computer. For the company in the throes of later-stage development, it offers a framework useful for identifying issues and evaluating and controlling the growth of EDP.

Mr. Gibson is assistant professor of business administration at the Harvard Business School, where he teaches in the organizational behavior area. He has done research and consulted extensively on problems of computer-resource management within organizations. Mr. Nolan is associate professor of business administration at the Harvard Business School and the author or coauthor of several recent HBR articles on information management. The work on which the following article is based was funded in part by the Division of Research of the school.

From the viewpoint of the executive vice president, "The EDP manager always waffles around when he has to explain his budget." From the viewpoint of the EDP manager, "The executive vice president never seems to understand why this department needs a lot of money."

The reason for this kind of impasse is clear enough: EDP, as corporations use it today, is so complex that controlling it, or even understanding it, is almost too difficult for words. However, through our work with a number of companies, we have reached certain conclusions about how EDP departments grow and how they should fit into the company's organization. These conclu-

sions offer a framework for communication for both the EDP manager and the senior managers to whom he reports.

There are four distinct stages in the growth of all EDP facilities, each with its distinctive applications, its rewards and its traumata, and its managerial problems. By breaking the evolution of the EDP department into four easy stages, it is possible to sort out the affairs of the department, if not into four neat, sequential packages, at least into four relatively small, sequential cans of worms.

The basis for this framework of stages is the recent discovery that the EDP budget for a num-

Exhibit I. Growth of applications

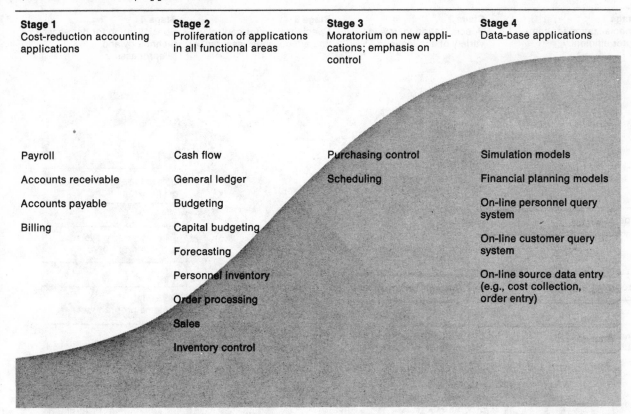

Stage 1 Cost-reduction accounting applications	Stage 2 Proliferation of applications in all functional areas	Stage 3 Moratorium on new applications; emphasis on control	Stage 4 Data-base applications
Payroll	Cash flow	Purchasing control	Simulation models
Accounts receivable	General ledger	Scheduling	Financial planning models
Accounts payable	Budgeting		On-line personnel query system
Billing	Capital budgeting		On-line customer query system
	Forecasting		On-line source data entry (e.g., cost collection, order entry)
	Personnel inventory		
	Order processing		
	Sales		
	Inventory control		

ber of companies, when plotted over time from initial investment to mature operation, forms an S-shaped curve.[1] This is the curve that appears in the exhibits accompanying this article. The turnings of this curve correspond to the main events—often crises—in the life of the EDP function that signal important shifts in the way the computer resource is used and managed. There are three such turnings, and, consequently, four stages.

In the companies we know, there are remarkable similarities in the problems which arise and the management techniques applied to solve them at a given stage, despite variations among industries and companies, and despite ways in which EDP installations are used. Moreover, associated with each stage is a distinctive, informal organizational process. Each of these seems to play an important role in giving rise to the issues which need to be resolved if the stage is to be passed without a crisis and if the growth of the resource is to be managed to yield maximum benefit to the company.

Our purpose here is to describe the four stages in turn, listing the key characteristics of each

and explaining the underlying organizational forces at work in each.

In the space of an article we can touch only on the main problems of EDP management at the different stages. Hence the view we present is bound to be somewhat simplified. Caution is advisable in another respect, too: history has not yet come to an end, and we are sure that the S-curve we describe and the stages it seems to follow do not represent the whole story. At the end of the S-curve of contemporary experience there will doubtless be more S-curves, as new EDP technologies emerge, and as companies become more ambitious in their use of EDP techniques and more sophisticated in systems analysis. However, we hope that the dynamics of later cost escalations will be clearer after the reader has finished with our description—clearer, and perhaps even predictable and controllable.

Four stages of growth

Three types of growth must be dealt with as an EDP department matures:

O A growth in computer applications—see *Exhibit I.*

1. Richard L. Nolan, "Managing the Computer Resource: A Stage Hypothesis," *Communications of the ACM,* July 1973, p. 399.

Exhibit II. Growth of personnel specialization

Stage 1 Specialization for computer efficiency	**Stage 2** Specialization to develop variety of applications	**Stage 3** Specialization for control and effectiveness assurance	**Stage 4** Specialization for data-base technology and teleprocessing

Operator

Programmer   Systems programmer   Computer systems programmer

Analyst   Scientific-applications programmer   Maintenance programmer

Data-base systems programmer

Teleprocessing systems programmer

Operating systems programmer

Business-applications programmer   Data-base and teleprocessing applications programmer

Systems analyst   Functional systems analyst (e.g., finance, marketing, manufacturing)   Data-base and teleprocessing systems analyst

○ A growth in the specialization of EDP personnel—see *Exhibit II*.

○ A growth in formal management techniques and organization—see *Exhibit III*.

The S-curve that overlies these three kinds of growth breaks conveniently into four segments, which represent the four stages of EDP growth: initiation, expansion, formalization, and maturity. Most notable are the proliferation of applications in Stage 2 (as reflected in *Exhibit I*) that causes the budget to increase exponentially, and the proliferation of controls in Stage 3 designed to curb this increase (as reflected in *Exhibit III*).

This sequence of stages is a useful framework for placing a company's current problems vis-à-vis EDP in perspective and helping its management understand the problems it will face as it moves forward. It is especially helpful for discussing ways to smooth out the chaotic conditions of change that have caused so many de-

railments in Stages 2 and 3. Even in our work with small companies, we have found the framework helpful—in obviating crises before they arise and in suggesting the kinds of planning that will induce smooth growth.

Thus one virtue of this framework is that it lays out for the company as a whole the nature of its task at each stage—whether it is a new company planning to buy its first computer, or a company in the throes of developing advanced applications, or a company with a steady, mature EDP facility.

Stage 1: Initiation

When the first computer is implanted in the organization, the move is normally justified in terms of cost savings. Rarely, at this point, does senior management assess the long-term impact of the computer on personnel, or on the organiza-

Exhibit III. Management techniques customarily applied in each of the four stages

	Stage 1 Lax management	Stage 2 Sales-oriented management	Stage 3 Control-oriented management	Stage 4 Resource-oriented planning and control
Organization	EDP is organized under the department of first-applications justification; it is generally a small department.	The EDP manager is moved up in the organization; systems analysts and programmers are assigned to work in the various functional areas.	EDP moves out of the functional area of first applications; a steering committee is set up; control is exerted through centralization; maintenance programming and systems programming become dominant activities.	EDP is set up as a separate functional area, the EDP manager taking on a higher-level position; some systems analysts and sometimes programmers are decentralized to user areas; high specialization appears in computer configuration and operation; systems design and programming take on a consulting role.
Control	Controls notably lacking; priorities assigned by FIFO; no chargeout.	Lax controls, intended to engender applications development; few standards; informal project control.	Proliferation of controls to contain a runaway budget; formal priority setting; budget justification. Programming controls: documentation, standards. Project management initiated; management reporting system introduced: project plan, project performance, customer service, personnel resources, equipment resources, budget performance. Chargeout introduced; postsystem audits. Quality control policies for computer system, systems design, programming, operations.	Refinement of management control system – elimination of ineffective control techniques and further development of others; introduction of data-base policies and standards; focus on pricing of computer services for engendering effective use of the computer.
Planning	Loose budget	Loose budget	Strong budgetary planning for hardware facilities and new applications.	Multiple 3-5 year plans for hardware, facilities, personnel, and new applications.

tion, or on its strategy. Thus management can easily ignore a couple of crucial issues.

The location question

In Stage 1, the priority management issue is to fix departmental responsibility for the computer:

▽ Initially it makes economic sense to locate the computer in the department where it is first applied—very frequently, in accounting—and to hold that department responsible for a smooth introduction and a sound control of costs and benefits. The costs and benefits can be clearly stated and rigidly controlled under this approach —and they usually are.

△ However, the department where the computer will first be used—accounting, say—may not be the best location for the EDP facility later on. The later and more complex applications, such as inventory control and simulation modeling, should ideally be located in an autonomous department of computer services or management information systems which reports through a high-level manager.

But granted this longer perspective, management may decide on a less rigorous application of payback criteria for judging the performance of the initial application. Costs for "future development" may not be scrutinized too closely at this stage, and budgets may expand very early under this arrangement.

Many companies resolve this issue in obvious fashion. Management simply locates the facility within the department of first application for an initial period; then, when its viability has been proved and other applications develop, management creates the autonomous EDP unit.

In practice, however, this seemingly simple resolution conceals a serious trap. The department that controls the resource becomes strongly protective of it, often because a manager or a group within it wants to build up power and influence. When the time comes for computing to assume a broader role, real conflict arises—conflict that can be costly in terms of management turnover and in terms of lingering hostilities that inhibit the provision of computer services and applications across functional areas.

Fear of the computer

Another priority issue is to minimize the disruption that results when high technology is injected into an organization. Job-displacement anxieties appear; some people become concerned over doing old jobs in new ways; and others fear a loss of personal identity with their work. These fears may lead to open employee resistance. While reactions of this kind may occur at any of the stages, they can be particularly destructive in Stage 1, where the very survival of the EDP concept is at stake.

In plain fact some of these fears are probably justified. For example, some employees (although usually relatively few) may indeed lose their jobs when the computer is first installed.

On the other hand, the concerns that develop from rumor or false information are usually overblown, and they are readily transformed and generalized into negative sentiments and attitudes toward management, as well as the computer itself. The wise course for management is to spike rumors with the most honest information it has, however the chips may fall. Such

openness will at worst localize fears and resistances that must be dealt with sooner or later anyway.

Unless management is willing to recognize the seriousness of this anxiety, it risks a more generalized reaction in the form of unresponsive and uncreative work behavior, a broader and higher level of uncertainty and anxiety, and even sabotage, as a surprising number of cases have demonstrated.

Management can make no bigger mistake than to falsely reassure all concerned that the computer will not change their work or that it will mean no less work for everyone. Such comfort blankets lead to credibility gaps that are notoriously hard to close.

Thus the key to managing this process of initiation to the computer is to accept the fact that people's perceptions of reality and their views of the situation are what have to be understood and dealt with, rather than some "objective" reality.[2] These perceptions will be diverse; management cannot assume that all organizational members are equally enthusiastic about introducing efficiency and reducing costs. Where you stand depends on where you sit and on who you are. In communicating its intention to introduce EDP, management should remember this and tailor its communications accordingly.

There will be variations from one situation and company to another in the manner and detail in which management releases information about future location and about the impact of the computer. Depending on circumstance, management directives may best be communicated downward by an outsider, by a department head, or by the new EDP manager. In settings where employees are rarely informed of management planning, it may even be wise to explain to the echelons why they are being given the explanation; again, in settings where the echelons have participated in planning, a formal presentation may be less effective than open group discussion.[3]

Stage 2: Expansion

The excess computing capacity usually acquired when a company first initiates an EDP facility, combined with the lure of broader and more advanced applications, triggers a period of rapid expansion. The EDP area "takes off" into new projects that, when listed, often seem to have been selected at random. As *Exhibits I-III* show,

2. For a related argument, see James G. March and Herbert A. Simon, *Organizations* (New York, John Wiley, 1958), Chapter 6.

3. For further discussion of this point, see Paul R. Lawrence, "How to Deal With Resistance to Change," HBR January-February 1969, p. 4.

Stage 2 represents a steady and steep rise in expenditures for hardware, software, and personnel. It is a period of contagious, unplanned growth, characterized by growing responsibilities for the EDP director, loose (usually decentralized) organization of the EDP facility, and few explicit means of setting project priorities or crystallizing plans.

It is a period, further, in which the chaotic effects of rapid development are moderated (if they are moderated at all) only by the quality and judgment of the personnel directly involved in the process. While top management may be sensitive to some of the ill effects of the computer, it tends to be attracted to and carried along with the mystique of EDP as well.

This stage often ends in crisis when top management becomes aware of the explosive growth of the activity, and its budget, and decides to rationalize and coordinate the entire organization's EDP effort. The dynamic force of expansion makes this a fairly difficult thing to do, however.

Dynamics of early success

Once Stage 1 has passed, and the management and personnel of the computer area have justified and assured their permanent place in the organization, a new psychological atmosphere appears as the users from other departments (the customers) grow in number and begin to interact with the technical EDP staff. Although some users stick to economic value in judging the utility of computer applications to their particular problems and functions, other users develop a fascination with the computer and its applications as a symbol of progressive management techniques or as a status symbol for a department or individual. This fascination breeds an enthusiasm not moderated by judgment.

For their part, the technically oriented systems analysts tend to overgeneralize from the successes they have achieved with transaction-oriented computer-based systems (e.g., order processing, payroll, accounts receivable) in Stage 2. They often feel that "now we can do anything"—in other words, that they have mastered problems of communication with users, that their expertise is solid, and that they are ready to select and deal with projects primarily on the basis of their technical and professional interest. In this heady atmosphere, criteria of economic justification and effective project implementation take a back seat.

When the users' exploding demands meet the technicians' euphoric urge to supply, in the absence of management constraint, exponential budget growth results. Overoptimism and overconfidence lead to cost overruns. And once this sharp growth has begun, rationales created in the mood of reinforced enthusiasm are used to justify the installation of additional capacity; this in turn provides the need for larger numbers of personnel and for more rationales for applying the now expanded resource to whatever new projects seem attractive to the crowd. So the spiral begins.

The spiral is fed by the fact that as the resource increases in size and ambition, it must have more specialists.[4] Indeed, even without this capacity expansion, the continuing pace of technological development in the computer industry creates a constant need for new specialist talent, especially in Stage 2 and beyond. This "technological imperative" is a driving force that has caused the growth of numerous and quite diverse professional groups of computer personnel in the industrial environment. (The reader might find it helpful to review *Exhibit II* at this point.)

Many of these personnel come into the company with a primarily professional orientation, rather than an understanding of or sympathy for the long-term needs of an organization. Like the EDP specialists already employed by the company, these people will be far more interested in tackling technically challenging problems than in worrying about computer payback. If they are allowed to pursue their interests at will, the projects potentially most valuable from the company's viewpoint may never be worked on. Moreover, the chores of program maintenance and data-base development may be neglected, sowing the seeds of costly future problems.[5]

All these factors together lead to the evolution of an informal structure among computer personnel and between computer personnel and users. The lack of clear management guidelines for project priorities, for example, often results in sympathetic wheeling and dealing between EDP systems analysts and the user groups with a preference for those projects which offer the greatest professional challenge. Without specific directives for project developments or new hardware acquisition, too, computer personnel develop expectations of a loose work environment.

4. John Dearden, "MIS Is a Mirage," HBR January-February 1972, p. 90.

5. Richard L. Nolan, "Computer Data Bases: The Future Is Now," HBR September-October 1973, p. 98.

Some of the users, at the other end of the string, are easily enmeshed in impractical, pie-in-the-sky projects.

For short periods such an environment may be highly motivating for some, but, as we need hardly point out again, the other side of the coin is a rapidly growing budget—and a number of vocal and dissatisfied users.

In view of these informal dynamics and structures, what can management do to make this period one of controlled growth? How can control be introduced that will head off the impending crisis and dramatic cutbacks characteristic of such situations but at the same time not choke off experimentation with the resource and not turn off the motivation of specialists?

Here it is useful to compare the lists of management techniques shown for Stages 2 and 3 in *Exhibit III*. For the most part, the problems that arise toward the end of Stage 2 can be greatly alleviated by introducing right at the start of Stage 2 the techniques that companies ordinarily use in Stage 3.[6] Before carrying out this step, however, attention should be given to two other important strategies: acquiring necessary middle-management skills and improving the company's procedures for hiring computer personnel.

Acquiring managers

The main key to successful management in this stage is acquiring or developing middle managers for EDP who recognize the need for priorities and criteria in project selection and who have strong administrative skills: the ability to prepare plans and stick to budgets, the ability to seek out significant projects from users who may not be demanding attention, and, generally, the ability to manage projects.

Finding such managers more often than not means going outside the company, especially since most potential middle managers among systems analysts are usually caught up in the computer growth spiral. However, where it is possible, selection from within, particularly from the ranks of systems analysts, can serve the important function of indicating that career paths exist to management ranks. This can show computer technicians and technical experts that there are career rewards for those who balance organizational needs with professional interests.

6. For an approach to introducing these steps in either Stage 2 or Stage 3, see F. Warren McFarlan, "Management Audit of the EDP Department," HBR May-June 1973, p. 131.

Once those at the general-management level have determined that the time has come to institute such "human controls," the EDP manager must be brought to recognize the need for them (if, indeed, he does not recognize that need already) and the fact that he has the countenance and support of top management.

For his part, the EDP manager himself must resist the tempting pressures to see his resource grow faster than is reasonable. He has a delicate and important selling job to do in communicating this to other department managers who want his services. Once he is shored up with competent subordinate managers he will be free to carry out this role.

Finally, in addition to applying administrative controls, management needs to assess continually the climate of the informal forces at work and plan growth with that assessment in mind. The formal organization of middle managers in the EDP department makes such planning, and its implementation, viable.

Acquiring diverse personnel

Senior management must also recognize the increasing specialization of personnel within the computer department:

☐ At one extreme are the highly skilled and creative professionals, such as computer systems programmers. Their motivation and interest are oriented to the technology with which they work; they have relatively little interest in organizational rewards. Their satisfaction and best performance may be assured by isolating them organizationally, to some degree.

☐ At the other extreme are the analysts who work closely with functional departments of the company. These people may be expert in particular fields relevant to only a few industries or companies, performing tasks that require close interaction with both users and programmers. Their interests and value to the company can coincide when they perceive that career-path opportunities into general management are open to them.

☐ There are also the operators with important but relatively low-level skills and training, with some capabilities for organizational advancement, and with relatively little direct interdependence with others.

To organize and control these diverse specialists requires decisions based on one basic trade-off: *balancing professional advancement of special-*

ists against the need for organizational performance.

To cater to specialist professionals, for example, a company might isolate them in a separate department, imposing few organizational checks and gearing quality control to individual judgment or peer review. Such an arrangement might motivate a systems analyst to become the world's best systems analyst.

Emphasis on organizational values, in contrast, suggests that the company locate and control the specialists in such a way as to increase the chances that short-run goals will actually be achieved on schedule. This strategy risks obsolescence or turnover among specialists, but it successfully conveys the important message that some specialists' skills can advance a management career.

However, in the early stages management is well advised to avoid the issue entirely: the highly sophisticated professional should not be hired until his expertise is clearly required. Moreover, at the time of hiring, the specialist's expectations for freedom and professional development should be explicitly discussed in the context of organizational structure and controls (these controls include those administered by the middle level of EDP management), as part of the "psychological contract." [7]

Such discussion can go a long way toward avoiding misunderstanding during the period of rapid growth of computer applications. In effect, making clear the terms of the psychological contract is an example of the management of expectations. In this instance, it is one of the means that can be employed to introduce the organization, controls, and planning procedures that are needed to head off the crisis atmosphere of Stage 3.

Stage 3: Formalization

Let us assume that Stages 1 and 2 have run their bumpy courses without too much direct attention from top management. More likely than not, top management becomes aware of the runaway computer budget suddenly, and it begins a crash effort to find out what is going on. Its typical question at this point is, "How can we be sure that we can afford this EDP effort?"

Top management frequently concludes that the only way to get control of the resource is through drastic measures, even if this means replacing many systems analysts and other val-

uable technical personnel who will choose to leave rather than work under the stringent controls that are imposed during the stage. Firing the old EDP manager is by no means an unusual step. [8]

From the perspective of computer personnel who have lived through the periods of initial acceptance and growth, but who have not developed a sense of the fit of the computer resource within company functions and objectives, the changes top management introduces at this time may seem radical indeed. Often what was a decentralized function and facility is rather suddenly centralized for better control. Often informal planning suddenly gives way to formal planning, perhaps arbitrarily. This stage frequently includes the first formalization of management reporting systems for computer operation, a new chargeout system, and the establishment of elaborate and cumbrous quality-control measures (again, see *Exhibit III*).

In short, action taken to deal with the crisis often goes beyond what is needed, and the pendulum may swing too far. In response, some computer personnel may leave. What may be worse, most will "hunker down"—withdrawing from innovative applications work, attending to short-term goals, and following the new control systems and plans to the letter. All of this can occur at the expense of full resource utilization in the long run.

In addition, there is a parallel development that dovetails with the budget crisis to reinforce the overcontrol syndrome. Studies of computer usage show that the machines are first applied to projects that reduce general and administrative expenses—typically, replacement of clerical personnel in such tasks as accounting. Next come projects that reduce cost of goods, such as inventory control systems. The crisis atmosphere of Stage 3 roughly coincides with completion of these first two types of applications.

At this juncture the applications that have real potential for increasing revenues and profits and facilitating managerial decision making are still untouched. Financial-planning models and on-line customer service systems are two examples of such applications.

As senior management ponders the problems of Stage 3, it tends to associate the applications of the earlier stages with preexisting manu-

7. Harry Levinson et al., *Men, Management and Mental Health* (Cambridge, Harvard University Press, 1962).

8. See Richard L. Nolan, "Plight of the EDP Manager," HBR May-June 1973, p. 143.

al systems and straightforward cost-justification and control. In contrast, it finds projected applications for revenue-producing and decision-making projects hard to envision and define. The natural tendency is to assume that these projects will call for a faster, higher spiral of risk and cost. Thus senior management tends to introduce inappropriately strong controls that are designed, consciously or unconsciously, to put a stop to growth. This clearly may be too strong a reaction for the company's good.

Three sound steps

In general, three control steps that are appropriate and not unduly restrictive are available for most large EDP facilities in Stage 3. First, certain of the more established and less complex operations and hardware can be centralized. Second, the increasing impacts of computer applications can be flagged and defined for the top by introducing overseer and resource-allocation mechanisms at the general-management level. Third, some parts of the systems analysis function can be decentralized and other parts centralized, depending on where the systems work can best be done (we shall say more about this shortly).[9] Of course, this final step requires that the decentralized systems work be coordinated through a formal integrative mechanism.

But the real problem in Stage 3 is not what steps to take; it is how to take them. Management here is introducing change into a web of informal relationships and expectations. *How* the changes are managed is as important as *what* the changes should be, but more difficult to define.

That is, although there are few formal controls in the first two stages, the *informal* social structures and norms that have grown up by Stage 3 are very much a reality to the personnel involved. While it may appear that systems are replacing no systems, this will not be true:

◊ Lacking guidelines for project selection, systems analysts will have projected their own sets of priorities, either individually, as a group within the company, or as members of their profession.

◊ They will have created criteria and standards, although these will not ordinarily have been written down or otherwise articulated for higher levels of management.

◊ Without project management guidelines, systems analysts and users will have developed their own rules and procedures for dealing with each other.

On the whole, the stronger these informal controls and structures are (and the weaker the formal controls and structures are, the stronger they will be), the more resistant the personnel will be to change and the more chaotic and traumatic the introduction of formal systems will be.

In managing changes as pervasive as these there is probably nothing worse than doing the job halfway. Doing nothing at all is disaster, of course; but management action that is undertaken on a crash basis—without enough attention to execution and second- and third-order consequences—will sharpen, not resolve, the crisis.

For example, management cannot afford to be either squeamish or precipitous in making personnel changes. Trying to introduce needed formalization of controls with the same personnel and the same organizational structure more often than not encourages conflict and the reinforcement of resistance rather than a resolution of the crisis; by refusing to fire or to enforce layoffs, senior management may simply prolong the crisis, create further dissension, and further demoralize personnel. On the other hand, management must be sure that it retains the experienced personnel who have the potential to function well in the mature stages of the operation—it may not always be obvious who these people are or what their future roles will be.

Thus, although the crisis of Stage 3 calls for action, it first calls for analysis and planning—planning that sets forth clear and explicit objectives for exploitation of the computer resource vis-à-vis the user departments.[10] Such a plan, once it is developed and understood, can turn anarchy back into evolution, while at the same time avoiding the kind of overkill control that results in underutilization and underrealization of the potential of the resource. Here are our suggestions for general plan direction.

1. Reposition the established components of the resource.

Whether or not EDP has been carefully managed in the past, most companies need to centralize some parts and decentralize other parts of the computer resource at about this point.

9. See the section which discusses the McKinsey study on effective users, in F. Warren McFarlan, "Problems in Planning the Information System," HBR March-April 1971, p. 78.

10. For mechanisms for improving the interface between EDP and users, see John Dearden and Richard L. Nolan, "How to Control the Computer Resource," HBR November-December 1973, p. 68.

Chris Argyris   Davis Chapter 15

"RESISTANCE TO RATIONAL MANAGEMENT SYSTEMS"

<u>Innovation</u>, 1970, Number 10, pages 28-35.

Resistance to MIS is a very prevalent phenomenon among managers. Based on his experience, Argyris provides a thoughtful analysis of this phenomenon, exploring its root causes, and drawing out five areas of MIS impact on managers. Although the article provides few prescriptions for the ills described, it does provide some useful insights.

Rationality is a universal pursuit of men and managers. Providing information and decision support to a manager through an MIS yields greater rationality. However, rather than welcomed as helpers, MIS professionals and their systems are often rejected. Argyris believes that MIS professionals have a sense of mission and genuinely believe that the only way to achieve effective management in complex organizations is through the expanded and deeped rationality available from sophisticated information systems. Theoretically, all valid knowledge is good, but when it reveals a maze of coverups, elaborate fictions, incompetence, missed opportunities, and mistrust, it is no wonder that MIS is considered such a threat and that we face the irony of irrational resistance to potentially rational processes. Resistance may also appear when managers begin to realize that the impact of MIS will eventually require fundamental changes in their personal styles of managerial thought and behavior. After presenting a picture of impending chaos in organizational life, Argyris discusses five areas of impact of MIS.

1. Middle managers will experience a greater restriction of their space of free movement, resulting in feelings of lack of choice, pressure, and psychological failure, turning to helplessness and decreased feelings of responsibility.

2. When the MIS sets goals for managers and makes their decisions, the manager feels psychologically unneeded if he follows the new rationality.

3. MIS emphasizes the use of valid information and technical competence to manage organizations rather than formal power which gets things done by simply giving orders.

4. MIS reduces the need for organizational politics between departments. The view of competing departments building up protective walls gives way to a view of interrelated activities that have to be meshed into a coordinated whole.

5. The use of intuition and experience to fill in the blanks for decision making will decrease because MIS requires managers with higher levels of intellectual and conceptual competence. They must be able to deal with interrelationships among the facts.

READING SUGGESTIONS

Read the first part quickly to get an impression of the nature of the problem of resistance to MIS and some of the causes suggested by Argyris. Then read to identify and understand the five areas of impact of MIS as summarized above. As you read, think about whether or not you agree with Argyris as he discusses each impact.

QUESTIONS

1. Identify three causes of resistance to MIS.
2. How does Argyris implicitly define MIS?
3. What is the consequence of withholding upsetting information from top management?
4. What are the human implications of developing an MIS to feed back data on the performance of a manager to the manager's boss before the data gets to the manager?
5. Why do managers and employees build elaborate defenses to hide the truth of their adaptations from the next higher level of management?
6. Give your own analysis and evaluation of the validity of each of the five areas of MIS impact discussed by Argyris.

Resistance To Rational Management Systems

Be more rational? Sure. Get a better feel for the future? Absolutely. Cooperate with the computer? Okay. Only keep that damn machine out of my operation! Follow along as • Chris Argyris • considers the natural history of resistance to rationality, in this case MIS (management information system), from his experience as management consultant and professor of administrative sciences at Yale.

Rationality is one of the highest order goals in civilization. To be sensible, to use the power of reason, to avoid emotionalism in making decisions—civilized people honor and value these characteristics and often strive to attain them. To be rational is to be good.

We have even created our organizations with rationality in mind: If every man behaves reasonably and sensibly, then bureaucratic structures (our dominant form of organization) can achieve their goals. Of course, for organizational managers and executives to conduct their affairs rationally, they also need to know a lot of things. In American industry, for example, management requires a virtual torrent of information about its own operations, plus knowledge of its market environment, those hard-to-control forces operating beyond its doors.

"If only we could cut the guesswork out of this decision. . . . . If only we had more information. . . . If only we could shape up Department X. . . . If only we knew the consequences of this new policy. . . ." Information, insight, foresight, in a word—rationality; with these we could do anything. We all go through this "if only" fantasy in our work (and personal) lives. Because we all go through the fantasy, technicians constantly develop new methodologies and technologies in the pursuit of rationality—operations research, PPBS, and computer models are only recent examples.

Because we all experience the fantasy, then obviously new systems that provide more information, more accurate models of the world we live in—in short, more rational ways of choosing our next steps—are welcomed enthusiastically. People who can make such things happen are universally acclaimed, adopted as blood brothers, given succor, comfort, and honor. So you might think. . . .

Unfortunately, the opposite usually happens. I've seen it over and over again. New developments for rational decision making often produce intense resentment in men who ordinarily view themselves as realistic, flexible, definitely rational. Managers and executives who place a premium on rationality, and work hard to subdue emotionality, become resistant and combative in the back-alley ways of bureaucratic politics when such new technologies are introduced.

These reactions sound paradoxical. Yet they stem from ingrained, almost unconscious processes in American organizational life. Waves of fear, insecurity, and tenacious resistance arise unbidden from the bowels of the organization. Strange but true.

It's also understandable in human terms. It does not happen because men are stupid. It happens because of their long and successful education in organizational survival, where they learn deceit, manipulation, rivalry, and mistrust—qualities endemic to our present organizational structures.

Professionals in the field of information sciences genuinely believe that work-life has become so complicated that the only way to achieve effective management is through the expanded and deepened rationality available from sophisticated information systems. These men have a sense of mission, expressed by one man I met recently in a multibillion-dollar corporation: "We want to unfreeze this colossus and push it into the twenty-first century."

A major assumption of information scientists is that if "real life" situations can be adequately modeled (with valid inputs to a computer model) then action will be more effective. To put it another way: more and more of the complex decisions of life can be influenced by rational thought.

I'm not a computer or information specialist. So my description of a sophisticated management information system (MIS) comes from experts in that field. It's the creation and anaylsis of data in such a way that a person can have it immediately available for his ongoing decision making. Not routine decisions. But important, critical, innovative decisions.

Decision makers can get overwhelmed by too much information. Overloads occur regularly. The beauty of a management information sysem (MIS from now on) is that with it one man can identify relevant patterns in two hours instead of a group taking up to two months.

These kinds of systems are still new. But they can be fully workable in the next twenty-five years. Even today it's not difficult to program the entire Swedish economy; who would have dreamed of that twenty-five years ago?

In the last three years, I have been working on some intellectual questions raised by these possibilites. For example, is it possible to bring information to our society in such a way as to make our society more effective? In this context, my definition of "effective" is: giving more people the opportunity for free and informed choice as well as personal commitment to that choice.

Things are not as simple and hopeful as they once seemed to me. In the university, we generally assume that all valid knowledge is good. What I'm finding as I study the impact of information systems on organizations is that some valid knowledge is considered bad—bad because it is threatening.

In many companies, valid data on important problems would reveal a maze of cover-ups, elaborate fictions, incompetence, missed opportunities, and distrust. All these things can impede an organization from reaching its goals, or even keep it from rationally defining its goals. Valid data for an MIS would reveal to many managements how much has been hidden from it all these years.

No wonder, then, that MIS seems such a threat and that we face the irony of irrational resistance to potentially rational processes.

With regard to MIS, there does exist some valid basis for resistance, or at least skepticism. Many executives agree that increased rationality is a worthwhile goal. But they express opposition in terms of two specific issues: 1) they don't understand the new information technology, and 2) they don't believe it's wise to use such technology when it still hasn't proved itself.

These are acceptable, albeit temporary objections.

But I believe there is a deeper reason for executive resistance. It's rarely discussed because executives themselves are rarely aware of it. This basic, unspoken reason usually surfaces after lengthy discussion about the *probable* long-range effects of MIS.

At this point managers slowly begin to realize that fundamental changes will be required in their personal styles of

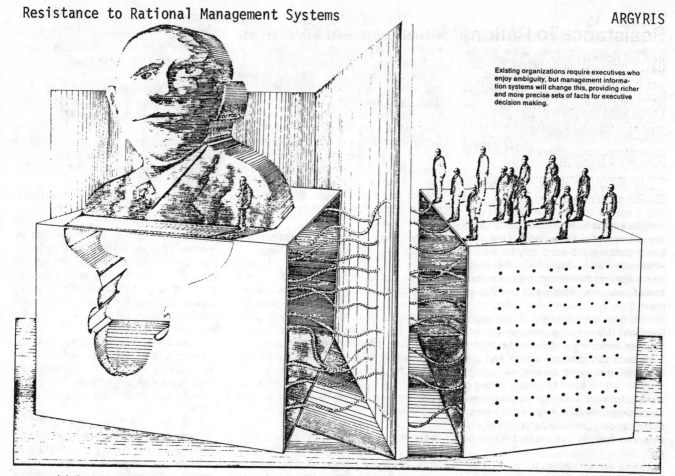

Existing organizations require executives who enjoy ambiguity, but management information systems will change this, providing richer and more precise sets of facts for executive decision making.

managerial thought and behavior. That's when the danger signals start.

Those other stated objections—lack of knowledge and the primitive state of the art—are important, but only temporary. Eventually they will be overcome by research and dissemination of knowledge. But concern and fear about what MIS will do to managers—what it will reveal about the way they've been operating all this time—is what creates the basic resistance.

Naturally, this is not easily admitted or spoken about. However, to make sense of this emotional block to rationality, to see both the human potentials and the human problems in MIS and other rational technologies we should face the issue squarely.

To understand this we have to think about the nature of organizations and about the ways men invent to carry out their own work. For the crux of the problem is there, in the lessons men learn along the paths to institutional power and security.

By far the most dominant organizational design used today is the pyramidal structure: Authority resides at the top; commands travel down through an ever-widening succession of levels to the bottom. The most fundamental property of the pyra-midal structure is its intended rationality; within respectable tolerances, men will presumably behave rationally. In other words, men will behave the way the design requires them to behave; they will do what the organization wants them to do. Or so the planners hope.

The personal effects of being in such an organization are central to the issues under consideration here. Three aspects of the pyramidal bureaucracy are especially crucial:

► specialization of work,
► a rigid chain of command,
► unity of direction.

This combination tends to make employees, especially lower-level workers, dependent upon and submissive to their superiors. They also experience very short time perspectives (get today's work done; don't think about tomorrow) and little sense of responsibility about their work. Employees who prefer some degree of challenge and to have some control over their work situations are not satisfied. They become frustrated. They experience a sense of psychological failure.

They can adapt to the frustration and failure, all right, but in such forms as apathy, indifference, slowdowns, goldbricking, creation of unions, absenteeism and high turnover.

At the upper levels, the pyramidal design has different impacts. To run well, it requires executives who need to direct, control, reward, and penalize others and, most importantly, requires men who need to suppress their own and others' emotionality. In this system there is much more conformity, mistrust, antagonism, defensiveness, and closedness than there is individuality, trust, concern and openness.

Just because things are that way doesn't mean executives like it. But they too adapt and continue to operate in such an atmosphere. And all along the line people build elaborate defenses to hide the truth of their adaptations from the next higher level, all the way to the top. The ignorance of the men at the top concerning the operations and state of health of their own organizations has been extensively covered in recent years.

Among the hidden truths, at the lower levels, are the sanctions workers develop against producing according to individual ability (while management experts blithely continue to design special incentive systems); against too much personal involvement in one's work; and against informing management of all the shortcuts employees discover or design to make their work easier.

247

At the upper levels, subordinates tend to "think positive" (remain within the tolerance limits arbitrarily set at the top); they react primarily to crises; they tend to create win-lose competitions between groups for resources and esteem; they hide information; and they create "just-in-case-the-president-asks" files.

Let's look at a few specific examples.

First the JIC ("just-in-case") file. In government, incidentally, it's known as the CYA ("cover-your-ass") file. This file documents a department's positions on various issues and policies. Most of the position papers are intended only for the file—they are rarely circulated. The documents state for the record, if the president should ever ask, what steps *our* department took to prevent *their* department from taking the company in the wrong direction. If something goes wrong, and the president starts to inquire, the department head can produce a copy and say, "We saw that crisis coming six months ago" or "We've been keeping a record of how Department X goofed." In most cases the original is never even sent to the president; why stir up trouble before it's necessary, and besides, Department X may be right.

There are variations, aimed at hiding the truth but not completely. In one company, a blistering six-page memo on policy was sent up through channels. At the level just below the general manager, people decided he would raise too much hell if he saw the memo and started asking tough questions. But they couldn't ignore it either. So they summarized the memo in one paragraph of a yearly report. Instead of saying "We're in big trouble," with six pages of documentation, the paragraph merely reported, "There might be some difficulty in the next year or two, but the difficulties are not insurmountable." When the general manager read it, he assumed someone had control of the situation.

He was wrong. Two years later, when I happened to be at their meeting, the trouble had erupted and the general manager was seething: "Why didn't someone tell me about this?" The author of the original memo replied, "We sent you a six-page memo on it two years ago." The general manager then exploded at the people from the intervening level: "Did you ever get that memo?" "We did," they stated, "but you kept telling us you were too busy to read long reports and we should compress things for you. All right, so we compressed it. Who are you going to nail for that?" Members of an organization can protect themselves with such tactics, but by hiding "illegal" activities they put themselves in a psychological bind. On the one hand, they know such behavior is administratively wrong; on the other hand, they honestly believe that survival is not possible without it. Upper-level executives can adapt even to this bind. They insist it's realistic and mature "not to make waves," to withhold upsetting information, to accept mistrust and destructive competition as part of unchangeable human nature. When management acts on these assumptions, their original pessimistic realism about "human nature" becomes a self-fulfilling prophecy.

What specific kinds of adaptations do workers use further down the line?

Lower-level employees realize that if they really get involved in the meaninglessness of their work, they might literally go mad. So then tend to become apathetic and uninvolved. This strategy reduces their capacity to care for themselves as human beings. They develop what Erich Fromm has called the market orientation. They now care more about how much they are worth in salary than the intrinsic value of what they are doing.

A young man can start working on an assembly line with a rather high degree of commitment. But he learns very soon that if he maintained that commitment, he could go mad. So he begins to withdraw psychologically. And as he withdraws certain things begin to happen: He no longer cares about the quality of the work as he used to; he also begins to see himself as a less responsible human being.

But how do you live with yourself if you see yourself as growing less responsible? One way is to say, "It's not so bad; we've got inspectors who'll catch things if they're really bad." Or, "There's a five-year guarantee and the customer can always bring it back."

I remember reading the diaries of two Detroit ministers who went to work on an assembly line just to see what it was like for their parishioners. It's fascinating to read their notes, "Well, today I've begun. Not only did I swear at the damned cars, but I put in the batteries incorrectly. I knew it was morally wrong. Yet I felt good about it."

These ministers took on the psychology of the workers even though they had no intention of remaining. Just imagine if you had to remain. The worker says, "I have to do this because everybody else does it; it's foolish not to." Eventually he sounds even worse than a top-line executive who guiltily admits, "Well, I had to do this thing to make a profit." As one worker once said to me: "The quality of work isn't your responsibility, it isn't my responsibility. It's the inspector's responsibility. What are you trying to do, take him out of a job?"

Now what does all this organizational analysis have to do with information systems and decision-making rationality?

Just this—as all this behavior becomes imbedded in the system, there is a reduction in the chances that accurate information will flow in either direction.

In such a situation, top management usually reacts by establishing even more rigid controls which only reinforce the original condition that began this sequence. (The irony about controls is that they are usually the wrong response to the right problem.) The problem is the apparent lack of responsibility of organization members. But the cause of the lack of responsibility may be the very impact of the controls (as well as of the structure and leadership styles) upon individual, group, and intergroup relationships. A better response would be to redesign the controls so that participants may give of themselves, rather than give up themselves.

All these reactions reinforce the initial conditions, so we have a closed loop creating a system with increasing ineffectiveness in problem solving, decision making and implementation. Consider this: In the social universe, where presumable there is no mandatory state of entropy, man can claim the dubious distinction of creating organizations that generate entropy, that is, generate slow but certain processes toward system deterioration.

To some, this analysis may seem overly pessimistic. But John Gardner has gone so far as to suggest that the "dry rot" in organizations will become so bad that eventually they will collapse. I share that view. What I think will happen at both upper and lower levels is that rather than clean out the dry rot, organizations will cover it up with a new layer of controls or a new set of people. Since everybody's dry rot is increasing, its cost is simply included in the price structure to the consumer. In government, hospitals, and school systems, dry rot is also included as part of the indirect cost, but there appears to be a limit to what the taxpayer will pay. There may be a lesson here for industry.

Now that I have presented this picture of impending chaos in organizational life, what happens when we add the potential impact of rational decision technologies such as MIS? They will only exacerbate the situation. Or, more accurately, the resistance generated by MIS, rooted in organizational dry rot, will make things even worse.

MIS is sometimes thought of as coping with relatively stable, static, and often trivial data that are easily programmed—providing information about such things as salary structure, employee attendance, warehouse inventory, number of production rejects. These data are rarely important inputs to problem solving by top management. I am not concerned with such a view of MIS.

I am concerned with MIS where it's use can alter significantly the way top managers make important decisions. These are the uses of MIS that help an executive to understand the complexity of the present. These are the systems that provide an opportunity to experiment with different future states of the environment. The state of the MIS art is too primitive for such uses at present. However, in studying the human problems associated with the introduction of MIS, the important thing is to focus on the potential of the system—because executives are smart enough to react to the potential at least as much as to present capabilities.

An MIS, like any formal bureaucracy, is based on the assumption that organizations are, and should continue to be, rational. The MIS designers are interested in modeling the system in accordance with how individuals actually behave. So they include both functional and dysfunctional activities. The criterion for inclusion is that the factors are relevant to solving problems, even if they are unwritten, unspoken, and "illegal."

The traditional management expert may limit his studies to the formal system—the table of organization, the chain of command. In contrast, the MIS expert tries to surface covert policies, practices, and norms. This requirement can be threatening to many people, as we have seen, because what has been hidden may be incriminating.

As the informal modes become explicit, information comes increasingly under the control of top management. The top level starts to see things it never saw before. Middle managers feel increasingly hemmed in. In psychological language, they will experience a great restriction of their space of free movement, resulting in feelings of lack of choice, pressure, psychological failure. These feelings in turn can lead to increasing feelings of helplessness and decreasing feelings of responsibility. Result: a tendency to withdraw or to become dependent upon those who created or approved the restriction of space of free movement.

Sound familiar? MIS can do to middle and near-top management exactly what the job specialization itself does to lower-level employees.

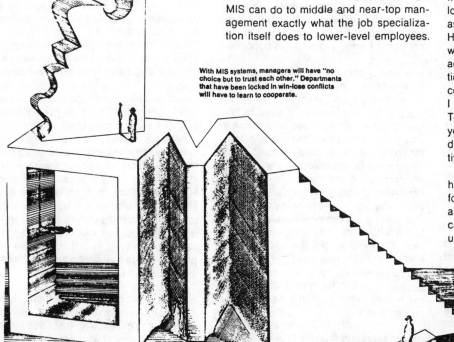

With MIS systems, managers will have "no choice but to trust each other." Departments that have been locked in win-lose conflicts will have to learn to cooperate.

The second psychological impact of MIS upon managers is another double bind.

MIS has the capacity to operate on-line in real time. There can be formal and continuous flows of information throughout the organization, and machines are involved in all decision making. In essence, the system can centralize all the important decisions. If a local manager sees an opportunity to alter a plan, he asks the console to evaluate his idea and give him a yes or no response.

Such a system can create a very unattractive world for the local decision maker; daily goals are defined for him, the actions to achieve those goals are specified; his level of aspiration is determined for him; and his performance is evaluated by a system over which he has no influence.

These conditions may lead managers to perform as expected. However, they will also lead to a sense of psychological failure. Those managers who aspire toward challenging work with self-responsibility will be frustrated; those who prefer less challenge will be satisfied. The former may leave, fight, or psychologically withdraw; the latter usually stay and also withdraw. In short, the manager, because of MIS, will experience frustrations that his employees once experienced when quality control engineers first designed their work and monitored their performance. The manager is now in a double bind. If he follows the new rationality, he will succeed as a manager and fail as a human being. Here's how it works: A manager sees a world in which he can be held increasingly accountable for wider ranges of information. He says to himself: "Ten years ago I could go to the board and say, 'I'm sorry, I didn't know this was going to happen.' Today the board can ask me, 'Why didn't you have a venture analysis made? Why didn't your model include other alternatives?' I have no out."

There's his dilemma. If his models are incomplete, he can be fired for not including all the data. If the models are complete, he gets frightened, not because he can be fired, but because he's useless. He's psychologically fired.

A third impact the MIS can have is on power. MIS emphasizes the use of valid information and technical competence rather than formal power to manage organizations. MIS emphasizes what is done and how it gets done, not just who does it or who gets credit for it.

There are serious human difficulties with making valid information and technical competence the new currency for power. It greatly reduces the ability of managers to give orders simply because they have been given power. This may be threatening to executives who are used to making the organization "move" even if they have incomplete or invalid information. Under MIS, the more one has valid information and competence in problem solving, the less one needs traditional power.

As we have seen above, the tendency of current management systems is to produce information about important issues which is invalid. An effective MIS will ask executives to produce precisely that information they have learned to withhold in order to survive.

MIS will do away with the kind of activities in this story: A large company made a decision to examine its computer technology. It had computers in four different places costing about $30 million per year. Two first-rate computer consultants were called in and they developed a plan to integrate the hardware into a $5 million a year operation. But to make it work, several competing departments would have to give up sovereignty over their computers and alter their ways of collecting data. The departments didn't want to go along. So the plan was rejected. The consultants' report was never sent to the top; it remains a secret. Under MIS that couldn't happen.

Existing organizations generally require executives who enjoy ambiguity, manipulating others, and making prophecies which only they can fulfill. The latter skill is particularly important. One mark of a successful executive is that he can marshall human and financial resources to make his decisions come true even if others feel that the goals could not—or should not—be achieved.

As MIS becomes more sophisticated there will be less need for such executives, less need for "taking hold of the goddam place and turning it around and tightening it up." In other words, success in the past may have come from selecting an admittedly ambiguous course of action but, with resources and power, make it come to reality. The manager, therefore, had good reason to feel essential and powerful. Sophisticated

quantitative models could reduce his magic powers and feelings of being essential.

A fourth impact of MIS is that a mature MIS reduces the need for organizational politics within and among departments. Traditional organizational theory states that a subordinate should focus only on his own department. His superiors will worry about integrating several departments into a meaningful whole. Because organizations foster competitiveness, lack of trust, and win-lose dynamics, the subordinate tends to build walls around his department to protect it from competing departments or arbitrary superiors. Thus interdependence becomes only partially effective and primarily through constant monitoring by the superior.

Many managers believe that interdepartmental competition is healthy. They see it as the best way to assure that departments will make the best possible demands upon the management.

In contrast, MIS does not view the organization as an aggregate of hungry, competitive, and angry units, but as a set of interrelated activities that have to be meshed into a whole. The MIS follows a principle that most managers agree with in the abstract but seldom follow in practice—the principle of interdependence. With MIS, departments which have been locked into win-lose conflicts will have to learn to cooperate with each other.

Departments with a long history of survival through combat will understandably be cautious and skeptical about being "required" to cooperate.

The one kind of cooperation they do practice, trading favors, may also have to change. Consider this hypothetical situation involving a shirt manufacturer. It used to take four to six weeks for sales information to flow from the field through regional offices, then up the ladder to the president's office. Along the way, the reports were censored with protective information to offset the harshness of that ultimate question: "Why didn't you sell all those shirts?" If a jam was coming up, the VP for sales could go to the VP for manufacturing and make a deal. Rather than tell the president the shirts didn't sell, they'll tell him that manufacturing didn't make as many as expected. The VP for manufacturing then has money in the bank in case he himself gets in a jam.

Under MIS, with its constant, instant sales information (like an airlines reservation system) the president is always up-to-date. He can use his information to be punitive, in the traditional manner:

"Why didn't you sell those shirts?" Or he can use MIS to find out what went wrong in the system. As one (real) company executive put it, "We now have no choice but to trust each other." That may be a strange feeling, but it's also a good one.

The final human impact of MIS is that it requires managers with higher levels of intellectual and conceptual competence. They must be able to deal with the interrelationships among the facts. Typically, this is not a skill possessed by many executives.

In the past, when data were incomplete a manager used intuition to fill in the many blanks with possibly valid data. Managers immersed themselves "in the facts" of their past experience. A sophisticated MIS is able to develop a much richer set of facts with past and present quickly summarized.

At this point, management science specialists might wish to state that the ultimate goal of a valid information system is to free the manager from the routine data and permit him to be creative and innovative. I could not disagree.

Unfortunately, our studies so far indicate that the majority of managers still do not know how to use models as the basis for creative experiments. This is partly due to the fact that experimentation, risk taking, and trust have been drummed out of our managerial systems. This assures that just those men who do not enjoy experimenting will become managers. Those few brave souls who prefer to experiment will be faced with an array of control systems that are still based on the principle of management by exception. Their behavior will come under audit the moment it deviates from expected norms.

The extent to which "management by exception" permeates management thinking cannot be overemphasized. Basically, its prevalence derives from one of the primary reasons why individuals organize in the first place: to reduce variance and increase the probabilities of achieving stated objectives. In a world where deviance is questioned strongly and, more frequently, looked down upon; in a world where there is little risk taking and innovation generally, it is understandable that people tend to be conservative in thinking and protective in orientation.

Since most of my attention has been directed to traditional managers, perhaps the reader might assume that I see the information specialist as a hero who can do no wrong. Not so. In an organizational context, the MIS specialist is a newcomer who experiences all the difficulty of entering near the top without having the social or organizational savvy to help himself very much. If he's being resisted, it's partially because he invites resistance in the way he goes about trying to get line managers to adopt MIS.

My research experience indicates that MIS is generally introduced through special task groups which are assigned to a small number of departments. In effect, MIS starts its test period in isolation from most of the company. In this setting, the MIS expert displays a combination of arrogant selling zeal and organizational defensiveness which does not make relations with suspicious managers any easier.

In one company I studied recently, MIS team members developed several ways to cope with their dilemmas. First, they convinced themselves it was their mission "To force people to become more explicit in their thinking, in order to be more effective." Another put it this way: "It's my job to make people think through what the hell their objectives are."

Given that their task is conceived as coercing others to become more explicit and rational, then any coercion they use becomes consistent with their mission.

In contrast, sometimes the MIS team tried to be diplomatic. Their diplomacy came in the form of translating their ideas into "simple" managerial language, by suppressing (they thought) their disrespect for the low intellectual caliber among the managers, and by not confronting the managers on any threatening issues.

But their diplomacy didn't last long. When they met too much resistance they either withdrew or became aggressive and competitive in return. To make matters worse, their feelings of intellectual superiority were no longer concealed and they came across to their intended clients as arrogant.

The manager's reactions to threats and arrogance can be predicted. His feelings of mistrust, suspicion, and fears of inadequacy find ways to influence other managers to let the MIS group atrophy or be disbanded. For example, not enough company departments will be persuaded to pay for the MIS services. Or management will find that people don't understand the value of the new systems and can't use an operations research group effectively.

What can be done to reduce the problems identified and to increase the chances for MIS to be accepted? Actually, there isn't much in my experience, or in the experience of other behavioral scientists, to suggest formulae with a great deal of certainty. We are dealing with emotional human problems that require interpersonal competence; they are not just technological systems.

The first step is for all concerned to become aware that MIS (or any other new system) is not the basic problem. The basic problem is that organizations are full of concealed dysfunctional actions and defenses that are revealed by MIS. Perhaps if ways could be found to make quantitative models more accurately reflect the world as line managers experience it, their fears and resistances would be lowered. But that is more a hope than a likelihood.

However, there is research and experience in some areas relevant to reducing such organizational problems. These are the areas of interpersonal, group, and intergroup functioning. Knowledge is beginning to be developed about how individuals can increase their interpersonal competence and the effectiveness of their group relationships. But this means modifying current organizational strategies which preclude dealing openly with personal, interpersonal, and intergroup problems.

My emphasis on interpersonal relations and expression of feelings does not mean that emotionality should be substituted for rationality and interpersonal competency for technical competence. Openness requires a particular combination of rational and emotional communication. The aim is to create a situation in which information scientists can express their feelings in such a manner as to help traditional executives express themselves in a similar open manner.

The theory is simple: Emotional problems within organizations do not simply disappear when they are not faced; instead, they remain to obstruct continually the implementation of rational plans. ✍

Comments the Editor (LZ):

If Chris Argyris (or his friends and colleagues) had solutions to the dilemmas identified in the article, you would have read them in the article. But they don't have handy suggestions for achieving harmony between today's managers and tomorrow's information systems.

Successful information systems have two extremely potential effects on an organization: They can free people for the creative work we all say we'd like to do; or they can become ultimate weapons in the hands of traditional, authoritarian chiefs. Based on organizational history, the latter is more likely to happen. In other words, more use-

ful information is more likely to be wielded in a punitive, "shape up or ship out" style than to be considered in a cooperative "let's get together and solve this" style.

Chris Argyris

As Argyris points out, to become more rational in planning is to become more cooperative than competitive, more open than secretive, more honest than deceitful. There are so few organizations operating that way, where can a man go to learn how? It may be that man's fears of the machine will, in this instance at least, defeat the machine.

The alternative requires a major reconsideration of what "management" is. And for all the reasons Argyris points out, this is unlikely to become a widespread phenomenon. His agreement with John Gardner that our institutions are heading for chaos is not merely an author's dramatic emphasis.

Chris Argyris's sights into the problems of rationality in organizations are based on extensive experience as consultant to a great variety of organizations in industry (IBM, Polaroid, Lever Brothers, DuPont, Shell Oil) and government (State Department, National Institute of Mental Health, National Science Foundation). He has also extended his work on executive development and productivity to other countries as special consultant to several governments including France, England, Norway, Greece, and Germany. His home base is Yale University where he is Beach Professor of Administrative Sciences and a member of the Board of Directors of the Institute for Applied Social Science.

Gary W. Dickson and John K. Simmons   Davis Chapter 15

"THE BEHAVIORAL SIDE OF MIS"

Business Horizons (13:4), 1970 August, pages 59-71.

This article presents a cogent analysis of the behavioral implications of MIS implementation. The perceptions grew out of a pilot implementation.

The development and installation of a computer-based
information system frequently focuses on technical problems
of hardware, software, data communications, etc. Yet,
major problems in the installation of an MIS result from
behavioral reactions of the four groups involved: operating personnel, operating management, technical staff, and
top management. The reactions may be very dysfunctional.
Three such reactions are aggression, projection and avoidance. The dysfunctional behavior appears in all groups
except the technical staff, the agents of change. Operating management evidences the greatest resistance. The
article concludes by suggesting ways in which the dysfunctional behavioral reactions to an MIS may be minimized.

READING SUGGESTIONS

The authors differentiate four types of systems that
may exist within the MIS -- clerical, information, information-decision, and programmed. This classification is important in the discussion of the behavioral reactions.

Five factors influence or explain dysfunctional behavior when an MIS is introduced:
1. The way the MIS affects the traditional formal struc-
    ture.
2. The extent to which the MIS disrupts the informal or-
    ganizational structure.
3. The personal characteristics of affected personnel
    (such as age, length of service, etc.).
4. The organizational climate for change and past exper-
    ience with it.
5. The method of making the change.

Note how the different organizational groups are assumed to react in terms of output behaviors of aggression,
projection or avoidance (Figure 1). These reactions are
then analyzed in more depth. Figure 2 summarizes the reasons for the reactions.

QUESTIONS

1. Describe the four types of systems the authors iden-
    tify.
2. Why do people in organizations resist information sys-
    tem changes?
3. What are the dysfunctional behavior patterns associa-
    ted with a new system?
4. Describe the probable dysfunctional behavior and its
    causes (or probable causes) for each work group.
5. List eight procedures or actions which may be used to
    reduce dysfunctional behavior.

THE BEHAVIORAL SIDE OF MIS

Some aspects of the "people problem"

G. W. DICKSON AND JOHN K. SIMMONS

Both authors are faculty members in the School of Business Administration, University of Minnesota. Mr. Dickson is also associate director of the school's Management Information Systems Research Center.

To enjoy the technical benefits of management information systems, it is often necessary to solve the dysfunctional side effects stemming from behavioral problems—in short, people problems. Reactions to the installation of MIS may range from failure to use the output to outright sabotage. The authors identify three types of dysfunctional behavior—aggression, projection, and avoidance—that may appear in four groups—operating personnel, operating management, technical staff, and top management. Only the technical staff—being designers and agents of change—shows no dysfunctional behavior. Operating management, the group that should enjoy most of the system benefits, goes farther than any other group in its resistance, and exhibits all three forms. The authors suggest ways of minimizing the behavioral problems that may follow introduction of MIS.

Time and time again it has been said that the "people problem" is the major difficulty firms encounter when they attempt to design, develop, and implement management infor-

mation systems. Recently, McKinsey and Company conducted a survey of thirty-six large computer users to investigate their computer practices and achievements. The analysis of the survey results strongly suggests that computer expenditures are not being matched by rising economic returns, and that the underlying reason is essentially behavioral in nature.[1]

The same point was dramatically brought home when we interviewed seventeen firms associated with the University of Minnesota's Management Information Systems Research Center concerning their research interests relative to the "management of management information systems." Such topics as project identification and selection, project time and cost estimation, project control and documentation, and the entire area of operations management were felt by the firms to be far less crucial than topics involving people problems in some way. The conclusion is inescapable that, in order to achieve the technical benefits of management information systems,

1. See, for example, J. Diebold, "Bad Decisions on Computer Use," *Harvard Business Review*, XLVII (January-February, 1969), p. 15, and *Unlocking the Computer's Profit Potential* (New York: McKinsey and Company, 1968), pp. 14-15.

the dysfunctional side effects stemming from behavioral problems must be minimized, and that any systems designer who "gives a complete hardware description to his charge without suggesting or forecasting problems in the social system does a disservice to himself and to his organization."[2]

This article will examine the effect of information systems on various levels of the organization and suggest ways of minimizing the dysfunctional consequences of introducing management information systems. The organizational groups considered to be relevant are: operating personnel (both nonclerical and clerical); operating management (first-level supervision through middle management); technical staff; and top management. One of our major propositions is that each group plays a different role in the development and use of management information systems, is affected differently by their introduction, and, therefore, must be discussed separately. Another of our basic points concerns the management information system (MIS) itself, which we will consider first.

CONCEPTUAL FRAMEWORK FOR MIS

Whenever managers or technical persons connected with organizational electronic data processing (EDP) systems get together and are confronted by the term "management information systems," the first question they usually ask is how the term should be defined. The typical response is to avoid the question or to combine several "buzz words" in order to so obfuscate the issue that the questioner becomes frustrated and passes on to other topics. In fact, it is quite safe to say that to our knowledge no satisfactory definition of MIS exists.

There is no doubt that the lack of an adequate definition makes discussion of the area as difficult as describing the daily activities of a resident of Shangri-la. In fact, it is highly probable that much of the trouble has been caused by speakers and authors, who, when referring to management information system, are actually speaking of EDP systems that do not provide (nor were they designed to provide) management with any information whatsoever. In order to clarify the discussion, we shall subdivide the term into four subareas differentiated by the objective that the system is intended to satisfy:

Clerical system—To substitute computer processing for manual record keeping

Information system—To supply information (not data) that is oriented toward management decision making

Information-decision system—To go beyond the simple provision of information to the decision maker and actually to assist the way in which the decision is reached

Programmed systems—To have the system rather than human decision makers make the decision.[3]

Later in this article we shall discuss how each of the organizational groups is affected by the different types of systems and what their behavioral reactions to each may be. Before getting to this level of detail, however, it is necessary to consider the general consequences of an organizational change.

CONSEQUENCES OF CHANGE

People tend to resist the new in favor of the old. Greenberger highlights this phenomenon in commenting that "explanation of human inertia would cite man's tendency to resist the new and espouse the old, his need for security, and his fondness for familiar objects even while exploring the unfamiliar."[4] Since

---

2. L. K. Williams, "The Human Side of a Systems Change," *Systems and Procedures Journal* (July-August, 1964), p. 199.

3. See G. W. Dickson, "Management Information-Decision Systems," *Business Horizons* (December, 1968) for additional discussion of these subareas.

4. M. Greenberger, "The Computer in Organization," in C. A. Walker, ed., *Technology, Industry, and Man* (New York: McGraw-Hill Book Company, 1968), p. 304.

unfavorable behavioral consequences often accompany any significant organizational change, it should not be surprising when a new management information system encounters resistance. In order to minimize or, better, to prevent these unfavorable consequences, management must not only recognize that introduction of an information system is likely to trigger trouble among personnel, but must also have some knowledge of the particular factors that underlie this type of behavior.

Factors Influencing Behavior

Many factors, including the magnitude of the change itself, may cause persons to resist change. Five factors, we believe, are especially related to dysfunctional behavior upon the introduction of MIS.

First, most complex organizations have definite departmental boundaries and divisions of formal responsibility, and changes in these boundaries and divisions often occur in connection with the introduction of a new information system. These changes may be planned in advance or occur as part of unforeseen adaptions necessary to the successful use of the system. Reif points out that "resistance will be inevitable as departmental boundaries are violated and entire functions are deleted or several combined in the name of greater operating efficiency."[5]

Second, the effect on the informal structure of an organization is also important. An organization tends to develop a system of values, ethical codes, taboos, special working relations, and sometimes even a special language among members. This structure often tends to be a strong force in the day-to-day functions of an organization. The impact of a new system on the informal structure can be

as serious in terms of creating behavioral disturbances as the impact on the formal structure.

Third, personal characteristics and background of the particular members of the organization will affect behavior toward the new system. These factors include age, length of service, personality, cultural background, attitude toward the computer, organizational level, and experiences with previous organizational change.

Younger people with fewer years of service with an organization tend to be less opposed to change than older people with many years of service. Over-all personality and cultural background are also important in determining reaction. Schlosser refers to these factors when he reminds system designers that the personal characteristics of those affected may cause difficulties and create a situation where the individuals may not be ready to accept change.[6]

Some people simply view the computer in a negative light. Greenberger emphasizes that to many people the computer represents the most recent intrusion of the machine into man's private domain.[7] In addition, publicity in recent years has tended to justify the cost of computers through replacement of people. When these two factors are combined with a possible feeling of awe and a lack of understanding, the likely result is an unfavorable predisposition toward any system that incorporates the computer.

Reactions are also likely to vary with the organizational level affected. Most writers tend to agree that the middle-level manager can and often does offer the most resistance to change. Beckett articulates this point with the comment that "there is no disrupting the resistance that precedes major system changes—particularly from members of the

5. W. E. Reif, *Computer Technology and Management Organization* (Iowa City: Bureau of Business and Economic Research, University of Iowa, 1968), pp. 37-38.

6. R. E. Schlosser, "Psychology for the Systems Analyst," *Management Services* (November-December,1964).
7. "The Computer in Organization," in *Technology, Industry, and Man*, p. 309.

middle management group."[8] The effect of organizational level and the role of the middle manager are, we believe, especially important regarding information systems.

Fourth, the members of an organization are more likely to respond favorably to a proposed change if the managerial climate maintains open communication and permits all grievances to be heard. The members of an organization can also sense the over-all attitude of top management toward the system and the extent to which it has top level backing or support. Past experiences with organizational change may have a great deal to do with how new changes are accepted; if previous changes have not established a feeling of trust, confidence, and cooperative spirit, then the members of an organization may come to feel that management or special staff groups are likely to try to "put something over on them." Under such conditions, changes (or new systems) face trouble.

Fifth, at least one writer, the late Douglas McGregor, implies that the method employed to introduce a change may be the most important variable affecting its likelihood of success: "A fair amount of research has pointed up the fact that resistance to change is a reaction primarily to certain methods of instituting change rather than an inherent human characteristic."[9]

Not everyone would agree that the method used to implement the change is the primary variable influencing acceptance of change (remember the earlier quotation from Greenberger). However, research studies in this area suggest that the method by which a system is introduced is highly pertinent to the reaction to be expected from the organization members.

8. J. A. Beckett, "The Total Systems Concept: Its Implications for Management," in C. A. Myers, ed., *The Impact of Computers on Management* (Cambridge, Mass.: M.I.T. Press, 1967), pp. 221-22.

9. Douglas McGregor, "The Scanlan Plan Through a Psychologist's Eyes" in *Technology, Industry, and Man,* p. 124.

Outputs of Behavior

Mention has been made of dysfunctional behavior associated with a new system. What specific forms do these outputs of behavior take? We have identified three general types.

Aggressive behavior represents an attack (either physical or nonphysical) intended to injure the object causing the problem. The most dramatic aggression toward the system occurs as sabotage—when persons attempt to destroy systems components. A less dramatic but more common aggression occurs when persons attempt to "beat the system." People are always smarter than systems and will be motivated to prove it if a system is operating in a way that offers a pay-off from heating the system (tangible or mere self-satisfaction). The authors saw this type of situation in a recent research investigation.

The setting was an information system in a complex organization designed to collect man-hours in different work stations on a daily basis. Workers were frequently rotating from one work station to another during the day, and were supposed to clock in and out each time they moved from one station to another. During the course of an interview, one worker indicated that there had been some "ganging up" on an unpopular foreman. Workers would not punch out of a particular area when leaving for another work station or would punch in at the unpopular foreman's area and then work in a different area.

In a systems setting, *projection* exists when people blame the system for causing difficulties that are in fact caused entirely by something else. In many instances, the system may be blamed for failings actually caused by such factors as excessively rapid implementation, unrelated factors such as the general incompetence of the individual or individuals involved, or a wrong decision properly made in light of the best information available at the time.

When people defend themselves by avoiding or withdrawing from frustrating situations, they are exhibiting behavior known as *avoidance.* In the area of MIS, this behavior often takes the form of ignoring the system approach. Along with participation in decisions pertaining to the structure of the system, an attempt should be made to achieve harmony between individual and organizational goals. Schlosser makes a strong point concerning the need for the systems analyst to create attainable goals for employees involved in the system if the employee is to accept and learn to use the system. He cites a case in which foremen who were convinced that their ultimate goal of self-advancement would be helped by the system became staunch allies of the system analyst.[13] Of course, relating the goals of the information system and those of the individual may be somewhat difficult in some cases; a substantial amount of probing may be necessary to find the key to obtaining the needed acceptance and support from those members of the organization affected by the system.

Clarity of the System

The purpose and characteristics of the system should be as clear as possible to those who have any direct contact with it; effective use or support cannot be obtained if there is confusion or a lack of understanding. This means that the nature and detail of a system must be fully explored and discussed with those affected before, during, and after installation. Generally, much more explanation is necessary than is usually thought to be required; those of us who have many years' experience in the classroom know that this basic problem applies to many situations. In order to minimize the dysfunctional consequences of a general lack of understanding of the system, a substantial percentage of the systems analyst's time—perhaps 25 to 30 percent—should be reserved for communication with users of the information. Full communication is essential.

13. "Psychology for the Systems Analyst," p. 206.

Another factor of importance is minimizing initial system errors. The authors have often encountered situations where confusion, misunderstanding, and failure to use output have been caused by numerous errors during the first few months of operation. Frequent mistakes can delay or even completely undermine a potentially good system. User reaction to errors must be recognized, and every effort made to have an error-free operation before implementation. Finally, with regard to system implementation, realistic goals and deadlines must be set. Implementation at too fast a pace creates confusion and numerous errors in addition to short tempers and tired minds.

Plan Scope

The fact that a computer has the ability to do something that a man can do—even more efficiently—does not necessarily mean that the computer should do it. In the over-all interests of the organization and for the most effective system, certain tasks may need to remain in the hands of individuals. Whisler points out that "managers with whom we have talked are reluctant to admit that computer systems, in any way, tell them what to do. The idea of 'sharing control' is somewhat more palatable." Hofstede calls attention to the possible need to deliberately plan a certain amount of scope for the individual within a computer-controlled system, resulting in a "calculated inefficiency" that can save the humanity within the system.[14]

The individual must retain his sense of dignity and importance as a human being along with the feeling of worthy contribution to the needs of the organization. Acceptance

14. T. L. Whisler, "The Impact of Information Technology on Organizational Control," in *The Impact of Computers on Management,* p. 40; G. H. Hofstede, *The Game of Budget Control* (Ansen, The Netherlands: Royal Van Gorcam, 1967), p. 304.

of the system is not likely if the individual has the feeling, rightly or wrongly, that the computer has usurped his position.

New Challenges

Calculated inefficiency may not be necessary in most cases. New challenges may be opened up by the installation of a computerized system. Although certain tasks may be taken over by the computer, there are often less routine and important jobs that, because of lack of time or pertinent information, have not been receiving adequate attention. Such situations are to occur most often at the lower and middle management levels.

Beckett comments that the loss of decision-making power by middle managers under advanced systems turns out to be in part an illusory loss. The decision-making prerogative that is given up may be of such low quality (routine) that it is questionable whether a manager should have devoted time to it in the first place. Whisler comments, similarly, that the real problem is that we have not discovered the new decision problems that are the real challenge for the people whose old decision problems are being removed by information technology. We have not taken a look at what decision makers ought to be doing that is more important and satisfying than what they did before.[15] The systems analyst should attempt to discover and emphasize these new challenges in his discussions with management at all levels if he is to obtain the most effective implementation of the system.

Reexamine Performance Evaluation

Neither tasks nor their relative emphasis should be modified in a new system without reexamining the performance evaluation criteria. Huse notes that "one of the things that struck me in some of my research is the fact that managers resisted the new computer programs because they could no longer maintain control of their own subunit and yet they were still being rewarded on this basis."[16] Huse also comments that there will have to be a shift from rewards based on individual accomplishments to rewards based upon group achievements if integrated programs are to be successful.

The most effective reward system, especially in complex situations, is a topic upon which there is substantial disagreement; there are few guidelines to offer the systems analyst. Yet it is an area with which he must be concerned, where tasks or the emphases on tasks change extensively in conjunction with the new system. Management must work out the reward system to the satisfaction of those affected if the system is to be accepted.

User Orientation

In order to design the appropriate management information system, the analyst must attempt to determine how user behavior will be affected by the manner and form in which the outputs are communicated. The design of the system must fulfill the needs of the user if he is to be satisfied with the output; otherwise, he is compelled to maintain his own system, which, of course, defeats the basic purpose of the installation. The longer the user runs his old system in parallel, the more difficult it is to get him to supply accurate data to a new one that is not serving his needs. The system designer should be careful not to overwhelm the user with a large volume of output which the user either cannot understand or cannot use effectively. Walker makes the pertinent point that the

15. "The Total Systems Concept: Its Implications for Management" and "The Impact of Information Technology on Organizational Control."

16. "The Impact of Computerized Programs on Managers and Organizations."

sional affiliations as in progress up the organizational ladder, we might expect more impersonal, problem-oriented behavior at the top, with less emphasis on loyalty to the firm and more on relatively rational concern with solving difficult problems.

Again, top staff people may follow their problems from firm to firm much more closely than they do now, so that ideas about executive turnover and compensation may change along with ideas about tying people down with pension plans. Higher turnover at this level may prove advantageous to companies, for innovators can burn out fast. We may see more brain picking of the kind which is now supposedly characteristic of Madison Avenue. At this creating and innovating level, all the current work on organization and communication in research groups may find its payoff.

Besides innovators and creators, new top-management bodies will need programmers who will focus on the internal organization itself. These will be the operations researchers, mathematical programmers, computer experts, and the like. It is not clear where these kinds of people are being located on organization charts today, but our guess is that the programmer will find a place close to the top. He will probably remain relatively free to innovate and to carry out his own applied research on what and how to program (although he may eventually settle into using some stable repertory of techniques as has the industrial engineer).

Innovators and programmers will need to be supplemented by "committors." Committors are people who take on the role of approving or vetoing decisions. They will commit the organization's resources to a particular course of action — the course chosen from some alternatives provided by innovators and programmers. The current notion that managers ought to be "coordinators" should flower in the 1980's, but at the top rather than the middle; and the people to be coordinated will be top staff groups.

Tight Little Oligarchy

We surmise that the "groupthink" which is frightening some people today will be a commonplace in top management of the future. For while the innovators and the programmers may maintain or even increase their autonomy, and while the committor may be more independent than ever of lower-line levels, the interdependence of the top-staff oligarchy should increase with the increasing complexity of their tasks. The committor may be forced increasingly to have the top men operate as a committee, which would mean that the precise individual locus of decision may become even more obscure than it is today. The small-group psychologists, the researchers on creativity, the clinicians — all should find a surfeit of work at that level.

Our references to a small oligarchy at the top may be misleading. There is no reason to believe that the absolute numbers of creative research people or programmers will shrink; if anything, the reverse will be true. It is the *head men* in these areas who will probably operate as a little oligarchy, with subgroups and sub-subgroups of researchers and programmers reporting to them. But the optimal structural shape of these unprogramed groups will not necessarily be pyramidal. It is more likely to be shifting and somewhat amorphous, while the operating, programed portions of the structure ought to be more clearly pyramidal than ever.

The organization chart of the future may look something like a football balanced upon the point of a church bell. Within the football (the top staff organization), problems of coordination, individual autonomy, group decision making, and so on should arise more intensely than ever. We expect they will be dealt with quite independently of the bell portion of the company, with distinctly different methods of remuneration, control, and communication.

Changes in Practices

With the emergence of information technology, radical changes in certain administrative practices may also be expected. Without attempting to present the logic for the statements, we list a few changes that we foresee:

❡ With the organization of management into corps (supervisors, programmers, creators, committors), multiple entry points into the organization will become increasingly common.

❡ Multiple sources of potential managers will develop, with training institutions outside the firm specializing along the lines of the new organizational structure.

❡ Apprenticeship as a basis for training managers will be used less and less since movement up through the line will become increasingly unlikely.

❡ Top-management training will be taken over increasingly by universities, with on-the-job training done through jobs like that of assistant to a senior executive.

❦ Appraisal of higher management performance will be handled through some devices little used at present, such as evaluation by peers.

❦ Appraisal of the new middle managers will become much more precise than present rating techniques make possible, with the development of new methods attaching specific values to input-output parameters.

❦ Individual compensation for top staff groups will be more strongly influenced by market forces than ever before, given the increased mobility of all kinds of managers.

❦ With the new organizational structure new kinds of compensation practices — such as team bonuses — will appear.

Immediate Measures

If the probability seems high that some of our predictions are correct, what can businessmen do to prepare for them? A number of steps are inexpensive and relatively easy. Managers can, for example, explore these areas:

(1) They can locate and work up closer liaison with appropriate research organizations, academic and otherwise, just as many companies have profit-ed from similar relationships in connection with the physical sciences.

(2) They can re-examine their own organizations for lost information technologists. Many companies undoubtedly have such people, but not all of the top executives seem to know it.

(3) They can make an early study and reassessment of some of the organizationally fuzzy groups in their own companies. Operations research departments, departments of organization, statistical analysis sections, perhaps even personnel departments, and other "odd-ball" staff groups often contain people whose knowledge and ideas in this realm have not been recognized. Such people provide a potential nucleus for serious major efforts to plan for the inroads of information technology.

Perhaps the biggest step managers need to take is an internal, psychological one. In view of the fact that information technology will challenge many long-established practices and doctrines, we will need to rethink some of the attitudes and values which we have taken for granted. In particular, we may have to reappraise our traditional notions about the worth of the individual as opposed to the organization, and about the mobility rights of young men on the make. This kind of inquiry may be painfully difficult, but will be increasingly necessary.

"MANAGEMENT IN THE 1980's REVISITED"

Personnel Journal (50:1) 1971 January, pages 35-43, 71.

In 1958, Leavitt and Whisler wrote an article with thought-provoking predictions about the future of management, given the increasing use of computers. Twelve years later, P. F. Newell (supervised by J. G. Hunt) asks the very relevant question as to whether or not the predicted changes appear to be taking place. The article contains no original research; instead it is a review of existing studies. Although the article is dated by the absence of studies subsequent to 1970, it is a useful and interesting look at the questions and the limited research available to answer them.

READING SUGGESTIONS

The authors have selected ten factors to discuss. Table 1 summarizes these factors. A suggested approach to reading the article is to start with Table 1, read the conclusions noting that the ten factors are summarized into four points relating to: centralization, reduction in employees at all levels, organization structures and duties, and heuristic programming. The final points of the conclusions are a commentary on the research they reviewed. They ask for more research involving several firms and for more study of the effect of organizational variables in determining the impact of computer technology.

Having obtained an overview, the article can be read more meaningfully from the beginning. Note especially the difference between opinion surveys and empirical studies of actual impact.

QUESTIONS

1. What were the predictions about the role of top and middle managers? What has happened?
2. What were the predictions about centralization? What has happened?
3. What was the prediction about the future role of the computer specialist? What has happened?
4. What were predictions of employment? What has happened?
5. What explanation is given for the apparent lack of progress in applying heuristic programming?

6. Referring to Table 1, what is the significance in the unanimous agreement of predictors and observed trends in the tendancy toward more decision making by computors?
7. In 1970 Hunt and Newell suggested a trend toward increased centralization of computer facilities. What new technological developments in the 1970s suggest that they were wrong?

The impact of the computer as predicted a decade ago is being seriously restudied. The authors conclude that projections to the 1980's do not appear to be materializing—at least not nearly to the extent predicted. They tell why and look hopefully to more multi-firm studies to test their hypothesis.

Management in the 1980's Revisited

J. G. HUNT
Associate Professor of Management
Southern Illinois University
Carbondale, Illinois

and

P. F. NEWELL
Systems Analyst
Allis-Chalmers Manufacturing Company
Springfield, Illinois

ONE way of arousing controversy is to put a number of computer "experts" in the same room and ask them to make predictions about the managerial impact of computers. A decade ago, Leavitt and Whisler in a now classic article made just such predictions concerning the computer.[2] In essence, they argued that by the 1980's the role of top and middle management would be radically changed. Most middle management functions would be eliminated, while the top manager's job would become much more innovative and creative in nature. Accompanying this would be a sharp shift toward centralization.

These predictions and others made shortly after have led to much discussion and controversy. In considering them after a number of years, to see how appropriate they seem to be in the light of new knowledge, we might start by asking whether it appears that computer development will be far enough along by the

1980's to allow the kind of changes prophesied by Leavitt and Whisler. The answer is probably a qualified "yes." What seems to be needed is a system built around a huge data bank or dossier of information which could be used to relate incoming data with recorded history. Feedback would be accomplished by linking the computer directly to the flow of information about various "commodities" such as cash, material, personnel, and the like. As these information flows moved from one position to another, the event would be automatically recorded and analyzed by the computer. The computer might merely add the commodity to a cumulative total or it might relate the event to predefined decision rules programmed into it. If it discovered a deviation, it would issue an exception report to top management.

Top management in such a system would be largely composed of those with programming and operations research backgrounds. They would react to an exception report by analyzing the external forces acting on the system and their relationship to company goals. They would be the ones with the knowledge and ability to modify the system as needed. Middle managers would monitor the system, making everyday adjustments to it. Their tasks would be largely pre-programmed and, therefore, repetitive and routine. Many of the tasks that could not be precisely pre-programmed would be accomplished by "heuristic programs" which would arrive at a

This article is based on a portion of the junior author's M.S. thesis, with the senior author as committee chairman. E. R. Ashworth and W. T. Greenwood were other members of the thesis committee. Appreciation is expressed to Thomas Hedges, Thomas Purcell and Robert Schellenberger for their helpful comments.

Since this article was prepared for publication, a book by Thomas L. Whisler has been published. The reader may wish to compare his latest conclusions with those of this article. See Thomas L. Whisler, "Information Technology and Organizational Change." (Belmont, California: Wadsworth, 1970).

[2] Harold J. Leavitt and Thomas L. Whisler, "Management in the 1980's," *Harvard Business Review* (November-December, 1958), pp. 41-48.

workable though not necessarily optimal solution. Such programs are considered to be a simulation of higher order thinking which can be used to solve ill-structured problems.[3]

The system, once designed, would exist largely by itself. It would have the capacity to instantly gain most of its input data and could make most of the routine corporate decisions. It would also have some ability to synthesize and make minor decisions on its own. Only external forces would cause it to seek advice outside its own environment.[4]

How close are we to such a system today? The answer seems to be "fairly close." Some of our larger companies are now developing certain segments of it. Ford, Westinghouse, Lockheed, and most major airlines have already developed the real-time information systems that would be an important part of such a system.[5] Perhaps the major area which is furthest from that described above is heuristic programming, and we shall have more to say on this later.

Thus, we conclude that a system such as that above would probably be largely feasible in a technological sense by the early or middle 1980's. With this as a premise, we next examine the likelihood of the managerial changes predicted by Leavitt and Whisler and others making early prognostications, and ask, "To what extent do present trends tend to support these predictions?"

Early Predictions

As indicated above, the major predictions of Leavitt and Whisler cover the areas of centralization and managerial job duties. They argue that information technology, i. e., techniques for high speed processing of data, the application of mathematical methods to

decision making, and simulation of higher order thinking through computer programs will spread rapidly and make centralization much easier. This is because it will allow more information to be organized more simply and processed more rapidly. Thus, top management will be able to act on a wider range of problems than before. It is argued that if centralization becomes easier to implement, top managers will probably revert to it since decentralization has been largely negatively motivated. Top managers have backed into it because they have not been able to keep up with size and technology.

Another predicted effect of the computer is the intensive structuring of many middle management jobs, while others will become much less structured. Computers are likely to lead to more structuring where: 1) measurement of results is relatively easy; 2) jobs call for big money decisions; and 3) where programming promises to significantly aid the present job holder. At the same time, it is predicted that such middle management jobs as research and development and computer programmers will move up in the organization and become less structured since innovation and creativity will become more important as the rate of obsolescence increases. Thus, middle management will break in two with the larger portion dropping organizationally and becoming more structured and the smaller portion becoming less structured and rising in the organization.

At the same time, it is predicted that top management will become far more innovative and creative with far fewer routine decisions. Top management will be assisted in this by high level innovators and programmers supplemented by "committors" who approve or veto decisions. Those committors will *commit* organizational resources to a particular course of action chosen from alternatives provided by innovators and programmers. As tasks become more complex, the committor may be forced to have the top men operate as a committee.

The organization chart of the future would then no longer be a pyramid but would instead be fairly heavy at the top and bottom. This occurrence would be largely the result of

---

[3] For a nontechnical discussion of this area see, Jerome D. Wiest, "Heuristic Programs for Decision Making," *Harvard Business Review* (September-October, 1966) , p. 129.

[4] For details of a model such as that described here se P. F. Newell, "The Managerial Aspects and Ramifications of Cybernetic Information Systems," unpublished Master's thesis, Department of Management, Southern Illinois University, 1968, Ch. III. This chapter also contains many references describing various components of this model.

[5] Newell, *loc. cit.*

the thinning of the ranks of middle managers. As the number of middle managers are reduced, the pyramid would become thinner at the middle. In time the over-all shape would resemble a football balanced upon a bell (see Figure 1).[6]

FIGURE 1
The Football and Bell Concept of Organization

SOURCE: Hak Chong Lee, "The Organizational Impact of Computers," *Management Services* (May-June, 1967), p. 41.

Another early set of predictions come from a 1959 seminar held at the University of Chicago. The conclusions of this group largely reinforce those of Leavitt and Whisler. They suggest that middle management will be the managerial level most affected by the new computer technology. They argue that lower managers have already had a great deal of programming done to their jobs and that the logical next step will be at the middle management level. Many of the middle managers coordinative duties will be diminished and hence, more freedom for other hard to program duties will exist. The football and bell concept is seen as only a temporary phenom-

enon. The group foresees a flattening effect upon the entire organizational structure occurring soon. The organization will be rearranged along the actual flow of information, with a reduction in the number of departments accompanied by a reduction in personnel within these departments. Management as we think of it today will disappear in time. The only form of management that will remain in the future organization will be the computer experts and the analysts who can control the computer information-coordination system.

Over-all, the predictions with respect to top and middle management are quite similar to the earlier ones of Leavitt and Whisler. Top management will regain the ability to centralize decision making and will have much more information at its disposal, while the duties of middle management will be substantially altered.

While there was general agreement on the points mentioned above, there was controversy concerning parallels with what had happened to blue collar work. One group felt that heuristic programs would cause the creative aspects of many executive jobs to be taken away in a manner not unlike what happened when the assembly line replaced the skilled craftsman. The remaining tasks would become routine and would be taken over by the computer when it was economical to do so. Another group believed that routine tasks would be swiftly computerized and the executive could spend his time at creative decision making. Thus, one group believed the computer would replace the executive, while another maintained it would free him. There was, however, common agreement that the number employed in managerial positions would be reduced.[7]

In 1962, a series of evening lectures concerning management and the computer were held at Massachusetts Institute of Technology. These meetings as a whole stressed the positive advances of the computer and computer programming. The question of computer simulation of the human mind was not

---

[6] Leavitt and Whisler, *op. cit.*, pp. 41-48.

[7] George P. Shultz and Thomas L. Whisler (eds.) *Management Organization and the Computer* (Glencoe, Ill.: The Free Press of Glencoe, 1960) .

discussed from the viewpoint of whether or not it was possible, but what man could learn about the human mind itself from the development of such programs.

The meetings ended with a general agreement that there could conceivably be a race of men and a race of computers, each with a different function. True cybernetic information systems, even extending beyond our model, were thought to be economically operable within a few years, but men were thought to be a necessary element to properly evaluate the output of the system.[8]

Perhaps the most controversial of all these earlier predictions came from Michaels in 1962. He foresaw thinking machines with the potential to be smarter than the engineer who designed them or the programmer who built the logic used by the machine. He predicted that computers could "learn" to recognize what they had "seen" before and "teach" themselves generalizations about what they recognized. Such machines might arrive at solutions hostile to mankind. If the system were of a closed-loop nature, humans might not be able to change the course of the paths these machines take.[9] He foresaw, as did those earlier, the drastic alteration and reduction of middle management and was concerned about the fate of those displaced.

Michaels also believed that the computer would have a large impact on the society of the country. Mass unemployment was predicted as the machines took over and a social upheaval would occur as society adjusted to more leisure time and changing personal roles within the family. Perhaps most important, he foresaw an elite class emerging. His elite class was somewhat similar to Leavitt and Whisler's elite computer specialists who virtually controlled the corporation. Michaels believed these men would become the governing elite as well, as they would be the only ones able to communicate with the machines they had built. The remainder of the population would be forced to accept such an elite. In a sense he believed, as did the men at the M. I.

T. seminar, that there could be a race of machines and another of people both trying to live together in one environment. Needless to say, he was alarmed by what he believed was beginning to happen.[10]

Trends Based on What Has Happened

While the evidence is not yet all in, and in many cases is not all that we would like, we can now begin to evaluate these predictions.

Centralization

Critics of management centralization contend that the decentralization concept was developed without regard for size or complexity in order to promote a profit center technique. This profit center technique has been widely used in both large and small firms. Thus, the defenders of decentralization claim that since the lack of information did not cause decentralization, the computer will not cause centralization where it has not been proved effective. It is argued that it is not a lack of information that causes organizations to use decentralization but the element of time. Managers cannot maintain an expertise in all the different activities in which their organization is engaged. The proper use of the ability to *use* information is more critical than the *flow* of information itself.[11]

The supporters of decentralization argue that the data processing activities and the logistics systems (flow of goods from raw materials to a marketed product) may become more centralized and account for most of the evidence pointing to a revival in centralization. Time sharing, low cost random access equipment and fast data transmission have made centralized logistics systems economically feasible. It may be cheaper to maintain a large central computer rather than several smaller ones, especially where two or more locations have a common data base. Yet profit and decision making responsibility can still be

---

[8] Martin Greenberger, (ed.) *Computers and the World of the Future* (Cambridge: The M.I.T. Press, 1962).

[9] This could happen in our model if the intelligence of the system could mature by itself.

[10] Donald N. Michaels, "Cybernation: The Silent Conquest," *Computer and Automation* (March, 1962), pp. 26-42.

[11] John Dearden, "Computer: No Impact on Divisional Control," *Harvard Business Review* (January-February, 1967), pp. 99-104.

delegated. Hence, it is possible to have a high degree of *centralization* of facilities accompanied by a high degree of *decentralization* of decision making.[12]

The Department of Defense has been frequently mentioned as proof that the computer causes centralization of decision making. The facts involved may have been distorted. Ever since Pearl Harbor, Congress has been enacting legislation causing greater centralization of decision making by the War Department and its successor the Department of Defense. Until Secretary McNamara rationalized operation of the Defense Department and put the burden of its routine on computers, this centralization by legislative decree made the department virtually unmanageable. Thus, in this instance, a force other than technology caused centralization of decision making through the use of computers.[13]

Just as Congress decided that centralization of decision making was preferable to other types of decision making, the same analogy has been found in the corporation. The type of decision making is frequently determined not by the computer, but by the personal preferences or philosophies of the chief executive.[14] In a rather detailed study, it was found that in a company with a centralized decision making philosophy a physically centralized computer works best, while one with a decentralized decision making philosophy obtains better results with a decentralized computer system. The over-all management of the computer was found to be centralized in 30 out of 33 firms, while the managerial philosophy of the firms determined the extent to which systems and planning and computer operations aspects of the computer organizational structure would be centralized.[15]

A recent study by Dale also reinforces many of these conclusions. He found that out of the 33 largest users of computers 14 reported no computer impact on their organization structure, 13 reported more centralization and six reported more decentralization. Thus, for about half of these organizations the computer has been fitted into the present philosophy and framework. This is consistent with those who argue that the computer's role here is a neutral one and can work for either centralization or decentralization or some combination of the two depending on desires of the organization. And while the figures seem to show that there is a heavy centralization emphasis among the remaining companies, Dale argues that much of this is centralization of facilities rather than centralization of decision making. He concludes that there seems to be a trend toward physical *centralization* within decision making *decentralization*.[16]

Middle Management

Here, as above, information from several different sources seems to make trends fairly clear. There is evidence that computers have not directly caused executive unemployment, but have instead cut into the need for middle managers. For example, a report by the American Foundation on Automation and Employment (AFAE) found that the volume of business at Metropolitan Life soared 75% since the first computer was installed in 1954, while the number of middle managers has hardly increased.[17] What seems to be happening is that normal attrition and increases in business have compensated for a good bit of displacement as a result of the computer. For example, Dale's sample indicates that 26 of 33 companies indicated no computer impact on span of control or chain of command, and seven reported "some impact," essentially the elimination of one management level (and the corresponding middle management jobs).[18] The AFAE, based on 35 interviews with business, government and university

---

[12] Dearden, *loc. cit.*

[13] Glenn Gilman, "The Computer Revisited," *Business Horizons* (Winter, 1966), p. 81.

[14] John Diebold, "What's Ahead in Information Technology," *Harvard Business Review* (September-October, 1965), p. 82.

[15] James W. Taylor and Neal J. Dean, "Managing to Manage the Computer," *Harvard Business Review* (September-October, 1966), pp. 104-105, 109.

[16] Earnest Dale, "The Impact of Computers on Management," unpublished manuscript, pp. 42-46.

[17] "Automation and the Middle Manager, What Has Happened and What the Future Holds" (New York: American Foundation on Automation and Employment, 1966).

[18] Dale, *op. cit.*, pp. 46-49.

spokesmen, suggests that the reason the computer has not advanced further into the realm of middle management decision making is because of management's resistance to change, skepticism about the potentialities of the computer, and the present hostility between traditional managers and computer technicians. It feels that once these difficulties are overcome, repercussions will be larger. One piece of evidence is presented to show that those middle managers who were really good at their jobs before the computer are not likely to be displaced by it.[19]

There is virtually universal agreement that the middle manager's duties will change as a result of the computer. Dale's study of 33 companies shows some impact in 23 cases and substantial impact in five cases, with no impact in only five cases. In all the companies where there had been a change, there was an expansion of the responsibilities of middle managers and an increase in the necessary job qualifications. With the advent of computers, middle managers spent more time on such functions as communication, interpretation, and counsel. These jobs required more analytical and planning ability, more judgment and greater communications skills. Repetitive, routine aspects of their jobs decreased or disappeared.[20] Fiock found a resistance to change among middle managers because the old ways of doing things which they were using would be changed. Hence, these managers would be useless in the new organization because their routine tasks were being eliminated.[21] Gilman expressed the view that in some instances, a manager doesn't manage at all. In essence, his duties are clerical in nature. As computers have been applied to such areas as production control, inventory management, shop loading, etc., the manager has been given more time on the matters that are more important. The manager has the time to better understand what prompts decisions and is in a better position to explain and anticipate what higher management

wants.[22] Thus, he is able to do his job better by utilizing the computer and will not be trapped in a "paper jungle," merely processing paper from one stage to another.[23]

Still other authors are in substantial agreement with these conclusions.[24] And finally, at least two studies agree with Leavitt and Whisler that the particular function of a middle manager is likely to influence the extent and direction of change in his job duties. For example, the buyer in a purchasing department has typically used his personal judgment in deciding such things as what vendor to use. Now, models run through the computer can determine decisions of this type, as a result of which one highly important part of the buyer's job has been taken out of his hands.[25]

In interpreting these studies we must bear in mind that most, if not all of them, have given no precise definition of the term "middle management." We would suggest that future studies make their concept of middle management quite clear so that where apparently different results occur, we can determine to what extent differing definitions are responsible for such results.

Computer Specialists

Although the role of the computer specialist has assumed increasing importance with the advent of sophisticated third generation computers, these specialists do not seem to have assumed the decision making importance of early predictions. Evidence indicates that companies tend to put operating people in charge of the computer function rather than vice versa because it is easier to educate them in computers than to teach computer

---

19 "Automation and the Middle Manager . . .," *loc. cit.*

20 Dale, *op. cit.*, pp. 47-48.

21 L. R. Fiock, "Seven Deadly Dangers in EDP," *Harvard Business Review* (May-June, 1962), pp. 91-92.

22 Gilman, *op. cit.*, p. 86.

23 This point is discussed in depth more in Neil H. Jacoby, "Impact of Scientific Change upon Business Management," *California Management Review* (Summer, 1962), pp. 36-37.

24 See, for example, "Automation and the Middle Manager . . .," *loc. cit.*, Melvin Anshen, "The Manager and the Black Box," *Harvard Business Review*, (November-December, 1960), pp. 90-91.

25 Joseph P. Schwitter, "Computer Effect Upon Managerial Jobs," *Academy of Management Journal*, Vol. 8, No. 3, 1965, pp. 233-236; "How the Computer is Changing Management Organization," *Business Management* (July, 1967), p. 30.

specialists about business. There is also a tendency to recruit computer specialists internally rather than externally, probably for the same reason as above, and because of the great shortage of specialists in the open market.[26] In addition, there is a tendency for over-all management responsibility for the computer to be retained at the top corporate level in no greater degree than any other important company function, and emphasis is being placed on operating management to plan applications for the computer.[27]

There is some evidence that the status and compensation of computer specialists is improving and that they are reporting to executives higher in the organization than formerly. However, they are regarded strictly as specialists and are not assuming middle or top management decision making responsibilities.[28] Some authors forecast that with the advent of newer, more sophisticated computers and further development of heuristic programming procedures, many routine programs can be dispensed with. Along with this is likely to come much pre-programming of simple procedures and the development of self-correcting programs.[29] To the extent that these forecasts are accurate, we can see a relative decline in the importance of programmers, though probably not systems analysis.

Organization Structure

Trends seem to indicate that instead of a football and bell shaped organizational structure the conventional pyramid is likely to continue. Instead of departments or functions as at present, however, the future pyramid will probably be designed as a system.[30] The information system will parallel the real flow of information within an organization.[31]

Here, each department might act in an independent fashion as part of an organization constructed along the lines of a systems concept. For example, the directing of materials and semi-finished work through successive manufacturing departments may be so complex that each department must act independently in processing of the goods. Ordinarily, because of this independence or lack of communication and control, inventory and buffer stock would have to be provided between departments to prevent fluctuations in production.[32] However, the systems concept utilized with the computer would allow the entire process to be scheduled and the buffer stock eliminated.

Employment

Dale's study shows that 25 out of 33 companies report no change in managerial employment due to the computer, and another study indicates there has been a 3.1 percent gain in white collar employment as a whole and a 3.9 percent gain in the clerical portion of white collar employment. However, in general, it is argued that as the full impact of the computer is felt we can expect a decline in clerical employment.[33] One study of 19 organizations showed that for every five jobs eliminated only one was created by computerization and those jobs remaining were drastically changed.[34] It is predicted that the impact of the computer will probably not affect separate levels of an organization, but will instead affect the entire organization, the higher levels being less affected than the lower levels.[35]

The growth of business is one factor which may limit layoffs due to the computer. The AFAE has found this to be true in many

---

[26] Taylor and Dean, op. cit., p. 103, Dale, op. cit., p. 32-33, "Computers, the 'Software' Snarl," Time (August 18, 1967), pp. 75-76.

[27] Anshen, op. cit., pp. 81-82.

[28] Ibid., p. 92.

[29] "Computers, the 'Software' Snarl," op. cit., John Diebold, "ADP—The Still Sleeping Giant," Harvard Business Review (September-Ocober, 1964).

[30] Ibid., p. 92.

[31] Diebold, "What's Ahead in Information Technology," op. cit., p. 77.

[32] Anshen, op. cit., p. 82.

[33] Dale, op. cit., p. 47, Paul Armer, "Computer Aspects of Technological Change," Automation and Economic Progress (Englewood Cliffs, N. J.: Prentice-Hall, 1966), p. 95.

[34] Ida Hoos, "When the Computer Takes Over the Office," Harvard Business Review (July-August, 1960), p. 103.

[35] Marshall K. Evans and Lou B. Hague, "Master Plan for Information Systems," Harvard Business Review (January-February, 1962), p. 102.

companies.[36] Not to be overlooked is the fact that technology has been traditionally a job creator and thus, the fears based upon the computer causing mass unemployment may be largely unfounded. If the computer is an entirely new phenomenon as Michaels believes, it might be wise to consider the five point policy advocated by Evans and Hague. These authors believe that the turnover in the ranks of clerical work is normally high. Thus, any reduction should be accomplished through attrition. Early retirement is another possibility. Reclassification and retraining are other possible solutions. Perhaps most important, the hiring of personnel today should reflect the needs of the corporation of the future. Long range planning and goals should be a significant factor in the selection of new employees.[37]

Heuristic Programming

Based on programs now existing, which allow computers to think and learn, Simon predicts that in less than twenty five years (but later than the 1980's), businessmen will have the technical capability of substituting machines for all human functions in an organization.[38] However, even if this prediction about technical capability is true, there is the question of whether it would be economically feasible to do so. In data processing tasks, computers are near the break-even point. They are now more economical than human labor only for large scale arithmetic calculations. One recent study showed that 18 of 27 manufacturing companies were losing money on the present installations.[39] Thus, economics looms large as a factor in influencing the extent to which the full potentials of computers will be utilized.

In 1965 Whisler had occasion to review the conclusions of his earlier paper. Those of most relevance here have to do with managerial levels, centralization, and middle management duties.

Whisler's 1965 Conclusions

He concludes on the basis of one military and two business organizations that information technology has led to a decrease in organizational levels. Our review above indicates that this may not be a typical occurrence.

Similarly, he concludes on the basis of a few organizations that his predictions with respect to increased centralization have been verified. And again, our data are not so unequivocal on this point.

Finally, he concludes that his earlier prediction of the routinizing of many middle management positions may be in error. He argues that the computational part of the manager's job will be computerized and the communications portion of his job will become more important.[40] This conclusion seems consistent with that of a number of observers discussed above.

Summary and Conclusions

Table 1 shows the stands taken by those making early predictions and the conclusions reached based upon actual experience and developing trends.

Based upon this table, we conclude the following:

1. The predictions concerning centralization do not appear to be accurate. Rather than leading to centralization, the computer appears to be a neutral element which will be fitted into the basic managerial philosophy of the organization. Indeed, it is quite likely that there will be centralization of computer facilities, with an accompanying decentralization of managerial decision making. This is especially true with the advent of time-sharing systems.

2. The issue of a reduction in number of managers and organization levels does not appear to be supported. Trends indicate that neither of these has declined, but there will not be future growth characteristic of that of the past. The firm will grow larger without substantially increasing its white collar and managerial work force. This is in sharp contrast to Michael's dire predictions about permanent unemployment for all personnel in the firm.

---

36 "Automation and the Middle Manager . . .," *op. cit.*

37 Evans and Hague, *op. cit.*

38 Herbert A. Simon, *The Shape of Automation for Men and Management* (Harper Torchbooks, Harper and Row, 1965), p. 30.

39 Gilbert Burch, "On Line in Real Time," *The Computer Age and Its Potential for Management* (New York: Harper Torchbook, 1965), pp. 10-11.

40 Thomas L. Whisler, "The Manager and the Computer," *The Journal of Accountancy* (January, 1965), pp. 27-32.

TABLE 1
Summary of Predictions and Trends

Tendency Toward:	Leavitt & Whisler	Chicago Seminar	M.I.T. Seminar	Michaels	Trends
Decision Making Centralization	Yes	Yes			No
Centralization of Facilities	Implied				Yes
Reduced Levels of Management	Yes	Yes	Yes	Yes	No
Reduced Number of Managers	Yes	Yes	Yes	Yes	No
Reduced Number of Middle Managers	Yes	Yes	Yes	Yes	No
Reduced Number of Top Managers	No	No	Yes	Yes	No
Formation of Elite Class	Yes	Yes	Yes	Yes	Yes/No
Perfection of Heuristic Programming	Yes	Yes	Yes	Yes	Yes/No
Affecting Number of Clerks			No	Yes	Yes
Decision Making by Computers	Yes	Yes	Yes	Yes	Yes

3. Predictions concerning organization structure and managerial duties seem to be partially confirmed. Leavitt and Whisler's football and bell organization seems instead to be pointing toward the use of systems within a pyramid. However, their prediction of the differential effect of the computer on middle management duties seems to be coming true. At the same time, their prediction of the rise of the computer specialists seems to be taking place. However, its form appears a little different from first predicted. First, it arrived sooner than expected. Second, the monetary reward has arrived, but the power within the organization does not seem to have arrived yet, nor is it likely to appear as earlier predicted. If, as some prophesy, less programming is required for fourth generation computers, we may see the role of the programmer diminish, though that of the systems analyst should increase.

4. The question of heuristic programming does not seem to have been developed enough to really predict its future role. Our state of knowledge here may be much as it was for the other areas when the earlier predictions were made. Thus, we cannot be as firm in our confirmation or rejection of these predictions as we were about the others.

Over-all, on the basis of the evidence reviewed, we conclude that the early predictions generally overestimated the probable impact of the computer by the 1980's and indeed, some of the early predictions will probably never come to pass. Though technology will likely make most of the predictions possible, cost and managerial operating philosophies will tend to substantially influence the use made of such technology.

Two final points should be made. First, we would like to argue for more multi-firm studies of the impact of computers. Much of the writing seems to be based on the personal experience of one author many times in only one or a very few firms. This is extremely difficult to generalize from and yet many of these authors appeared to do just that. More large scale, in-depth studies of the nature of those by Dale, and Taylor and Dean would certainly make it easier to better determine what is actually happening and to get a more accurate estimate of trends. Also, as we indicated earlier, these studies should carefully define their terms, especially the term "middle management."

Second, a study by Woodward has shown that technology can have a striking impact on a number of organizational variables including organization structure and the job of the manager. These factors are dramatically different as we move from small batch to mass-production to continuous process technologies.[41] It seems to us that there might also be a corresponding difference in the state of the computer system model developed. In turn, the computer impact would probably be substantially different. Thus, instead of trying to make predictions that seem to be generally applicable, we would expect them to differ sharply as a function of technology. A multi-firm study of organizations using each of the three kinds of technologies could test our hypothesis. We might then project from this to the future.

---

41 Joan Woodward, *Industrial Organization: Theory and Practice* (London: Oxford University Press, 1965)